Losing Her Crown

Book One

Tywana Ashley

Copyright © 2023 Tywana Ashley
All rights reserved
First Edition

Fulton Books
Meadville, PA

Published by Fulton Books 2023

A book based on true events.

ISBN 979-8-88982-252-3 (paperback)
ISBN 979-8-88982-253-0 (digital)

Printed in the United States of America

I would like to thank my daughter Babie for her talented hands drawing the image for my book's cover. I dedicate my book to my deceased mother Nadine, sister Terri and niece Krystal. I love and miss you guys deeply.

CONTENTS

Chapter 1 1
Chapter 2 10
Chapter 3 21
Chapter 4 28
Chapter 5 38
Chapter 6 54
Chapter 7 65
Chapter 8 82
Chapter 9 91
Chapter 10 109
Chapter 11 124
Chapter 12 154
Chapter 13 164
Chapter 14 181
Chapter 15 197
Chapter 16 212
Chapter 17 241
Chapter 18 263
Chapter 19 289
Chapter 20 322

CHAPTER 1

"I love you, and I love you too," Jonathan said to his wife and daughter. "We can stay connected with one another through our cell phones. This is something that I must do, and I don't care about losing my family."

Melanie cried out, "Jonathan, please, baby, don't do this to us and leave. We can work this out through marriage counseling."

Jonathan ignored Melanie's attempts to entreat him to remain in their marriage. He removed himself from the apartment they shared with tears streaming down his face. Melanie and their daughter stood in the now empty apartment. Tears streamed down their faces uncontrollably. She couldn't believe this was happening to her and Honey. Poor Honey. She rushed behind her father, trying to talk to him, but he ignored her attempts to get his attention. Melanie saw the hurt look on her daughter's face. Honey's pain cut through Melanie's soul, and there was nothing she could do to make it better. Melanie wanted to rush to his side like Honey, but instead, she fell to her knees, lamenting.

Honey made her way back in the house to comfort her mother. Mommy and Daddy breaking up, this wasn't how this story was supposed to end. It's not fair that she should be feeling this pain at such a youthful age. Melanie wished she could protect her from this pain.

JJ, their son, looked at his dad in anger. JJ knew the truth and spared his mother's feelings. He wanted to hurt Jonathan for the pain he caused them all. JJ cried internally for his mother and sister. He felt it necessary to leave with Jonathan and help care for him.

That was it. Melanie looked around the apartment, remembering the laughs, the talks, and all the cries they shared. It was all over now. She thought, *How could this happen on my birthday?* She looked at Honey, wondering, *How does a child fathom having her family together one day, and the next day they are separating?*

She took Honey and left the empty apartment. Melanie turned the ignition on as tears streamed down her face. Honey asked Melanie, "Mom, where are we going? Who are we staying with now?"

They were on their way to a family member's home. Melanie answered, "We're staying with a family member until I can get us an apartment."

Melanie was twenty-one and Jonathan twenty when they married. Melanie was beautiful. She had a beautiful light-skinned complexion, long beautiful hair, a killer smile, and no children. This was attractive to Jonathan, and he wanted to make her his. When he first laid eyes on her, he thought, *Damn, she got some big ass titties.* There were others expressing interest, but he knew he had to secure her for himself.

When Melanie met Jonathan, he was not a productive member of society. He was just hanging around the hood, slanging drugs and banging. He certainly did not worry whether Melanie would accept him or not. His motto was "I'm that nigga." He could care less about a female not reciprocating his advances. He just moved on to the next one. Jonathan was handsome, and Melanie fell in love with him when she first laid eyes on him. She heard that voice tell her, "That's your husband." Melanie couldn't approach him to disclose her feelings. She was with someone, but it didn't stop them from flirting. Jonathan didn't care about her boyfriend. He was determined to extract Melanie from him.

Melanie's boyfriend was on drugs. Jonathan knew, because he was selling drugs to him. Melanie was very naïve and never looked at the signs that were right before her eyes. He was very clever in covering up his tracks, keeping Melanie in the dark. You see, Melanie's father used drugs, and he was an abusive, violent soul toward Melanie and the family. Melanie thought all drug users behaved this way. Her boyfriend did not display the behavior her father had. He was able to maintain his character with her and her family. Melanie had never been around drug users, so she only knew abusive behavior from her father.

LOSING HER CROWN

The day came when Melanie's boyfriend could no longer hide his drug habit. He faced incarceration for succoring criminals in the act of committing burglary to his place of employment. The crime could easily have him incarcerated for at least fifteen years. The judge found him guilty, but he only served about four months because he snitched on the guys involved in the robbery. Since this was his first offense, his lawyer worked a deal for him. His incarceration broke Melanie's heart. Her family tried to tell her that he had a drug habit, but she would not believe them because he was not violent nor abusive toward her.

Jonathan didn't have to fight for Melanie. She became his after a couple of months of her boyfriend's incarceration. Melanie was not going to wait for him, and since Jonathan had already stolen her heart, she wanted to be with him. Honestly, the relationship between Melanie and her boyfriend had started to run its course before the crime was committed. The feelings just weren't the same. With his untidy appearance, seldom haircuts, body odor, and disappearing acts, Melanie should've figured out something wasn't right. These all should have been signs for her. Those drugs had clinched a grip so deep into his soul that it caused eviction from their apartment. The two had to stay with a friend that Melanie had known for years. Living with the friend intensified his habit because unbeknownst to Melanie, she was using drugs as well.

Sandra couldn't keep this news from Melanie's family. She had to share the secret she knew about Melanie's boyfriend. Sandra, and Melanie's families had known each other prior to Melanie's existence. Melanie's family couldn't fathom why Melanie was so blind to what was before her eyes. They told her mother, Lashon. Lashon knew it to be true and would try to talk to Melanie, but she just wouldn't believe them. She stood by him until it was evident to her by his confession that he was a lost soul to drugs.

One day, Jonathan caught Melanie outside, where she lived with her mother. They began to converse. Their talk was going well until he angered her when he began to make disparaging remarks about her ex-boyfriend being on drugs. She felt embarrassed about what he was disclosing, and she didn't want to hear it. Here was another soul knowing things about someone she loved at one point. Melanie didn't want to relive the lies and hurt her boyfriend caused. She began to argue with Jonathan.

Jonathan asked Melanie while they were arguing, "Did he leave you with a habit?"

Melanie looked at Jonathan, answering him with anger, "No! He didn't leave me with a drug habit!"

The quarrel between the two became intense. Jonathan walked away, leaving her. She didn't want him to leave, but she said nothing. She thought, *Why did he not just say sorry to me? He started this. We could've still been here sitting, talking, and getting to know each other.* This didn't make sense to her. A little while later, Melanie was outside talking with a friend. Jonathan had returned and sat next to her. He apologized to her for his words. She tried to act nonchalant after receiving his apology. She finally dropped her guard, and the rest was history.

Going with the Flow of Things

In the beginning of their courtship, Melanie discovered quickly that Jonathan wasn't the type of guy to hang around his lady, spend time with her, take her places, none of those things. And he wasn't into sharing feelings. He acted detached, like he had never been in love nor had a girlfriend. When holidays rolled around, he never bought her anything for her birthdays, Valentine's Day, Christmas, nor their anniversary. She bought him gifts in hopes that he would catch on and start reciprocating. It didn't matter to her what it was. She just wanted him to think about her. It never happened. And it hurt her that he did not understand how to be attentive to all of her. She kept her feelings to herself because she did not want to scare him off nagging about spending money nor time with her. She accepted his flaws. Their sex life was not what she expected. There were no complaints. She enjoyed every encounter. And he had a nice size instrument too and knew how to use it. The problem was, he wasn't giving it to her as often as she wanted.

This was a strange relationship. She only saw him every two months or so. This confused her and had her wondering if there was someone else. She thought, *Why would he stay away from me for months at a time? Why are we even together? Why do I feel like I am the only one working to cultivate a healthy relationship? Am I just a trophy to him?* She kept being clouded with thoughts. A voice would calm her, reminding her, *Always expect the unexpected when it comes to a man.*

Melanie laughed, stating, "Yep, Dad, you are right. Always expect the unexpected when it comes to a man. That way, you won't be surprised." She never said anything to him about how he made her feel. She just went with the flow of things. She knew somewhere deep in his heart, he loved her. They both had battles within that needed conquering. His flaw was the need to share his feelings with Melanie and be attentive to her. Melanie's flaw was the need to have a voice for herself and always following someone else's lead. You see, as a child up to adulthood, Melanie diligently followed orders from her dad. When to talk, when to participate with family television time, when to sleep, when to eat (if he allowed her to eat), when to do everything. Her mother endeavored to talk to him about the way he treated Melanie and her sister, but he didn't listen. He was too busy instilling fear in his children's hearts.

Melanie and Jonathan had been dating for about one year now. They were riding to work together. Melanie always remained silent, afraid to initiate affection and a conversation with him. He made her feel he had no interest in anything she had to say. As soon as she would end her speech, he would nod and then turn the radio back up for his entertainment. When all stations would play songs he disliked, he would reduce the volume until a station played a familiar tune to his liking. Never mind if Melanie liked the song or not. But she never said anything. She just went with the flow. After a while, Melanie began to dismiss any music on the radio that was not to his liking by reducing the volume on the radio. Didn't matter if she liked it. She knew he didn't. She knew what he favored and what he detested.

Melanie could not fathom why she felt as though she was walking on thin ice when she endeavored to converse with him. Why was she afraid to say anything to him? One day, after being with him for a year, she asked, "When are you going to start spending time with me? Why do you never take me anywhere?"

Jonathan answered, "Spend time with you? Say, let me tell you something. I am not into all that spending time and being emotional. That's not me."

Melanie said not one word. She just did the usual when her dad would disappoint or hurt her. She hung her head low and became silent. He never noticed her sad face. And to add insult to injury, when Jonathan picked her up from work, she would be happy to see him with a smile on her face, ready to greet him with a hello.

As soon as Melanie entered the car, Jonathan would ask her, "Why are you smiling? There ain't nothing for you to be smiling about. You need to walk around with a frown on your face. Stop smiling so much. People will take advantage of you if they see you smiling all the time."

Melanie wasn't sure how anyone would take advantage of her because of her smile. Imagine this soul full of smiles, just spreading the love, hearing from a loved one, "No smiling." This marked the beginning stages of the second time her smiles would wither away. It took years for Melanie to get her smiles back from the wounds caused by her dad. She didn't realize that she would repeat that same cycle again, reliving the same situation but different circumstances. She reflected on her past hurt, and if her eyes were open, she would have seen the turmoil Jonathan would inflict on her. She committed a myriad of self-inflicted treasons staying in this relationship. No one was making her stay. She just felt safe and secure being with Jonathan. He was her protector, her everything. She had never dated someone who coast their way through life. So she figured she would coast along right by his side.

Living a Boring Life

Melanie had a great relationship with her mother. Her mother was the only parent she felt loved her. After all, Melanie was her cupcake. Whenever you saw the two of them, you were guaranteed to become overwhelmed with their energy. Their smiles were extremely powerful, forcing others to smile. People thought they were sisters. Melanie could tell her mother anything. Her mother was beautiful, with a youthful visage.

She was not a fan of her daughter's boyfriend. She would often state to Melanie, "I don't understand. Where is your boyfriend? Why are you always at home on Friday and Saturday nights? You need to find someone who will take you out on dates. You never do anything. You never go anywhere. You're living a boring life at such a youthful age."

Melanie knew her mother was right, and she would respond, "Mom, I know. I really do need someone in my life." On occasions, Melanie would think, *Mom is right. You are living a boring life. There is no way I should be sitting around in the house not doing anything. I should be living life. I really need to find me someone who will treat me like the lady I am.*

But as quick as she would think this, she would dismiss the thought. She often told herself, "There is too much going on out here in the world. No one is trustworthy these days. Besides, I am comfortable with the way things are between Jonathan and myself. There is something special between us. I just know there is."

She held on to the thought that Jonathan would one day recognize who she was to him, so she talked herself away from the thought of seeing someone else. Family members who encountered Jonathan didn't favor him at all. They tried to warn Melanie of what type of person he was. They all knew that he would end up hurting Melanie one day. Melanie was just too blind from being in love with Jonathan to see how accurate they were. Her heart wouldn't allow her to think of him being any other way but how she saw him.

She always told herself, "Love will kill the monster inside Jonathan." Melanie should have realized that the monster in Jonathan could always resurface when the proper opportunity presented itself.

Melanie always wondered when Jonathan would ever tell her he loved her. This was something she never dared discuss with him. She knew men did not like to talk about nor display these natural feelings and emotions. It had been about a year since they met on January 4, 1994.

One day, while riding home from work, Jonathan turned and faced Melanie while at a red light. He grabbed her hand and looked at Melanie, stating, "You know I love you, right?"

She was shocked at him and asked, "You do?"

He responded, "Yeah, man. You know I love you. I know I don't show it, but I do."

She felt so good on the inside. "I love you too, Jonathan."

He drew close to her and said, "Give me a kiss."

Melanie leaned in and gave him what he asked of her. She thought, *It finally happened. He told me he loved me! Oh my god, he said he loved me! I knew it! I knew it! Yes! I knew my baby loved me. I just had to be patient and wait for it.*

She was all smiles the entire ride home. On the inside, she felt this was one thing conquered, but how much more conquering before he revealed all of him to her? She wanted to be a part of his world. She wanted to meet his friends and the remaining family members. So far, she had only met his mother, aunt, and grandmother. She knew a couple of Jonathan's friends. Now that he had told her how he felt, she thought this meant she had access to him. She quickly learned this was not the case. He gave bits and parts of himself when he was ready to her.

Melanie had moved out of the apartment she was living in with her mother, sister, and brother. She moved in with a friend and had her own room. It already had a bed and a little couch. This was perfect for Jonathan because the complex was his stomping ground. So there was nothing that would stop them from seeing each other on a regular basis. Jonathan was good friends with the boyfriend of Melanie's roommate's. They had known each other for years before Jonathan met Melanie. Melanie was so happy. Jonathan was spending more time and nights with Melanie. Melanie's roommate never complained because Jonathan's presence was keeping her boyfriend at home. The four of them had fun together. It was heaven for Melanie.

Jonathan eventually started living with Melanie. This was all Melanie wanted. A place where Jonathan would be welcome and to begin living out her dreams with Jonathan. Everything she had ever wanted from Jonathan was happening.

LOSING HER CROWN

Melanie was driving home, thinking about her life. She thought, *Thank you, God. You answered my prayers. I asked you to open Jonathan's heart and eyes about me. He's spending time with me and tells me he loves me. We're closer, and he lives with me.* Melanie prayed for those things, but did she really understand what she was asking from God?

CHAPTER 2

"Melanie!" Jonathan shouted.

Melanie walked to Jonathan, asking, "Yes, Jonathan?"

Jonathan commanded Melanie, "Drop them panties."

With a smile, Melanie replied, "Okay." While she removed her clothing, Melanie performed a little striptease for him. Jonathan ogled Melanie with excitement. He loved how she swayed those hips as she did her figure 8 dance. Those hips were moving in slow motion, and then she picked up a little speed. Jonathan's member stood erect as he continued to watch Melanie.

Jonathan thought, *Damn. I'ma tear that pussy up.* Jonathan pulled Melanie close to him, asking, "Are you ready for me?"

Melanie responded, "Yes, I am."

She lay back on the bed and took a deep breath as he entered her. She had to prepare herself because he always thrust inside her. His thrusts were painful, causing her to squirm and scoot. She would often confide in him about the pain he inflicted.

Jonathan always responded, "But it feels good to you, doesn't it?" To calm her, he would use his tongue to tickle her ear, taking her mind off the pain. It worked a little, but she could still feel the pain he was inflicting inside her.

Melanie answered, "Yes, it does feel good, but it still hurts, Jonathan."

When Jonathan was ready to relieve himself, he asked Melanie, "You want to have my baby?"

She replied, "Yes, I do."

Jonathan's thrusts would become even harder inside her. Melanie always clenched onto Jonathan, holding him tightly. As she said yes to him, Jonathan relieved himself and planted his seed in her that night. This was different from their normal routine because they always practiced the rhythm method. Jonathan did not like wearing a condom with Melanie. From that night, in every sexual encounter, Jonathan planted his seed in Melanie. Melanie never stopped him.

Pregnancy Symptoms

Weeks went by, and Melanie started feeling funny, with awkward taste buds, sleepiness, nausea, and vomiting after a meal. Melanie went to see her doctor. She had submitted blood and urine samples to be examined. She waited quietly for the doctor to return to the room. She always liked reading the literatures on the wall with pictures of the body's anatomy. That seemed to pass the time while waiting.

Her doctor stepped in the room, stating, "Well, Melanie, I looked at your test results. It confirmed just what I thought. You're feeling tired, nervous, and you haven't had your period this month. Congratulations. You are going to be a mother."

There was a smile that invaded Melanie's face. She absorbed the information asking, "Oh my god! Are you serious? I am? I'm pregnant?"

Dr. Gharma replied, "Yes, you are pregnant. You are about five weeks into the pregnancy. Would you like to hear the baby's heartbeat?"

Melanie replied, surprised, "Yes, ma'am! I would love to hear the baby's heartbeat!"

She had Mel lay on the exam table and slide her clothing down to her hip. She placed some cold gel on Melanie's stomach, placed the detecting wand on her abdomen, and started to move back and forth, searching for the heartbeat. There it was. She had detected it. Melanie was so excited. The baby's heartbeat sounded like a washing machine to her. The heartbeats were rapid. After Mel heard the heartbeat, Dr. Gharma reached into a drawer and handed her a baby book, prenatal vitamins, and literature about her pregnancy.

Melanie already knew she was pregnant with Jonathan's baby. She just needed to confirm it. She was having all the symptoms of being in this condition. On her trip home, she did nothing but smile.

She was so excited and anticipated telling Jonathan her good news. There was a thought that surfaced. What would she do if he told her the baby wasn't his? She had witnessed guys spew this out to their expecting girlfriends. She thought, *I'm having his baby. What will he say? God, please let this bring joy to him. I don't want to feel rejection from him.*

When Melanie arrived home, Jonathan was speaking to a friend. He noticed Melanie walking through the door. He asked, "What did the doctor say?"

She could not help but smile as she walked toward the room they shared. Jonathan was smiling, too, and followed her into the room they shared.

Jonathan asked, "So what did the doctor say?"

Melanie replied with a big smile on her face, "You're going to be a daddy."

Joy went through Jonathan's body. He asked, "For real? You pregnant for real?"

Melanie replied, "Yes, I am."

Jonathan was happy now that Melanie had a confirmed pregnancy. He thought, *Yeah, I'm about to be a daddy!* He walked out the room to share the news with his friend.

Melanie went to see her mother to tell her about the news. She didn't know how her mother would respond. She knew her mother wasn't fond of Jonathan.

"Hey, Mama, guess what? You are going to be a grandmother!" Melanie was so excited and didn't wait for her mother to guess what her surprise was. Her mother wasn't surprised, nor was she happy.

She stated, "Melanie!" She was so disappointed in Melanie. She rolled her eyes at Melanie.

Melanie knew her mother was not pleased with her news. This saddened Melanie and hurt her. She wasn't expecting this type of resistance from her mother. She asked herself, "Why is she not happy about me being pregnant? Should not matter who the father is. It's me, her cupcake, having her grandbaby."

Lashon wanted grandkids by Melanie, but why did she have to allow herself to get pregnant by Jonathan? It was all she could think of. He was no good for her. She despised her daughter's decision to not take any precautions to protect herself. Her cupcake had ruined her life. She secretly didn't care for him but tolerated him because of Melanie. She always thought Melanie was meant to be with someone who treated her like the queen she was. Lashon thought, *I just don't understand why she would get pregnant by him. He treats her like she is just a home girl to him. He disappears on her for months at a time. I wish I had shown her better. I know she is following my footsteps. She is going to end up taking care of his ass. I just know it. He is already displaying the same characteristics her father had. He's not a responsible person. And how will he take care of the baby if he's not working? My daughter will end up taking care of this baby alone. Why could she not see this? My daughter deserves better.*

Lashon could see her daughter getting hurt. She witnessed the toxic relationship and couldn't understand why her daughter was blind. Her mother knew better than to talk against him to Melanie. She knew her daughter loved him deeply and knew her disparaging remarks about him would only draw her closer to Jonathan. Melanie was always defensive when people would try to talk about Jonathan to her. She didn't want to hear their opinions. She let them talk, but she did just what she wanted, which was ignore them and love Jonathan more. Their advice went in one ear and right out the other. She thought, *How can any of them fix their mouths to say anything about my relationship? Look at the relationships they are enduring. My mom should refrain from saying anything to me about him. She was married to and stayed with my worthless dad all those years. Everything he put her through, she still stayed with him. Jonathan is nothing like him. He loves me, and he wants to be with me.*

Melanie's morning sickness was becoming more intense about six weeks into her pregnancy. She couldn't hold anything in her stomach. Everything she tried to eat, she would regurgitate immediately. She was losing weight and could barely function. Her mother noticed her symptoms, stating, "When I carried you all, I never had symptoms like you're experiencing. I was able to work and move furniture around with no problems."

At six weeks, Melanie scheduled an appointment for a sonogram. She was excited and couldn't wait to hear the heartbeat and see the baby that was growing inside her. The tech appeared and asked Melanie to lay back and pull her clothing down to her hips. She applied the cream across Melanie's belly. She was looking at the sac in which the baby resided. There was no heartbeat and no evidence that the sac was growing. The tech called in colleagues to look at the screen so that they would confirm her diagnosis. They agreed that the diagnosis was right. The tech gave Melanie a hug and told her she didn't need to be home alone. Melanie couldn't process what was going on with her baby.

She thought, *What's going on? Why is she hugging me? What does she mean the sac isn't growing and there's no heartbeat?* Melanie asked, "Ma'am, what's going on with my baby?"

She told Melanie her doctor would be calling her to expound. She couldn't tell Melanie her baby had no life, and her body would soon reject and terminate the pregnancy.

Melanie walked out of the office with a stoic look on her face. She drove home crying. She couldn't believe what was happening. "God, please don't take my baby from me. I was so excited when I heard the first heartbeat. How will I tell Jonathan our baby will terminate itself? What am I going to do? Oh, God, I want my baby!"

At this time, Jonathan wasn't living with Melanie any longer because of a confrontation he erroneously involved himself with a friend. A fight occurred, and Jonathan had to leave before the police arrived. She had no way of contacting him to deliver the bad news.

A couple of days after her sonogram, her doctor called her and explained to her the details of the sonogram performed. Dr. Lindsay expressed how sorry he was, stating, "Since there is evidence the sac isn't growing and no heartbeat, the pregnancy will eventually terminate. Melanie, you shouldn't be alone when this happens."

Melanie replied, "Yes, Doctor. I understand."

Dr. Lindsay added, "Melanie, I want you to come in for an examination after the miscarriage occurs. Please call us to schedule the appointment."

Melanie agreed and hung up the call. She was heartbroken and couldn't believe what she absorbed. When she released the line, she lay in her bed, wondering what went wrong. Was there something she or her doctor could have done to prevent this? Melanie knew this would be one of life's mysteries. Sometimes the body would reject the pregnancy because of an unknown genetic deformity.

Jonathan called Melanie to check on her. Her roommate called her to the phone. When she heard it was Jonathan, she braced herself to deliver the news. "Jonathan, the doctor says the baby isn't growing, and there is no heartbeat. I will eventually miscarry this baby."

Jonathan was sad to hear that Melanie wouldn't be able to carry his baby. He asked, "For real, baby? Awe man, I'm so sorry. Are you okay?"

Melanie answered, "Yes, I am."

Jonathan added, "Melanie, I love you, okay?"

Melanie replied, "Okay, I love you too." They released the lines. Melanie didn't hear from Jonathan after that call. No checking on her, nothing. She felt even more alone.

Melanie went to stay with her mother until the pregnancy terminated itself. She wanted to be around people who loved and cared for her most. Two weeks dragged by, and in the wee hours of the morning in March, Melanie began to experience abdominal pain. Her stomach felt as though it was twisting into a ball, knot, or something. It hurt. It hurt bad. Her mother called Jonathan to let him know she was losing the baby, and paramedics were on their way. Jonathan rushed to be with her. He was there within minutes. Melanie heard him arrive. He hit the curb trying to park the car to get to Melanie. She lost the baby while on the toilet. She was wiping herself. She looked at the tissue, and there it was. A white tissue-like, lifeless embryo with black eyes. She thought, *My baby.*

She was still in pain after the miscarriage happened. The ambulance arrived and wheeled her to the ER at St. Paul Hospital. Jonathan followed the ambulance. A DNC removed any and all remnants of the miscarriage.

Jonathan joined her in the room. He looked at her, asking, "Melanie? When are we going to try this again?"

Mel answered, "Jonathan, I don't know if I want to ever go through this again in life."

He stated with shrugged shoulders, "Okay."

Melanie had decided she would move back home. She just didn't want to be away from her mother. She needed to feel love and attention. She knew Jonathan wouldn't be there for her. She packed all her belongings and left the apartment she once shared with her roommate. She was angry at Jonathan for not being there for her. She didn't understand Jonathan intervening in a fight that didn't concern him, causing him to be away from her when she needed him most. If these signs weren't eye-opening, nothing would be. Only an act of betrayal would be the eye-opener for Melanie.

It took Melanie a long time to get over the miscarriage. She fell into a realm of self-pity. Melanie just couldn't understand why it had to be her. She sat on the patio, wondering why she miscarried her baby. What did she do wrong? She started drinking beer, smoking weed, and sitting out on the patio late at night, thinking about her baby. Tears would roll down her face.

"Why, God? Why did you take my baby from me? I don't exhibit qualities of abandonment, neglect, or abuse. Just ain't fair."

Whenever she would endeavor to converse with Jonathan about it, he would brush her off and tell her, "Look, man, you can't be dwelling on this. You need to get over this."

As true as it was, this wasn't what she wanted or needed to hear from him. No one understood how she felt. She kept it inside and dealt with it the best way she could. No support made everything worse for her. If she had a caring boyfriend to hold her and tell her everything would be fine, she could have found the strength needed to a speedy recovery. Jonathan didn't exhibit any of those simple human compassions she was looking for. Eventually, Melanie decided she would eliminate feeling sorry for herself and make this better for herself.

LOSING HER CROWN

Melanie brought herself out of depression and started to live life as before without drowning herself in beer and weed. Melanie focused on her writing and wrote a short story about her struggle.

On the Outside Looking In

It was early Sunday morning. The day most people get up and prepare themselves for church. I decided today would be my day to worship the Lord. I ate breakfast and dressed myself. Dashed out the door because I was running late. I got in my car and was on my way to church. When I pulled into the parking area, a young man met and helped me out the car. He looked at me stating, "We've been waiting for you." He escorted me to the door. Stunned with his chivalrous act, I thanked him. I started to wonder, what did he mean by, "We've been waiting for you?" He excused himself and said, "Enjoy the service." I opened the door and saw that everything and everyone were in somewhat a mannequin state. I looked at the preacher, his face had impressions of a preacher profusely preaching. The congregation was standing with their hands in mid-clap. I became fearful wondering why I was discerning this still audience. There appeared a white light before me, and a man clothed in white. He immediately took me by the hand, leading me to a bench where three individuals were seated. As I drew closer, I saw that these three individuals were me. The young me, the current me and the person God wanted me to be. He placed me in front of the young teenaged girl. She sat there with her head hung low looking sad. He asked, "What happened?" I looked at her and said, "I don't know what happened." He stated,

"The eyes are the window to your soul." I looked deep into those eyes and jumped back. I remembered what turned her beautiful smile to somber. Again, He asked, "What happened?" I said, "She was hurt. Hurt by those who were supposed to care for and nurture her as a child. And You, You said humble yourselves little children and I will fight your battles for you. But when she cried out to You, You were nowhere to be found." He led me to the current adult me and asked, "What happened?" I looked at her as she sat there with clenched fist and a look of defeat on her face. I said to Him, "She grew older and wiser. She promised to close off her heart and go to battle with uninvited guests who entered her life." He stepped away from me and began to disrobe His upper body. I viewed the scars that had taken up residency on his body. His body was severely disfigured. Blood began to drip from his head from the crown of thorns that mysteriously appeared. He said, "My daughter, because of your many trials here on earth, you are a better person. I was there when you cried out to me. And I understand being human is the hardest being to live here on earth. Every time wrong came against you, there was an angel taking record and reporting to me. You have a testimony to give." The marks on his body, the dripping blood and crown of thorns disappeared. He led me to the third body and placed me before her. I knew what he wanted me to do. I looked at the young broken-hearted girl and the adult who didn't trust anyone with those clenched fists. I said farewell to them both. They faded away. There sat the new and improved me. I sat where she sat, and we became one. Once united, He disappeared, and the preacher and the congregation were once again singing and praising His name. Amen.

One morning, Melanie was ready to pick up Jonathan for their commute to work. She called him, "Are you ready for work?"

He replied, "No, baby, I'm not going."

Melanie replied, "Okay, well, I'll talk to you later." She felt so uneasy driving alone. She loved him driving her and picking her up from work. The next day, it was the same response. Melanie wondered what was going on with him. "Why is he not going to work?"

One day, she called, and he told her, "Melanie, I quit the job."

She asked, "Why? What happened?"

Jonathan replied, "I just quit, okay?"

Melanie knew this would start the cycle again of her seeing him every two months or so. She replied, "Okay, Jonathan. Talk to you later."

Soon after, Jonathan stopped talking to Melanie. He was never reachable at his cousin's, where he lived. She couldn't figure out his reason for abandoning her. She missed him. She had never felt this way about anyone. She moped around the house, crying. She often thought, *What did I do to deserve this from him? I did everything right. I love him. I let him drive, use, and keep my car. Why is he acting this way toward me?*

Her mother saw the hurt on her face. She knew how Melanie was feeling and gave her the space she needed to heal.

Secret Revealed

One day, Melanie was lying in the bed with her mother. Melanie looked at her mother with those sad eyes, stating, "Mom."

Lashon responded, "Yes, baby? What is it?"

Melanie took a deep breath, saying, "Remember when you and Dad used to send Rita and me to Grandma's for the summer when we were little girls?"

Lashon replied, "Yes, I remember. Why?"

Melanie answered, "Well, one night, Grandma had us all sleeping in the same bed. Rita, Aunt Sherry, Uncle Stan, and me. Mom, I was next to Uncle Stan. I felt funny that night. Something disturbed my sleep, but it didn't fully awaken me. When I woke up in the middle of the night, my undergarment wasn't on but at the foot of the bed. Mom, I didn't remove the garment and place it at the foot of the bed. I never thought anything about it until I got older. I blocked it out because I was so young and felt they could've just slipped off from me."

Melanie started to remember what happened to her when she became older. She always wondered why she felt uneasy when she was around him. As an adult, she thought about how he was always hugging and hitting her and her sisters on their asses when he saw them. He hugged them and gave them about four hits on their asses. Her mother looked at her with such remorse and sadness.

"Melanie, I'm so sorry. Please forgive me. If I had known, I would have never sent you nor Rita there."

With tear stained eyes, Melanie responded, "It's okay, Mom."

They both knew Melanie wouldn't be okay. They knew this would always follow her. It would always be in the back of her mind. That one question. What exactly happened to her that night? A conundrum that remained unanswered. More importantly, why did Grandma have the four of them sleeping in that bed? Lashon couldn't take her eyes off her baby girl. She felt she had failed Melanie for the entire time she had been here on earth.

Melanie went on to tell her, "Mom, he and Aunt Sherry were very mean to us. They always made us feel as though we were imposing on them. Cramping their style or something. Every day we were there, they made us feel uncomfortable. Especially Uncle Stan. He made Rita and I lay on the floor and lift our bodies up with our butts resting in our hands. We had to stay that way until Grandma arrived home from work. He told us we better not tell on him to her. I was afraid of him, Mom."

Lashon saw the hurt in Melanie's eyes and wished she could take the pain from her baby. Lashon asked herself, "How could this monster touch his own brother's child? Why didn't I as a mother see this?" She beat herself up on the inside about this.

CHAPTER 3

Hospital Blues

Lashon was no longer with the children's father. They were married twenty-seven years, not yet divorced. There were four children—Rita, Melanie, Tosha, and their only brother, Justin. Justin was the baby of the bunch. Melanie was her fragile one. She warred inwardly with herself when it came to Melanie.

"I should have protected my baby from her father and his brother. Should have protected both of my daughters."

Lashon remembered how Melanie's dad used to treat Melanie and Rita. The things he would say to them as children should never have parted his lips. Melanie adored him. She desperately sought his approval. She always tried to make him proud of her. She was getting good grades in school. She was a good daughter who made mistakes here and there, but nothing that would cause him to treat her so terribly. She strove to be the best daughter she could be. She was thirsty for the attention of her dad. After countless endeavors over the years, she finally gave up on him. It no longer mattered to her if he was proud or not. She just became numb to his disinterest in her.

Lashon came home one day from a doctor's visit. She called Melanie into the room, stating, "Melanie, baby, I'm sick. They found ulcers in my stomach. They want to run more tests on me. I must be admitted to the hospital."

Melanie stated, "Okay, Mom. You'll be fine." Melanie didn't know how to react and just told herself there was nothing to worry about here. She told herself, "They're just ulcers. They can cure easily. She'll be back home in no time."

Time passed, and Lashon was still in the hospital. The doctor had discussed the tests with her and told her his findings. She had cancer and needed to start chemo immediately. They kept her in the hospital, and Lashon was fine with it. She needed the rest from home. Melanie and Tosha were always at each other's throats. Lashon wasn't looking forward to telling her kids she had cancer. When her daughters came for a visit, she broke the news to them. The baby girl, Tosha, immediately started crying and got into the hospital bed with Lashon. Tosha was the one who truly felt and understood what her mother was going through. Tosha had lupus, high blood pressure, and kidney failure. She was familiar with the hospital stays, the poking, prodding, and needle sticking. Tosha had more sympathy for her than any of the children.

Tosha was no more than seven years of age when that uninvited guest, lupus, invaded her body. Melanie remembered just like it was yesterday. It started out with a bad nosebleed. Her parents called 911 for an ambulance. When the paramedics arrived, they looked at Tosha and dismissed it as just a nosebleed. Later that night, Melanie was in the bathroom with Tosha. Tosha became light-headed and was vomiting chunks of blood. She fell backward for no reason. Her nose had started bleeding again. This terrified Melanie. She was nine, and her baby sister was only seven. They called the ambulance again. They rushed Tosha to the emergency room. A myriad of tests was performed to determine her diagnosis. Finally, the tests revealed she had lupus. One sure way they ascertained it was lupus was the image of a butterfly appearing on her nose. Tosha did not like being hospitalized as a child nor as an adult. She was mean to everyone. It didn't matter who you were. And if a doctor or nurse had bad breath while talking to her, she would turn her body the other way and tell them their breath stunk. She didn't mind letting you know. But because she had a cleft palate, they didn't understand what she was saying.

The hospital released Lashon with instructions to follow-up with chemo treatments. Melanie saw how frail her mother was becoming. But that was what happened when you were on chemo. It depleted all your energy; hair would fall out, and you would feel extremely ill.

To encourage her, Melanie would tell her, "Mom, you will beat this, okay."

Lashon was not as optimistic as Melanie and would reply, "Melanie, you know there is a chance that I may not make it, right?"

Melanie would reply, "Mom, I don't want to hear you talking like that. You are going to pull through this. Stop saying that."

All Lashon could say was "I love you, Melanie."

Melanie would tell her, "I love you too, Mom."

Lashon's sessions for chemotherapy increased. The treatment burned her internally, and she developed mouth sores. It was taking a toll on Lashon and her body. She was so tired and stayed to herself. She didn't want anyone seeing her in this state. She rarely went outside the door. After so many doses of the chemo, she lost weight, her confidence lowered, and that glorious head of thick hair was gone. This grieved her so much. She always received compliments for her beautiful head of hair. There was nothing she could do but rely on time. Time would give her back her beautiful mane. She accepted the inevitable side effect of chemo and purchased a wig. Lashon slapped on the wig and went on about her business.

One day, Lashon woke up feeling extremely good. The best she had felt in months. She told Melanie, "Melanie, I feel so good, and it's scaring me."

Melanie couldn't fathom what she meant. She asked, "How do you feel good but it scares you? Mom, if you are feeling good, that is a good sign. It means you are getting better, and your body is fighting this monster."

Lashon replied, "I'm still scared."

Lashon started showing signs that she was not getting better. The chemo was not working. She was constantly vomiting after the chemo treatments. She walked around the house every day and approached her children to hug them and whisper to them, "I love you, and I'm not going to make it."

The children would tell her how much they loved her. They would always tell her she would be okay and that she would make it. Lashon knew the inevitable would happen and accepted her fate in life.

Melanie became angry toward God, and she expressed it to Lashon. Lashon asked if Melanie would watch a program with her and Tosha on TBN. Melanie folded her arms in defense mode. Melanie replied, "No. I don't believe in Him."

Lashon stated, "Baby, don't say that. Why?"

Melanie replied, "Mom, why is this happening to you just when you rid yourself of Dad, started getting your life on track, and looking good, only for Him to take it away from you? You were just starting to live your life for the first time. Why would He do that? He was never there for me when I cried out to Him. He allowed the abuse from Dad to continue. He said that He would be there for us. But when we needed Him the most, He was nowhere around and turned His back on us. Why did He not answer us? Hurt and pain flooded us. What happened to Him fighting His children battles, Mom? So no, I don't believe in Him." Melanie saw her mother's eyes fill with tears.

"Melanie, you shouldn't feel that way, baby. You shouldn't give up on God."

Melanie replied, "Well, until He shows me otherwise, I'm abandoning Him the way He abandoned me."

This didn't compute with Lashon. Melanie's grandmother had them faithfully going to church every Sunday when they visited for the summers. Melanie believed in God and heard the scriptures, but she had never experienced losing someone she loved who was terminally ill. She could not fathom why God was taking away her mother when she was not prepared to step out into this world on her own. She was always with her mother, except for a couple of times she moved out, but she soon found herself back home.

Her mixed feelings about God was getting the best of her. Melanie wasn't herself. She thought about how God took her baby, separated her from Jonathan, and now He was taking her mother. Melanie thought, *This is so unfair. How do you give life, only to take it away? How am I supposed to be happy with so much grief around me?* Melanie didn't know that it was just anger she felt toward God. She didn't stop believing. She was just angry, and it was okay to be angry. Melanie battled inwardly about her beliefs and became overwhelmed with this shameful feeling. She couldn't believe she allowed her anger about her mother's illness question her beliefs. She cried out to God and apologized for the crime she committed against Him.

"God, I'm so sorry. Please forgive me for being angry toward You. I feel so full of shame. I allowed what is natural in life to question my belief in You. I hope you won't hold this against me." Melanie stopped being angry and accepted that her mother might not make it.

The children's father came by one day, not knowing his wife was sick nor the extent of her illness. He was on Lashon's patio, knocking on the sliding door. Lashon went to the patio to let him have it. She yelled, "You get away from here! Never come around here anymore!"

He looked at his wife, asking, "Baby, what's wrong with you? Why are you looking like this? You look sick." This grieved Tee. He knew something bad was going on with her body.

Lashon again stated, "Get away from here! I don't want you coming around here!"

He did as Lashon asked and walked away. He began to cry, asking, "What's wrong with my wife? She doesn't look herself." Rejection from his wife ignited the fire for a drug binge. He called the home one day with the children disclosing their mother had cancer. He cried uncontrollably. He thought about all the things he should have done, along with the things he regretted doing to her. This was his wife of twenty-eight years.

"I can't lose my wife. She is all I got. I love her, and I know she loves me. Lashon, oh my sweet Lashon!"

Being Hospitalized Again

Lashon's condition worsened. Still, she wasn't able to keep anything in her stomach. She just couldn't stop the vomiting at all. Melanie called her nurse at the cancer treatment center. She explained Lashon's condition. The children were asked that she come into the center to be examined. Once assessed, it was determined hospitalization was necessary. Once she went into the hospital, everything went south, and she never came back home. She was not living in and couldn't remember the present. She was living in the past. It only got worse as the days went by. She was speaking about things and people who just were no longer in existence, and she could see them. Melanie knew that at any time, her mother could leave this earth. Tosha spent every moment she could with her mother.

Melanie was grieving horribly in her own way. No one understood her grieving process. To get her mind off things, she left to attend a wedding in Chicago for peace of mind for about four to five days. People just couldn't understand and asked how she could leave knowing her mother was sick and on her deathbed. Melanie feared that her best friend was leaving her. Going away and not facing it made it unrealistic. Like it was all just a dream, and she would soon awaken. There wasn't a moment while in Chicago she didn't think about her mother. She smiled her best. She didn't want anyone feeling sorry for her. This was a happy time for the couple getting married. She didn't want to place a damper on such a joyous occasion.

To take her mind off things, her friend and their family kept her busy. There were family activities for her to involve herself. She was grateful for them all. Melanie had so much fun there that she found herself momentarily forgetting her worries back home. This made her feel terrible on the inside, making her feel guilty that she was enjoying life. She felt she was betraying her mother. She wanted to get home as soon as possible. Fun time was over for her. Melanie accepted the invitation to this wedding not knowing the bride or groom. She had to wait until her travel companions were ready to head back home. Her travel companion asked if she was okay and if she needed to get back home. Melanie didn't want to be selfish and ask her friend and his family to end their fun to take her back to her ill mother. She couldn't bring herself to do it. On the fourth day after the wedding, it was time to head back home.

Melanie thought about her mother constantly on their way back home. When Melanie arrived home, her mother's condition had worsened. Lashon had fallen into a deep coma while Melanie was away. When she walked in and saw her condition, she lamented. There was no one in the room with Melanie.

She took her mother by the hand, saying, "Mom, I love you so much. I went away for a while. Were you mad at me for leaving? Squeeze my hand once for yes and twice for no."

Lashon heard her cupcake speaking to her, and she tried to open her eyes, but she couldn't. Lashon squeezed her hand twice. Melanie felt relieved by her response. It didn't matter how the family felt about her leaving. Her mother was at peace with her.

"Mom, are you ready to go be with your mother?"

She squeezed Melanie's hand once.

"Okay, Mom. You go ahead and be with your mother. It's okay."

A couple of days later, Melanie and Tosha were home cleaning their mother's apartment. They all were anticipating Lashon would make it despite what the doctors told them. She was still hanging on to dear life. They wanted to have the house cleaned when she came home. While they were cleaning, they received a call from the hospital. It was the chaplain. She was expressing how sorry she was that Lashon had passed away. Lashon's older sisters had just left the hospital and were with her when she took her last breath. The chaplain was not supposed to call Lashon's children until her sisters had broken the news to them. By the time they arrived, Melanie and her siblings were already crying. Lashon died on July 16, 1997, and they buried her on July 19, 1997, in Koran Louisiana, right next to her mother and father. Melanie cried a little at the funeral. There were too many tears shed during the last six months of her mother's life. She was able to maintain composure until one, day it hit that she was never coming back. She would never see her mother again. Melanie cried uncontrollably. That feeling in her gut, the lump in her throat, and the pain in her heart all happened at once.

CHAPTER 4

Melanie was angry at Jonathan. Before her mom died, she called and told Jonathan about her mother's illness. He never followed up with her to ask how she was or anything. When Lashon died, Melanie called him to let him know. He gave his condolences but never came to check on Melanie. He never called Melanie to see if she was okay. No hug, no assurance to Melanie that everything would be okay from the person who was supposed to love her. If there was any crime for him to commit toward Melanie that would tarnish her feelings toward him, this should have been it. Not checking on her should have been the ultimate betrayal. All this she thought about, and still she refused to address him with intense persecution. She should obliterate him from her life. But as usual, she dismissed his behavior and forgave Jonathan.

During the one-year break between Melanie and Jonathan, they saw each other two times. Jonathan did miss Melanie, but he fell heavily into that lifestyle. He was in those streets badly, doing things that could easily provoke retaliation. So he dared not bring trouble around anyone he cared about or loved, so he had to stay away. He never disclosed this to Melanie. She just thought it was something she did that the reason he withdrew himself from her. Melanie became overwhelmed with emotions. She lost her mother, and now she might be losing Jonathan. She cried, cried, and cried.

"Why is he doing this to me? What have I done that was so bad that he had to leave me?" While drowning in sorrow and tears, Melanie heard a voice tell her, "Melanie, Jonathan fathered a baby with another woman, and he doesn't know how to come to you and tell you what he has done." Melanie cried more. This piece of news wasn't what Melanie wanted to hear. She asked herself, "A baby? But with whom? How could this be? I was supposed to have his child. Is this why he won't talk to me?"

Melanie often heard her conscience speaking to her when questions needed answering.

A Moment of Weakness

It had been six months since Jonathan left Melanie. She began to feel anger and vengeful toward Jonathan. Melanie remembered, here was this guy who lived in her apartments. Whenever he walked by Melanie, he would just smile and stare at her, mesmerized by her beauty. Melanie thought about him and had a moment of weakness. Jonathan left her without an explanation. There was no telling what he was doing and with whom. Melanie thought, *Forget this. He is doing what he wants to do. So am I. I don't care anymore.* Revenge plagued Melanie's mind.

Melanie went to this young man's apartment and knocked on his door. Before he could open the door, Melanie asked, "You ready for me?"

He looked at her and invited her into his home. He knew exactly why Melanie had come to him.

Melanie asked, "Do you have a condom?"

He checked his drawer and didn't have a condom. He told Melanie, "Sit here. I'll be right back." He wasn't gone long at all. He returned with a condom and led Melanie to his bed. He was excited inwardly. Never in a million years did he think Melanie would look his way. This was only a one-time thing for Melanie, and he knew it. She still loved Jonathan. She was getting her licks back for all he had done. When it was over, Melanie dressed and left. Neither of them mentioned this one-night stand, nor did it happen again.

Before Melanie's mother died, Melanie began to feel lonely. She needed someone to just talk to and be there for her. Her sister, Tosha, had a best friend named Daisy. Daisy knew Melanie was a good woman and wanted to introduce her to someone who would take her mind off Jonathan. Daisy had explained to him that Melanie was not looking for a relationship. She wanted to spend time with someone with all she was going through because her boyfriend wasn't there for her. His name was Chase.

When he first met Melanie, he was pleased. His friend looked out for him. Melanie was at her aunt's home. Daisy, Charley, and Chase pulled up in his van, ready to extract Melanie to hang out a bit. They exchanged names and went off to enjoy the remainder of the night. Melanie had a wonderful time with Chase. Her friend had done her justice.

Chase was a wonderful person. He adored Melanie and introduced her to his family. They adored Melanie and wanted Chase to pursue a relationship with her. Every opportunity given, he would go to her and take her away from those cares that had her sulking in grief. Melanie was fond of Chase. She played with the thought of being with him, but Melanie knew where her heart was. It was with Jonathan. Chase was everything Melanie needed in life. Chase would be the perfect match for Melanie. A soul worth taking home to meet her mother. Lashon would have loved to see those two together. Jonathan, on the other hand, was an embarrassment. Melanie struggled inwardly about Jonathan. She wondered if she even loved him. Was it just lust boiling on the inside of her?

She thought, *I wish I could release myself from Jonathan and be with Chase. Everything about Chase is right. He cares about my feelings. He adores and spends time with me. Chase is everything I could ever want in a man. Hell, even his family adores me.*

Melanie's mother was pleased with Chase. She had never met Chase because of her illness. But she was happy that her daughter was spending time with someone, taking her places, and being attentive to her. All the things Jonathan never did. Sometimes, when Chase came to visit Melanie to whisk her away, no one was home to care for her mother.

Melanie would tell him, "I can't leave my mother. No one is here."

When Lashon would hear her say this, she would yell to her, "Melanie, you can go with him! I'll be okay."

Melanie asked, "Mom, are you sure?"

Lashon replied, "Yes, baby. You go on. I'll be fine." Lashon wanted her cupcake to find happiness. It was good that she was getting out, having fun, and enjoying life. She didn't want to hold Melanie back from spending time with this young man who adored her daughter.

Melanie met Chase's parents and siblings the second week of knowing each other. They all adored Melanie and thought she was the right person for Chase. They always invited her to go places with them. They even invited her brother, Justin, to come with them too. They accepted Melanie and really wanted her and Chase to be a couple. He invited her to family outings in Six Flags, Sandy Lake Park, and to that wedding in Chicago she attended. This was all new to Melanie. No one ever treated her this way. She wished that Jonathan was the type of man Chase was to her.

Chase loved taking her around his homies and showing her off to them. He had a smile on his face while introducing her that would say, "Look what I got with me." Chase understood the situation Melanie was facing with Jonathan. She had already explained that she had someone and that he had abandoned her. Chase never pressured her about anything. He was very patient with Melanie. Chase was just happy to be in her company. He knew what existed between them would not last. Eventually, Chase couldn't stand the thought of being around Melanie, knowing he wanted more from her. His trips to her faded away about a month after her mother had passed. Melanie understood and accepted the distancing.

After her mothers' funeral, Melanie tried to move on and keep busy, but losing her mother was hard for Melanie. She had always been with her mother. She had never been on her own as far as having her own place. She wondered how she would find the strength to go on in life. One sure way for her to move on was finding another job. She had been unemployed for two months after her mother became ill. Her mother found out in November of 1996 that she had cancer. She passed in July 1997. She was gone eight months after finding out cancer invaded her body.

Melanie and her sister Tosha already had a strained relationship, but the death of their mother caused an increase in the strain. They weren't getting along as usual and not speaking. The arguments and not talking to each other amplified now that Lashon was no longer with them. Tosha always criticized Melanie about everything. She especially despised Jonathan. Tosha felt the same as Lashon. Melanie shouldn't have been with him. He made her sister cry, and Tosha didn't like this at all. Tosha and Lashon both knew that one day, Jonathan would cause Melanie pain. Instead of Tosha trying to help Melanie rid herself of him, she always had negative things to say about him. It just made Melanie have more faith that Jonathan would prove them wrong. She knew her loyalty was with him, but she wondered about his loyalty to her. She had doubts about how he truly felt about her. Things were still the same with no changes between them.

About a year passed since Jonathan had been away from Melanie. Jonathan started to miss her more than ever and was warring inwardly about a secret he had to disclose to Melanie. He knew this secret would hurt her. Jonathan had never loved anyone the way he loved Melanie. He was shameful and in disbelief he was so careless to allow this to happen. He thought, *How do I tell the person I love that I have fathered a child with someone else? She will leave me for sure. I know she will. How could I have been so careless?*

There was no official breakup between them, but still he knew he had to get Melanie back.

Jonathan had to see Melanie, and he drove to her apartment. When he arrived, Melanie was sitting in the car with another man and talking to him. Melanie had no interest in him. She was just trying to occupy her time and keep Jonathan off her mind. Jonathan saw her in the car. He didn't like what he saw, but what could he do? There was no way he could get mad about her spending time with someone after he left her open to these wolves out here. He always prepared himself for the run-in he might encounter from seeing Melanie with someone else. How would he respond seeing another man enjoy what was once his?

Jonathan stood there after Melanie's brother, Justin, pointed her out to him. Melanie, stunned at her brother pointing her out, immediately said good night to her company and exited his car. She walked over to Jonathan. He just looked at her and followed her into the apartment.

He asked, "Melanie, who was that you were sitting in the car with?"

She replied, "No one, Jonathan. Just a friend."

He asked, "If he's a friend, why did you not introduce us?"

Melanie replied, "Jonathan, he had to go, okay?"

Jonathan stated, "Mighty funny he had to leave when I pull up."

Melanie went into the room where her mother slept. Jonathan followed her. He was angry about Melanie sitting in that car.

Melanie wondered if it slipped his mind to ask her how she was doing since she lost her mother. How long would it take him to show compassion to her? Did seeing Melanie with another help aid in him forgetting to ask how she was feeling? He never uttered one word about her losing her mother.

Jonathan discerned Melanie had on a pair of leopard print shorts that were for bedtime and a T-shirt. Jonathan stuck his hand down her shorts, and no panties were present.

He shouted, "You were out there sitting in the car with oh boy with no panties!"

Melanie replied, "Nothing happened! He just showed up to the apartment after I took my bath." Melanie was telling a lie. She knew he was coming to see her. But she had no interest in this man. Melanie's brother was present and listening to them while playing his game. Jonathan told him to get up and go take his bath. Jonathan wanted to know if someone else had been dipping in his sugar bowl. He pulled Melanie toward him, touching her breast and ass that he had neglected now for a year. He removed those shorts and laid Melanie down, abandoning foreplay and thrusting himself inside her. She jerked her body. She had been without sex since that one moment of weakness. Her vagina was giving Jonathan a hard time to enter.

Jonathan whispered, "Damn, it's tight. Is it still mine, Melanie?" Melanie said nothing. He asked again, "Is this still mine, Melanie?" Jonathan started going deeper and thrusting harder in her.

Melanie could no longer stay silent. She screamed, "Yes, it's still yours!"

Jonathan said, "Tell me you still love me, Melanie." He was kissing Melanie passionately on her lips and started kissing and sucking on her neck. Those enthusiastic kisses and missed thrusting had Melanie's head in another dimension. She had forgotten how good Jonathan made her feel, and she could no longer control what was about to spew from her lips.

She shouted, "I still love you, Jonathan!"

This dismissed any thoughts Jonathan had about Melanie allowing someone else to enjoy his wonderland. Jonathan was careful not to plant any more seeds by using the rhythm method he always practiced with Melanie. Once their sexual encounter ended, they talked for a while. Jonathan didn't stay long. It was time to go after confirming no one had touched nor played with his wonderland. So he thought.

Melanie felt as though she betrayed herself. She cried internally. She thought, *How could you let him do this to you? Why are you so weak for this man? He left you, and here you are letting him dick dance all in you. You don't know where and who he has been with since leaving you. No protection, Melanie? Come on, you are smarter than that.*

When Jonathan left her and stayed away, she promised herself she would no longer permit him to finagle his way back into her life. That was an epic failure. She was weak for him. What was this hold he had on her? She had no explanation. She searched for answers and concluded they were meant to be. She craved this man like she craved no other.

It pleased Jonathan that he confirmed that Melanie had not been with anyone. But Melanie had a secret. Just that one time, she allowed her neighbor a pass into her wonderland. He did no damage, so Jonathan was clueless. Now that he knew Melanie had not been with anyone, his ego amplified ten times.

He stated, "Melanie, I gotta go and take this car back to its owner. I better not catch you in the car with no one else. You hear me?"

Melanie had dropped her head and looked at the floor. Not once did he ask how she was doing.

Jonathan raised her head, asking, "Melanie, do you hear me?"

She replied, "Okay, yes, Jonathan."

He felt like he had put his foot down.

Melanie remembered she needed to ask Jonathan's advice about her father's recidivist behavior since their mother died. She asked, "Jonathan, can I talk to you for a minute?"

Jonathan replied, "What is it, Melanie?"

She said, "Dad has been coming around here. He's been stealing from us and acting crazy."

Jonathan pulled out a gun to hand it to Melanie. Jonathan stated, "Okay, here, take this. It is clean. I had a dope fiend purchase it from the pawnshop." Jonathan handed Melanie the gun. He stated, "If he comes here messing with y'all, you light his ass up. You hear me, Melanie?"

Melanie replied, "Okay, Jonathan."

Jonathan kissed Melanie and gave her a hug. Melanie watched Jonathan as he entered the car and drove away. Melanie shut the door and looked at the gun. She stroked and examined the gadget. "I need to put this away. I cannot let this get in Justin's hands. He's just a child." Melanie put the gun in a safe place, out of Justin's reach. Melanie lay down and was ready for bed.

Jonathan drove home, thinking, *If she's thinking about getting with another, I just obliterated that idea.* Jonathan was not able to erase the image of the stranger spending time with Melanie in his car. He wanted to hurt this man, but he knew this was all his fault. If he had never left Melanie, there would be no reason for her to entertain the thought of being with another.

Heart Walk of Shame

The next morning, Melanie felt shameful. She sat on the bed and held her head in her hands, crying. "Why can't I get him out of my system? I knew exactly what he was doing. His ass thinks he is smart trying to see if another had been inside me. He will never know my secret unless I divulge it to him. His ass was itching to dance in me and never even asked how I was doing, knowing my mother had passed. This should have given me ammunition to dismiss his ass. Inconsiderate ass bastard! He was away from me a year. That was enough time for me to get over him and find someone who would treat me with respect. This is my fault. I was praying, crying, and pleading my case before God, petitioning to bring him back to me. What was I thinking? Can't be mad at any one but me."

Melanie thought of how stupid it was of her to just take this man back with no explanation of why he left her. Jonathan expressed no emotions, refused to spend time with her, take her out on dates, and seldomly told her how much she meant to him.

Melanie was no stupid person. She was just a woman who happened to be in love with a man who had no idea how to treat her. You see, Jonathan's father left when he was a toddler. His mother solely raised him. When he became a teenager, the drug dealers, hustlers, and gangsters took him under their wing. They educated him well about the streets and hard knocks of life. Survival of the fittest. That was the motto of the streets. This meant in the hood, for males, you get down or you lay down. He chose to get down with the program, and he loved it.

No one in Jonathan's eyes was worthy of preaching to him how he could be a positive product of his environment. There was no father in the home to steer him in the right direction and give him pointers on how he should treat a lady. All he saw was how to disrespect and use them, especially for their throats. Even though the streets showed love, this type of love came with a cost. The love they had for you was determined by loyalty. Family love and street love were not the same. Your family loves you unconditionally and has the choice of disowning you or severing those ties. The streets love you for the influence it has on you. If you walk to the beat of its drums, you're ok. Once you execute disloyalty, there's no more love. It's your ass they're after.

Jonathan was careless, and lived life as if he wouldn't make it beyond his twenties. He figured if he made it to twenty-one, he did what hindered most males in the hood. He dodged that bullet and survived. In the Black male's realm, making it to eighteen was an accomplishment, and it was amazing if they could reach twenty-one. So if he had any goals in life as a child, they were quickly dismissed as a teenager. He just lived for the moment.

After Jonathan realized the streets were no longer tantalizing for him, he began warring inwardly about who he needed to be and all the things he needed to lay to rest. He couldn't understand what was going on with him. His spirit was endeavoring to influence him. He often heard, *Melanie is all you need. Love her and start a family with her. She loves you and is loyal.*

Jonathan already knew what his conscience was telling him was the truth about Melanie. "I love her and want to make a change in life. Losing her wouldn't be good for me." Jonathan made up his mind that he would bury his street life to dedicate himself to Melanie. "She's worth it. She has shown nothing but loyalty to me. She never pops up on me. There are no demands that I spend time with her. No hanging around or clinging to me. Melanie is the opposite of these other women. I think of her as a diamond in the rough. I love all those things about her. She is beautiful, smart, no kids when I met her, and still no children. Why is she with me? What does she see in me? Why would she want to be with someone who fucks up all the time? She deserves better. I was away from her an entire year, and she still lights up with that shimmer in her eyes when I see her. Melanie is my baby. I love her."

Jonathan, after allowing this to marinade in his mind, decided that from now on, whatever Melanie wanted within reason, Melanie would get.

CHAPTER 5

One morning, Melanie was getting ready for work. A familiar uninvited guest showed up to the apartment. He was seeking compassion from the children. "I've been out in these streets drug binging, I'm tired and need to rest." He jumped the patio, tapping on the patio door. Melanie heard the knock and knew it was her dad. Melanie didn't want to hear any more lies from him. She called the police on him. They came to the property. Melanie told them their mother had passed away and he was trespassing. None of the siblings wanted him there. The officer explained to their dad he needed to leave. Melanie asked in front of her dad, "Sir, if he comes back causing problems or break in the apartment, am I at liberty to protect my home as I see fit?"

The officer replied, "Ma'am, you are at liberty to do as you see fit. Mr. Tee, did you hear your daughter? She doesn't want you here."

Her dad responded, "Okay, Officer."

Melanie decided not to go to work that morning. She parked her car in another section of the apartments. She had a gut feeling her father would come back as soon as he saw her leave. After parking the car, she walked back to the apartment. As soon as Melanie opened the door, she heard him coming through the shattered window covered with cardboard he had broken after their mother passed away. Melanie grabbed the gun and shot blindly at the window. *Boom!*

She heard her dad scream, "Oh! Melanie, baby, is that you? You shot me. Take me to the hospital, honey."

Melanie yelled, "I'm not taking you nowhere!"

He walked off, and Melanie called the police. Within minutes, Melanie heard sirens and a helicopter. The officer who just left had returned.

The officer asked, "Ms. Ashley, where is he?"

LOSING HER CROWN

Melanie replied, "I'm not sure, Officer." Melanie was shaking.

A neighbor had heard the gunshot and noticed the police were at her apartment. He knocked on the door to check on Melanie and the family. He saw that Melanie was shaking. He walked in and held her.

The officer stated, "Ms. Ashley, I was here earlier. You are not in any trouble. You told him not to come back. He knew the consequences. May I see the gun you used to shoot him?"

Melanie handed him the gun. He looked at it, emptied it, and examined the bullets.

He stated, "Oh, wow, these are hollow points. They do some damage."

They had to confiscate the gun and told Melanie she could have it back after their investigation. Melanie had no choice but to cooperate.

Once the police left, Melanie called her job to let them know she wouldn't make it to work that day. After speaking to her job, she called Jonathan. Jonathan answered, "Hello?"

Melanie spoke, "Jonathan, it's Melanie."

Jonathan asked, "What's up, Melanie?"

Melanie replied, "Um, I shot Daddy."

Jonathan chuckled and replied, "You did? Well, he deserved it. He had no business coming there. You okay? Melanie, you have no reason to feel guilty. You know that, right?"

Melanie answered, "Yes, I know. I just never thought I would do it. It felt good to pull that trigger."

Jonathan asked, "Melanie, are the police still there? You better not let them hear you saying that."

Melanie replied, "No, they are already gone."

Jonathan told Melanie, "Baby, I must get back to work, okay. I'll talk to you later."

Melanie replied, "Okay."

Jonathan thought, *My baby has been inducted into the bust a cap in your ass hall of fame.* Jonathan called out to his coworker, "Shay, guess who was on the phone."

Shay asked Jonathan, "Who was it, Jonathan?"

Jonathan replied, "It was Melanie on the phone. Guess what she just told me."

Shay asked, "Can you just tell me what she said? What did she tell you?"

Jonathan stated, "She told me she just shot her daddy."

Shay asked, "Melanie shot her daddy? Boy, quit lying. That girl did not shoot her daddy."

Jonathan laughed, stating, "Shay, yes, she did. I'm telling the truth."

Shay said, "But, Jonathan, Melanie so quiet, and she look like she wouldn't hurt a fly. What happened?"

Jonathan replied, "Well, looks can be deceiving. She with me now. I been preparing her for stuff like this. He was breaking into the apartment when she shot him."

Shay stated, "Boy, shut up. You been shaping and molding her to your liking?"

Jonathan replied, "Hell, yes. She smiles too much, and that bothers me. I know when people look at her, they see a target and feel they can take advantage of her. She is naïve to this world I am in, and I must show her the way. My influence on her will be so great, she will bar none."

Shay asked, "Really, Jonathan? That may come with consequences. There is a reason for her smiles. If you take her smile from her, she won't be the same person. You just may create or bring out the monster deep within her."

Jonathan replied, "I doubt that would happen. I am just making her a little less trusting to these wolves out here. The people who want to impose harm to her."

Shay stated, "Jonathan, she may become confused and think everyone is out to get her. You just can't take a kind soul like her and discard all those beautiful attributes about her."

Jonathan replied, "Well, that's the chance I'm willing to take. I'm looking out for her." Jonathan didn't understand how this would affect his relationship with Melanie. He had good intentions, but they would later prove to be intoxicating.

Jonathan went to Melanie one night while everyone was sleep. He couldn't wait to get to her. "I'm going to surprise her. Anticipating her reaction when I try what I have mastered on her. I been looking at these flicks, learning how to please her orally. Listening to the fellows and taking notes." Jonathan had performed an oral act on Melanie when they first started seeing each other. He just didn't know what he was doing the first time, and she did not care for him trying again.

When he arrived, Melanie was already ready for bed. She had taken her bath and was lying in the bed that she once shared with her mother. Melanie was surprised to see Jonathan. Jonathan hugged Melanie and kissed her.

Melanie asked, "What are you doing here, Jonathan? I was about to go to bed."

Jonathan ignored her statement and started touching Melanie all over her body, places that he once again had neglected for months. He laid Melanie down and told her to open her legs. She opened her legs, and he started pleasuring her orally. Melanie's eyes rolled to the back of her head.

She thought, *He is making this feel so good. And he knows what he is doing too. How does he know to do this? He didn't know what he was doing the first time. Who taught him this? I'm just going to enjoy this and not say anything.*" Melanie could feel herself about to climax. She confessed, "Jonathan, you better stop before you…oh my god, baby!"

Jonathan could feel her body twitching. It was one of the signs his friends told him to pay close attention. This was a sure sign that she was climaxing. They also told him, "Don't stop, even if she asks. Keep going and you got her. She will be yours."

Melanie called Jonathan's name out, "Jonathan! Oh my god! Oh God, this feels good!" Melanie's body was shaking and trembling. She felt flutters all over her body. Tingling sensations rushed through her body. She had never experienced this feeling. He paid close attention to her anatomy and had her head swimming with thoughts.

Melanie had forgotten about her concern to inquire with Jonathan of his newly acquired skill. Too many times she told herself she would just stay quiet and go with the flow. She just allowed things to surface without questioning. Melanie was losing herself while she stayed with Jonathan. Nothing mattered but her becoming Mrs. Jonathan Taylor. She loved the thought of having his last name, but her last name, Ashley, she adored. Melanie Ashley rolling off your tongue just had a better sound. She would be more than happy to take his last name. This would make it official and tell everyone that they belonged to each other. Melanie promised herself that there would be no smothering Jonathan at all if he married her. She didn't want to be another statistic and watch her marriage crumble. Always being around him, smothering him. She wanted to make sure she balanced this all. She would endeavor to approach any situation with finesse and delicacy. She would endeavor being an adult without the screaming, yelling, and pointing the finger.

She thought, *Easy how we can plan out everything, but getting it to play out the way I'm picturing it won't be so easy. It is going to take arduous work.*

Melanie didn't want to end up like her mother and father. All they ever did was argue, and sometimes, fists were thrown, and her mother would be the one hurt and in tears. This hurt Melanie to see her mother cry. She loved both parents, but her relationship with her father wasn't the best. All little girls wanted to be Daddy's little girl. Her baby sister won that title with him. Melanie required just a little attention. She had no problem sharing him. But he never made it possible for Melanie to embrace the "daddy's little girl" title. He favored Tosha because of her illnesses. She was able to get away with doing things Melanie and Rita knew better than to do. He always felt that Tosha's life span would be short. So he wanted her to enjoy her life as much as possible.

Melanie knew what caused her relationship with her father to go awry. She witnessed her dad hurting her mother one night. Melanie was only seven. She heard her mother screaming. Her dad had her mother pinned down on the floor. Lashon was on her stomach, and Melanie's dad was on top of her. He had Melanie's mothers' right arm pulled back, pushing it up her back like he was trying to break it. Melanie grabbed a broom and went into the area he had her mother pinned.

Melanie yelled, "You better get off my momma!"

She angered her dad and made him feel that she was choosing sides. He looked at Melanie with disdain, stating, "You better get your ass out of here before I beat your ass!"

Melanie saw the look on his face. That evil look on his face frightened her. She turned her face, walked away, and cried.

After he removed himself off her mother, he yelled out, "Melanie, bring your ass here!" He beat her with a clothes hanger that night. From that day on, he looked at Melanie as an enemy who would side with her mother. Melanie didn't figure this out until she became much older. It all made sense to her now.

"He had disdain for me because I was the only one to make him cognizant that I saw him hurting my mother. No child wants to see their father beating their mother for any reason." She had no explanation as to why her mother didn't save her that night. "I saved her from him possibly breaking her arm. Why was I not saved from that ass whipping?"

Melanie understood the entire time her parents were together that her mother was afraid to leave him with nowhere to go. At the time, Lashon and Tee had three small children. Justin came ten years after Tosha was born.

Melanie thought, *Where would she have gone with all of us at such young ages? Leaving a marriage with children is easier said than done.* Melanie had anger toward her mother as she progressed into adulthood. Her mother should have left their father to protect her and her sibling.

Entering Womanhood

Melanie was outside playing with friends and had to go to the bathroom. When she looked at her underwear, she saw blood and knew what this meant. She remembered reading the book about Margaret praying to God to get her period. Melanie was nine when she started her cycle. She was so afraid and didn't know what to do. She wrote her mother a letter and handed it to her sister to give to her mother. Melanie was afraid and went outside to hide behind a tree.

Her mother read the letter, which stated, "Dear Mom, I am on my you-know-what." Her mother came outside, calling for Melanie to come to her. Melanie slipped from behind the tree to approach her mother. Lashon talked to her about what she was going through and how she needed to keep herself extra clean to avoid odor in that area.

Melanie's mother had her handling business for her at such an early age. She was talking to the phone and electric company as if she was a grown woman. She was incredibly mature for her age. No wonder she started her cycle so young. Rita, on the other hand didn't get her cycle until she was fourteen. She suffered every month. She couldn't eat and would lose at least five pounds within three to four days of her cycle being active. She wasn't prepared for adulthood the way Melanie was. Melanie looked older and was bigger than Rita. So people often mistook Melanie as the oldest.

Melanie's father started abusing her right after the incident with her mother, when he almost broke her arm. Melanie was plump for her age. He would make fun of her size. He would call her fatso, porky pig, you get the idea. By the time she became a teenager, the abuse intensified. He called her a bitch, whore, outcast, and black sheep of the family. He would deny her food, making her miss meals because of her weight. This would anger Lashon. She would argue with him about not letting her eat. Her mother would fix her a plate and bring the food in the room to feed her.

At night, he would turn the air off and yell out to her, "I'm turning this air off so you can sweat some of that fat off you." He told her often that she wasn't his daughter, and she would never amount to anything in life. Not long after that, he started to abuse Rita as well. All those nasty words he would call Melanie, he said them to Rita. He also called her dumb and stupid. How could a father speak to his daughters with such disdain? These girls had never done anything to him but love him and thirst for their father's affection.

The Wrong Daughter Taken

Prior to his relationship with Lashon, their father had a daughter with another woman. She was about a year or two older than

Rita. Her name was Sandy. Sandy lived in the projects of Shreveport. So she lived a fast life and assumed the role of adulthood at such an impressionable age. Sandy's life on earth ceased after she turned seventeen. She suffered a gunshot wound by the hands of her boyfriend. He accidentally shot her under her eye while playing with the gun. The young man, after shooting her, didn't run from the scene. He immediately ran upstairs to Sandy's mother and told her what happened. When Tee received the news about Sandy, he procured a small amount of information. Her condition was worse than he thought. He thought it was a simple flesh wound or an injury from which she would expeditiously recover. When he arrived at the hospital, he found out it was far more serious than disclosed to him.

Her mother greeted him to explain what happened, ensuring it was an accident. He held no grudge nor was he angry at the young man since he didn't run and confessed. The young man loved and cared about Sandy. It was just one of those unfortunate situations.

Tee left the hospital and drove home to break the news to his wife and children, explaining Sandy was on life support and brain dead. Melanie, at the time, was thirteen. Their father didn't show any emotions when he divulged the news to them. Lashon wanted to see her before they pulled the plug. Tee drove his family to the hospital where his daughter lay lifeless. Melanie wanted to see her sister. After Lashon saw Sandy, Melanie asked to see her. The adults were against it, but Melanie was much stronger than everyone thought. She plead her case to her mother, and Lashon allowed her to see her sister.

She never forgot the day she walked into the hospital room to see her sister. Her head was bandaged and terribly swollen. Her tongue was hanging out of her mouth. The vision of the life support machine pumping her chest like a balloon being inflated was shocking. Melanie just looked at her. She couldn't believe what she was seeing. The girls weren't close at all. They saw her sporadically. Melanie started to feel bad because she remembered how cruel she was to her sister when she came to spend the holiday with the family for Christmas. She remembered she snatched her doll from Sandy while she was playing with the doll. Surely, Melanie at that time didn't think anything about it. But remembering that event just made her feel the unpleasantness she imposed on Sandy, making her feel like an outsider in the family.

Sandy hadn't graduated high school yet and was seventeen years old when she ceased to exist on this earth. After the death of his daughter, Tee constantly told Melanie that God took the wrong daughter. He should've taken Melanie. This hurt Melanie deeply and caused her to fall into depression. The one person she fought so desperately for approval shunned her. Melanie was fourteen when she started praying to God to remove her from earth. Melanie felt her dad detested her, and she wanted to give him what he had spoken. Since God took the wrong daughter, she would make it easy for him and pray that death would come for her.

Until God saw fit to grant her petition, Melanie kept her mind intact by shoving her face in her studies. Her studies took her away from it all. She anticipated going to school every morning. If she had it her way, she would go to school on the weekends. She looked forward to being away from him. She wished school occurred year-round. She hated summers. At least there at school, she had positive people and surroundings to compensate what she lacked at home.

Melanie and Rita were confined to their room all day every day. They couldn't have any visitors, and if they had a phone, they weren't to receive any phone calls. Girls couldn't visit them because Tee always thought they were there to hook his daughters up with their brothers, cousins, or a random boy he didn't know.

Melanie did have one friend who witnessed his abuse toward her and Rita on multiple occasions. She felt so bad for Melanie and wished she could do something to release Melanie from the hell she was living. These girls were best friends. They had known each other for three years and became very close to each other. She was the only person Melanie confided her troubles to. She loved Melanie like a sister and was heartbroken when Melanie moved away. Her dad would often move the family to a different school district when their friends would discover how he treated those two girls. The girls would tell their parents, and well, you know how that goes. It spread like an infectious disease to the adults.

So the adults would question him, "Why do we see Tosha out and about but never see Melanie and Rita?" He would give them a lame excuse that Tosha's life expectancy would be short due to her illness.

These girls who witnessed his abuse could hear him yelling obscenities to Rita and Melanie through the door when they would try to visit. They were afraid to knock on the door but knocked anyway. When he would answer, it was with aggression. He would ask the visitor's, "Who are you and what do you want with my daughter!" They would explain they were friends and were just coming by to visit. He would reply, "My daughters don't have friends and they don't take company!" After saying this, he would slam the door in their faces. When their friends would see them at school, they would tell them that their dad was a scary man and that they will never knock on their door again. Melanie felt she couldn't trust any adult with her story. Adults back then felt children didn't have a voice. They were always told to shut up with their claims being dismissed. Figuring they were disobedient children who didn't want to be governed by their parents. But this was not the case.

Along with praying for her life to end, Melanie began having nightmares about killing her dad. She had a recurring dream that she drove a knife through his body. She would wake up disappointed, knowing it was all just a dream. She thought God was telling her since she was praying for death, He would do her one better and take him. It would certainly end the nightmare these girls were living every day. Melanie warred inwardly about how she felt about her dad. She didn't want to feel this way about him. This wasn't how a daughter was supposed to feel toward her father. He was very ignorant and noncognizant that his future relationship with his children would be unhealthy.

Lashon always told him, "You better mind how you treat these kids. They are going to end up resenting you."

His response was "Them damn kids ain't going to hate me, and if they do, so the fuck what!"

The only child given the freedom to do as she pleased was Tosha. She was the exception to the rule. She could come and go as she pleased, and a myriad of friends would visit her. This grieved Rita and Melanie. They both cried often because their dad's foot was constantly on their neck. He never released his clench on them. His cruelty toward Rita angered Melanie. Often, she would take the blame for the things Rita did because Melanie felt sorry for her. She didn't like to hear him fussing at Rita. Just as Lashon predicted, those girls began to abhor their father. There was no justification for the abuse he invoked on them. He was a big ass bully. He bullied everyone in the home. He treated strangers with the utmost respect, but his wife and two of his four children, he treated them worse than you would treat an animal. These girls wished for the day for them to spring into adulthood. They couldn't wait until they were of age so they could leave home to get away from him. They were tired of his Dr. Jekyll and Mr. Hyde attitude. Nice to them for a couple of days, but then it was back to him being mad at them for weeks for no reason.

Whenever he and Lashon were arguing, he would get mad at those two girls and send them to their room. It became evident to Melanie any time an argument broke out, she would just go to her room. She denied him the satisfaction of running her out the family room. She knew the routine. Why sit there until he decided to tell her, "Get out of here and go to your room!" Lashon would enter the girls' room to entertain them, letting them know she loved them.

After he felt she had been in the room with them long enough, he would yell out to her, "Lashon, come out of there! You been in there with them long enough!" He was very envious of her relationship with those two girls.

Tee often made promises to his family that he would change for the better and not fuss at them anymore. Who was he kidding? That evil spirit had a grip on him that was out of this world. That spirit was riding him, and it refused to unclench its grip it had on him. That spirit knew it had found itself a fool, and it took pleasure in taking up residency in his temple. His spirit was willing, but his flesh was compelled to do the opposite. Tee claimed the reason he was so strict on them was because they lived in a small town where everyone knew them. He didn't want people coming to him reporting what they saw his daughters doing. To justify his abuse, he would often place reproach on his mother. He always told Lashon his mother didn't show him love. She never kissed, hugged, or told him and his siblings she loved them. Only the two youngest, Stan and Sherry, received those gifts. She favored them over the other children. He couldn't see he was repeating the same cycle. He showed his daughters what was familiar to him. Melanie would hear him talking to Lashon about how bad his childhood was.

Melanie would think, *If he knew what his mother did to him was hurtful, then why would he inflict that same pain on us girls, but ten times worse? This should've been a reason to cultivate a healthy relationship with us.*

Melanie longed for that daddy/daughter relationship. She would forgive him for everything. She loved her dad and always wondered why she was so forgiving when it came to him. After all he did to her, she just couldn't cut ties with him.

Melanie's father became addicted to drugs when she was sixteen years old. He started out with mixing crack with marijuana. They called them pre-mos. The addiction amplified the abuse toward Rita and Melanie. Soon, he was hitting the pipe. The lies and stealing from his family followed the addiction. He would stay off for days at a time and come back home as if nothing had happened. A bunch of apologies for his wrongdoings followed by beating Lashon for refusing to fund his drug habit. Anytime she refused to give him money for his addiction, he would become angry and threaten physical harm on Lashon. She would give in because she didn't want him harming her. He coasted through life with no responsibilities. Anytime he was blessed with a job, it went well for a while. But after a few weeks, the drugs would take over, causing him to binge and lose his job, claiming he was sick or had a toothache, even after Lashon begged him to go to work. It was Lashon who carried the family. His mission in life was to put fear in his family's heart. The entire household with the exception of Justin and Tosha was afraid.

Disappearing Act

Rita endured all she could take and had left the home once she was nineteen years of age. No one heard from her for years. She dropped off the face of the earth. After giving birth, she decided to leave. Lashon didn't want her taking the baby, so she left her with Lashon and the family. Melanie wondered, *How could she leave her daughter in a home where abuse existed?* It never occurred to Melanie, Rita just wasn't ready to be a mother.

One day, while Melanie was at work, their father threatened Lashon with a machete because he wanted drugs. Lashon had no other choice but to give him money to support his habit. Lashon was in tears and frightened. Melanie came home from work to her mother crying.

Melanie looked at her grief-stricken face, asking, "Mom, what's wrong?"

She replied, "Tee pulled a machete on me because I wouldn't give him money for drugs."

Melanie discerned the look on her mother's face. She saw the hurt in Lashon's eyes. She asked, "He did? Where is he?" Nothing amazed her when it came to him because he had done so much to them.

Lashon answered, "Yes, he did. He's not here. He left. I had to give him the money, or he would have hurt or killed me."

Melanie was fueled with anger and disappointment and thought, *This man is going to pay for the pain he put this family through. The crimes he committed against the ones who love him dearly will have grave consequences. God is going to make him suffer dearly for all that he has done to us.*

His addiction was so bad, he made trails to jail and prison. Tee had been in and out of jail and prison for seven years. Prior to her illness, Lashon lost respect and interest in him due to his recidivist behavior. This last prison sentence gave Lashon the time she needed to break free of his abusive and drug-addicted behavior.

The entire family was at peace whenever he was away in prison. There was harmony in the home with his absence. They all felt relaxed and at ease. Everyone was smiling in the home. Their subjection to abuse existed for so long that peace and harmony were strangers to them. Lashon started to self-improve. She lost weight, and her hair had grown tremendously. She was looking good too. When she made an entrance, all eyes were on her. The young dudes would see Lashon, and they would comment, "Damn, who is that?" Her entrance and her smile demanded attention. She was not looking for it. That was just how it was.

One day, Lashon confessed to Melanie, "I feel good. Never thought I would ever have peace in my life."

Lashon lost her way after being married to someone who had no idea how to appreciate and love his family. Twenty-five years she was married to this man and never prospered while with him. Her reward while with him was pure hell. But she did have that chance to transform into a shining star before her life expired here on earth.

Tee was finally released from prison after seven years. He saw how beautifully his wife had transformed. He was on his way to the apartment Lashon lived in to try to get in her good graces, but Lashon wasn't the least interested. Before serving that long stretch, he used to beg and plead with her how much he loved her and how sorry he was for the addiction and the heartache it caused. Lashon was over him and didn't want to be married to him any longer. There were some things you could do to a person or take them through which would prove there was no coming back from it. You could hurt and misuse someone for so long until one day they become numb to it, and they no longer want any dealings with you.

Lashon had started dating a male coworker. He would visit her in the wee hours of the morning. They both worked the graveyard shift, 9:00 p.m. to 5:00 a.m. One morning, Tee saw Lashon walking with the gentleman leaving her apartment. This angered and hurt him deeply. He thought, *Who is this nigga, and why is he coming out of my wife's apartment? Those kids told me she was not seeing anyone.*

Tee remembered those phone conversations with the girls when he would ask them, "Is your momma seeing anyone? Do she have a boyfriend?"

They would tell him, "No, she has no time for a boyfriend."

But they weren't being honest. The children didn't care to be truthful to him. They felt their mother deserved someone in life who would love, respect, and cherish her. Melanie wanted to burst his bubble and hurt him by telling him, "Yes, she sure does have a boyfriend, and she's divorcing your sorry good-for-nothing ass!"

Melanie knew not to say this because Lashon knew this would drive him crazy and cause him to commit atrocious acts against her. Melanie always asked Lashon, "Why not tell him? He is going to find out about you two."

Tee, fueled with anger after seeing this man, thought, *I'll fix her ass. She is my wife, and I am her husband. It's until death do us part.*

He found a huge rock on the property and walked toward her car. *Crash, crash, crash, crash!* went her car windows. He lost control and ran as soon as he burst the windows. Glass was everywhere. Lashon heard the crash and looked outside at her damaged vehicle. There was a lady who witnessed what he had done. She approached Lashon, stating, "Ma'am, I saw him when he vandalized your car. He had a large rock in his hand and went from window to window, bursting out each one."

Lashon called the police to press charges. When the police arrived, they told Lashon, "Ma'am, you are married to him. This is his car too. There is nothing we can do about this. Did he touch you? If he touched you, we can charge him with domestic violence."

Lashon stated, "No, Officer. He didn't touch me."

The officer stated, "Okay, ma'am. I'm sorry, but there is nothing more we can do."

Lashon stated, "Okay. Thank you, Officer."

Their father was hiding from a distance, watching.

Lashon and the children walked back into the apartment. Melanie thought, *I don't ever want anyone to act a fool over me like that. This man is crazy. If he had loved and cherished his family, this wouldn't be happening. He treated my mother and us like garbage. And once she started making transformations, he wants to come back and finagle his way back in because he knows he messed up in life. He can't accept that she has someone in her life wanting to wine, dine, and put her on a pedestal. I know this irritates him.*

LOSING HER CROWN

Before Lashon fell ill, Tee repeatedly burst her car windows and stalked her. He would also call her place of employment, leaving unpleasant messages for her. This wasn't her personal line but a line for employees to call. These messages weren't secure, and there were people who heard his messages. This grieved Lashon. She never told the children the things he said in the voice mails. All the bad he caused outweighed the little good he did. He was never a good husband to Lashon throughout the entire marriage.

She was the breadwinner of the home. She took care of everyone and everything. He was a pitiful excuse of a husband and father. Melanie missed her mother and always felt God took Lashon away because God knew Melanie's dad would eventually kill Lashon. As much as she loved him, this would be the one thing to obliterate longing to have that daddy-daughter relationship. Melanie knew that she would never forgive him for taking the one person/parent who meant everything to her. So if God took her so that her father wouldn't, Melanie was okay with that and understood her mother's short stay here on earth.

CHAPTER 6

She Deserves the Best

Two weeks had passed since Jonathan walked back into Melanie's life. He was showing her how much he loved her and wanted to be with her. He was spending time with her, telling her he loved her and abundantly having sex with her. He was doing the things that she had been wanting from him. This was new to Jonathan. He was hearing Melanie, but there was no influence to push him until he saw her in the car with that guy. He thought, *I have this all figured out now. She deserves the best from me. I love her and will show her that I am serious about her being in my life. I want to marry her. I want her to be the mother of my children. She is nothing like these other females hanging around me. She makes me feel good about myself. And I love being between her thighs. She gives me a reason to want to change and be a productive citizen in life. Time for me to leave these streets and hood rats alone and focus on a life I could have with Melanie. But how am I going to tell her about this baby that's already here?*

Before their separation, his family adored Melanie. They were excited and shocked to hear Jonathan had a girlfriend. They had heard so many things about her from Jonathan and his mother. When the separation occurred, they weren't happy, and they were disappointed in Jonathan. They kept telling him she was the person for him, and he needed to get Melanie back in his life. Jonathan knew they were being truthful. When Jonathan finally got Melanie back into his life, they were happy. They knew about the child and were hoping Jonathan would confess his sin so that he and Melanie could work things out.

It was New Year's Eve, going into 1998. There was a party at his grandmother's home. Everyone was enjoying the music, company, and food. Melanie loved attending family gatherings at his grandmother's. When the clock struck midnight, Jonathan's mother was full of alcohol, and she rung in her new year by stating, "All right, I'm still here alive with my grandchildren." Melanie was confused about what she said. Melanie only knew of one child that Jonathan had.

She wondered, *What did she mean by her grandchildren?* This reminded Melanie of her being in bed that night and crying about Jonathan. She heard that voice tell her Jonathan had impregnated another woman, unable to find the words to tell her. Melanie allowed it to marinade and dismissed it until she could talk to Jonathan herself about his mother's statement. She continued to enjoy the festivities of the night. Melanie wasn't the type to confront and cause a scene in front of others. She needed to think about how to approach it. When the party was over, they drove back home, and Melanie said not one word to Jonathan.

Why Did You Leave Me?

The next morning, when Melanie woke up, the words from his mother kept playing over and over in Melanie's mind. Melanie became angry. Jonathan was sitting in the room, watching television. She went inside her mother's closet to clear it and was tossing items toward Jonathan's direction. The items almost hit Jonathan.

He shouted, "Hey, stop throwing stuff! You almost hit me!"

Melanie became her angriest. That question that lingered in her head for so long was surfacing. She yelled, "Why did you leave me! I want you to tell me now! Why did you leave!"

Jonathan saw the look in Melanie's eyes. She wasn't joking around with him. Jonathan said, "Okay, I'll tell you. Just calm down, okay? I met this bitch one night at the club. I slept with her, messed around, and got her pregnant. I'm sorry, but I didn't know how to tell you. How do you tell the one person you love a secret like that? I knew this would hurt you. I was trying to figure out when was the best time to tell you about it, but every time I thought about it, I saw how much it would hurt us. I'm sorry, Melanie."

Melanie covered her face and cried. Jonathan reached out to hold her. Her body sank down to the floor as she cried. He pulled her up toward him and wrapped his strong arms around her to secure her. He stated, "I'm sorry, baby. Can we please work this out between us?"

Melanie replied, "How could you do this to me, Jonathan? Why did you have to cheat on me? And then you left me, making me feel as though I did something! When all this time, it was you. I'm not ready for this. All this time, I could've been with someone who loved and cared about me. I was spending time with him. He treated me like the lady you never once did. I really liked him too." Melanie couldn't stop. Those words flowed like vomit. She finally had a voice for herself and let it be known. She was not the woman Jonathan once knew.

Jonathan felt unease after hearing Melanie say this. He thought, *So she was spending time with someone while I was away.* Jonathan stated, "Melanie, I was afraid of losing you. And I could care less about this other guy."

Melanie explained, "Jonathan, you don't know how I would've taken this. You never even gave me a chance. I would've stood by you no matter what. I'm not these other females, but you decided in your mind that I was. If you slept with her, there is a possibility you could be the father. I would've told you to get a paternity test. Stuff happens. If you had approached me with honesty, we could've dealt with your betrayal correctly. This is how this is going to go since you hid her from me. She will continue to be hid. When I'm ready to accept her, I will let you know. And there will be no rushing me. It will only prolong it. And if I want to talk about it, I'll talk about it on my terms."

Melanie finally had a voice and spoke up for herself. Jonathan's absence made her a stronger person in life.

She asked, "How old is she, Jonathan?"

Jonathan replied, "She is almost two years old."

Melanie grew angrier. "Two years old! But, Jonathan, that is how old our baby would've been. So you had her pregnant the same time I was pregnant, but I lost my baby! When was she born, Jonathan?"

Jonathan replied, "She was born in August, Melanie."

Melanie asked, "August? Jonathan, our baby was due in October of that same year. Oh my god, do you love this woman, Jonathan?"

Jonathan replied, "No, I don't love her. I love you, Melanie. And if you are not ready to accept the child, then I am not either. I'll accept her when you are comfortable."

Poor Melanie. Jonathan placed this burden on her. She just couldn't see the damage her choice to stay would lead to her being unhappy. She didn't give herself time to process and heal from what she received. Her love for Jonathan blinded her.

Jonathan had finagled his way back into her life without disclosing to her he had a daughter who was two years old. Melanie made a quick decision about her future to stay with Jonathan, but on her own terms. Jonathan didn't make the matter any better. He should've never allowed Melanie's decision to influence his relationship with his child. This, too, would cause damage to their relationship.

Melanie felt betrayed and swore Jonathan would pay for his betrayal. One of them should've walked away. Better to have loved and lost, get over the hurt and pain, rather than stay for years, only for it to cause resentment and problems.

Melanie and Jonathan were living in her mother's apartment with Tosha and Justin. Tosha wasn't a fan of Jonathan and didn't want him in the apartment. Tosha expressed to Melanie how she despised him living with them, so Melanie and Jonathan found themselves renting a motel room. It felt good to have their own place. They lived there weekly until the approval of their apartment. This was Melanie's first time having an apartment in her name. They settled into their place and were making plans to marry.

Melanie, as much as she tried, couldn't forgive Jonathan for producing a baby with another woman. She constantly brought this up to Jonathan.

Jonathan could do nothing but state, "I'm sorry, Melanie, but you can't keep holding this against me. How long are you going to make me pay for this?"

Melanie responded, "I'm going to keep bringing it up for as long as I feel like it! I told you, if you stay with me, this is how it is going to be!"

Jonathan couldn't do anything but accept it. He knew if he stayed, he would have to be reminded of what he did to Melanie. Just selfish. He didn't want anyone else to have her and was willing to put his relationship with his daughter on the line. This was a different Melanie. He had never seen her so aggressive. He thought she would be the same sweet, kind, gentle soul. Wrong, wrong. We're talking about a woman who was deceived and tossed to the side by someone she trusted. He hadn't prepared himself for her constant lashing out at him.

Option for Home Dialysis

Melanie missed her baby brother, Justin. She worried about him being with Tosha because of her multiple illnesses. Tosha was given the option for home dialysis and decided to welcome the idea. She loved not waking up so early in the morning. Her treatments left her feeling extremely exhausted. She called Melanie, hoping Melanie would agree with her, but Melanie didn't answer. She was already on her way to visit Tosha.

Melanie knocked at her door. Tosha answered the door, allowing Melanie to enter. Tosha greeted her, stating, "Hey, Melanie, the hospital has given me home dialysis options, and I'm doing it."

Melanie wasn't comfortable with this. She asked, "Tosha, are you sure you should do this?"

Tosha replied, "Yes. They have been training me for two weeks now. Besides, I'm tired of driving to that hospital."

Melanie asked, "Tosha, what if something goes wrong and you're not aware of it? I don't think you should do this."

Tosha replied, "I have all the equipment ready for setup here." Tosha had thought long and hard about the question she wanted to ask Melanie. There was no way around it but to ask. She asked, "Melanie, would you be my nurse? I can train you, and you will be compensated by the state for this."

Melanie replied, "I'm not comfortable doing that. I'm not a trained professional for this. Something could go wrong, and it will devastate me if I make a mistake and cause harm to you. Please, Tosha, don't do this."

Tosha stated, "I can show you how it's done. They have been training me."

Melanie stated, "No, Tosha, I can't do this, and neither should you."

Melanie had a job of her own and wouldn't have been able to accept the position as Tosha's nurse. Melanie endeavored to talk her sister into remaining at the hospital for her treatments, but Tosha wouldn't entertain Melanie's pleas. Her mind was made up, and there was no changing it.

The strain on Tosha and Melanie's relationship still existed, and it was incredibly rocky. Melanie would've done anything to bandage the rip caused in the relationship by their father, but her attempts were unsuccessful. She always tried to cultivate a healthy relationship with Tosha, but she didn't reciprocate. Tosha was always mean to Melanie. The same overweight statements her father inflicted on her, Tosha practiced by repeating them, hurting Melanie even as an adult. Melanie felt as though her dad trained Tosha to be this way toward her. It was like he purposefully played her against her two sisters. Sisters should be close and not divided like they were. Melanie didn't feel any love from Tosha. Those feelings resulted in a distant relationship between the two sisters. Melanie loved Tosha, but she didn't care for the yo-yo moods of wanting to be sisters one minute, and the next minute, she's treating Melanie harshly.

Melanie endeavored for Tosha to save herself from being hospitalized. She dreaded going to the hospital to see her. No matter how long she stayed there with her visiting, it was never enough. Tosha felt because they were sisters, Melanie should stay with her the entire day. As if Melanie had no life of her own. As soon as Melanie would inform Tosha she was leaving, Tosha would become angry at her, and most times, she would cry. In the beginning, her crying made Melanie feel guilty, so she'd stay a while longer. After so many cries, one day, Melanie walked out, not allowing her cries to affect her.

Melanie always thought, *She must be crazy if she thinks I'm sitting up here all day with her. She better be grateful that I even came up here to see her as bad as she has treated me in life.*

Before she was offered home dialysis, Tosha allowed her health to decline. She missed Lashon deeply and wanted to be with her mother. She endeavored to go on in life, but she faced difficulty. Her mother had been the only parent/relative who cared for her. She knew Melanie and Rita wouldn't be as nurturing and caring as their mother. Their dad had done this to them. He showed noticeable favoritism toward Tosha and Justin. He degraded Melanie and Rita in front of her. Tosha made no attempts to talk to him about how he treated them. She'd rather laugh at his degrading remarks and use them against her sisters while absorbing all the attention from him. He had her so spoiled, she felt she was entitled to have things her way.

Tosha had been doing home dialysis for a while. Everything was going okay. She was living her life and coped with accepting their mother's death. To cope with her death, Tosha made a trail to her mother's sister's house where family members congregated every day. Before Tosha started home dialysis, family members would find her slumped over in her car exhausted from the dialysis treatment. She felt she had no one, especially her sisters. She didn't feel loved by them, but she never understood why. They were there for her, just not to her liking. She continued home dialysis, and soon, mistakes were made. Her home dialysis treatment failed, requiring hospitalization. She had no feeling in her toes, and they started to change colors. They turned purple and continued to progress to a darker color.

Justin had to live with his older cousin during her hospitalization. This was a major adjustment for him. Family members focused on keeping him happy but didn't know how these unattractive events would influence him. Losing his mother at the age of twelve, an absent father, and now his sister requiring hospitalization devastated him. Justin didn't know how to express himself and talk to someone about the roller coaster of feelings inside him. He dealt with them the best way he knew.

Melanie visited Tosha when she left work. She walked into her room one day and found their dad staying at the facility with Tosha. He was homeless and needed a place to crash and eat, so the hospital was his solution. Melanie also noticed he had Tosha's room filled with their mother's pictures. Melanie couldn't understand why he had done this. This would only cause Tosha to fall into a deeper depression, wanting to be with her mother. Melanie thought, *What is wrong with him? Why would he torment her this way? Does he not know she will miss mom more?*

Melanie never said anything because she knew Tosha would side with her father and keep the pictures visible in her room. She sat with Tosha for almost two hours. It was time to go home to cook dinner. Tosha became upset, stating, "You can stay longer. I'm your sister."

Melanie responded, "I'm going home to cook. I can't stay up here all night. I'll be back tomorrow."

She refused to understand that Melanie had a life with Jonathan. Their dad didn't make things any better. When Melanie would leave, he would call his brother and talk about how Melanie could stay longer with her sister. But he still had a grudge against Melanie for shooting him in his hand, leaving him disabled.

Doctors performed tests on Tosha's feet that brought grieving news. Tosha's body was plagued with all types of toxins from improper dialysis treatment. This was the cause of her feet turning black. They tried to control the infection, but it spread to her legs. She would face amputation of her legs. The treatments and antibiotics failed her. Tosha grieved and cried more. She had no other options. If she didn't have the surgery, the infection would spread throughout her body, killing her. Doctors scheduled surgery as soon as possible to prevent the spread. After the amputation of her legs, Tosha gave up and didn't want to live anymore. She wanted to be with Lashon now more than ever.

Melanie hadn't been feeling well. She couldn't keep anything in her stomach and felt this pain in her pelvis. She shortly found out she was pregnant with Jonathan's baby. She was about six weeks and was having problems. Melanie's pregnancy proved to be difficult. Her body wasn't responding well to this pregnancy. Her pelvic and anal areas felt inflamed and extremely painful. She had no problems with the first pregnancy. This pregnancy had her on bed rest, not being able to walk. There were times she crawled around on the floor just to be mobile. When she urinated, she felt as though she was passing razor blades. Melanie tried to continue her visits with Tosha before the pain became unbearable. It wasn't long before Melanie had to stop visiting Tosha.

Pulling the Plug

Tee returned to his recidivist behavior while he was caring for Tosha, resulting in another incarceration. Tosha, left without any visitors, felt alone. Her condition worsened, and eventually, she slipped into a coma.

The doctor who examined her stated, "There are no signs of life. The machine is keeping her body alive with no brain activity. It is time to pull the plug. Nurse, please call the family and let them know to come say their final goodbye to her."

Melanie was home when the hospital called about her sister. Melanie couldn't understand the caller because she had an accent. So she hung up the phone, thinking it was something minor with her sister. They called back, and this time, Melanie was able to fathom her words. The hospital staff were calling Melanie to inform her they were pulling the plug on her sister. Melanie succumbed to hurt. There was nothing she could do but pray for her sister. She called Rita to share the sad news. The sisters made plans to meet at the hospital the following day to see their sister. She called Jonathan to share the news. Jonathan was at work.

With a quivering voice, she said, "Jonathan, they're pulling the plug on Tosha."

Jonathan asked, "Baby, are you okay? I'm coming home."

Jonathan couldn't imagine the pain Melanie was feeling. He drove home, speeding to get to Melanie. Once Jonathan arrived, he hugged and kissed Melanie, keeping an eye on her, making sure she didn't upset herself and causing harm to his baby. He made sure to keep her spirits up with tons of laughter. He would do whatever it took to keep her happy. When she needed to cry, he held her and made it all better.

Melanie remembered to call her Uncle Stan to let him know the hospital would be pulling the plug. The next day, the sisters convened at the hospital to see Tosha and make peace with her. Thru her uncle, the staff knew about Melanie's condition and made sure a nurse would be in the room to monitor Melanie. They were worried about Melanie and how she would respond seeing them pull the plug. He and his wife made the trip to be with Melanie and Rita. Melanie wanted time alone with Tosha, but they were afraid to leave Melanie alone in the room with Tosha, but she insisted.

Melanie walked into the room and saw her sister in a nonresponsive state. She talked to her sister, apologized for the distant relationship between them, and told her she loved her. Her uncle was peeking in on her to make sure she wasn't crying, but Melanie held it together. This brought back memories. She remembered when she went to see her sister, Sandy, when she suffered a gunshot wound to the head by her boyfriend. She remembered seeing her sister on a life support machine breathing for her, how the gunshot left her head swollen, and her severely swollen tongue hanging out of her mouth. So Melanie was no stranger to seeing lifeless patients on life support. She made peace with her and exited the room.

It came time to pull the plug. Both sisters were there when they saw their sister take her last breath. As she took her last breath, Rita screamed out, "No!"

Melanie looked at her sister as she held her tears back. She refused to cause unnecessary stress to their baby. Jonathan thought, *Damn, my baby a soldier. Not a tear shed.*

The nurse maintained her position, watching Melanie, ready to comfort her should she burst out crying. The date was August 16, 1998. It was the day their baby sister's life ceased to exist on earth. She was gone and could finally be with their mother. Melanie's uncle and aunt kissed and hugged them both and went back home.

Jonathan slowly walked Melanie to the car. He was proud of her for being a soldier and not crying. He thought, *I'm incredibly amazed she shed no tears. She understood this would hurt our baby. She fought to keep those tears from streaming down her face. She's an awesome being.*

They were on their way to break the news to Justin. Justin had been living with their mother's niece when Tosha went to the hospital. During the ride there, Melanie thought, *No more of you missing and wanting to be with our mother. No more worrying about your health. No more worries of this world. No more arguing with me. No more baby sister for me.* It hit Melanie. She yelled, "No more baby sister for me! My baby sister is gone! I will never see her again! Oh God, maybe if I had tried more, this wouldn't have happened!" This is what we tell ourselves—if only. But there was nothing Melanie could do to make it better because she was the only willing participant. Even though the relationship between the two was a strained one, Melanie always wished the bad energy would disappear. There was no doubt that she loved Tosha. Jonathan pulled into a parking lot to comfort his Melanie.

Melanie and Jonathan arrived at her aunt's house. Melanie thought about how she would break the news to Justin. Losing their mother and now their sister would devastate Justin. He just lost his mom thirteen months ago. Now they must tell him one of his big sisters was gone. When they reached Justin, he was outside playing. They called him into the house and broke the news to him. Melanie saw the hurt look on her baby brothers' face. He fell to the bed and cried. Melanie felt so bad for him. She felt bad for them all.

Melanie thought, *No fair. We have lost our mother and our sister in a span of thirteen months.* She sat on the bed, comforting her baby brother, ensuring him it would be okay.

CHAPTER 7

Graveside Burial

Melanie was not able to travel to Koran, Louisiana, to attend Tosha's burial. Melanie was four months pregnant and was restricted from any activities. She was able to see her sister one last time at her wake. It broke her heart that her attendance at the burial service was impossible. Melanie wanted to place a rose on her casket as they lowered her to the ground. Jonathan hated that he couldn't take Melanie to attend her sister's burial. They both knew it wouldn't be good for her or the baby. He endeavored to keep Tosha off her mind and keep her laughing. There was no funeral, just a viewing and burial, like Lashon. They buried her next to Lashon, who was buried next to her parents, John and Desire Lott.

Melanie's pregnancy was taking a toll on her body. Melanie struggled daily to function. Every step taken brought excruciating pain to her pelvic and anal areas. She often went to the emergency room because of her continuing symptoms. Still, no answers as to why she was hurting. Jonathan tried to take care of Melanie the best way he could. He couldn't understand why she was having so many problems. He communed with female coworkers, searching for answers. No one could tell Jonathan why Melanie's body was responding negatively with this pregnancy. He wanted to make the pain go away. He had never seen Melanie in so much pain. He was worried about her and the baby. He thought, *I feel part of the reason she's hurting is my fault. She is carrying my baby, and I see her struggling every day. I wish I could take away the pain. I despise seeing her this way. Lord, please look over Melanie and my baby. They mean everything to me.*

Melanie had no one to care for her during her pregnancy while Jonathan was away working. She struggled every day to perform normal daily activities. She often cried. She was missing her mother and her sister. She thought, *I want my mom. I need her so much right now. Why did she have to die and leave me? So not fair that I had to lose her at a young age.*

Melanie thought about her baby brother, Justin. He was only twelve when their mother died and thirteen when Tosha passed away.

Justin lived with Melanie and Jonathan prior to Melanie's pregnancy. When Melanie became pregnant, because of her inability to take care of herself and him, she arranged for him to live with their mother's niece for a while. After Tosha died, the family gravitated to Justin, showing him love. The love they showed didn't fill the void that Justin missed being with Melanie and Jonathan. He understood Melanie couldn't currently care for him. He wanted to be with one of the two remaining sisters he had. He decided to live with Rita until Melanie could bring him back home with her and Jonathan.

Justin had no problems cultivating friendships with the children in the neighborhood. His friends' mothers loved him as if he was their own child. They all adored him and noticed how respectful he was. He was always welcomed to their homes, especially once they knew about his mother and sister. They took him under their wings. Lashon had taught him right about manners before she passed. He had an angelic face, and those brown eyes of his shimmered whenever he smiled.

Melanie thought about the day she had to say goodbye to her brother. She hugged him, stating, "Justin, I promise I will get you back after the baby is born. I love you, baby boy."

Justin didn't believe Melanie. Justin stated, "Sure, Melanie. I love you too, sis."

Everyone he ever loved left him. His dad abandoned him. His mother and sister died. And now his big sister had to make arrangements for him to live elsewhere because of her inability to care for him in her condition. Jonathan made the trip to Rita's apartment to get Justin settled into his new home.

Before leaving, Jonathan stated, "Boy, I love you. We are coming back for you."

Justin said, "I love you too, bro."

Ruptured Bag

Melanie's pregnancy continued to progress, along with the aches and excruciating pain. She was now a little over five months pregnant. One day, she was urinating and saw blood when she wiped. A phone wasn't in the home at that time. Melanie, in pain, had to walk down the stairs to their neighbors to use the phone. She knocked on the door. The neighbor answered her knock.

Melanie said to herself, "Thank God he answered." Melanie asked, "Hey, Toot, how are you? Could you please call Jonathan for me? Tell him please come home. I'm bleeding."

Toot replied, "Yes, okay, I'll call him right now and let him know."

Melanie replied, "Thank you." Melanie went back upstairs.

Toot called Jonathan, stating, "Say, kinfolk, your girl came downstairs and asked me to call you. She says for you to come home. She's bleeding."

Jonathan replied, "Okay, I'm on my way."

Jonathan left work. He thought about nothing but Melanie and the baby. *I hope the baby and Melanie are okay. God, please don't let anything happen to her and the baby.*

Jonathan didn't waste time putting the pedal to the medal. He was trying to get home to Melanie and the baby expeditiously. He kept surveying the area, making sure no police officers were lurking around him. He finally arrived home. He jumped out the car and rushed to the apartment. He entered, asking, "Melanie, baby, are you okay? You still bleeding?" Jonathan was always home with Melanie. He only left her alone to work, and he would come home. This had become his routine. If he wanted to hang with his boys, he brought Melanie along to sit and talk to their girlfriends. He was so happy to start a family with Melanie. Jonathan leaned in for a kiss from Melanie.

She replied, "No, I haven't seen any more bleeding."

Jonathan stated, "Let me know when you have to pee."

Melanie replied, "Okay, I will."

Jonathan didn't leave Melanie's side that night. Jonathan asked, "Are you hungry, baby?"

Melanie replied, "Yes, I am."

Jonathan made her favorite dish. She craved this dish more than anything. It was a pack of noodles, ground turkey meat, and broccoli. She loved this dish, and so did the baby. She could keep this meal down in her stomach.

Melanie called Jonathan, "Jonathan, I have to pee."

Jonathan replied, "Okay, baby. I'll go with you to the bathroom."

He followed Melanie into the bathroom. Melanie stood and hovered over the toilet to urinate while Jonathan watched, making sure no blood was present. Jonathan stooped so that he could see her stream. There was no bleeding in the urine nor when she wiped. Jonathan watched Melanie each time she urinated. Relieved there was no evidence of blood present, she could now eat. Jonathan brought her plate to her. The food smelled so good to Melanie. Melanie enjoyed every morsel. And so did the baby.

Another week had passed. Melanie was now five and a half months pregnant. The bleeding started again. Melanie was scared. This time, she had to walk to a pay phone to make a collect call to his job. A coworker accepted the charges and answered her call.

Melanie stated, "Julia, I'm bleeding."

Julia stated, "Melanie, hold on. Oh my goodness. Just a minute." Julia was able to contact Jonathan.

Jonathan rushed home. This time, it was in Melanie's best interest to go to the ER. Jonathan didn't want to take any chances this time. When they arrived, a medical assistant assessed Melanie's vitals then led her to a room for examination.

Once the doctor examined her, he stated, "Ms. Ashley, your water bag has ruptured, and it's bulging out of your cervix. You have a weak cervix. We need to place you on bed rest here at the hospital. We will endeavor to get you to six months, induce labor, and place the baby in neonatal care to continue development. You are in danger of losing this baby."

Melanie, devastated, agreed, "Okay, I will do whatever it takes to keep my baby."

Jonathan accepted the news. He knew it was in Melanie's and the baby's best interest to be hospitalized. Melanie prayed to God that she would be able to hold her baby without the bag rupturing any further.

She asked God, "God, if you can hear me, please save my baby. Don't take my baby away from me. I've already lost one baby. Please allow me to be a mother." Melanie cried herself to sleep every night while there.

Jonathan was there for her, except for those times he needed to go home for rest and to work. Melanie was always on his mind. He thought, *My baby is so strong. I don't know how she does it. Losing her mother and sister in just thirteen months is enough to depress a person. Now she is having to deal with this. God, this is my baby she is carrying. We've gotten this far. Please allow her to go full-term with this pregnancy.*

Another Loss

Jonathan brought his friend Slim to see Melanie on his next visit. Jonathan excused himself to smoke a cigarette. Slim gave Melanie a hug. He asked, "How are you doing, Melanie?"

Melanie replied, "I'm okay." They talked for a while, enjoying each other's company.

Melanie felt the urge to sneeze. When she sneezed, she could feel something touching her inner thigh. The baby had been released from her womb. Melanie, in shock, cried, "Oh no. No, no, no! Please, God, no!"

Slim asked, "What is it? What's wrong?"

Melanie stated, "The baby is here."

Slim yelled, "Nurse! Nurse, help! Something is wrong!"

Melanie had pressed the button to summon the nurse to her aid. A voice answered, "Yes, Ms. Ashley? How can I help you?"

Melanie said, "I sneezed, and I can feel the baby coming out of me."

The nurse stated, "Okay, we'll be there to get you to labor and delivery."

Slim stayed behind to let Jonathan know what happened. The staff rushed her to delivery. Melanie could feel the baby slipping out of her inch by inch. Finally, the baby was completely released from her body.

Melanie cried out, "Nurse, the baby is out now!"

The nurse looked under the cover and saw that the baby had been discharged from Melanie's body. Melanie could feel the baby moving. It gave her hope that the baby just might make it. But deep down inside, Melanie knew the odds were slim that her baby would survive. Once they arrived in delivery, the staff asked Melanie if she wanted them to endeavor saving the baby. She wanted them to do whatever they could to save her baby. While they tried resuscitation, Jonathan had arrived. He held Melanie and told her he loved her. The staff's endeavor to save their baby had failed. They explained to Melanie that the baby didn't survive because there was minimal development. A few minutes had passed. A nurse presented the baby to Melanie and Jonathan for them to have a couple of moments alone with her to say their goodbyes. They told them to expect movement from the baby. It was normal.

Melanie held her baby and asked if she could lay her baby to rest. The staff informed her they couldn't release a partially developed baby. Melanie and Jonathan didn't argue with staff about the matter. They just accepted the staff's decision. When Melanie handed Jonathan his baby, Jonathan looked at her, wishing she could have held on longer. He stated to his baby, "I love you, baby girl." The baby was moving. Jonathan stated, "Melanie, this baby is moving."

Melanie said, "Yes, Jonathan. Remember, they said we are to expect this. It doesn't mean anything. It's just reflexes." It came time for them to say goodbye to the baby. Melanie told her baby, "Bye, my sweet baby girl. Mommy loves you dearly, and I'm so sorry."

Melanie couldn't control her emotions. She cried for her baby. Jonathan and Melanie went back to her room. Jonathan stayed with

LOSING HER CROWN

Melanie for a while but soon grew tired of the hospital scene. He had to get away so that he could talk to Slim alone. He needed to grieve his own way. Melanie wasn't the person he needed. She was already distraught from losing the baby.

He said to Melanie, "Melanie, baby, I will be back tomorrow. I need to get away from this hospital. I love you, baby." He kissed Melanie and exited the room.

Jonathan drove to Slim's home. He didn't want to hear any music, just the sound of the engine of the car getting him to his destination. His mind was swimming with thoughts. He finally reached his destination. Slim met him at the door before he could knock.

Slim stated, "I'm going to get you high. Here, hit this blunt and play Madden."

Jonathan inhaled the blunt about four times and started feeling relaxed. Jonathan was in his feelings the whole ride there. He beat himself up on the inside because he left Melanie. He felt guilty about leaving her, but he just couldn't bear being in that hospital one more minute. He thought, *I hope Melanie's not mad at me for leaving. I hope she understands why I had to leave.* Jonathan, after witnessing Melanie lose two of his babies, thought, *No more getting Melanie pregnant until I marry her. This has to be the reason she keeps losing my babies.*

Melanie tried to fall asleep after Jonathan left. She cried the entire time. "Why does this hurt so bad, Father?" Melanie was angry. She was angry about three losses within a span of fifteen months. She had blamed God for taking her first baby, and now here He was again, taking another child from her. She asked, "What did I do, Father? What did I do that was so bad that You deemed it necessary to take my babies from me? This isn't fair. All these unfit women walking around here just spitting out babies, but me? You couldn't allow me to have just one of them, if not both? Why are you doing this to me?" Her eyes were christened with tears, and her heart was broken. She was crying uncontrollably.

She had a roommate in the room. Melanie kept her back turned from everyone. She didn't want them looking at her cry for her baby. Melanie's roommate dared not say anything to Melanie. She completely understood. Melanie didn't want to hear any empathy nor sympathy from anyone. She wanted God to answer her questions.

Leaving for Home and a Reunion

It was time for Melanie's discharge. The doctors had spoken with her about her next pregnancy. They explained to Melanie that the next time she was with child, they would perform a cervical cerclage. This procedure entailed Melanie's cervix getting stitched after three successful months of pregnancy. Since she had an incompetent cervix, this procedure would help keep the baby and the amniotic fluid secure. The procedure required sedation. She wouldn't be able to withstand the tugging and pulling on her cervix. Melanie kept this in mind to make sure she divulged this to her gynecologist. Having an incompetent cervix occurred in one out of one hundred pregnancies.

Jonathan arrived to pick up Melanie. He helped her with her things. She was so happy to be going home. She still thought about her baby and how it would've been had they caught the problem prior to the rupture. Too late now. She would just have to deal with the fact that she lost another baby that belonged to her and Jonathan.

Melanie and Jonathan had been living together now for about six months and moved into a two-bedroom apartment. They were both working. She had been calling Rita to talk to Justin, but each time she called, Rita would tell her that he wasn't there. Melanie would ask his whereabouts. She would tell Melanie he was at a friend's house. This went on for months. Melanie felt that she had failed her mother. Melanie promised her mother she would take care of Justin. She missed her baby brother and wanted to see him. After months of not talking to him, he finally called Melanie one day. Melanie's phone rang. She answered, "Hello."

She heard a familiar voice stating, "Hey, Melanie, how you doing? This Justin."

Melanie's heart jumped. She replied, "Justin! I have missed you. Where have you been? I have been asking to speak to you, but you were always away. Are you ready to come back and live with us?"

Justin replied, "Yeah, I'm ready. When can you come for me?"

Melanie answered, "I can come for you whenever you're ready to come back. You just let me know."

Justin said, "I want to come home today, Melanie. I miss y'all."

Melanie said, "Okay, baby brother. Jonathan and I are on our way."

Melanie went to Jonathan. "Jonathan, Justin just called me. He wants us to come get him now."

Jonathan asked, "For real? My brother ready to come back home to us?"

Melanie replied, "Yes. I just talked to him, and he wants us to come for him."

Jonathan asked, "Okay, you ready to go now?"

Melanie replied, "Yes, I am."

They began the thirty-minute trip ahead of them. Melanie was still processing the phone call with her brother. She was finally bringing her baby brother back where he belonged. With her and Jonathan. She was anxious to see Rita and Justin. She hadn't seen Rita since they lost their baby sister. They finally arrived. Justin had all his belongings packed and was ready to leave.

Melanie asked, "Justin, where is Rita?"

Justin replied, "She's in there, crying."

Melanie asked, "Crying? Why is she crying?"

Justin replied, "Because I'm leaving, Melanie."

Melanie walked inside the apartment. She witnessed her sister's demeanor, stating, "Hey, Rita. How are you doing?"

Melanie heard a broken voice. "I'm all right. Just hate to see him go. I had gotten used to the idea of him being here."

Melanie walked up to Rita. "I know, sis. I did the same thing when Jonathan had to bring him to you. It broke my heart to see him leave. It'll be okay."

They hugged each other and said bye. Melanie jumped inside the car, and they were on their way back home. Melanie felt full of joy while they were heading home. She could now feel that she was activating their mother's wish to take care of Justin.

After arriving home, Melanie showed Justin his room. He settled in and was happy to be with his big sister and brother-in-law-to-be.

Justin and Jonathan had already known each other before Jonathan met Melanie. Justin was just a little boy when he met Jonathan. Jonathan knew that their dad was an absent parent, and he was on drugs. He took Justin under his wing. He and the other hustlers in the apartments practically raised Justin. They would send Justin on errands, like going to the corner store or the hamburger joint for them. When Justin would return with their items, they would ask for their change. Justin would look at them and run off, telling them, "Ain't no change."

They would yell out, "You little bad ass. Wait until I see you next time!"

They still sent him, and he would continue to keep their money. They all thought it was funny though. There was no harm done. They all laughed and cracked jokes and figured he needed the change.

Melanie's body had healed, and the thought of trying again plagued her mind. But she was starting to feel a certain way about her and Jonathan living together in sin. She felt this was the reason she kept losing her babies. She was ready to get married and was pestering Jonathan about it.

"Jonathan, I'm tired of living in sin. When are we getting married?"

Jonathan answered, "Melanie, baby, as soon as I get my identification card, we can get married."

It was taking Jonathan too long. Melanie often asked, "Jonathan, when are you getting your identification card?"

Jonathan stated, "Melanie, I told you, I need to work some things out to get my identification card." Jonathan meant he had warrants out for his arrest from past traffic tickets. Jonathan had fallen off the radar without an identification card. He hadn't had a valid identification card since his last renewal in 1991. Melanie tried to wrap her mind around how Jonathan allowed his identification card to expire without renewing it. This didn't make sense to her. Another red flag that Melanie just casually ignored. It was 1999, and he wasn't legal, as far as the eyes of the law. But eventually, Jonathan was able to get his state identification. But only because police officers caught him from past tickets.

Melanie and Jonathan started making plans for their union. Most of their guests were Jonathan's family members. Not too many people were invited. Melanie asked one of her cousins if she would attend the wedding, knowing she would spread the news, but she seemed disinterested in Melanie's wedding. Her behavior caused Melanie to not tell anyone else for fear they would react the same way. Melanie figured they would end up not attending. So why even bother inviting them? She had her siblings there. Her uncle Stan and his wife were there as well. Her uncle had to be there because Melanie had asked him to give her away. Her own dad didn't know she was getting married because he was in prison. Melanie had spoken with her grandmother sharing her wedding plans. She would've loved to have her grandmother at the ceremony, but she was busy helping her daughter take care of her four small sons. She didn't feel comfortable leaving her daughter alone with the children, and honestly, her grandmother wasn't in any shape to travel alone and lived in another state. So Melanie understood why her grandmother wasn't able to attend her wedding.

A Joyous Occasion

It was the day of Melanie and Jonathan's wedding. Melanie had her hair and makeup done for her day. She was nervous and wouldn't eat anything. She wondered if this was right for her.

"Am I making the right decision? Jonathan is good to me, I think. I can always call this off if I want to. But I am here now. There's no turning back."

The ceremony was beginning. Melanie's uncle was crying. He felt honored to walk his niece down that aisle. When Melanie joined him, they began to walk. Melanie was trying to get this walk over because her stockings were slipping in her shoes, causing her to walk funny. Her uncle kept it at a slow pace and didn't bother to speed the process. Melanie forced herself to walk at his pace and endured the slipping she felt.

Melanie thought, *Oh my goodness! I need to get out of these shoes! I'm slipping in them!*

Jonathan hadn't laid eyes on his bride. When he saw her entering, he thought, *Oh my goodness, she looks beautiful.*

Everyone had their eyes on her. Jonathan's aunt on his father's side was present at the wedding, along with her husband. This was their first encounter of Melanie. The guests all thought Melanie and Jonathan were an attractive couple. Anyone who encountered them both freely spoke how attractive the two were together. This validated Melanie's thoughts that Jonathan was meant for her, and she was meant for Jonathan. All those compliments from people just made Melanie believe that there was no one out there for her but what was right in front of her. Jonathan meant everything to Melanie.

There were no written vows. They both repeated the traditional vows after the pastor. Melanie and Jonathan both said their I dos. Jonathan kissed his bride, and it was official. The pastor announced, "This day, September 14, 1999, I present to you Mr. and Mrs. Jonathan Taylor."

Jonathan and Melanie danced. Melanie wanted the first song entitled, "Kiss of Life" to be played. It was a lovely ceremony. All who attended the ceremony enjoyed themselves. Tosha's best friend, Daisy, and her boyfriend arrived late to the wedding. They missed the ceremony.

Jonathan's employer rented a room at the Holiday Inn for the newly wedded couple. A meal, strawberries, and champagne were ordered for them as well. They didn't get a chance to enjoy the meal because they were oblivious that it came with the room. They enjoyed being away from the apartment even if it was for just one night. Daisy and her boyfriend came to visit the couple for a while at the hotel. They all talked for a while and had a few drinks. The two left Melanie and Jonathan so they could have some private time alone. Melanie and Jonathan enjoyed each other for the remainder of the night.

The couple checked out the next day going home. Jonathan had two more days off from work. Upon returning to work, Jonathan's boss asked, "Did you guys enjoy the room and food?"

Jonathan answered, "Food? What food?"

His boss said, "We paid for you guys to have dinner and a bottle of champagne and strawberries."

Jonathan said, "We didn't know those items were purchased, and staff didn't say anything about it."

His boss called immediately and received a refund for those items.

Jonathan and Melanie settled into their new lives as Mr. and Ms. Jonathan Taylor. Melanie started getting ideas of Jonathan impregnating her. Melanie asked, "Jonathan? When can we start trying to have a baby?"

Jonathan replied, "I want you to go to the doctor first to make sure your body is ready for another pregnancy."

Melanie said, "Okay, will do."

See, that type of concern was why Melanie just knew Jonathan was right for her. He approached things delicately with caution. Melanie made an appointment with her doctor to have herself examined. She was able to get in that following week.

Melanie informed her husband, "Jonathan, the doctor will see me next week."

Jonathan stated, "Okay, baby. We will see what the doctor says. If they say you are good to go, then we will try again."

Melanie said, "Okay, that sounds reasonable." Melanie couldn't wait to see the doctor. She felt that since her and Jonathon were married now, God would bless their union with additional members to the family. "God has got to grant my petition. Jonathan and I are married now. We are legal and legit. No way He should deny my request."

Conducting Tests

The day finally arrived for Melanie to see her doctor. She didn't require Jonathan to be with her for this appointment and drove herself to attend. She arrived, and staff checked her in for the appointment and led her to an exam room. The nurse gathered vital information, gave her a gown, and told her to disrobe, and the doctor would be right with her. Melanie disrobed and put the gown on to cover her body. She sat on the exam table, looking at the different models of the human body and posters with detailed information. She was a little nervous. She thought, *I do hope this will be a productive visit. I just can't take hearing now isn't the time for me to start a family yet.*

Her doctor entered the room and asked, "Hi, Melanie. What brings you in to see me?"

Melanie responded, "I've had two miscarriages, and the last one, I was able to hold my baby for almost six months until my water bag started to bulge out of my cervix. A weak and incompetent cervix was the culprit. I was told a cervical cerclage after three successful months of my pregnancy would be required. They need me to get to and little past the first trimester. So I am here to get examined to make sure my body is ready for another pregnancy."

Dr. Gharma asked, "When were those two pregnancies?"

Melanie replied, "The first one occurred in 1996, and the second one was 1998."

Dr. Gharma replied, "Okay, and it's almost two years later from the last miscarriage. Enough time for your body to heal. Melanie, I need to examine you. Go ahead and lay back. Place your feet in the stirrups." Melanie did as the doctor instructed her. "Melanie, open your legs, and you will feel some pressure."

Melanie opened her legs, and as the doctor promised, she felt pressure. She always hated these exams. They were incredibly uncomfortable. Cold steel was inserted into you, stretching parts of your body just so the professional could observe your innards. Melanie thought, *I wonder what it looks like in there.* She could feel the doctor expanding the device for a better view. Melanie thought, *Oh my goodness. I detest these examinations. I can feel her scraping my wall with that Q-tip. Please hurry up!*

Dr. Gharma had completed the examination. "Melanie, I'm done with the examination. I took samples and will send them off to the lab. For now, on my end, everything is looking good. Here, let me help you. I will contact you in a couple of days with the results. Do you have any questions for me?"

Melanie replied, "Yes, I do. What do you think my chances are of having a successful pregnancy, seeing that I've had two unsuccessful ones?"

Dr. Gharma replied, "It's hard to say because all pregnancies are not alike. Since you have had two miscarriages, it would be wise to place you on bed rest immediately once your pregnancy has been confirmed and perform the cerclage after three months. You were able to carry the second baby about five and a half months. There is evidence that you can hold a baby, but you will require assistance. Do you have any more questions for me?"

Melanie answered, "No, I have no further questions."

Dr. Gharma concluded, "Okay, Melanie. You just call me if you think of anything. I will talk to you soon, and you take care."

Melanie said, "Okay. You take care as well."

Dr. Gharma made her exit from the room.

Melanie stepped down from the exam table, removed the gown, and got dressed. She exited the room and went home.

Jonathan was home when she arrived. "Melanie, what did the doctor say?"

Melanie replied, "She had to take some samples and send them to the lab for observation. She will call me with the results in a couple of days. But so far, all is looking good. She elucidated since I was able to carry our last baby almost six months that the baby will have a good chance of a full-term pregnancy with the assistance of the cervical cerclage."

Jonathan stated, "Okay, good. We'll just wait to hear from her then." Jonathan was keeping his fingers crossed that everything would be all right for them to start trying to have a baby.

Melanie had been so busy that she forgot about the doctor calling her with her test results. It had been past the time for her to call to discuss the results. Melanie decided to call the office to discuss the results. She worked at a clinic and knew doctors were incredibly busy. Melanie called and asked to speak to her doctor to discuss her test results. The friendly voice transferred Melanie directly to Dr. Gharma.

Melanie kept repeating to herself, "These results will show it's okay for us to start trying again."

"Hello, Melanie. How are you?"

Melanie replied, "I'm doing well, Doctor. How about yourself?"

Dr. Gharma replied, "I'm doing well. Let us get on with these results. I know you are anxious to receive them."

Melanie stated, "Yes, ma'am, I am."

Dr. Gharma stated, "Okay, well, the tests came back, and there is nothing preventing you from trying again. Everything looks good."

Melanie stated, "Yes! Thank you so much, Dr. Gharma. You made my day."

Dr. Gharma stated, "You are welcome. Were you needing anything else?"

Melanie replied, "No, ma'am. That was everything."

They both released the line.

Melanie entered the living room, stating, "Jonathan! Guess what? We can start trying!" Melanie blurted out the answer before Jonathan could guess her question.

He asked, "Really, Melanie? We can start trying?"

Melanie said, "Yes, baby. She is giving the green light to start trying."

Jonathan was happy and had a big grin on his face. Jonathan thought, *Finally, we don't have to practice the rhythm method.*

Melanie conversed with Jonathan about spacing out their sessions. Too much sex and no breaks would cause contraindication. They would have sessions twice per week for three months, resulting in no missed periods. Melanie was concerned. She could not understand what was taking so long.

Melanie approached Jonathan. "Jonathan, we have been trying for months now and no success. Something must be wrong."

Jonathan replied, "Just be patient, baby. We already know you can get pregnant."

Melanie started thinking, *Why was it so easy to get pregnant while we were not married? Now that we are married, it's taking forever.* She stated, "Okay, Jonathan, I'll be patient. If I am not pregnant in the next two months, I'm going to see a fertility specialist."

Jonathan stated, "Okay, baby. Sounds good to me." Jonathan responded to Melanie without realizing what she said because he was watching a game. He asked, "Whoa, wait a minute. What kind of specialist?"

Melanie replied, "A fertility doctor."

Jonathan shouted, "Fertility doctor! Melanie, are you sure you want to do this?" Jonathan knew what going to a fertility doctor meant. Multiple babies. Jonathan thought, *With Melanie having a weak cervix, her body would react severely to multiple babies. She could barely walk and function from the pain with one baby. Why won't she just wait and be patient? I hope she knows what she's getting herself into with this.*

Jonathan knew too many miscarriages wouldn't be good for Melanie. Melanie answered, "Jonathan, yes, I'm sure this is what I want to do. Why are you asking this?"

Jonathan replied, "Baby, I'm just concerned. I witnessed the pain you endured with this last pregnancy. I felt helpless, Melanie. Looking at you and the expressions on your face, there was nothing I could do to ease the pain. You looked exhausted just from taking a couple of steps, in excruciating pain, and you looked defeated all at the same time. I just know that with a fertility doctor, it may mean multiple babies. I don't want your suffering amplified, is all. Melanie, you know I still love you even if you're not able to carry children, right? We don't have to have children to be happy. I'm happy with it just being you and me."

Melanie replied, "I know, Jonathan. But I just feel incomplete. I feel less of a woman if I am unable to give my husband a son. You have children. Two daughters. Easy for you to say this. I am without a child. It is my duty as a wife and woman to bear children for my husband. You've already experienced fatherhood twice. I want to experience motherhood. I don't care about pain I must endure, being out of breath, exhausted, and the amount of time I would spend on bed rest. It is all worth it just to have my bundle of joy in my hands. That's just how I feel."

Jonathan understood Melanie and said no more about her decision to see a fertility specialist.

CHAPTER 8

Seeing a Specialist

Two months whisked by. Melanie was still not pregnant. She called her doctor to request a referral for a fertility specialist. Her doctor referred her to the closest specialist to Melanie. The specialist was well-known in the community, and he could help Melanie. Melanie told Jonathan about the referral. Jonathan wasn't as excited as Melanie. He wished Melanie would give more time for her body to naturally give her what she wanted.

Melanie immediately contacted Dr. Brooks and scheduled an appointment. She was able to see the doctor the following week. "Jonathan, I have an appointment with the specialist next week."

Jonathan thought, *I hope he recommends anything other than her having to swallow some fertility pills or injections. Her body is sensitive to one baby. How will she carry two or more?* Jonathan responded, "Okay, baby. You need me to go with you?"

Melanie replied, "I would love for you to accompany me. If you don't mind. The appointment is scheduled for next Wednesday at nine thirty."

Jonathan answered, "Of course, I don't mind. I'm there for you."

Melanie was shocked. Normally, husbands refused to accompany their wives to doctor's appointment. But Jonathan wanted to show Melanie he wasn't like the other men. She showed him that she wasn't like other women, and he wanted to pay it back to her and show support.

Melanie asked, "Really, Jonathan? You will accompany me to the doctor's office? Thank you, baby." Melanie rushed over to Jonathan and gave him a big hug and kiss.

Jonathan had a big smile on his face. He thought, *That made her this happy? Just offering to go to the doctor with her? This marriage thing is easy.* Melanie wasn't hard to please at all. The simplest things in life made her happy.

The date of Melanie's appointment came quickly. She was up at 7:30 a.m., getting herself together. All she could think about was what type of treatment the doctor would offer her. There was no question in Melanie's mind if she could get pregnant. The two first pregnancies were evident she could. The question was why, now that her and Jonathan were legal in God's eyes, they couldn't conceive.

Melanie exited the bathroom to wake Jonathan. She stood over him, stating, "Jonathan, get up, baby. Today is my appointment to see the fertility doctor. Remember, you said you would go with me? Are you still going with me?"

Jonathan opened one eye and was struggling to get the other eye open. He let out a loud yawn and stretched. Jonathan replied, "Of course, I'm going with you. I know this is an important day for us, and I remembered. Let me jump in the shower and get dressed."

Melanie stated, "Okay, I'll make us some breakfast. After we eat, we will leave."

Jonathan said, "Okay, baby. I will be done in about thirty minutes."

Melanie made bacon, eggs, and French toast. Jonathan inhaled the aroma just before jumping out of the shower. After he showered, he got dressed and sprayed on some cologne. He went into the kitchen, stating, "Boy, that smells good, baby." Jonathan made his breakfast into a sandwich. He noticed Melanie wasn't eating. Jonathan asked, "Did you already eat your breakfast, Mel?"

She replied, "Oh, no, I can't eat anything. I feel a little nervous about the visit."

Jonathan said, "Melanie, you must eat something, even if it's just French toast or some bacon. Eat something."

Melanie replied, "Okay, you're right. I will eat just enough to put something in my stomach. I don't know why I feel so nervous about this visit."

Jonathan stated, "It's nothing, Melanie. Subconsciously, you're thinking he may deliver unwanted news to you. That is why you're feeling nervous, Melanie."

You see, it was statements like this that Jonathan would say to her that always put her at ease. He was that voice that she needed to hear that would dismiss her fears. Jonathan always knew what to say to her to make her feel better. It was 8:45 a.m., almost time to leave. The doctor's office was about twenty-five minutes away. Melanie wanted to leave early just in case traffic was present.

"Jonathan, let's go." Melanie grabbed her purse and the keys.

"Okay, baby," stated Jonathan. "I'm getting my hat and will be right there."

Before leaving, Jonathan told Justin they were on their way to see Melanie's doctor and asked if he wouldn't mind cleaning the kitchen prior to their return home. Justin didn't mind at all. He would enjoy the time alone and play some music during their absence.

Melanie and Jonathan exited the apartment together, locking the door behind them. Melanie handed Jonathan the keys to drive them to the doctor's office. Once in the car, Jonathan made Melanie put on her seat belt. She didn't like wearing them at all. She always thought they were risky, especially when they imprisoned people trying to escape a fiery vehicle or an eighteen-wheeler coming toward them, unable to stop. But she slapped it on to appease Jonathan.

Jonathan kept Melanie's mind off the visit. He knew she plagued her mind with wanting to have his child and the waiting game of conception. Jonathan thought, *I wish she would enjoy us first before having a baby. I would like to enjoy my wife. There are so many things I would like to do with her. So many things we haven't done together. I never was available to her for the entire time of our relationship like I should have. But I promised myself, whatever Melanie wants, she gets.* Jonathan was true to his words and wanted to make Melanie happy. He wanted to spoil Melanie in every way possible.

Melanie saw the building and excitedly stated, "There it is, Jonathan! Right here on the right. Oh my, this is a beautiful building. Look at the waterfall in the front, Jonathan. Oh my goodness, it's beautiful!"

This was one of the things Jonathan loved about Melanie. Simple beauty moved her. It excited her. He loved how she appreciated the simple things in life.

Melanie asked, "Jonathan, do you want to valet park for $5 or park in the garage?"

Jonathan replied, "We'll just park in the garage for free. No need to pay someone to park the car." Jonathan parked the car in a space that was close to the entrance. He opened the door and exited. Melanie was getting her things together. Jonathan walked over and opened the door for Melanie.

"Thank you, baby."

Jonathan stated, "You are welcome." He grabbed Melanie by her hand and walked into the building with her.

Jonathan asked, "Melanie, what floor is the doctor located?"

Melanie replied, "We need floor 8." Jonathan pressed the number 8 on the elevator. Jonathan asked, "Melanie, are you still nervous?"

Melanie replied, "Not as much. You being here with me makes it better. Thank you for supporting me with this. I really appreciate you, Jonathan."

Jonathan stated, "Baby, you don't have to thank me. I am your husband. I'm supposed to support you." They stepped off the elevator and approached the check-in desk.

A young man asked, "Yes, how can I help you guys?"

Melanie replied, "Yes, I have an appointment. My name is Melanie Ashley. It's at nine thirty with Dr. Brooks."

Jesse stated, "Yes, ma'am. I'll get you checked in for the appointment. Did you complete the questionnaire we sent you?"

Melanie replied, "Yes, I do have it completed. Here you go."

Jesse stated, "Great, you have a $35 copay. How will you be paying?"

Melanie replied, "It will be cash." Melanie handed Jesse her money. She received her receipt, and Jesse directed her to the waiting room.

While they were sitting, Jonathan discerned multiple posters on the walls with women having successful pregnancies, some with more than one baby. They sat in the room until a nurse came through and asked if she was Melanie Ashley. After confirming with Melanie that it was indeed her, the nurse led her to the patient exam room. Jonathan felt uncomfortable hearing them state her maiden name. Jonathan owed child support and back pay for two kids, and he knew if Melanie had changed her name, they would be coming after her, deducting from her checks. He didn't want this burden on her. Nor did he want it to cause financial problems in the marriage. So he told her to leave her name as is. Melanie agreed and was relieved to keep her name as Ashley. She despised Melanie Taylor. It just didn't flow right to her.

The nurse led them to a room and asked, "Mrs. Ashley, what brings you in today?"

Melanie thought, *Now when I made this appointment, I told them why I was coming. It seems anytime an appointment is made, you inform the person scheduling why you are coming, only to be asked, what brings you here?* Melanie replied, "Yes, ma'am. We have been trying to get pregnant for months with no success."

The nurse asked, "Have you ever been pregnant?"

Melanie replied, "Yes, I have."

The nurse asked, "How many pregnancies, and were they successful going full-term?"

Melanie replied, "I've had two pregnancies. They both resulted in miscarriage. My first baby, I was about six weeks. And the second pregnancy, I carried her until I was almost six months."

The nurse, with compassion, stated, "Oh, I'm sorry. What happened with the six-month pregnancy?"

Melanie explained, "I have a weak cervix. The water bag was bulging out of my cervix, and the amniotic fluid was leaking. I was told on my next pregnancy going into the second trimester, a cervical cerclage will be necessary."

The nurse stated, "Oh, wow. I know that was a rough time for you. They didn't discern that you had a weak cervix after you graduated to the second trimester with the second pregnancy?"

Melanie replied, "No, ma'am, they did not. I was in the emergency room at least two to three times per month. They examined me each time I went. I was having severe pain with that pregnancy. The pregnancy prevented me from walking. I had to crawl around the apartment just to be mobile. When I tried to walk, each step taken I felt excruciating pain and inflammation in my pelvic and anal regions. There was nothing they could do, nor could they prescribe medication without harming the baby."

The nurse stated, "Oh, wow, I've never heard of those symptoms. You're the first patient to tell me this. I will inform the doctor of this and let him know that you are ready for him. Good luck to you."

Melanie and Jonathan replied, "Thank you."

Melanie thought about what she told the nurse. "Jonathan, maybe all those trips to the emergency room and them examining me with that vaginal speculum may have caused my cervix to open."

Jonathan replied, "Maybe so, baby. Maybe so."

They both sat there for a moment in silence. There was a knock on the door. A handsome man with a big smile and nice physique walked into the room and introduced himself. "Hi, I'm Dr. Brooks. How are you doing today?"

Melanie and Jonathan both replied, "We're doing fine."

Dr. Brooks asked, "So, Mrs. Ashley, you are trying to get pregnant? I have received your history from Dr. Gharma, and the nurse gave me a little background about your trials and failures to carry a baby full-term."

Melanie thought, *Thank God he didn't ask so what brings me here.* Melanie said, "Yes, that is correct, Doctor."

Dr. Brooks stated, "Okay, I can get you pregnant but won't be able to help with the weak cervix. You will need an obstetrics or gynecologist for that. Since we know you have no problems getting pregnant, we will prescribe Clomid to speed up the process. This medicine is known to produce multiple babies. Are you okay with that?"

Melanie replied, "Yes, Doctor. I am okay with that."

Jonathan sat there and rolled his eyes to the back of his head, thinking, *He just had to use those words. Multiple babies.*

Dr. Brooks noticed Jonathan's expression and laughed. He asked Jonathan, "The words *multiple babies* give you a scare?"

Jonathan laughed, answering, "Yes, they do."

Dr. Brooks asked Melanie, "Mrs. Ashley, are you ready? If so, follow me." Melanie rose to follow Dr. Brooks. The doctor took Melanie by the hand and led her to the in-house pharmacy.

He handed her a bottle of Clomid, saying, "Mrs. Ashley, the instructions for consumption are already on the bottle. Follow the instructions, and you should have no problems conceiving. Do you have any questions for me?"

Melanie jokingly thought, *Yes, are you married?* Melanie chuckled, stating, "No, Doctor, I don't have any questions."

Dr. Brooks stated, "All right then, Mrs. Ashley. You are free to go. Just check out where you checked in for the visit."

Melanie stated, "Okay, thank you, Dr. Brooks. I appreciate you being available to see me."

Dr. Brooks said, "Mrs. Ashley, you are welcome."

After Melanie checked out, Jonathan expressed a concern. "Melanie, baby, are you sure you want to do this? The possibility of multiple babies is scaring me."

Melanie replied, "Yes, I am sure, Jonathan. We'll just have to pray to God about it."

Jonathan reiterated, "I saw what that pregnancy did to you. You were always in pain, and that look on your face made me wonder if the pain was worth having you in that condition. You always looked as if you were exhausted and ready to give up."

Melanie rebutted, "Well, Jonathan, you know what they say. No pain, no gain. Since my body already hurts in that condition, when it comes time for me to deliver, it will be a piece of cake." Melanie couldn't have been more wrong. Those labor pains were worse than the pain she was experiencing.

Jonathan opened the door for Melanie and closed it. He thought, *Remember, whatever Melanie wants, she gets.*

Melanie wasted no time. When they were home, she immediately started her regimen of those Clomid pills. She was following the directions as instructed by her doctor. She made sure to take them with water.

Justin was home. He asked, "Hey, guys. How was the visit?"

Melanie replied, "I had a nice visit. And the doctor was handsome too."

Justin stated, "Cool. I will see you two later. Going to a friend's house. A group of us are playing some games. Pairing up as teams."

Melanie and Jonathan said, "Okay. See you later."

Jonathan asked, "What do you mean he was handsome too? Was he flirting with you?"

Melanie laughed, stating, "Well, he was handsome. I don't have a problem when you call other women pretty or beautiful. So don't get mad or jealous that I just so happen to find a man attractive. And no, he did not flirt with me."

Jonathan responded, "I never thought of it that way."

Melanie stated, "You men never do. You think you can say whatever you want, and the woman must put up with it with a closed mouth. Well, not me. If you can point out beauty, so can I."

Melanie went in the bedroom and slipped into her lingerie. She called out to Jonathan with a seductive voice. "Jonathan, come here, baby. I want to show you something." Melanie jumped on the bed and lay there.

When Jonathan walked in, his eyes almost popped out from his head. "Baby, where did you get that?"

Melanie had purchased this lace catsuit that had an opening for easy access so Jonathan could insert his throbbing member into her. It fit Melanie just right too. It didn't help that she had on her heels with it. This turned Jonathan on even more. He felt himself growing in his pants. Melanie rose from the bed. She had let her hair down. When she walked, her hair bounced up and down.

Jonathan let out a grunt and said, "Bring your ass here." He pulled Melanie toward him, grabbed her by her ass, and squeezed it. Melanie grabbed Jonathan's face and kissed him passionately. Jonathan walked Melanie backward to the bed and laid Melanie on the bed. He was throbbing so hard, it was hurting. To calm himself, he pleasured Melanie. She was enjoying every tongue stroke too. He had mastered his craft and was now making Melanie have multiple orgasms. And she enjoyed them all. She was due these strokes. He was making up for those past encounters of being clueless to her anatomy. He loved driving Melanie crazy. He loved feeling her pound on the bed and shaking her head from left to right as if she was having a fit.

Jonathan asked, "Are you ready for me? Are you ready to feel me? Raise them legs up and keep them up for me."

Melanie raised her legs up for Jonathan, and he thrusted into her. Melanie screamed out, "Jonathan! Oh my god! Wait a minute!"

Jonathan replied, "Wait a minute for what? You can take this. Long as I have been thrusting inside you, you should be used to this by now." He grabbed Melanie's legs and placed them on his shoulders and drove deeper into her.

Melanie screamed again, "Jonathan, you are hurting me!"

Jonathan asked, "Yeah, but it hurts so good, right?"

He began to kiss and suck on her neck to get her mind off the pain. He demanded Melanie, "Get on your knees. I want your ass up and face down, okay?"

Melanie replied, "Okay, Jonathan." She turned around.

Jonathan rubbed his penis up and down her vagina and rammed himself inside Melanie, causing her to jump. She tried to pull away.

He asked, "Where are you going? Why are you running? Come on back here."

He pulled Melanie back each time she tried to pull away. Jonathan would slap Melanie on her ass. She loved when he spanked her ass. Jonathan made the ass slapping sound off too. Melanie started moving with Jonathan. This drove Jonathan crazy. He could no longer contain himself and climaxed.

Jonathan kissed Melanie, saying, "You always make me feel good."

Melanie said, "Yeah, and don't you forget it."

Jonathan slapped Melanie on her ass and asked for a towel to clean up. Melanie delivered a towel with soap and water on it.

After handing him the towel, Melanie stated, "No way I can just take a wash off and feel comfortable. I need me a shower."

Jonathan laughed, asking, "What are you trying to say? I'm taking a ho bath?" They both burst out laughing.

CHAPTER 9

It was time for Justin to be enrolled to attend school. He approached his sister and asked, "Melanie, what school will I attend this school year?"

Melanie replied, "There's a school right up the street you can attend. I'll enroll you one week prior to school starting."

Justin stated, "Cool. My friends here attend that school, and they've given me information about it."

Melanie asked, "Okay. Did they have anything negative to report about the school?"

Justin answered, "No. No bad reports."

Melanie stated, "Okay, well, I'll get you enrolled."

Two weeks had passed. Melanie enrolled Justin into school. Melanie also made sure his name was on the list for bus services. Melanie was curious and asked Justin, "Baby brother, have you thought about college?"

Justin answered Melanie, "School isn't my cup of tea. The thought of having to sit through four more years of jibber jabber is a waste of time for me."

Melanie didn't fight him about this. She stated, "Okay. It's your choice. If you ever change your mind, you know I'm here for you and will help all I can." Justin thanked Melanie.

Justin and Jonathan were conversing one day. Justin said to Jonathan, "I'm glad y'all came for me. I was afraid I would never see y'all again. I cried often from missing y'all. In my mind, everyone I cared about either died or abandoned me. I thought you all had abandoned me. It hurt when y'all took me to Rita. It was as though I was going from home to home. I felt like there was no stability."

Jonathan stated, "You here with us now for as long as you desire. You know Melanie and I love you. Our intentions were to never make you feel abandoned. We thought we were doing the right thing by you. Melanie wasn't able to take care of you in her condition. We are grateful to have you here, and we're making memories, baby boy."

Justin added, "I spent nights at my friend's house and sometimes in the Laundromat."

Jonathan looked at him, asking, "Justin, why were you sleeping in the Laundromat? Why were you not living with Rita?"

Justin replied, "I was accused of going through her boyfriend's things, and they asked me to leave."

Jonathan yelled, "What! They asked you to leave and go where? Justin, she was receiving monthly checks for you, and you had nowhere to stay? Why did you not call Melanie and me?"

Justin replied, "Every time I asked Rita for Melanie's number, there was always an excuse. I would walk in the house while she would be on the phone and asked if she was talking to Melanie. She would say no, it was someone else on the phone. I knew sometimes she would be lying because she would talk low when I asked her."

Jonathan was furious. He thought they were leaving Justin with a responsible adult. Jonathan stated, "Justin, I'm sorry you had to go through that. But like I said, you home with Melanie and me. You can stay long as you want. Okay?"

Justin replied, "Okay."

Later that night, Jonathan strove with himself, wondering if he should tell Melanie. After pondering, he confessed to her the details of Justin's stay at Rita's. Melanie was furious. She began to question her baby brother about Rita. Melanie couldn't believe the details disclosed to her. He began to cry while telling her the story. Melanie remembered the promise she made to her mother to take care of Justin. She had failed her mother. She called Rita and didn't ask any questions. She lit in on her. "Rita, Justin is over here crying! He told Jonathan and I that you kicked him out the house! He was staying over at a friend's and sometimes in the Laundromat! How could you do this to him, Rita? He shouldn't have been out there in the streets like that!"

Rita replied, "Melanie, I don't want to hear that shit! Don't call me with that!" Rita hung the line up on Melanie. Melanie grew angrier. She didn't care to continue this conversation with Rita. So there was no callback made. She said what was on her mind and released everything.

Melanie asked, "How dare she hang up on me! How could she do this to her own brother? She could have called me! As bad as my pregnancy was, I would have taken him back!"

Jonathan stated, "Melanie, calm down, baby. He is home now. Just forget about it. You've said your peace." It made sense.

Melanie agreed, "Okay. It is in the past now. You are right, Jonathan. I will just leave it alone. I'll drop it." Melanie apologized to Justin and hugged him tightly. Melanie cried, "Baby brother, I'm so sorry. Please forgive me."

Justin stated, "It's okay, Melanie. None of this was your fault. You had no idea what was going on then. I don't blame you for what happened."

Melanie couldn't forget about this. She knew her mother was watching from heaven. She made Melanie promise she would take care of Justin.

Melanie went to bed with Jonathan. Still troubled from her talk with Justin, she had to eradicate those feelings inside her. She turned to Jonathan, stating, "Mom made me promise to take care of him, and I let her down, Jonathan. Why did I not see that this would happen? I should have known not to leave Justin with her. Dad is the reason she became detached from us. He mentally abused us both. She took the abuse and used it to part ways with us. After she had her son, she left home. We rarely ever saw or heard from her. We had no way of contacting her, nor did we know where she lived. She became so distant toward us. It was like she fell off the radar."

Jonathan was cognizant about how abusive their father was to them. He despised Melanie's father, and there was no love lost at all. He wanted to hurt him for hurting Melanie and the family.

Jonathan stated, "Mel, I don't understand how someone could have a beautiful family and treat them like garbage. It just doesn't make sense to me."

Melanie stated, "We all have wondered that ourselves. We never understood how a father abuses and commits crimes against the ones who loved him. He thinks that he did nothing wrong. He feels that saying sorry to us and God fixes everything. But he continued his recidivist behavior and caused us to resent him." Melanie felt angry, stating, "I'm done with this entire ordeal. I want to go to sleep now. Good night, Jonathan."

Jonathan agreed, "Okay, baby. Good night."

What Was I Thinking?

Melanie had been taking her fertility pills faithfully. She loved the idea of having twins, triplets, or even more. But she knew one was all they needed. She thought, *I could have waited a bit longer before taking those drugs. What was I thinking? We don't need a litter of babies at one time. Is it too late to stop taking them? I've barely had enough time with my husband.*

Melanie had been taking the pills for three weeks now. She discussed with Jonathan if she should stop taking the pills. Jonathan went along with whatever Melanie wanted. He didn't sway her to cease consumption of those pills. Jonathan knew it was too late for her to stop.

Melanie was two weeks late. She made no big deal about it because she often had irregular periods. Jonathan kept track of her periods and already knew she was late but kept it to himself. He wanted Melanie to feel as though she was surprising him with the big news.

Melanie made an appointment with her obstetrics/gynecologist. She had been feeling sick and could barely eat anything. She was hurting the same as her previous pregnancy. On a scale of 1 to 10, her pain level was an 8. Her previous pregnancy was a full-blown 10.

Melanie thought, *Maybe this pregnancy will not be as hard as the first one. I wish the doctor would hurry up so I can get home. I don't feel well, and I'm hurting.* Melanie had already urinated in a cup prior to entering the room.

The doctor tapped on the door and entered the room. She discerned Melanie's visage, asking, "Hello, Melanie, how are you?"

Melanie replied, "Dr. Gharma, I'm not feeling too good, and I'm hurting."

Dr. Gharma continued, "There is reason for your discomfort. I conducted a test utilizing your urine. Congratulations, you are pregnant. When was your last period?"

Melanie replied, "It was October 20."

Dr. Gharma calculated Melanie's pregnancy utilizing a pregnancy wheel. She faced Melanie, stating, "That would put you right at six weeks. You should be having this baby toward the end of July or early August. I want to take a look at you to make sure everything is okay. Good thing the nurse had you undress to get a sonogram to confirm a heartbeat or two. Then we will conduct a vaginal exam. We'll see just how those fertility drugs impacted your uterus." The doctor and Melanie both burst out laughing.

Dr. Gharma pulled the sonogram machine toward her. She reminded Melanie the gel would feel cold across her belly. She provided Melanie with a paper sheet to cover up her lower body. Dr. Gharma moved the wand around Melanie's belly until she was able to find a heartbeat. She increased the volume on the machine so that Melanie could hear the heartbeat.

She asked, "Melanie, do you hear that? That's the baby's heartbeat."

Melanie was melting internally. She could hear the baby's heartbeat. Melanie replied, "Yes, Doctor. I can hear it."

Dr. Gharma stated, "Well, Melanie, it looks as though you only have one baby." Dr. Gharma moved the device over to an untouched area to ensure no other heartbeats were present. There were none. "Melanie, it sounds like a healthy baby. Good thing that this is only one fetus tucked away. The symptoms experienced in your previous pregnancy are proof that your body wouldn't be able to withstand multiple babies."

Melanie agreed, "Yes, I do think it's best for me to only carry one baby."

Dr. Gharma had laid a baby book, prenatal vitamins, and some other literature about her pregnancy on the counter. Dr. Gharma asked Melanie, "Will you scoot down for me and place your feet in the stirrups?" Melanie lay back and placed her feet in the stirrups. Dr. Gharma added, "Melanie, you will feel a little pressure, but I will be gentle. I know you are in pain. I'm going to take a sample and send it to the lab."

Melanie stated, "Okay, Doctor."

The exam was quick, and the doctor slowly extracted the speculum from inside Melanie. Dr. Gharma stated, "Okay, we are all done. Everything is looking good. Here is a baby book, sample of prenatal pills, and literature about mom and baby. Call me seventy-two hours prior to depleting the sample, and I will call in a prescription to your pharmacy. Make sure to take them every day. These pills will help the baby grow and provide nourishment. I need you to make sure that you endeavor to make the right food choices. I will have biweekly visits with you starting next month until your delivery date. Do you have any questions for me?"

Melanie replied, "No, I don't, Doctor."

Dr. Gharma concluded the visit and walked out the room.

Melanie dressed herself and made her way to her car. Melanie cried. Not because she was sad. She was internally happy. She cranked up the car and drove home to share with Jonathan the exciting news. Her foot was a little heavy on the gas. Melanie thought, *Oh, shoot. I better slow down.* She looked at the speedometer. She was going twenty miles over the speed limit. *I am not trying to pay the city my hard-earned money for a speeding ticket.*

It was too late. A patrol officer was behind her. Melanie hesitated to stop until she was in an area in view of the public. She pulled into a grocery store parking lot, far from the other cars but close enough for any witnesses should the officer get out of hand.

The officer exited his car. He approached Melanie and stooped a little to get a better view. "Evening, ma'am. Are you in a hurry? You were going twenty miles over the speed limit. Do you have an emergency?"

Melanie replied, "I'm so sorry. No, Officer. There is no emergency. I was just driving from my doctor's office. She gave me some good news. We are expecting a baby. I guess the news had me excited and rushing home to tell my husband he's going to be a daddy."

The officer stated, "Congratulations. I am going to let you off with a warning. Slow down, okay?"

Melanie replied, "Thank you, Officer. Will do." Melanie's heart was pounding. She praised God, stating, "Thank you, Jesus. Thank you." Melanie watched as the officer entered his patrol car and drove away.

Melanie left the parking lot and drove home to Jonathan. When she arrived home, Jonathan and Justin sat in the living room, watching television. Jonathan asked, "Hey, how was the visit?"

Melanie replied, "It was a successful visit, Jonathan." Melanie cracked a smile.

Jonathan, excited, asked, "For real? No way, baby. You are pregnant?"

Melanie answered, "Yes, Jonathan. You are going to be a daddy. She says I'm due around the end of July, early August."

Jonathan rose from the couch and walked over to Melanie to give her a big hug and kiss. Justin walked over to Melanie, stating, "Congratulations, sis. I am anxious to be an uncle." He graced Melanie with a hug.

Melanie smiled, saying, "Thank you, baby brother."

Jonathan asked, "How are you feeling? Do you need anything? Here, why don't you sit down and tell me what I can do for you."

Melanie replied, "I'm hurting, Jonathan. I will take your offer and sit down for a spell."

Jonathan stated, "Yes, this happened with your last pregnancy at such an early stage. How far along are you?"

Melanie answered, "About six weeks, exhausted, out of breath, and of course the pain. Oh, and there is only one baby."

Jonathan mentally thanked God. He stated, "Melanie, I'm relieved to hear that. I was against those fertility drugs and prayed to God for only one baby. Multiple babies wouldn't be good for you. Melanie, I want you to just sit down and take it easy. When do they plan to place you on bed rest? You need to be home and not working if you are already hurting, baby. What did Dr. Gharma say?"

Melanie answered, "With all the excitement, I forgot to ask her about that. I'll call her."

Jonathan stated, "No, I will call her. You take it easy. I have her number in my phone."

It shocked Melanie to see him taking control and being responsible with the pregnancy. It made her feel at ease and that Jonathan would always have her back and take care of her.

The next morning, Jonathan called the doctor and explained to her Melanie's symptoms. Since the doctor was cognizant of Melanie's previous miscarriages, she agreed with Jonathan. Melanie needed to be at home on bed rest if she wanted to keep the baby.

Dr. Gharma added, "Mr. Taylor, you make sure she doesn't walk any farther than from your door and to the car. If she is hurting, exhausted, and out of breath as you are describing to me, this could cause harm to her and the baby. I told her she needs to come in to see me every two weeks instead of monthly. Also, you all may want to pump brakes and not have sex. I need you two to understand that Melanie is extremely high-risk."

Jonathan agreed, "Yes, Dr. Gharma. I understand. No sex and no stress."

She told Jonathan to call her back with the specifics of whom to address the letter and have the company fax to her office the FMLA forms to complete. Jonathan was taking charge, and it pleased Melanie.

Jonathan was waiting on Melanie hand and foot. He was taking the necessary precautions to prevent Melanie from losing any more of his babies. When Melanie was ready for her baths, Jonathan went with her to make sure she didn't slip in the tub. He even ran her bathwater for her. Any part of her body she couldn't wash, Jonathan helped. He was great with Melanie. If he had to leave, he would have Justin to care for her until he made it back.

Justin made sure to not let Jonathan down when it came to Melanie. Justin often thought about being an uncle and would succumb to excitement. He thought, *I can't wait until this baby arrives.*

LOSING HER CROWN

I hope she has a boy. He can run in behind me. Crazy about his uncle Justin. Justin laughed.

Melanie asked, "What are you laughing about, Justin?"

Justin replied, "I'm just thinking how cool it would be to hear one of your babies call me Uncle Justin."

Melanie stated, "I know, right? I have to take it easy and be careful. I want this pregnancy to be successful."

Justin added, "No need to worry, sis. Jonathan and I both have your back."

Melanie rebutted, "Okay, G. I. Joe." They both laughed. His friends named him this before their mother passed away.

Justin had formed a gang in the apartments they lived in prior to Lashon's passing. He was only ten at the time. No one in the family knew about the gang. It was after Lashon passed that the subject surfaced. Jonathan somewhat knew and confided in Melanie one day after he talked to Justin. The gang Justin formed was called PTT, a.k.a. Plum Tree Thugs. They ran around the apartments, tagging property and committing all types of petty crimes. One day, an officer caught Justin tagging property and brought him home to Lashon, disclosing his mischievous acts. Justin tried to lie, but Lashon knew the officer spoke the truth about his actions. She wasn't one of those parents quick to believe her child's lies.

Justin, at an impressionable young age, grew up too fast without his father in the home. Justin had no respect for his dad and spoke to him with disdain. Tee felt that since he was a disappointment and wasn't in Justin's life, he had no business correcting him. He left it up to Melanie and Tosha to discipline Justin. Tee knew he messed up in life and wasn't there for him the way he should've been. He knew this concerning all his children. None of them had respect for him. Now that they were all adults, whenever he cursed them, they cursed him right back. It was tit for tat. Melanie didn't like speaking to her father this way at all. The things he would say to his children were outrageously disrespectful. A good father wouldn't say the things to his children that spewed from his mouth. Melanie would convince herself each time it happened that this was the last straw.

She would tell herself, "He will never ever get a chance to speak to me that way again. I'm grown and refuse to take this verbal abuse from him."

No matter how often she told herself this, after each tongue-lashing from him, once enough time passed, Melanie was willing to forgive and give him another chance. She loved her dad despite the way he treated and verbally attacked her.

Procedure Day

Melanie was growing with a small bump. She had reached three months. Her clothes were starting to feel tight on her. She was looking forward to her next visit with the doctor. It was time for the insertion of the cervical cerclage. Melanie made an appointment with Dr. Gharma for the procedure weeks ago. She wanted to make sure she would get Melanie in two weeks after entering her second trimester. She waited two weeks after just in case Melanie's body recognized the baby as a foreign object and decided to discard the baby.

Jonathan drove Melanie to the appointment. He noticed that Melanie was quiet and gazing out the window. Melanie focused her attention on a field of corn they were passing. Jonathan grabbed her hand, asking, "Melanie, why are you so quiet, baby? Everything okay? You feel a little nervous?"

Melanie replied, "Yeah, just a little. Not too much. They will need to put me under for the procedure. Dr. Gharma says I won't be able to stand the tugging and pulling required to place the cerclage. The procedure takes less than an hour."

Jonathan stated, "Yeah, baby, I know. I spoke with Dr. Gharma, and she explained the procedure to me. You know I love you, right? Everything will be okay, baby."

Melanie replied, "Yes, I know you love me, and I love you too. I know this procedure will be a success. Can you believe it, Jonathan? You and I will finally enjoy the joys of a full-term pregnancy this time. Only thing is, I can't share my pregnancy with the world since I am on bed rest for the entire pregnancy."

Jonathan stated, "Yes, baby, I know. The world doesn't matter. Just the souls living under our roof. Did I tell you how beautiful and glowing you look?"

Melanie laughed, answering, "No, you didn't. Thank you though. You know, once you tell me this, you will have to continue telling me this, right? I'm soon entering the big belly stage and will feel very unattractive to you and myself."

Jonathan assured her, saying, "You don't have to worry about that, Melanie. You will always be attractive to me." He pulled Melanie's hand toward his lips and kissed it.

They arrived at the hospital. Jonathan helped Melanie out the car. He latched his hand to hers and led the way. They entered the hospital and went to the surgery department. Dr. Gharma was there waiting and noticed Melanie entering the waiting room after she was checked in for the procedure. She had just finished her coffee and walked toward the couple.

She greeted them, stating, "Melanie and Jonathan, glad you made it safely. How are you, Melanie?"

Melanie answered, "I'm not well. I am still tired and can only walk so far before I feel exhausted. Thank you for completing those forms to place me on bed rest. That was a huge help."

Dr. Gharma stated, "No need to thank me. I know the importance of you being on bed rest for your pregnancies. Jonathan, how are you feeling today? I wanted to tell you thanks for being so proactive in caring for her. I am impressed with your concerns about her pregnancy. Not too many husbands or fathers take control the way you have."

Jonathan replied, "I'm well, Dr. Gharma. I always want to be a participant in Melanie's pregnancies. She's carrying my baby, so we both are pregnant."

Dr. Gharma said to Jonathan, "You just keep surprising me. Melanie, he's a keeper."

Melanie admitted, "Yes, Dr. Gharma. Jonathan is the best."

Dr. Gharma requested the nurse get a wheelchair for Melanie. She led Jonathan to a waiting room. "Jonathan, you can wait in here. We will be back in two shakes."

Melanie undressed herself in the patient room while the nurse stood outside the door. Melanie opened the door, alerting the nurse she was ready. The nurse wheeled her into the operating room, where Dr. Gharma was waiting. Melanie was prepped, and when it was time for surgery, Dr. Gharma said to Melanie, "We are giving you your anesthesia. I want you to count backward from ten."

Melanie started counting. Before she could get to 8, the anesthesia expeditiously affected her alertness, sending her to la-la land.

Melanie's feet were on the stirrups. Dr. Gharma inserted the speculum. She began the procedure and asked for the tools necessary to complete the mission. She carefully grabbed a hold of Melanie's cervix and placed a stitch around the cervix to close it. Another successful procedure for the doctor. There was no harm imposed on the amniotic sac nor the baby. They removed the anesthesia mask at the doctor's orders.

Dr. Gharma stated, "Melanie, wake up. The cervical cerclage was a success. We will give you a couple of hours to recover and let Jonathan know. After leaving here, you will still feel drowsy and sleepy. Also, there will be some spotting from the procedure. That is normal."

Melanie, still under the effects of the anesthesia, vaguely understood what the doctor said to her. As soon as they wheeled her to recovery, Melanie was out again.

The recovery team watched Melanie carefully. Dr. Gharma walked to the waiting room. She approached Jonathan, stating, "Jonathan, the procedure was a success. Melanie is resting in the recovery room. If you like, you can go in to see her or go downstairs or outside the hospital to get a bite to eat to kill time. She'll be out for a couple of hours. Also, she will experience some spotting from the procedure. It's normal. No reason to be alarmed."

Jonathan agreed, "Okay, Dr. Gharma. I will look in on her and get something to eat. Please call me as soon as she opens her eyes. I will be close by."

Dr. Gharma stated, "Will do. I have your number in my cell phone. I'll call you as soon as she opens those eyes."

Jonathan went to the recovery room. He could hear Melanie snoring before approaching the nurse's station. Jonathan began laughing. He asked, "Nurse, she at it, huh?"

Nurse replied, "Yep, she's been at it since they wheeled her in here." They both laughed.

Melanie was snoring loudly. Louder than being at home. He blamed it on the anesthesia. Jonathan left the hospital feeling confident. All he thought about while sitting in that waiting room was Melanie and their unborn child. He was relieved to hear Dr. Gharma confirm Melanie was fine. That was one less worry he had on his mind.

Jonathan had another worry, but he dared not say anything to Melanie about it. He thought about his daughter and how he abandoned her to please Melanie. He felt as though he was betraying his own child. Jonathan struggled inwardly about this subject. He prayed to God that someday, He would take this bitterness in Melanie's heart and replace it with forgiveness and acceptance.

"God, I know You can hear me. Please open Melanie's heart to forgive me for what I did to her so that she may accept my child. I know I hurt her. I was such an immature person, living life with no care in the world. Just out there wild. I love her, and I want our marriage to work. Forgive me for abandoning my child, Father. This hurts me deeply. I want Melanie and myself to be part of her life. Amen." Jonathan wiped away tears that streamed down his face.

Jonathan walked out of the hospital to get lunch at a place he and Melanie frequented. It was just around the corner from the hospital. There they had a variety of foods that he could choose. Jonathan sat there to eat his lunch. He took his time eating. He played games on his phone to help kill time.

After eating lunch, Jonathan decided to head back to the hospital and visit their gift shop. He purchased a beautiful helium-filled balloon, card, and one of Melanie's favorite candy bars. He paid for the items and exited the gift shop. Jonathan thought, *I hope she likes her gifts and is ready to return home.*

Jonathan entered the surgery department and found himself in the waiting room. He sat there for about ten minutes, anticipating a call from the doctor.

The staff alerted Dr. Gharma that Melanie had awakened. While speaking to her nurse, she noticed Jonathan walking into the waiting room, so there was no need to call him. She checked on Melanie first and entered the waiting room, stating, "Jonathan, Melanie is awake, and she is getting dressed. We will bring her here to the waiting room for you. She is still a little groggy and may go back to sleep when you all get home. She is to do no form of exercise, bending, and no reaching. In her case, very minimal walking for two to three days. She needs to rest her body."

Jonathan responded, "Yes, Doctor. I will make sure Melanie is well rested."

Dr. Gharma added, "Jonathan, you have my number. If Melanie needs me, just call. It was good seeing you, and take care."

Jonathan stated, "You too, Dr. Gharma."

No sooner had the doctor exited than they were wheeling Melanie into the waiting room. Jonathan looked at his wife, asking her, "Hey, baby, how are you feeling?"

Melanie looked at Jonathan, sluggishly laughed, and replied, "Jonathan, is that you? Jonathan, I feel sleepy."

The nurse stated, "Mr. Taylor, Melanie is still a little groggy. This is expected. She will be sleeping off and on for a while. There will be spotting from the procedure. Did the doctor give you the instructions? If not, here is all the information you'll need to care for your wife."

The nurse handed Jonathan discharge papers with instructions. Jonathan replied, "Yes, ma'am, she did give me instructions, but it doesn't hurt to have written instructions for assurance. Thank you."

The nurse stated, "Okay, you are good to go. I will wheel her out to the curbside and help you get her inside the car."

Jonathan said, "Okay. Let me bring the car around to the front." It only took about five minutes. The nurse began helping Melanie up from the wheelchair. Jonathan exited the car to help get Melanie out of the wheelchair. She was able to rise and walk, but not too fast. She had to pace herself. She could still feel the effects of the anesthesia. She held on to the car to help the nurse and Jonathan get her settled.

LOSING HER CROWN

Once in the car, Melanie was incredibly exhausted. The walk from the wheelchair to the car had her feeling as though she had run a marathon. Jonathan closed the door and thanked the nurse. He entered the car and asked Melanie, "Melanie, baby, you okay? You ready for our commute home?"

Melanie answered, "I'm okay. I'm tired." She had slurred speech, but Jonathan knew exactly what she was saying.

Jonathan stated, "Okay, baby, you just rest. Justin waiting for us to get home. He's going to help me get you out the car."

Melanie replied, "K, Jon."

Jonathan laughed inside, thinking, *They got my baby on some good stuff.*

Their drive was quick, and they were finally home. Justin was looking out for them and ran to the car door to help Melanie. Melanie looked at Justin, laughed, and stated, "Hey, Justin, I love you."

Justin laughed, asking, "Jonathan, she loaded, huh?"

Jonathan replied, "Yep, she been halfway talking and giggling since we left. Come on, Melanie. Let us get you inside, baby." They both entered the apartment with Melanie between them.

Jonathan asked Justin to help him get her in the bedroom. From there, Jonathan undressed Melanie and put her to bed. Melanie smiled at Jonathan and drifted off to sleep. Jonathan kissed Melanie on her forehead. "Rest, my two babies."

It was 8:00 p.m. when Melanie woke up to use the bathroom. A little more of the anesthesia had worn off. She called out to Jonathan. "Jonathan! Jonathan!"

Jonathan dashed into the room. "Yes, Melanie? What you need, baby?"

Melanie replied, "I need to use the bathroom. Please help me get up from the bed. How long was I asleep? When did we leave the hospital? I'm so exhausted."

Jonathan replied, "We left at three this afternoon. You been sleep for about four and a half hours. Yes, you are going to feel this way until the anesthesia runs its course. Are you hungry, baby?"

Melanie replied, "No, I just want to lay down and watch television until I fall back asleep. I will eat something tomorrow. Can you make me an omelet for breakfast?"

Jonathan replied, "I sure can. Anything for my two babies." Jonathan turned on the television after helping Melanie back in bed. When he turned around, Melanie was already fast asleep. Jonathan kissed her on her forehead. Melanie cracked a smile in her sleep.

The next morning, Jonathan was awake before Melanie. He made her two loaded breakfast omelets. He knew she would be hungry. Her last meal was yesterday morning. He asked his brother, "Justin, grab that tray for me. I need to get Melanie's food to her."

Justin replied, "Okay, here you go." Justin was helpful to Jonathan when it came to caring for Melanie. He loved his sister and would do anything for her.

Jonathan marched in the room to surprise Melanie with her breakfast. He had a big smile on his face. He opened the door, stating, "Melanie. Melanie. Wake up, baby. Sit up so you can eat your breakfast."

Melanie yawned, opening her eyes to Jonathan. Melanie asked, "Jonathan, what time is it? What day is it? You made me breakfast? Feels like I've been sleeping for days."

Jonathan replied, "It's the day after your procedure. It's ten in the morning, and yes, I made you breakfast. How are you feeling this morning? Are you in any pain? You need help sitting up to eat?"

Melanie answered, "Yes, I do feel some pain, and I do need you to help me sit up, please. I need one of those pain pills too."

Jonathan helped Melanie. He reached for her medication, stating, "Here is your pain medication. And drink this water with it."

Melanie placed her pill on the tray, stating, "Jonathan, I can't take this yet. I need to eat something first." Melanie had a weak stomach when it came to taking any pain medication. Taking them on an empty stomach would cause her nausea and vomiting. She ate her breakfast and took her medication as Jonathan instructed with water.

Melanie felt flutters in her womb. "Oh my, Jonathan. I can feel flutters! Come feel the flutters, baby. These flutters are powerful." Melanie laughed.

Jonathan placed his hand on Melanie's stomach. He stated, "Oh, wow. I felt a little flutter." He decided to place his head on her stomach. "Whoa! I felt that flutter too. Hey there, baby. You're a boy, aren't you? Daddy loves you and can't wait to see you."

Jonathan was so excited and knew in his heart they were having a boy. He often daydreamed about bringing Melanie and their son home from the hospital. Nothing or no one had ever influenced or made an impact on him to make that change in his life the way these two would.

Jonathan's father had missed seeing him grow up from the time he left. His first bicycle ride, first year in school, first fight, first girlfriend, etc. He would see him occasionally on holidays and summers. This affected Jonathan in a way that life just didn't seem attractive to him. When he became older, he was numb to how his dad basically ignored him. In his world, it no longer mattered. His presence was no longer desired. He often asked that one question all children asked when their father was absent: Why did my dad leave?

Melanie and their baby were all the reasons he needed to be a better husband and father than his dad. His issues with his dad no longer mattered, so he thought. His mission was to prove to his dad and show him, he is nothing like him. He didn't want to be that husband who turned his back on his family.

Melanie asked, "Jonathan, what makes you think this isn't a girl?"

Jonathan replied, "Did you not feel that powerful flutter? We are having a son, baby. When will you have the sonogram to determine the sex?"

Melanie asked, "Do you really want to know? I thought maybe we should be surprised in the delivery room."

Jonathan replied, "Nah, not me. I want to know. But I already know I have a pair of nuts in there."

Melanie stated, "Okay, well, when I'm further into my pregnancy, the doctor will take pics anyway. The sonogram will ensure our little bambino is growing properly. Would you like to be there when she looks at the baby?"

Jonathan replied, "Of course! I told you, I will be there every step of the way. I want to make every appointment with you." Jonathan promised himself he wouldn't let her go through this alone, no matter if the pregnancy would be complicated or not. He wanted to see the baby growing anytime a sonogram was offered.

Jonathan kept his promise to Melanie. During one of Melanie's visits, he could see his seed turning flips and swimming around, being active in Melanie's womb. This brought excitement to his heart. He wanted to give Melanie and their baby the world. They both filled the room with new parents-to-be gestures as they watched the active baby.

CHAPTER 10

Melanie was now six months and growing rapidly. She was still in pain and on bed rest. She struggled to walk and was easily out of breath. She thought, *I wonder how many other women have suffered the way I have.*

As much as Dr. Gharma tried to figure things out, there was no explanation as to why Melanie was hurting in the reproductive region and anal area. There were no known documented cases of pregnant mothers having confessed these symptoms Melanie was having.

It was time for Melanie's biweekly appointment to see Dr. Gharma. Dr. Gharma had to prepare Melanie for her suggestion of future pregnancies. When Melanie came in for her two-week checkup, Dr. Gharma brought her and Jonathan into her office. She looked at Melanie, stating, "Melanie, I am puzzled about your condition. There are no documented cases for what you are going through with this pregnancy. This is a first. There may be a chance your body is allergic to this condition. Your body looks at your babies as being an unidentifiable object, and it reacts in the worse way. So you two may want to discuss if it is worth the risk to have more children. You have complicated high-risk pregnancies."

Melanie replied, "Okay, Dr. Gharma. I understand, and it makes sense." Melanie didn't care about the pain. She always wanted at least three children. She sat in the chair half listening to the doctor. The doctor's soliloquy went in one ear and out the other. Nothing would keep her from having more babies.

After their discussion, Dr. Gharma stated, "Okay, guys, let's get you in an exam room to take a look at the baby." Dr. Gharma had her nurse to room Melanie. She wouldn't have to change into a gown. She just needed to lower her pants for the doctor to view images on their little one. Dr. Gharma tapped on the door and entered the room. "Okay, Melanie, let us get the images of the baby. I can print some off for you if you'd like."

Melanie and Jonathan both replied, "Yes, we would like that."

Dr. Gharma began the exam. She moved the wand up, down, and across Melanie's growing abdomen. She stated, "The baby is looking good and is growing. Looks like the baby is sucking its thumb. I'll image this for you."

Melanie and Jonathan both replied, "Oh my god. The baby has the thumb in its mouth." The connection between Melanie and Jonathan was so strong, they were stating sentences together.

Melanie replied, "The baby gets that from me. I sucked my thumb until the age of twelve."

Dr. Gharma asked, "Would you like to know the sex?"

Jonathan didn't waste any time responding, "Yes, I want to know."

Melanie replied, "I guess it wouldn't hurt to know. We need to start preparing for this baby."

Dr. Gharma replied, "You guys are having a boy."

Jonathan threw his hands up as if he had just won a boxing match. He stated, "Told you we were having a boy. I have a pair of nuts in there."

Melanie stated, "I just want my baby to be healthy."

Dr. Gharma stated, "And a healthy baby boy he is. Well, guys, here are pictures of the baby. We are removing the stitch from your cervix close to your due date. You won't need any anesthesia. I just need to snip the stitch. We will need your cervix to start opening."

Melanie stated, "Okay, we will be here. Just let us know when."

Dr. Gharma reminded Melanie, "Okay. I will see you in two weeks. Do you all have any questions for me?"

Melanie and Jonathan both replied, "No, thank you."

Dr. Gharma concluded, "Okay, make sure to schedule before leaving."

Melanie replied, "Yes, ma'am, I will. Thank you. See you in two weeks."

Dr. Gharma exited the room.

Jonathan asked, "Melanie, are you hungry? We can stop by Fine Market for some food."

Melanie replied, "Yes, I want some food from there. I want a little of everything they have for us to self-serve. You know what I like, right, Jonathan?"

Jonathan answered, "Yes, I know exactly what you like. You will have enough food for leftovers. What you don't eat today, you can finish tomorrow."

They left the doctor's office and made their trip to Fine Market. Jonathan filled Melanie's container with all her favorite foods. He had to get another container just for her. He didn't get her too much of each item. Just a little of everything she liked. He was out in no time. Melanie kept thinking about the delicious food that would soon hit the palate of her mouth. Jonathan made it back to the car. As soon as he made his way inside, Melanie could smell the food. The smell of the food must have awakened the baby. He started kicking her.

She responded, "Calm down, little one. We will be home in about five minutes. Mommy will feed you until you've had your fill."

Melanie was growing bigger and becoming more tired and out of breath. Every day was a struggle for Melanie. Steps to the bathroom were becoming difficult for Melanie. Jonathan made sure she didn't do anything that would cause her to put his son's life in danger.

During one of her visits, Dr. Gharma warned Melanie and Jonathan that she shouldn't lay in bed all day. She wouldn't want to develop pain in her hips and bedsores from lying on her sides too much. Walking would be good for Melanie. Even if it was just walking back and forth from one end of the hall to the other end. She needed to stretch her legs out as much as possible. Every day Melanie made herself get out of bed to walk around the apartment and sit in the living room for as long as she could stand. When it was evident from the increased aches and pains that her body had enough, she would go back to her room and watch her favorite cartoon shows. She loved her cartoons. They helped take her mind off the pain and suffering. Laughter was how she was going to get through this.

Melanie was starting to miss Jonathan. Miss him making love to her and holding her. Melanie and Jonathan have had sex about two times since her pregnancy. The longevity of no sex didn't bother Jonathan. At least that's what Melanie felt in her heart. He was always careful not to hurt Melanie. They were told they should consider abandoning the act, but he took cautious measures to not hurt his darling wife. Melanie didn't want Jonathan to stray during her pregnancy, so she took a chance every three months for intimacy with her husband.

Jonathan was an impeccable husband to Melanie. He waited on her hand and foot. He was always at home and never left her alone, with the exception of running errands. Even then, he endeavored to not leave her home alone for no more than an hour. He was more cautious than Melanie was with his baby. Jonathan wanted to make sure nothing would prevent Melanie from having a successful full-term pregnancy and delivery. He knew Melanie thought his eyes would wander, so he would give in to her, but with extra precautions of being extremely gentle. Jonathan always made her feel she was still attractive to him.

Tornado and Death

Jonathan had been watching the news. There was a tornado coming through, violently ripping neighborhoods apart. The sirens were alerting everyone to take cover. Jonathan gathered Melanie and Justin, stating, "I need you both to get in the bathroom and get in the tub now! I will bring a mattress in there to cover you all. That tornado has hit the interstate coming this way."

Melanie and Justin went into the bathroom, and in the tub they went. Jonathan brought the mattress in to cover them. Jonathan had been monitoring the whereabouts of the tornado. They could hear the sirens sounding off loudly. Melanie was scared. But Jonathan was there, and he was taking over with no problems. Melanie was at ease because of his actions. By the time they were in the tub, ready for the mattress to cover them, the tornado had averted its attention elsewhere to cause destruction. Melanie was relieved. Not as much as Jonathan. He was worried about Melanie, the baby, and Justin.

LOSING HER CROWN

He didn't care about his safety, just the safety of those three was his concern.

He asked, "Baby, you okay? Let me help you out the tub."

Melanie hadn't sat down in the tub yet when the tornado's direction took a turn. Jonathan helped her out the tub, and she went back into her room to relax and sleep.

While Melanie was asleep, her uncle who gave her away at her wedding called Jonathan to check on Melanie and to deliver a bit of sad news, but he didn't want Jonathan to tell Melanie because of her condition. Melanie's aunt Sherry had passed away from lupus. Lupus had claimed the lives of her uncle, baby sister, and now her auntie. All on her father's side of the family.

After Jonathan concluded his conversation with her uncle, he went to Melanie. He couldn't withhold this information from her. When he entered the bedroom, Melanie saw the look on his face. It was a face that said, "I have come to bear bad news."

Melanie asked, "What is it, Jonathan?"

Jonathan answered, "Melanie, baby, I have to tell you something. Your uncle called me, and I just don't think I should keep this from you. Your uncle asked me not to tell you because of your condition. Your Aunt Sherry died, baby."

Melanie's eyes began to water, and tears began to flow. She couldn't believe her aunt was dead. She asked, "What? What happened to her?"

Jonathan replied, "Your uncle says she died from lupus."

Melanie was shocked. She never knew her aunt had lupus. She often heard her aunt complain of the same symptoms her sister had, but while they lived in Louisiana, Melanie never knew this to be confirmed by a doctor. This was another funeral she couldn't attend because of her pregnancy. First her baby sister, and now her aunty.

Jonathan looked at his wife, stating, "Baby, I'm sorry, okay? I am so sorry. Are you okay?"

Melanie replied, "Yes, I'm okay. I have to be strong for the baby. Just please keep me in good spirits. I don't want to be in this room by myself please."

Jonathan stated, "Sure, baby. I don't mind at all."

Melanie couldn't control the waterworks. She cried more knowing she would not be in any condition to say her goodbyes to her aunt.

Melanie called her grandmother after the funeral. Her grandmother was in good spirits at Melanie's surprise. She told how she laid her baby girl to rest. She stated, "She loved pink, Melanie. I made sure I laid her to rest in pink."

Melanie's grandmother wanted to know how Melanie's pregnancy was progressing. She asked, "How are you doing, Melanie? Is everything okay with the pregnancy?"

Melanie replied, "I'm doing well, Grandma, and so is the baby. I am almost ready to deliver. Grandma, would you come out and help me with the baby after I have him?"

Mawmaw Ashley asked, "You want me to come out there?"

Melanie replied, "Yes, Grandma, I do."

Mawmaw Ashley stated, "Okay, I sure will come and help you. I want to get away from here for a while. You make sure you call me and let me know. I will come before he is born. That way, I can be there before the baby's arrival."

Melanie replied, "Really, you will? Thank you, Grandma." They said their goodbyes to each other and told the other how much they loved each other.

Melanie went into the living room to share the news. She waddled to Jonathan, stating, "Jonathan, Grandma is coming to spend some time with me before and after the baby is born. Her and the boys. She's going to help me out with the baby. I'm sorry. I should have asked you first. Are you okay with this?"

Jonathan responded, "Okay, baby, that's cool. When are they coming?"

Melanie replied, "She'll be here a few days before they induce labor. She's coming by Greyhound."

Jonathan replied, "Okay, that sounds good, baby. I'll pick her up from the bus station."

Melanie felt relieved. She would have more than just Jonathan and his mother there for the birth. She was so excited. Her grandmother would share her experience with her.

Stitch Removed and Grandma's Arrival

It was two weeks before they were to induce labor on Melanie. Dr. Gharma scheduled Melanie to have her cerclage removed. She waddled into her doctor's office, extremely exhausted. Dr. Gharma looked at Melanie, stating, "My Melanie, you look overwhelmingly exhausted. More than normal. Good thing your date is approaching. I wouldn't want you to go any longer than you need carrying this baby. Are you ready for the big day?"

Melanie replied, "Yes, I am eager to deliver this baby. I feel like I'm going to pop anytime now."

Dr. Gharma stated, "You hang in there. It won't be long at all. Jonathan, I see you're continuing to be an awesome husband with Melanie. You're one of a kind. I have said it before, and I will say it again. You don't witness many husbands making every appointment, taking care of the mother of their child the way you do. It's rare that I see this behavior."

Jonathan said, "She's carrying my baby. I have to make sure they both okay. I'm the reason she is in this condition."

Dr. Gharma replied, "At least you do get the idea of the woes of a woman carrying a baby. You have proven to me and Melanie that you have everything under control. So are you all ready to remove the stitch?"

They both replied, "Yes."

Dr. Gharma stated, "Okay, let's remove the stitch. This won't require any anesthesia, just sharp hands."

Jonathan stood up to help Melanie lay on the examining table. There was a little struggle because of how big she had grown since her last visit. But Jonathan was able to get her up on the table with the help of a step stool.

Dr. Gharma stated, "Okay, Melanie, position your feet on the stirrups. You're going to feel the cold speculum and some pressure." Dr. Gharma had her nurse help remove the stitch. One had to hold the stitch in place while the other snipped it. One mistake of cutting her cervix instead of the stitch wouldn't be good. Admission into the hospital from bleeding would be necessary. The removal of the stitch was successful. They had a challenging time trying to cut it, but they were finally able to do so.

Dr. Gharma pushed back and removed her gloves. She stated, "Guys, everything is looking good. No lifting of any kind and rest as usual. Melanie, I will be calling you with the specifics for you to check into the hospital. You have any questions or concerns?"

Melanie replied, "No, Doctor, I don't."

Dr. Gharma said goodbye to the couple and exited the room. This would be Melanie's last office visit here. They gathered their things and made their trip home.

Melanie called her grandmother the week before to let her know her doctor would induce her in two weeks. The phone rang. Melanie heard a familiar voice on the other end. Melanie stated, "Hey, Grandma! It's Melanie. How are you?"

Melanie's grandmother answered, "I'm doing good, Melanie. Is it time for me to come on out there?"

Melanie answered, "Yes, it is, Grandma. When can you be here?"

Her grandmother stated, "I'll be there this weekend."

Melanie asked, "Okay. You do want Jonathan to come for you, right? I'll have him come for you. Just let me know what time your bus will arrive, and he will be there."

Grandma replied, "Okay, baby. I surely would like him to come for us."

They conversed for a while and released their lines. Melanie went to Jonathan to inform him Mawmaw was coming so that he would prepare himself to pick her up from the bus station.

The weekend arrived. Melanie was grateful her grandmother was delivering on her promise. She couldn't wait to see her Mawmaw. Her bus was coming in at 3:45 p.m. Jonathan made the trip to pick them up from the bus station. He was there early. He recognized the familiar small-framed and aged lady and the boys who accompanied her. Jonathan approached her and gave her a big hello and hug. He took Mawmaw's bag and walked her and the boys to the car. The ride back home wasn't far at all. Jonathan thanked Grandma for coming to help him. He had been doing everything for Melanie since she found out she was pregnant. Jonathan was mentally and physically exhausted.

But he always put himself in Melanie's shoes. No matter what negative thought surfaced, he would expeditiously revamp his thinking. He constantly told himself he planted his seed in her. He was the reason why she was suffering. He meant what he told her. They were both in this condition, and he was sharing the pregnancy with her.

They pulled into the apartments. Grandma looked at the beautiful landscape, the beautiful trees, nicely trimmed hedges, and fresh cut grass. She loved smelling fresh cut grass, especially in the country where she lived. Melanie was standing at the door, waiting for her arrival. When the door opened, Melanie was there to greet her with a hug.

Melanie shouted, "Grandma! Oh, I have missed you so much. How are you doing?" Melanie hugged and kissed her grandmother.

Grandma answered, "Melanie, I'm doing well. I see you are ready to pop any day now. Are you ready?"

Melanie replied, "Yes, Grandma, I am ready to have this baby. I hope you won't mind sleeping with me. I made sure Jonathan washed the sheets on the bed."

Grandma stated, "I don't mind, sweetie. I would love to bunk with you."

Melanie asked, "Grandma, are you tired from the trip? You want to lay down for a while?"

Grandma replied, "No, baby. I am fine. I just need to sit down for a while."

Once she rested a little, she started getting up to clean the house. She couldn't sit still. It was hard for her to not clean constantly. She wanted to make sure the apartment was degermed and smelled clean and fresh every day. Sometimes Jonathan would tell her to just sit down. He would do the cleaning. She wasn't paying Jonathan any attention. She did the cleaning anyway.

Complicated Delivery

The big day had arrived. Dr. Gharma called Melanie and gave her the specifics one week prior. She explained to Melanie her colleague would be delivering the baby because she had an out-of-town family emergency. Dr. Gharma explained they would be inserting a pill inside Melanie to help open her cervix. Inducing labor was worse than natural labor. They couldn't wait any longer for the baby to arrive on his own. She was already two weeks overdue.

They arrived at the hospital. Staff led them to the labor and delivery ward. Jonathan's mother met them there and walked in with them. She met Melanie's grandma. Hellos and hugs were exchanged.

Jonathan asked Melanie, "Baby, are you okay? You ready to do this?"

Melanie replied, "Yes, I am. I have been ready." Melanie, the night before, enjoyed a big meal. She was cognizant the staff would not provide her anything to eat or drink. She could only have ice chips. Food and drink would cause her to vomit. After she dressed in her gown, she laid in her bed and only disrupted her relaxation to use the bathroom.

The nurse came in with the pill to insert behind Melanie's cervix. This would break her water, and the labor pains would soon start. It took about four hours after the insertion for Melanie's water to break. When she felt her water bag had broken, she alerted the nurse. It was time for them to start checking Melanie's cervix to see how far her cervix dilated. They came in every hour or so and checked. The labor pains surfaced and were hurting Melanie. She would grab on to the bedrail each time she felt a contraction. They lasted for about twenty seconds or so. Melanie was in labor for about twelve hours that day. This was the worse feeling. Melanie had heard other mothers talk about labor horror, and others had it easy with no labor pains at all. Melanie thought since she was already feeling excruciating pain from the pregnancy, the delivery would have mercy on her and spare her the contractions. This was not the case. She still felt the labor pains.

Melanie endured all the pain she could. She couldn't take it anymore and asked for an epidural. The staff brought in the epidural with a trained professional to insert. "Mrs. Taylor, I need you to remain still while I insert this in your back. One wrong move and it could paralyze you."

Melanie replied, "Okay. I will."

Staff instructed Melanie to sit up on the side of the bed and slightly bend over to expose her spine. They inserted the epidural

LOSING HER CROWN

with no problems. Melanie didn't flinch. It started to immediately take effect on Melanie. There was no more pain. The last cervix check gave them all they needed for Melanie to start pushing. Jonathan's mother remained in the room to see her grandchild come into the world. Once it was time for Melanie to start pushing, her grandmother excused herself out the room. She didn't have the stomach to witness this event.

Melanie asked, "Grandma, where are you going? You don't want to stay?"

Grandma replied, "No. I'll be in the waiting room."

It was time for Melanie to push. The nurse stated, "Mrs. Taylor, when I tell you to push, you push. If I tell you to stop, I want you to stop no matter the pressure you are feeling. Melanie followed the nurse's instructions. There was a problem. The baby's heart rate was dropping. The cord was wrapped around his neck. They were paging the substitute doctor. He couldn't be located. The nurse and Jonathan practically delivered the baby. Jonathan held one leg, and the nurse had the other, pulling each one back toward Melanie to help her push the baby out of her.

Finally, the doctor showed up when the baby was crowning. He required the assistance of special scissors and cut Melanie to get the baby out of her. The baby finally arrived. They immediately took the baby and placed him in a small bed-like device that had blankets covering the bottom. They placed a tube down his throat, trying to revive him.

Melanie could hear the nurse saying over and over, "Come on, baby, breathe for me. Breathe for me." Baby JJ, was forgetting how to breathe on his own. They had to keep him on the breathing machine until he could learn to breathe on his own.

Jonathan's mother was crying. Jonathan looked at his mother and looked at the doctor. He walked toward the doctor and stood over him with clenched fists, stating, "He better be all right!"

The doctor was putting Melanie back together from cutting her. He ordered the nurse, "Give him an update." The baby began breathing as the doctor requested for the update.

Melanie couldn't hold her baby. After reviving him, staff immediately delivered him to intensive neonatal care. For the first two weeks of his life, Baby JJ was in neonatal care. Melanie was exhausted and had to rest. The following day, she was finally able to hold her child. It broke Melanie's heart to see her baby lying there with these stickers attached to his head. They shaved his hair in the front to help keep stickers attached for conducting tests when needed. Nothing she could do to make this better for him. He received so much love from the staff there. They couldn't keep their hands and eyes off Baby Taylor. He was a beautiful baby.

Each passing day, the doctors were presenting to mother and father discouraging news. Baby Jonathan was experiencing back-to-back seizures requiring phenobarbital to control them. Brain damage developed during his delivery. His frontals had been damaged. The doctor explained to the parents he wouldn't process information as normal people would. He would suffer from developmental delays, but they couldn't ascertain how far behind Baby JJ would be from normal babies his age. He would have a learning disability and emotional behavior issues. Melanie cried even more. This was too much for a new mother to ingest. Jonathan saw the hurt but didn't understand how Melanie felt.

He told Melanie, "Melanie, stop crying so much. Everything will be okay. He's going to be fine."

Melanie screamed, "I know he will be Jonathan! But I am his mother! How dare you tell me not to cry for my baby! I carried him these ten lunar months! Not you! I felt his kicks! Not you! He felt my feelings! Not yours! I felt him growing inside me! Not you! Jonathan, I have a bond with him that you will never understand. Don't you ever tell me not to cry for my child!"

Jonathan realized his statement was unnecessary and revealed to Melanie he was inconsiderate to the hurt stabbing through her heart. This pain was worse than the pain of carrying him.

Melanie didn't want to leave the hospital without her baby after she was discharged. The hospital was able to rent a room to the couple for about $30 per night. That way, they wouldn't have to travel from home back to the hospital should something happen to their baby.

They lived in that room four days straight. Jonathan grew tiresome of the hospital scene. He wanted to get Melanie and himself away from it all. He knew this would be good for Melanie. He had been sleeping on a reclining sofa in the hospital room that was uncomfortable for him. They rented a room for one night at a motel close to the hospital. Melanie felt relaxed and was able to sleep a full night for the first time. She felt refreshed the next day, and so did Jonathan. They returned to the hospital the next day after check-out time.

Jonathan's coworkers were coming to see Baby Taylor. One of his coworkers visiting noticed when Jonathan talked, Baby Jonathan would follow Jonathan's voice and look for him. She stated, "Jonathan, he's following your voice. He's looking for you."

Melanie would get the hardest kicks from Baby JJ when he heard Jonathan's voice. Jonathan had talked and sang to Baby Jonathan while he was in Melanie's womb. Jonathan had established a rapport with his son before he entered this world. He wanted little Jonathan to know his daddy was here for him. Jonathan finally brought grandma to see little JJ. Grandma adored Baby JJ when she finally saw him. Everyone who visited the baby greatly adored him. He was just that adorable.

Melanie prayed to God regularly while Baby Jonathan was residing in neonatal care. She had never attacked heaven with such intense exertion. Even when her mother was dying, her prayers for her were not as intense as they were for little Jonathan. Melanie attacked God to heal her baby. "God, please, whatever was taken from him during birth, restore it back to him."

It was time for Baby Taylor to go home. Melanie and Jonathan were happy to bring him home. When they were getting the baby ready for home, all the nurses came to say goodbye to him. They loved him so much and hated to see him leave. Grandma and Justin both were waiting for him to come home. Justin was only fourteen when Melanie had his nephew. The hospital wouldn't allow Justin to see him because he had to be at least sixteen years of age to enter neonatal care.

Grandma had sanitized the entire apartment since her stay with Melanie and Jonathan. She had visited Baby Jonathan once while he was in the hospital and thought he was the most beautiful little baby she had ever seen. She had been praying for him the entire time he was at the hospital. She just finished cleaning when they walked through the door. She stated, "Lord, have mercy. Look who is finally here. Give him to me, Melanie. Y'all get yourselves changed out of those clothes. That hospital full of cherms up there."

Melanie chuckled inside, thinking, *Mawmaw still using that word instead of germs.*

Justin looked at little Jonathan, stating, "Melanie, he looks like a White baby. He's going to have them girls after him."

Melanie replied, "Yeah, he already has stolen my heart."

Melanie averted her attention to her grandmother ordering them to change from being at the hospital. She chuckled inwardly again. It had been a while since she heard her grandmother say that word and others. She missed hearing her grandmother use words like *cherms*, *qiver*, and *rench*. *Germs*, *cover*, and *rinse* were the words she was saying.

Melanie reminisced about her summers with her grandmother. She used to have her and Rita in the backyard with this huge pale for them to help her shell peas, shuck the corn, snap peas, you name it. Melanie never thought she would miss those times until there was no more childhood. She was happy her grandmother was visiting. She remembered how she used to spoil her and Rita. Looking at her grandmother reminded Melanie how happy and carefree she felt at that age. Except for the times Melanie felt their aunt and uncle were mean to them and that incident after Grandma had them all sleeping in the same bed. Melanie would never be able to fathom why her grandmother would allow a grown ass man to share a bed with little girls. Grown men shouldn't be sleeping in the bed with little girls. She didn't hate her grandmother. She was just hurt that it happened. Melanie had been through so much hurt by the men in her life who were supposed to love her unconditionally. She was a forgiving soul. Too forgiving, if you ask me.

Melanie was going outside before she was ready. She had become imprisoned in the house for so long, she couldn't wait to enjoy the outside and its fresh air. Grandma didn't like this at all. Whenever

Melanie would come in from being outside, Grandma expressed her thoughts. She stated, "Melanie, you shouldn't be outside. Your body is still open to infections."

Melanie didn't care. It went in one ear and straight out the other. Melanie didn't like anyone having authority over her. She ignored her grandmother. The whole time Grandma was there, she had to keep the boys inside the apartment. They couldn't go outside and be kids. Melanie was receiving section 8 and was trying to keep them undetected from office staff. She didn't know her lease would allow visitors to stay up to two weeks if she informed the office. Since their time outside was very limited, Grandma decided it was time for her to leave. She felt that Melanie didn't need her because she rejected receiving her advice, and the grandboys were working Grandma's nerves. Melanie understood her reason for leaving. She hated to see her go but understood. Grandma packed their things. She gave Melanie a hug and kiss. Jonathan drove them to the bus station for their trip back home.

CHAPTER 11

Woes of Developmental Issues

Melanie and Jonathan had to start making appointments for Baby Jonathan's evaluation by developmental providers. They would need to conduct tests on little Jonathan to discern his mental capacity. They received a referral to the Child Study Center. They had excellent providers there. They worked with children with delayed developmental skills and behavior/emotional issues.

All appointments attended resulted the same—a five-year developmental delay. There would always be emotional/behavior issues. He would have to be on medication for the rest of his life. Melanie and Jonathan were against him taking any prescribed medications because they caused cancer. They swore together that this wouldn't be an option for their son. They researched online for natural remedies. Cancer had already claimed the life of her mother and Jonathan's grandfather. She swore this monster wouldn't clench its grips into their baby, claiming his life. Jonathan's mother was doing her own research to find natural remedies as well.

Jonathan was torn. This was his son, and he wondered if his delay would impose on activities he wanted to engage with his son. Jonathan prayed to God, "My boy. This is my only son, God. I need to teach and show him things in life. Things I didn't get a chance to do with my own father. I want to teach him things my grandfathers taught me. I don't want him to be a target to others. These children will make fun of, use, and abuse my son."

Succumbing to Prescribed Medications

Baby Jonathan had reached nine months when he was taken to the center. Their prognosis was the same as the doctors from the neonatal unit. He was scooting, crawling, walking, and grasping objects at the normal rate. Their concern was him talking at the appropriate age. He wasn't talking like the other children his age. He had limited vocabulary. He could say *daddy, momma, yes* and *no* but all other words were a challenge. The denied oxygen to his brain deprived him of a normal vocabulary required at his age. He endeavored to get his words out, but it was difficult for him to do so. Not understanding him would cause him to experience frustration, which led to angry episodes. This wasn't easy for Melanie and Jonathan. They could see the frustration on his face as he endeavored to talk.

His diagnoses intensified as he progressed with age. He was showing signs of aggression, nonchalant attitude, and no respect for authority outside the home. They had tried everything. Spanking and yelling at him were not the answers. They tried online natural medications, but nothing succored.

At the age of three, they enrolled him into a school specifically for children with attention deficit disorders and emotional, and aggressive behavior. His teacher had been observing him in class and taking record of everything he was doing. The school scheduled a meeting, requesting the attendance of the parents. There was so much li'l JJ had done. He committed offenses the school hadn't disclosed to Jonathan and Melanie.

On the day of the meeting, little JJ's teacher told them he slapped her in the face one day and how he abused another student who was handicap and blind. Little Jonathan assaulted the child and took a toy from him.

Melanie, shocked, asked the teacher, "Why did you not tell us about this? We could have corrected this. You all gathered all this evidence against him and never informed us of the aggressive behavior. This behavior takes precedence over the insignificant things you were calling us to discuss. I feel as if we are on trial for our son's life."

The teacher had no answer for Melanie. It was true. They had to make their case against him to show them how desperately he needed to be on prescribed medication.

The reports of assaults toward teachers and students resulted in visits to the school for Melanie and Jonathan. They could no longer fight this. It was time for Melanie and Jonathan to accept the fact that he would have to start his journey with prescribed medication. When they visited with the prescribing doctor, they expressed their concerns against those cancer-causing treatment drugs. They were relieved to hear that those medications no longer contained the ingredients causing cancer. This was huge news for concerned parents. Little Jonathan started his path with prescribed medications. Melanie and Jonathan were cognizant that if they didn't take action to suppress the behavior, once he was older, the law would be more than happy to either take him off their hands and institutionalize him, or worse, kill him because to them, he would be a threat. Officers had no training to deal with a suspect with mental challenges. They wouldn't even know how to look for the signs of a mentally disturbed suspect, especially a Black one. They witnessed it too many times, seeing the media exposing officers abusing their authority against the Black men in the communities, whether if mentally challenged or not. They always kept Jonathan Jr. at home so he wouldn't succumb to their abusive behavior.

Jonathan Jr. had been placed in remedial classes to be around students who were his equal. His teachers had no problems with him since he was taking his prescribed medication. As Jonathan grew older, students outside his classroom would tease him at school. They knew he didn't comprehend class work on their level, so he became a target. They weren't cognizant that Jonathan Jr. was a smart soul; he just learned at a slower pace. Also, his light complexion made it worse. To the bullies, he was a dumb light-skinned pretty boy, and they practiced ridiculing him. They always provoked him. But because of the aggression suppressed inside him, no matter how big or small his opponents were, he always came out on top as far as whipping their asses. Li'l Jonathan had brute strength, so one of his punches, if thrown hard enough, could knock someone out cold.

When the kids saw this for the first time, they would cheer him on, and he gained their respect. But there were those who still wanted to test him, thinking he wouldn't be able to dominate them in a fight.

By the time li'l Jonathan reached high school, the school district eliminated remedial classes forcing, Jonathan Jr. to integrate with the students who were either smarter or those who knew how the world operated around them. Jonathan Jr. felt out of place being around the "smart" kids in class. Jonathan and Melanie sheltered him all his life. He never played nor mingled with the neighborhood kids. Jonathan witnessed some kids making fun of him and knew the bullying would increase once his son started high school. Jonathan sat him down and had a talk with him.

Jonathan stated, "Son, don't let anyone pick on you at school. They can say and talk all they want, but don't let them touch you, son. You are an easy target to them. You're a little slower than they are, and you are a light complexion. You have two strikes against you, and people will provoke you. When they touch you, make an example out of their asses. Let it be known you are a force to be reckoned with. Okay, son?"

Jonathan Jr. replied with a big smile, "Okay, Dad. Don't let anyone bully me. Gotcha, Dad."

Not long after talking to JJ, Jonathan received a call from the principal, informing him that Jonathan Jr. had been in a fight with another student. The way he fought this student raised brows at the school. Jonathan Jr. had no mercy for this student. He kept hitting him as if he were losing control. A teacher was able to pull Jonathan off the student and calm him. The teacher could see the enraged look and his bucked eyes. The teacher asked, "Jonathan, are you okay? You good?"

JJ had no problems with the teachers and adult authority. It was the older kids at school that caused problems. Jonathan replied, "He walked up to me and said, 'What's up, dumb yellow boy?' I ignored him, but he pushed me into the wall, yelling, 'You're ignoring me, yellow boy?' That's how it started."

Mr. Snow replied, "Okay, let's take a walk to the principal's office. This incident needs his attention."

Mr. Snow escorted Jonathan Jr. and the other student to the principal's office. Jonathan explained what occurred to the principal. There was no questioning why he reacted this way. The principal understood Jonathan was defending himself, but school policy stated both the offender and the defender must face suspension for the remainder of the week. After contacting Jonathan and explaining to him what transpired, he called Melanie to inform her.

"Melanie, Jonathan has been in a fight, and they are asking that we attend a meeting."

Melanie asked, "What happened, Jonathan? I know he wasn't the aggressor. They need to leave my baby alone. He bothers no one. They are always picking on him." Jonathan filled Melanie in on the details.

Jonathan informed his mother of the incident and the scheduled meeting. She wanted to be a part of the meeting as well. When he told Melanie she wanted to participate, Melanie was not happy at all. She despised Jonathan for involving her in their own family matters.

Melanie asked, "Was that necessary? She doesn't have to be involved in everything going on in this family. This is our family, not hers. She always wants to put her two cents in on everything. In the beginning, I remained silent. When will she learn to let go and let us? You are a grown ass man with a wife and child. She is overstepping her boundaries, Jonathan."

Jonathan did this often. He called his mother, telling her everything going on with their son. Jonathan replied, "This is his grandmother, Melanie. There's no harm."

Melanie stated, "Bullshit! Stop telling her everything that goes on with him! We can handle this on our own!" Melanie was extremely stubborn. She feared feeding too much information would cause his mother to start telling her what she needed to do with her own son. Melanie despised any advice given to her about her son.

On the day of the meeting, when the trio arrived, staff displayed amazement that they all participated. And they voiced what they were discerning before them. You see, when it came to Black American kids, it was easy for them to assume that there was only one parent in the home. Especially if only one parent attended these meetings. Their presence eliminated thoughts of stereotypes. A two-parent home for Black American kids compared to all other races was not normal in the hood. A single Black mother raising kids alone was the norm. And the fact that Melanie and Jonathan were married was a plus.

The principal stated, "Wow, guys. We have never had a conference with both parents and grandmother attending. We appreciate you all for coming and are surprised to see all of you here supporting him."

When Melanie heard this from the faculty, she understood the importance of having a support system for JJ. She thought, *Okay, maybe it wasn't a bad idea having her attend. Maybe I should let my guard down just a little.* Melanie was fooling herself. There was no way she would be letting her guard down. She was too bull headed.

The principal continued, "We know that this isn't Jonathan's fault, but we still have to suspend him for the remainder of the week."

Jonathan asked, "So even though it's not his fault, he still has to be suspended? He's supposed to just allow people to touch him?"

The school administrator replied, "Yes, sir. We understand the concern, but he still fought, and it is school policy to suspend both parties in the matter. But we can tell you this. He made the other student bleed. We strongly believe Jonathan will not have any more problems from this student. He really did a number on this kid."

Hearing this didn't make the situation better. Melanie and Jonathan were against him fighting and certainly didn't want him hurting others. But they did support him defending himself.

Melanie thought, *Great. He will be behind in schoolwork. No school equals no explanation of his work.* But the teachers knew about his condition and didn't expect Jonathan to have the same responses as his fellow students. They didn't require lengthy paragraphs for his answers. One to two non-lengthy sentences for his answers proved satisfactory with teachers. The school and teachers endeavored to assist him by offering their tutoring services to JJ. They all loved Jonathan Jr.'s mannerisms. His parents baptized him in politeness. He always used yes; no, sir; yes/no, ma'am; and opened doors for the ladies. He would say to them, "Ladies first." No matter the ladies' age, his father made sure JJ was a gentleman.

Suffering Another Miscarriage

Melanie was feeling sad. She was looking at a show about women surviving miscarriages. Melanie had suffered another heartbreak. When little Jonathan was three, they tried to have another baby. They wanted their children to be close in age and grow up together. Once she found out she was pregnant, she experienced the same symptoms with Jonathan Jr. and her previous pregnancy. She always wanted a girl for herself. Jonathan was content because he had his son and two daughters. But Melanie wasn't content. She wanted her pair, a boy and girl. Melanie dreamed of having a host of grandchildren from their children. No one understood why she would want to continue putting her body through the torment of her carrying a baby. Jonathan was against her being in this condition. But he promised that whatever Melanie wanted, Melanie would get. No matter the issue with her pregnancy, he would be there for her. Before entering two months, she miscarried the baby. This was her third miscarriage, and she wondered if she was only meant to have one baby.

Such a Selfish Person

Following her miscarriage, she returned to work. Melanie received a call from Jonathan. He stated, "Melanie, something isn't right. I am experiencing pain and swelling in certain areas of my body."

Melanie stated, "I've always told you to get yourself examined. I have the insurance. Use it. Stop telling me if I have a clean bill of health, it means you have one too. There could be some things going on with you internally that won't surface until it is too late."

Jonathan stated, "Yeah, baby, I know. It is time for me to start seeing someone before my condition fails to improve or worsens. My balance has been off too, baby."

Melanie said, "Okay, call your doctor and make an appointment to be seen. Let me know what date it's scheduled, and I'll record it in my calendar."

Jonathan asked, "Can you call for me, baby?"

Melanie replied sarcastically, "Jonathan, I'm at work. But yes, I'll find time to call for you."

Jonathan replied, "Okay, thank you, baby." Jonathan did not recognize the sarcasm in her voice. Melanie had assumed the role of being the breadwinner and secretary in the home while Jonathan stayed home with JJ as a toddler up to his teenage years. He worked here and there, but not enough to claim his crown as the king of the castle. Melanie was wearing that title and was queen of the castle. She thought, *Why in the hell couldn't he schedule the appointment? Very inconsiderate of him asking me to call while I am at work. He could call himself and get the appointment quicker. I would need to find time to do so. What sense does that make? I should have told him to schedule the appointment himself.*

Melanie was upset and irritated with Jonathan. But she remembered how he catered to her during pregnancy. So she quickly dismissed the thoughts of being upset with him.

Intimacy Leading to Pregnancy

"Ouch!" screamed Jonathan. Jonathan was making dinner for Melanie before she arrived home from work. He wanted to surprise her with her favorite dish. Fried chicken, hot water corn bread, cabbage, mashed potatoes, and corn on the cob were being prepared while she was on her way home. Jonathan had cut himself while slicing the cabbage. It was a nice size cut. He stopped cutting the cabbage and went into the bathroom to rinse his finger. He applied alcohol, holding his finger tightly. Alcohol and an open wound just did not mix. It burned. He applied pressure to his finger to allow the excess blood flow through before applying an antibiotic cream and Band-Aid. Jonathan went back to the kitchen to finish preparing the meal. He examined the cabbage. There was no blood on it. He continued slicing the cabbage. He was grateful to Melanie for allowing him to be at home with Jonathan Jr. while she worked.

It was only the three of them, so there was no need for a big dining room table. Jonathan had removed the two leaves in the middle of the table and stored them in the built-in compartment. The apartment they were living in had a dining room big enough for the table Melanie purchased. When they had extra mouths for dinner, Jonathan would add one or both leaves with extra chairs to accommodate their guests. So the small table with four chairs sufficed for them. Jonathan Jr. sometimes ate in his room. Tonight, he ate before his parents because Melanie was arriving home late. He wanted to get everything such as homework, showering, and eating out the way before it was bedtime for him. His medicine had him out by 9:00 p.m.

Jonathan finished preparing their plates just as Melanie was coming through the door. Melanie walked in, and Jonathan was standing there in front of her, leaning in for a kiss. He gestured for her to hand over the things in her hands and on her shoulder so that he could put them away for her. He led her to the table and pulled the seat out for her. She asked, smirking, "What's all this for, Jonathan?"

Jonathan replied, "Oh, I'm just trying to show my diligent and hardworking hot wife how appreciative and grateful I am to have her in my life."

Melanie asked, "I smell food. Did you cook?"

Jonathan replied, "Yes, I did. I made your favorite fried chicken, mashed potatoes, corn on the cob, cabbage, and hot water corn bread."

She stated, "No way. You did not cook all that. It smells good, and it's making me hungry."

Jonathan stated, "Hold your horses. Let me finish here and we can sit down and eat. Jonathan Jr. has already eaten. He has completed all his homework, and he is in the shower now. I didn't want him to wait for us to eat because you were coming home late tonight. He says waiting that long makes him overeat."

Melanie stated, "Okay, I'll see him after he gets out the shower. I know he'll want to watch a little television before turning in tonight."

Jonathan went into the kitchen and returned with their plates. Melanie, amazed, stated, "Oh, wow, Jonathan. Everything looks scrumptious." Melanie took a bite of everything and was savoring every bite taken.

Jonathan asked, "You approve, baby? Is it good?"

Melanie replied, "Yes, it is, Jonathan. It's good and tasty."

Jonathan followed up with a glass of wine for her to enjoy. He picked out her favorite, Moscato. Jonathan knew a little wine in Melanie made her a tiger with him in bed. This was all an earnest effort for what he was expecting back in return. Not so much as expecting it but just wanted to feel acknowledged and appreciated for his work at home.

Melanie asked, "My favorite wine, Jonathan? What are you trying to tell me?" Melanie put her glass down and asked, "Okay, what's going on? Why all this?"

Jonathan replied, "I just wanted you to come home and relax. Now if you want to reward me later tonight, I am open to it. I miss my wife. You have been working so hard and taking care of us financially. I just wanted to show some appreciation."

Melanie stated, "Aw, Jonathan. That is so sweet of you. I miss you too, baby. I know I have neglected you. I am sorry. Will you forgive me?"

Jonathan answered, "Yes, I do, baby."

Melanie was looking for him to answer her with a different response. She thought, *This selfish ass man. He could have told me no need to apologize. Acknowledge I do everything and more. He should be apologizing to me for him not working, halfway cleaning, and rarely having dinner ready for me when I come home. Maybe if I didn't have to come home from a full-time job just to cook and clean, I wouldn't be so tired and would want to have relations with him!* Melanie started feeling unappreciated.

Once Melanie ate her fill, she went into Jonathan Jr.'s room to say hello to her son. She tapped and entered. "Well, hello, son. How are you doing this evening?"

Jonathan Jr. replied, "I'm doing well, Mom. How are you, and how was your day at work? Did you have fun?"

Melanie laughed and replied, "I had a wonderful day, son. I didn't have fun, but I did manage to put smiles on people's faces today." Melanie always received compliments from patients about her beautiful smile while greeting them.

JJ stated, "So you spread your smiles to others and received compliments? Sounds like a fun day to me."

Melanie never thought about it that way. She had worked that same job for years, and it became repetitious for her to smile, so after a while, she didn't notice nor pay any mind how her smiles impacted others. Melanie replied, "You are right. I did unknowingly have fun today. I love you so much. Thank you, son."

Jonathan Jr. stated, "You're welcome, Mom."

Melanie gave him a big hug and kiss before exiting his room.

Melanie thought, *I better have my shower and get all cleaned up so I can give this man some tonight.* She alerted Jonathan, stating, "Jonathan, I am going to take my shower. I'll see you in about thirty minutes."

Jonathan rebutted, "Okay, baby. I have a movie for us to watch. I picked out one of your favorite movies."

Melanie replied, "Okay, cool." Melanie got in the shower and wondered which of her movies he picked out for her. It didn't matter to her which one he picked. She loved them all. It had been a while since they had a movie night ending with passion in the bedroom. She made sure to tidy up and trim the area Jonathan loved tasting. She was getting excited just thinking about it and thought about skipping the movie to make up for lost time.

After showering and shaving, Melanie put her clothes on and went into the living area to join Jonathan. She inquired, "Okay, baby, what have you got for us to watch? I am ready to watch and play."

Jonathan replied, "I picked out *Cain and Oh Dog.*"

Melanie agreed, "Yeah, okay. It's not too long and will be over before ten." Melanie, no matter how often she watched this movie, would always fall asleep on it. She would awaken after hearing the very first song play ending the movie. The lyrics "Wake your punk ass up" would play, and she would wake up, stating, "Aw, man, I missed it again!"

Jonathan would burst out laughing. He secretly didn't like the movie as much as she did. Whenever she fell asleep, he would fast-forward to the end of the movie, making her believe she missed it. Sometimes Melanie couldn't get past the first twenty minutes of the movie before she fell asleep. This time, she stayed up to watch it.

After the movie was over, she gave Jonathan that look, and he knew what was next. They both led each other to the bedroom, hand in hand. Melanie closed the door behind them and locked it. She didn't want Jonathan Jr. accidentally walking in on them. She removed her pajamas, and underneath, she had on a sexy red teddy for Jonathan. She had a pair of red slip-on high heels with red fur on the top that she slipped into to spice up things. Jonathan eyes bucked, and he ogled his wife's shape. She asked him to sit on the bed. He was starting to grow in his shorts. Melanie did a little striptease for him. She was shaking her tail, bending over, dropping it like it was hot, and much more. Jonathan sat there watching her for three minutes. He couldn't take anymore. He stood, pulling Melanie toward him. He grabbed and rubbed her, starting with her breasts. He worked his way down to her butt. He grabbed her butt with both hands, squeezing it. He whispered in her ear, sending sweet sensations throughout her body. She placed her arms around his neck, pulling him toward her neck for him to gently kiss and caress her with his tongue. Melanie released him and began massaging his shaft that was standing so beautifully erect.

He moaned, "Oh, Melanie."

Melanie instructed Jonathan, "You just lay back and enjoy this." Jonathan lay back with the biggest smile on his face.

He shortly stopped Melanie. He stated, "Come here. You ready for me?"

Melanie answered, "Yes."

Jonathan stated, "Lay down and open them legs."

Melanie followed Jonathan's orders. First, he rubbed his shaft on her clitoris and went inside her to get her all wet. He retracted and started pleasuring her. His tongue was going back and forth like a windshield wiper, only faster.

Melanie started to moan, stating, "Oh my god, Jonathan, your tongue feels good."

Jonathan placed his fingers inside her. He had mastered making her squirt too. Melanie was about to climax. Melanie whispered, "Goodness, Jonathan." Melanie squealed as she climaxed. Jonathan made her have multiple orgasms. She was losing control. She started beating on the bed, and her head was moving from side to side. Jonathan wouldn't stop. He kept going until she squirted. He loved making her squirt.

Once he satisfied Melanie, Jonathan asked, "You ready for me now?"

Melanie replied, "Yes, I am."

Jonathan stated, "Hold them legs up for me, and don't let go of them."

Melanie held up her legs, and he thrust himself into Melanie. Melanie expeditiously released her legs, letting out a scream. Jonathan covered her mouth, saying, "Melanie, be quiet, baby."

Melanie rebutted, "Jonathan, that hurt. You can't do me like that."

Jonathan stated, "I'm sorry, baby, but you should be used to this by now." Jonathan didn't let up at all. He continued thrusting in her. He placed Melanie's legs on his shoulders, digging deeper into her.

She asked, "You trying to tear another hole in me or something? You're hurting me!"

Jonathan stated, "I know, baby, but don't it hurt so good?"

Melanie replied, "Yes, but it still hurts."

As usual, Jonathan started sucking and kissing her neck, averting her attention from the pain. This was another tactic of his that drove Melanie crazy. Melanie would endeavor to stop him, but he would just grab her by her hands and imprison them. He loved being inside Melanie. Once she was able to endure his thrusting, she would squeeze her vaginal muscles. She repeated this, and it drove Jonathan crazy. She started moving her ass back and forth, getting into a rhythm with Jonathan. He could no longer contain himself and released inside Melanie. He had to lay there for a minute before exiting Melanie. He stated, "Melanie, be still. Don't move. Let me just lay in you."

Melanie thought, *You getcho ass off me!*

Jonathan remained inside Melanie for a moment and slowly retracted. He kissed Melanie and lay on his back. Melanie went back into the bathroom to jump in the shower. Before doing so, she knew to supply Jonathan a towel with soap and water so that he could wipe himself. She thought, *That was well worth the wait. I'm so exhausted and ready to go to bed.*

Once Melanie finished showering, she reached for her towel to pat herself dry, retaining her skin's natural moisture. She stepped out of the bathroom into the bedroom. She asked, "Jonathan, how are you feeling, baby?" Melanie looked at Jonathan and noticed he was fast asleep with the towel still in his hand. She murmured to herself, "Yeah, I put your ass to sleep." Melanie reached for the towel, rinsed it, and placed it on the towel rack to dry. From there, it would be placed in the dirty clothes basket. She returned to bed, laid her head on her pillow, and fell asleep from exhaustion.

Melanie was at work and started feeling nauseated. She had been so busy with daily wonts that she hadn't noticed she missed her period. She looked at her calendar. "Oh, shoot. I am two weeks late. Last time we had sex was two weeks before JJ's sixteenth birthday."

Melanie and Jonathan's sex life suffered for weeks due to Jonathan's symptoms worsening. Jonathan resisted telling Melanie that his symptoms progressed. He was happy she didn't pursue sex with him. And if it was the wrong night for her to do so, he would tell her the extremely painful headaches were present, or he would tell her he would like to hold his wife in bed for intimacy. Melanie didn't mind at all since she was always tired.

Melanie, a month ago, made Jonathan's appointment with his doctor. He couldn't get in sooner because the schedule was full. She had taken time off work to accompany him to the appointment. They were sitting in the exam room. Jonathan felt a tad nervous, but Melanie being there with him eased his nerves. They talked about his condition and tried to come up with reasons why it was happening.

The doctor came in and greeted them with a smile and hello. "Good morning, guys. Mr. Taylor, what brings you in today?"

Jonathan replied, "I have experienced joint pain and swelling all over my body, along with losing my balance."

Dr. Henry asked, "When did these symptoms begin?"

Jonathan replied, "It started when I was walking up the stairs about six months ago. Each step taken, I could feel pain. I tried pulling myself upward, and there was pain present in my fingers. Later that day, I noticed swelling in my fingers. The pain progressed to my back and legs."

Dr. Henry asked, "Do you have a family history of arthritis?"

Jonathan replied, "Yes, my mother and my father's mother both suffered from rheumatoid arthritis."

Dr. Henry stated, "Okay, I will run some labs on you to see how your levels are, if that's okay?"

Jonathan stated, "Yes. Whatever needs to be done to pinpoint the culprit."

Dr. Henry placed a sheet of paper on his clipboard, circling blood panels needed. He asked Jonathan, "Did your mother or grandmother become crippled?"

Jonathan answered, "No, my mother isn't crippled at all, and my grandmother is deceased, so I'm not certain how it affected her."

Dr. Henry asked, "Okay. Would you be open to physical therapy?"

Jonathan replied, "Sure, if you think it will help."

Dr. Henry stated, "In the meantime, I will prescribe ibuprofen with a sleep aid for the pain until we know what it is we are dealing. You may want to take it easy and avoid using stairs and any activity that worsens your pain. Nothing strenuous. I want to see you back in one month. My phlebotomist will be in to extract your blood, and I will refer you to physical therapy. I will send this medication to your pharmacy and call you with the results to discuss with you. Does that sound like a plan?"

Jonathan answered, "Yes, Doctor."

Dr. Henry asked, "Would you have any questions for me?"

Jonathan replied, "No, I don't, Doctor."

Melanie interjected, "I have a question, Doctor. Will you be checking for other ailments just in case it's not arthritis but something else?"

Dr. Henry smiled at Melanie, replying, "Yes. I am ordering extensive blood work to rule out other ailments."

Melanie placed her hand over her heart with the expression of relief, stating, "Okay, good to hear."

Dr. Henry asked, "Okay, any other questions?"

Melanie and Jonathan both replied, "No, thank you."

Dr. Henry added, "Remain here, Mr. Taylor, to have those labs drawn. Take care." The doctor exited the room.

Jonathan grabbed Melanie by the hand. Melanie felt that there was something wrong. She asked, "Are you okay, Jonathan?"

Jonathan replied, "Melanie, I'm scared. This isn't something that I want to hear at my age. I need to be ailment-free. Physical limitations can't exist for the things I have in mind for you and Jonathan Jr. No one in my family has experienced the symptoms I'm having."

Melanie replied, "That's why we are here. We are addressing the culprit early before it progresses. You should have a complete exam and get your rectum checked and all."

Jonathan looked at Melanie with a bizarre look, replying, "You may as well forget about that. Nobody will be sticking their finger up my ass. I don't care who it is. Couldn't they just take a sample of waste material?"

Melanie replied, "Jonathan, they administer that exam to make sure you are free from enlarged prostate, nodules, and tumors. It is important that you have it done. Labs won't tell them anything."

Jonathan replied, "Like I said, my ass will not be getting violated by no one. I mean that, Melanie. So end of discussion."

Melanie replied, "Okay, Jonathan, have it your way. I won't bring it up again."

As they sat waiting, there was a light tap. A small framed lady walked in, stating, "Hi, guys. Mr. Taylor, I am here to draw your blood. Can you give me your full name and date of birth?" Jonathan gave her the information. She drew his blood and told them they were free to go. Jonathan made his follow-up, and they were out the door.

Melanie's symptoms of feeling very fatigued and nauseated had progressed. Every morning, she was in the restroom vomiting. She thought Jonathan wasn't cognizant of what was going on with her. Jonathan knew Melanie's period was late and knew she was pregnant. He was waiting for Melanie to confide in him. He kept track of everything. There was nothing missed by Jonathan when it came to Melanie. He knew her body better than herself.

Melanie wanted more children, but at her age and with previous complications, she would be extremely high-risk. She also considered Jonathan's condition. She felt it was in their best interest to not have any more children. She was thinking ahead. "He wouldn't be able to take care of me like he did when I was pregnant with Jonathan Jr. I will be too much of a burden for him."

Her decision was final. She made an appointment at the Family Planning Clinic for the procedure. It wasn't easy, but it was for the best. She made an appointment prior to Jonathan's follow-up with his doctor.

Melanie cried often when she was alone. The hormones and the thought of aborting her baby was overwhelming for her. This was one of the most complex decisions she would have to face. She didn't believe in abortions. But how would she carry a baby at her age and be a burden on Jonathan with his ailments? She saw how difficult it was becoming for Jonathan to perform easy tasks. How he would grip his hands because one of them was in pain. Jonathan's ailment and complicated tasks were justification to terminate the pregnancy.

On the day of the procedure, Melanie felt scared and revisited her decision. She convinced herself to follow through with the procedure. She drove herself to the clinic and checked in for the appointment. She looked at all the faces in the clinic. There were faces who didn't look sure about the decision they were making, and others were happy about getting rid of their unwanted child. Melanie sat down and grabbed a magazine.

"Good. I need something to take this off my mind before they call me back." Nothing took her mind off what she was about to do. She tried playing a game on her phone. Melanie's thoughts were interrupted by a loud cry coming from one of the rooms. She heard a young lady screaming, "Oh, God, no! What have I done? I am so sorry. Please forgive me!"

Staff started rushing to the room to calm the young lady. But it was too late. The entire lobby heard her. Melanie, feeling conflicted, placed the magazine back and walked out of the clinic in tears.

Melanie opened her car door and entered. She prayed, "God, forgive me for what I was about to do. I am so sorry. What was I thinking?" She drove home in silence with no music to rock and bop her head to. When she arrived home, there was no one there. She turned on the television, and the evangelist just so happened to tell a story about a nurse who witnessed an abortion for the first time.

He stated, "The nurse told me the state doesn't consider abortion murder if the baby hasn't been fully released from the mother's body. They just need the head out to perform the procedure. If the mother is in her second trimester of pregnancy, they induce her, breaking her water. Once the baby's head is out, the doctor takes an object and pokes it through the back of the baby's head. The nurse could see the baby jolt. Folks, this baby felt what this doctor was doing."

Melanie began to cry and knew that was why the mother was crying out so loud. "Oh God, I can't believe I entertained the thought of aborting my baby. I want my baby, Father."

Jonathan Pushing Himself

Jonathan was outside with Jonathan Jr. They were playing a game of one-on-one basketball. They were enjoying the taunting between the two of them. "What you got, old man? You know you can't hold me."

Jonathan stated, "Try to shoot, and I'll show you what I got."

Jonathan Jr. dashed for the goal. Jonathan blocked him. Jonathan Jr. did a quick spin, but Jonathan already knew this was one of his son's moves and was already where he needed to be. He stopped Jonathan Jr. in his tracks, jumping up and blocking his shot. As Jonathan was coming down for his landing, he let out a loud cry.

Jonathan Jr. released the ball, asking, "Dad! Are you all right?"

Jonathan was curled up in agony. He had pushed himself too far. This wasn't what his doctor meant when he instructed Jonathan to remain active. This was a contact sport that involved agility, jumping, and quick response. Jonathan was in no shape for this type of activity. Jonathan Jr. called his mother. "Mom, Mom! Come quick. Dad hurt himself while we were playing one-on-one at the court!"

Melanie replied, "Okay, son. I'm on my way."

Melanie expeditiously jumped in her car to get to her two boys. She knew exactly which court they were playing. It was within walking distance from their apartments. When she arrived, she saw Jonathan Jr. helping his father. Melanie ran toward them. She had not even turned the ignition off the running car. She left the door wide open. "Jonathan! What happened? Are you okay? What did you do to yourself?"

Jonathan replied, "It's nothing, Melanie. I just hurt my back, is all. I am fine, baby. Please just take me home so I can get off my feet and rest."

Jonathan Jr. stated, "Dad, you can lean on me. I will help you. Old man."

Jonathan rebutted, "All right, I can still show you a thing or two. This is just a minor setback."

Melanie interrupted, "I don't think you should be showing him any more of your moves. If any, you should be walking, running, or doing aerobics with him. No more putting your body in danger, Jonathan. Okay?"

Jonathan let out a long sigh and replied, "Yes, Melanie. I understand."

Jonathan Jr. deposited his father into the car carefully. Melanie placed his seat belt on him. Jonathan Jr. made his way to the back seat. Melanie drove them home. They all exited the car. Jonathan Jr. carefully assisted his father out of the car. "Dad, place your arm around my neck and just lean on me. I got you, Dad."

Jonathan said, "Thank you, son."

Jonathan Jr. stated, "Dad, you don't have to thank me. This is my fault anyway. I should have never challenged you, making you give all you had."

Jonathan stated, "Son, it's not your fault. I knew my limit. I didn't want you to think your old man wasn't a challenge for you. I didn't want to let you down, son."

Jonathan Jr. stated, "Now see, I told you, you were old." They all burst out laughing as they entered the apartment.

JJ walked his dad to the living room and gently helped him sit. JJ stated to his dad, "Dad, you don't have to impress me physically. You impress me in other areas."

Jonathan and Melanie both looked at their son, confused. Jonathan asked, "How so, son?"

Jonathan Jr. replied, "Well, Dad, you have been here for me since the beginning. I have friends, and a portion of them don't have a father in the home. If they do, they are not their biological father. Just a man they cannot stand but tolerate because he makes their mother happy. I'm impressed that you haven't abandoned Mom and me."

Jonathan assured JJ, "Oh, son, I would never abandon the two of you. Well, the three of you."

Melanie and Jonathan Jr. both simultaneously said, "The three of us?"

Jonathan replied, "Yes, the three of you. I know you are pregnant, Melanie."

Melanie looked at Jonathan with tearstained eyes. "Oh my god, Jonathan. How did you know?"

Jonathan replied, "Well, baby, you were giving me signs. For one, you haven't had your cycle. You haven't been able to eat without vomiting, and you have been extremely moody." Classic symptoms of pregnancy."

Melanie stood to get a glass of water. She thought, *How do I tell him about my visit to the clinic?* Melanie was nervous but strengthened herself to tell Jonathan. She returned and sat next to him, stating, "Jonathan, I have to tell you something."

Jonathan asked, "What is it, baby?"

Melanie's lips were quivering, and tears were streaming down her face. Jonathan Jr. went to his mother and held her. "Mom, it's okay. You don't have to cry."

Jonathan pushed himself up from the couch and held his wife's hand, stating, "Melanie, whatever it is, we can get through this. Okay?"

Melanie replied, "You are going to be mad at me. I went to the family clinic to abort the baby."

Jonathan asked, "What? Baby, why?"

Melanie looked around to fix her focus on something other than the hurt look on Jonathan's face and replied, "Because I remember how bad my other pregnancies were. You are not well, Jonathan. I didn't think you would be able to take care of me in that condition. And my age was a huge factor. Before I could have the procedure done, I heard a young lady screaming, crying, and regretting what she had just done to her baby." Melanie looked at Jonathan, adding, "I just couldn't go through with it. I left the clinic and drove straight home."

Jonathan took Melanie into his arms, stating, "Oh, Melanie, I'm so sorry you felt you had to be alone with this. You know I am with you in any decision you make. We could have talked first, and if you felt this was best, I would have been there for you. I am glad you didn't go through with it. It's time to hear the pitter-patter of little feet roaming around again." Melanie felt blessed she had an understanding husband who supported her.

Jonathan Jr. interrupted, "So wait, I will be a big brother after all? Seriously?"

JJ had always wanted a baby brother or sister but never asked his parents why they never tried. He preferably wanted a baby sister. Jonathan and JJ embraced Melanie. She felt relieved, as if a heavy burden was lifted from her. Melanie thought, *Thank you, Lord Jesus. Thank you, Father, for giving me an understanding husband.*

Jonathan pulled away, stating, "Melanie, you have been through a lot today. Relax and rest yourself."

Jonathan Jr. stated, "Yeah, Mom. You sit down and relax. Dad and I got you. Okay?"

Melanie replied, "Okay. You all are right. But wait a minute. What about dinner? I need to start dinner."

Jonathan Jr. answered, "Mom, I told you. We got you. What would you like me to cook? Dad has been showing me a thing or two."

Melanie asked, "You have been learning how to cook?"

Jonathan Jr. replied, "Yeah, Mom. And I have been having fun too. I think I may want to go to cooking school."

Melanie said, "Well, all right then, son. Surprise me, and make it good too. Your little brother or sister and I are hungry."

JJ stated, "You got it, Mom."

Jonathan took hold of Melanie's hand, stating, "Hey, you know we are a team, right? We can talk about anything. No need for either one of us to be alone in these types of decisions. You should know this by now, Melanie."

Melanie replied, "I know, Jonathan. I was just thinking of you. But I forgot JJ can help you out as well. Forgive me, Jonathan?"

Jonathan replied, "Of course I do. There is nothing you can do to me that wouldn't be forgivable."

Melanie stated, "Okay, I'm going to hold you to that."

Jonathan asked, "Have you spoken to Dr. Gharma, Mel? Is she aware that you are pregnant again?"

Melanie replied, "That's on my to-do list. I will call her first thing tomorrow."

Jonathan stated, "Okay, I'm going to take a quick shower."

Jonathan made sure to check on JJ while he was in the kitchen cooking. He needed a little help with one of the items he was cooking and used the internet for guidance. He was making his mother fried pork chops, mashed potatoes, broccoli, and whole kernel corn. The aroma coming from the kitchen made Melanie hungrier. But she was a patient soul. She didn't mind waiting for a home-cooked meal. Jonathan, after returning from the shower, had removed her shoes from her feet. He felt pain in his back but dared not make a whimper. He didn't want Melanie to worry about him. He needed her to remain calm and stress-free. Melanie could hear JJ fixing plates. She stated, "Oh good. He will be in with the food soon. I can't wait to taste my son's cooking. How long have you two been cooking in that kitchen?"

Jonathan replied, "For about three months now. Jonathan is good at it too, Melanie. Some things just came naturally to him."

JJ exited the kitchen with Melanie's food on a tray. "Mom, here you go. I hope you enjoy. Dad, have a seat. I have your plate fixed too, and I'll bring it to you."

Jonathan said, "Okay, son. I'll have a seat and let you cater to me too."

JJ brought his father's food on a tray and reminded them both no eating until he sat with them. He wanted to eat as a family. He entered with his food and brought them all a glass of iced tea. Melanie said grace. "Father in heaven, thank you for this food we are about to receive. Help this food to be nourishment for our bodies. Amen."

Jonathan and JJ stated, "Amen."

They all began eating. Melanie was amazed. She asked, "This is your cooking, son? Oh my goodness, this is delicious. You really did this? This pork chop is good. And the mashed potatoes and broccoli are the bomb. I know the corn was from the can, so you get no credit for that. But overall, you did good, son, and I'm proud of you."

JJ replied, "Thanks, Mom. I knew you would like it."

Jonathan stated, "Son, I must hand it to you. You almost as good as your old man." They all laughed and continued eating their meal together.

When everyone had their last morsel of food and finished their drinks, JJ collected their plates, glasses, and trays. "I've got these, and I'll wash the dishes too. You all just sit back and relax. You all have some discussing to do about my little brother or sister."

Melanie and Jonathan stated, "Thank you, son. That was good."

Paying a Visit to the Doctor

It was time for Jonathan to see his doctor. Melanie was still feeling nauseated and exhausted, and now the pain had settled in her reproductive and anal areas again. "Melanie, baby, I want you to stay at home. I prefer you not travel. You need to take it easy and rest. Have you spoken with Dr. Gharma? When is she placing you on bed rest?"

Melanie replied, "Yes, Jonathan. I have spoken to her office. I am waiting for her to call me back. I have already sent in the necessary forms for her to complete. You know I can still come with you. I can bear the pain."

Jonathan stated, "No. You stay home and take it easy. JJ, make sure your mother stays off her feet. Okay, son? I don't want her doing anything."

Jonathan Jr. responded, "Yes, Dad. I will make sure to wait on her hand and foot. Did you hear that, Mom? Dad is placing me in charge because you can be stubborn at times."

Melanie couldn't help but wonder what his agenda was. She knew he was only looking out for her, but did he have another reason for not wanting her to come with him? She wondered, *Is his condition worsening and he doesn't want me to know how it has progressed? He has, in the past, kept me in the dark about things because he thought he was protecting me. Trying to keep me from worrying. But this is his health. I am his wife, and I need to know what we are to expect. I'll call his doctor after his visit.*

Jonathan was heading out the door. "Melanie, I'm getting ready to go. I will see you two in a little bit. JJ, remember to take care of your mother while I'm away."

JJ stated, "Sure thing, Dad."

Jonathan headed to his appointment. Jonathan felt that deep inside, out of all things he had kept from her, this was justifiable. "I want to make her pregnancy as easy as possible. She should only be focused on her pregnancy and not what's going on with me."

He was right. Melanie need not worry about Jonathan. It was too risky for her pregnancy. He knew how delicate her body was to pregnancy, and adding stress would surely cause her to lose his baby. He wasn't willing to take that chance with her. Besides, Melanie, at her age, was already running the risk of a complicated pregnancy.

Jonathan arrived at his destination and checked in for his appointment. The nurse called Jonathan to assess his vitals and room him. Dr. Henry came in and greeted Jonathan. "Well, Mr. Taylor, how are you feeling today? Have you felt any better or worse since our last visit?"

Jonathan answered, "I'm doing okay, Doctor. Nothing has changed. I am no better and no worse since the last visit. Only thing is, I hurt myself playing basketball with my son. Trying to show him I still had it. I ended up pulling a muscle in my back. It tightens up on me, and there is some pain."

Dr. Henry stated, "I bet the missus gave you an earful. What would you say your pain level would be today?"

Jonathan replied, "Yes, she did. It's about an eight. The pain awakens me about two or three in the morning. I get about four or five hours of sleep."

Dr. Henry stated, "I will prescribe a muscle relaxant." Jonathan agreed the relaxant was needed.

Dr. Henry recalled speaking with Melanie. He stated to Jonathan, "Your wife asked that I talk to you about having a prostate exam. Now hear me out for just a second. This exam, for most men, is uncomfortable to think about, but it rules out anything that we can't find through blood work. You should really think about this exam. You would want to have a clean bill of health and be here for your son and the arrival of your second child. Do research on the internet. This exam has saved a myriad of lives from early stages of cancer and other diseases."

Jonathan stated, "All right, Dr. Henry. I will think about it."

Jonathan was furious with Melanie but kept a smile on his face while visiting the doctor. Dr. Henry continued, "Your lab results came back, and I am concerned. Your markers are higher than normal. They show evidence that you have rheumatoid arthritis. I am wondering how long because you are struggling to walk up the stairs, and your fingers were hurting while you were trying to pull yourself up those stairs. Would you approximately know when this started?"

Jonathan replied, "The first time I experienced pain was about ten years ago. I dismissed it because the pain was bearable, and I attributed it to playing sports back in high school and occasional football with the fellows during my twenties."

Dr. Henry stated, "I see now. You dismissed it because it was minor. Now it has progressed." Dr. Henry thought for a moment. He stated, "I will refer you to a friend. He is a rheumatology doctor.

He is the best. He diagnosed a patient with kidney failure just by examining her nails. He is impressive and not a prescription pusher if you prefer not to consume medications. He can refer you to his nutritionist to enlighten you about foods to eat that would eliminate the progression of rheumatoid arthritis. Cease trying to show your son you still got it. You need to preserve whatever mobility and use of your joints remaining to keep you active. Keep exercising. You are exercising, right?"

Jonathan replied, "Yes, Doctor. I walk forty-five minutes per day, and I stretch my body twice per day for about ten minutes each time."

Dr. Henry stated, "That's good, Mr. Taylor. Keep that up, and you will feel better."

Ready to end the visit, Dr. Henry stated, "I will electronically send the muscle relaxer to your pharmacy. I will have my staff send a referral for you to see Dr. Salazar. Do you need a refill for the ibuprofen? I can electronically send the refill to your pharmacy."

Jonathan replied, "Yes, please send in a refill. I only have three remaining."

Dr. Henry stated, "Okay, it's done. Now I want to see you back in three months. Make an appointment with Dr. Salazar before coming back to see me. He has a Saturday clinic if the weekdays are not good for you. Do you have any questions for me?"

Jonathan replied, "No, Doctor, I don't."

Dr. Henry added, "Okay, I'll see you in three months, and here is Dr. Salazar's card. He's right here in the same building, right around the corner."

Jonathan stated, "Thank you, Doctor."

Jonathan was ready to leave and go home. Before he left the building, he stopped by the front desk to check out and have Melanie removed as his PHI. She could no longer call to inquire about what was going on with Jonathan. Only thing she could do was update them about his condition, but they wouldn't be able to discuss any health information with her about him. Jonathan drove home, angry. He thought, *How dare she talk to my doctor behind my back when I clearly told her I will not have that exam. She is overstepping her boundaries.*

When Jonathan arrived home, Melanie was so happy to see him. She had a smile on her face and asked, "How was your visit, baby? What did the doctor say?"

Jonathan answered, "Everything is okay. He prescribed more ibuprofen, a muscle relaxer, and to keep up with the exercising. Says my labs weren't as alarming as he thought. You hungry, baby?"

Melanie replied, "No. JJ made something for me while you were out at the doctor's office. I just finished eating it too. I was craving ramen noodles, ground turkey meat, and broccoli. The baby full too and satisfied."

Jonathan stated, "Okay, well, since you have eaten, I will just make me something quick, like some chili dogs." Jonathan entered JJ's room, asking, "JJ, you want some chili dogs?"

JJ replied, "No thanks, Dad. I ate what Mom had. After I cooked and mixed it together, I had a taste, and it was good."

Jonathan stated, "Okay, I'll make just enough for me then. Melanie, you need anything while I'm in here?"

Melanie responded, "A glass of water, please, if you don't mind."

Jonathan stated, "Okay, baby."

Jonathan placed his wieners in a pot to boil. He retrieved a can of chili and emptied the contents in a pot. He delivered a glass of water to Melanie and went back to the kitchen to prep his food. Jonathan grabbed hot dog buns from the pantry once the wieners boiled. He placed them on the buns and drenched them with chili. He grabbed a glass to pour him some iced tea. He thought, *Maybe I should have some water instead.* He grabbed a bottled water and exited the kitchen.

When he came back, Melanie looked at him. Jonathan saw her looking at him. He asked, "What is it, Melanie?"

Melanie asked, "The doctor didn't discuss anything else with you?"

Jonathan replied, "Yes, he did. He told me you called him about convincing me to have that prostate exam. I told him I would consider it. Melanie, you have enough to worry about, okay? I want you to cease calling there and consulting with him about me. I need you to concentrate on carrying our baby and taking it easy. You need not stress yourself out with what is going on with me. Okay, baby?"

Melanie answered, "Yes, Jonathan. I understand. I will cease contacting your doctor. But I am just looking out for you like you are looking out for me. I meant no harm at all. Just want you to be healthy for me and the kids, is all."

Jonathan stated, "I know, baby. And I do understand your concern, but I got this. Okay? Now let us talk about something else or watch one of your favorite movies."

Melanie shuffled through the library of movies. She wanted a heartfelt movie. She found *Krooklyn*. She loved this movie, but not the part about the mother dying. It brought tears to her eyes every time she saw it. She empathized with the mother because sometimes she felt the same. She was primarily the breadwinner. She cooked, cleaned, did her wifely duties, nursed Jonathan and JJ, was the appointment setter, all the above. Sometimes she felt overwhelmed as if she were drowning. She hadn't watched the movie yet while pregnant. She knew the waterworks would soon start running. She wondered if she should watch it.

She stated, "Jonathan, I want to watch that funny movie about not being a menace. I am in the mood for comedy. I don't want to watch anything sad."

Jonathan agreed, "Okay then. Funny it is."

The Difficulties of Life

"Melanie, when will you be seeing your doctor for your cerclage? It is time, right? You are past three months of pregnancy."

Melanie replied, "Oh, I'm sorry. I thought I told you. I am seeing the doctor next week to have the procedure done. Can you take time off from work?"

Jonathan replied, "Yeah. I'll let Trent know when I go back in tomorrow."

Jonathan had applied for a job and became gainfully employed. He was working eight hours per day because Melanie was pregnant and on family leave. She was getting a percentage of her check every month. It wasn't enough to cover all their bills. Jonathan knew the owner of the bakery. He hired Jonathon as a supervisor. The work wasn't hard at all. Jonathan kept his crew busy. There was rarely any time for fun and games. But Jonathan didn't abuse his authority with them. The crew loved him and didn't mind the work. He managed teenagers and one adult. Since there was only one adult, Jonathan helped with opening the store.

The teens bragged to their parents about Jonathan. Jonathan was easygoing. If they were a couple minutes late, it didn't bother him. He understood because he, at one time, was a teenager himself. But he always talked to them about their dilatory actions and how this would affect them if they didn't have a boss like him. They managed to cut being late to work down to a minimum.

Jonathan enjoyed his job. It was easy work with good employees. There was one teenage girl who adored Jonathan too much, and she confessed her love to another coworker. Tina and Sherida were the only girls working on his shift. They were both seniors in high school and were able to work the one-to-five shift. Sherida always knew Tina had a crush on Jonathan and would discern her ogling his entire body. Tina asked Sherida, "Girl, don't you think he is just the finest thang you've ever seen? He can rock my boat anytime."

Sherida replied, "Tina, you are too young for him, and he is married."

Tina stated, "And so what, girl? Married men be the first to cheat. They can't avoid looking at us young girls. They have those hags at home and be wanting something young, tight, and firm. We a delicacy to these older men. And they pay too, girl. I had one who knew he couldn't touch me without shelling out at least $200. Don't call me nor come around me if you don't have any cash."

Sherida replied, "Tina, you a ho. I dare not have my man around you." They both laughed.

Tina stated, "Sherida, tell the truth though. Isn't he fine as hell and good-looking?"

Sherida replied, "If that's your type. Not mine."

Tina stated, "Well, his wife better watch out, because I'll be taking some of that check like I do the others. They should take care of their men."

Sherida stated, "Tina, if a married man cheats on his wife, it's not because she's not taking care of him at home. You know most men are just unfaithful, and they can't help themselves. Too many big booty, big breast, beautiful women for them to be with one person. If they could, they would poke every woman passing their way and still wouldn't be satisfied."

Tina added, "Whatever, girl. I still don't care. I'm jumping his bone, and he's going to break me off some cash too."

Sherida stated, "Nothing good will ever come out of messing with a married man."

Tina rebutted, "There will be some good. We both will be making each other feel good."

Sherida shook her head at Tina and walked to the front to begin her shift. She thought, *This is one stupid sex-driven ho.*

CHAPTER 12

Jonathan and his crew's shift had ended. The store had closed, and he walked to the back to gather his things. Tina saw him walk to the back and followed him. She asked, "How are you doing? Would you like a little company? Can I ride along with you, if you don't mind?"

Jonathan replied, "Hi, Tina. No, you can't ride home with me. Where are your parents?"

Tina answered, "My mom is working late, and Dad is out of town. So may I ride home with you?"

Jonathan answered, "Tell you what I'll do. I can give you bus fare."

Tina replied, "I don't want no ride from no bus. I want you to take me home. Come on, you know you want to ride me home. Let me grab my things, and I'll be with you in just a few." Tina was aggressive, and she was not taking no for an answer. Jonathan knew he had to put his foot down with her when she returned.

Tina returned smiling from ear to ear. Jonathan stated, "Tina, I meant what I said. I will give you fare for the bus."

Tina stepped close to Jonathan, saying, "Stop playing. I am riding with you. You know you want me to ride with you. Come on, Jonathan."

Jonathan took all he could stand. He yelled, "Tina, get up off me right now! You take that somewhere else away from me! I am a married man, and you are a child! I am not a pedophile! What is wrong with you? You trying to get me put in prison or something? Get out of my face right now, little girl!"

Tina stepped back and ran back to the front of the store, crying. She thought, *He didn't have to speak harshly to me. Bastard! I will ruin him!* Tina's feelings had been crushed, and she would do anything to get back at him for dismissing her.

Jonathan left the locker room, locked up, exited the store, and jumped in his car angrily. "What is wrong with this damn girl? Is she crazy or something? I better call Trent and tell him what happened." Jonathan pulled out his mobile phone and called his friend.

Trent answered, "Hello."

Jonathan stated, "Hey, Trent. Jonathan here."

Trent asked, "What's up with you?"

Jonathan replied, "Your employee Tina just made a move on me, man. She doesn't fathom the word no. I had to speak harshly to her to get my point across. She is a persistent one. She got all up on me in my personal space, Trent."

Trent responded, "Wait a minute. You said Tina did what? Aw, man, Jonathan, I am so sorry. I will have to speak to her about this. In fact, let me call her now."

Jonathan stated, "Okay, Trent, man. Handle that for me." Jonathan released the line with Trent.

Jonathan arrived home. Melanie could hear the key turning in the keyhole. Jonathan entered the apartment. She asked, "Hey, baby. How was work today?"

Jonathan replied, "Melanie, I had a terrible end of day."

Melanie asked, "What happened, baby?"

Jonathan replied, "One of the teenage girls made a move on me, baby. I had to speak harshly to her to get my point across. She was not hearing me while speaking to her kindly. I had to pull out the hood Jonathan on her."

Melanie asked, "Are you okay? Have you spoken to Trent?"

Jonathan replied, "Yes, baby. I talked to him right after it happened on my way home. He told me he would call and talk to her. I can't believe this happened to me. I'm sorry, Melanie."

Melanie asked, "Why are you apologizing? You did nothing wrong."

Jonathan answered, "Well, baby, not only did I yell at her, but I also completely crushed her. So she may be feeling some type of way and may try to flip this on me."

Jonathan had never been in a situation worrying about a teenage girl accusing him of sexually harassing her. Melanie said, "Baby, don't get yourself worked up about this. Just go back to work and keep your distance from her. She sounds like trouble."

Jonathan said, "Yeah, you are right. I didn't do anything wrong. I will just wait for Trent to call me after he talks to her." Jonathan averted the conversation elsewhere. He asked, "So how is my baby in there?"

Melanie replied, "Oh, doing well. Just keeping me hungry all the time. My clothes are getting tighter and tighter. I know JJ is tired of me by now. Oh, I almost forgot. Justin came by to see me. Seeing him had me missing him more. I wish he had remained at home with us. But I knew he missed his friends when he left Rita's. I knew once he became older, he would return to that side of town."

Jonathan asked, "Justin came by? He didn't even stay around to visit me. He's the closest thing to a brother I have. Guess I'll see him next time."

Jonathan excused himself to use the bathroom. When he returned, he asked, "Are you hungry, Mel? It's after five?"

Melanie replied, "No, Jonathan. I am full. I may want a snack later tonight. A combination of fruit and raw vegetables. Nothing heavy. I prefer to be heartburn-free tonight."

Jonathan stated, "Okay, I'll make it in advance. It will be ready when you want it."

JJ walked into the living area. "Hey, Dad, what's up? You good, Dad?"

Jonathan replied, "Hey, son. How are you? Come out on the balcony. Let your old man wrap to you for a minute."

JJ replied, "Sure thing, Dad." They stepped on the patio. JJ asked, "What's up, Dad?"

Jonathan wasted no time. "Son, I just want to thank you for taking care of your mom while I'm away. I know this can be a job itself. She has you doing this and that when I am away, doesn't she? Tell the truth, son."

JJ replied, "Honestly, Dad, she doesn't require a lot. I am always getting up, making sure she doesn't need anything. Her calls are limited. Not constant as expected. I was thinking we should purchase a bell for her. She is in pain, Dad. Calling us hurts her. I can hear it in her voice."

Jonathan said, "Son. No. You will never hear that bell stop ringing. That bell will give her the okay to test how quick we respond. The system is fine the way we have it. You don't want to complicate it. Okay?"

JJ replied, "Okay, I didn't give any thought to it. Just thought it would be easier than her yelling out to me when I miss her phone calls."

The Lies of a Teenager

Trent called Tina to speak to her about what happened between her and Jonathan.

"Tina, I need to talk to you. What happened at the store today?"

Tina answered, "The supervisor made a pass at me, and when I turned him down, he yelled at me."

Trent stated, "Okay, tell me what happened."

Tina replied, "It all happened fast. I was in the locker room gathering my things. I was about to leave. He came into the locker room and stopped me in my tracks. He pressed his body up against mine, asking if I felt his member and that it was for me. I told him to get away from me and I am just a teenager. I asked him what his wife would think about him trying to sleep with a teenager. He didn't seem to care. He tried to kiss me. I pulled back from him and walked out of the locker room. You need to fire him or I will be telling my mother."

Trent stated, "Okay, Tina. I'll be in contact with you soon." Trent released the line.

Trent was a block away from Jonathan's apartment and called Jonathan while parking. "Jonathan, can you come outside, man? I need to talk to you."

Jonathan replied, "Okay, Trent. Give me a minute. Melanie, I'm going outside to talk to Trent for a few minutes."

Melanie responded, "Okay, Jonathan." Jonathan walked out of the apartment. He jogged over to Trent's car. Trent motioned for him to get in the car. Jonathan entered and asked, "What's up, man?"

Trent replied, "I spoke to Tina."

Jonathan asked, "Okay. What did she say?"

Trent replied, "You will not like what she told me."

Trent told Jonathan exactly what Tina had told him. Jonathan, in anger, stated, "What! Come on, man. She trying to say I was all over her and I tried to kiss her? I did none of what she told you. I told you what happened, Trent. That girl was all over me, man. I am no pedophile. She is lying, Trent."

Trent stated, "Jonathan, for now, I need you to lay low until I can get more information. I will still pay you. Just don't come to the store for now. I will be in contact. If she is threatening to tell her mom, that means the authorities will be involved. I wouldn't want them coming to the business and escorting you out in handcuffs. You may want to watch yourself."

Jonathan agreed, "Okay. I will lay low and not come to work. I didn't do anything, Trent."

Trent stated, "Jonathan, to be honest, her story sounds a little suspicious. But please understand my position here. A teenager accusing a grown man of sexual harassment isn't good business for me. I will keep my eyes and ears open and call you if anything changes. Okay?"

Jonathan replied, "Yeah, man, whatever."

Jonathan exited the car and walked toward his apartment. Trent yelled, "Hey, Jonathan!" Jonathan turned toward Trent. Trent asked, "We still cool, right?"

Jonathan replied, "Yeah, man. We still cool."

He turned and walked back to his apartment. Jonathan knew Trent was right about lying low. He went inside to tell Melanie what happened. She would need to know about this. Jonathan walked in, stating, "Melanie, I can't believe she told Trent that I initiated this. He told me to lay low with pay until he can get answers. He said her story sounds fishy."

Melanie asked, "Really? She said you initiated? Jonathan, was anyone else around to witness?"

Jonathan replied, "No, baby. And the worse part, Trent says she will be telling her mother if he doesn't fire me, which is why he asked that I lay low."

Melanie thought, *She will not tell what happened unless Trent fires him? This is a bunch of nonsense. This girl is lying.* Melanie asked, "Baby, did you act, say, or show any type of affection that would have led her to make a move on you? Sometimes teenagers can assume erroneously."

Jonathan replied, "No, baby. I was the same with everyone there. I never showed favoritism toward any of them there. I wish I could understand why she would lie."

Trent covered Jonathan's shift until he could get to the truth. The afternoon crew had arrived. One of the guys asked Trent about Jonathan. Trent announced, "Listen up, guys. Jonathan is no longer here." Trent looked toward Tina and noticed she had a devious smile on her face. Sherida looked her way as soon as Trent announced the news. She saw the look on her face as well. She knew what Tina had done. She was furious with Tina. She liked Jonathan. He was a cool boss. He wasn't like the others who came and went. He cared about the people he supervised.

Afternoon rush proved to be hectic. Sherida couldn't wait until the traffic died out so she could talk to Tina. She watched Tina as she galloped around the store as if nothing had happened. She was smiling and being unusually friendly to customers. This was all an act, and she knew it. She was covering up something. Sherida was compelled to extract the truth from Tina. She would freely divulge just enough for Sherida to figure out what happened.

After the rush, Sherida confronted Tina. "All right, Tina. Spill it. What did you do? Why is Jonathan not here? I saw you walk into that locker room yesterday after him."

Tina replied, "Sherida, what do you mean? He made a pass at me, and I told Trent about it."

Sherida walked away from Tina. She thought, *That lying heifer. She expressed to me how she would make advances toward him. I knew she had something to do with him not being here.* Sherida and Tina had been friends for as long as she could remember. She knew that Tina was a little loose around the guys.

When Sherida's shift was over, she clocked out and wished everyone a good evening. She entered the car with her mother. Her mother saw the look on her face. She asked, "What is wrong, Sherida?"

Sherida replied, "Mom, can we talk, please?"

Mom answered, "Sure, baby, what's on your mind?"

Sherida replied, "Mom, Tina has done something bad. She was always talking about our supervisor. How she wanted to jump his bone with no care that she's a minor. Mom, this guy is married, and he is expecting a baby."

Mom asked, "Okay, what has she done?"

Sherida replied, "Mom, I saw her walking into the locker room yesterday after him. All day she talked about having sex with him. I know she made a pass at him, and he rejected her. Trent announced today he was no longer employed. Mom, he treated us all with respect and as equals."

Her mom interrupted, "You know, baby. I have heard stories about Tina but always gave her the benefit of the doubt because she was a close friend of yours."

Sherida continued, "Mom, I am conflicted. What if she goes to the authorities with this? She will destroy him and his family. He would be another Black man accused of something he didn't do all because of a rejected teenager. What am I supposed to do? I've known her all my life, but I've only known him three months or so."

Mom replied, "Baby, you have got to do what is right. Sweetie, this man and his family don't deserve lies and embarrassment. Especially his pregnant wife. This will be a burden on you if you choose to be silent. I taught you better. Friend or no friend, Tina is wrong."

Sherida stated, "You're right, Mom. If I don't say anything, I am just as guilty. Thanks, Mom."

Mom stated, "You're welcome, baby. Would you like to stop for some ice cream?"

Sherida replied, "Sure, Mom. Thanks!"

Unveiling of the Truth

Sherida couldn't sleep that night. She tossed and turned. She knew her friend would feel betrayed, but she couldn't stand by and allow her to accuse Jonathan of trying to sleep with her. She went in early before Tina would arrive. When she arrived at work, she approached Trent.

She asked, "Trent, may I talk to you?"

Trent replied, "Sure, you want to talk here or in my office?"

Sherida answered, "Can we step into your office away from listening ears and prying eyes?"

Trent walked toward the back and opened his office door. Sherida walked closely behind him.

Once they were in his office, he offered Sherida to sit. Trent asked, "Okay, what is on your mind? Are you quitting?"

Sherida had dropped her head low after she sat. She looked up and answered, "Oh, no. Nothing like that. I wanted to talk to you about Jonathan."

Trent braced himself for another accusation. Two in two days. Sherida began her soliloquy. "Jonathan has been nothing but nice to us all and treats us with respect unlike the other past shift leaders. I must tell you something. Tina confided in me that she wanted to have relations with him. She was straightforward. She doesn't care about his family. She will practice extreme measures. Trent, I don't want her to destroy him and his family."

Trent, relieved, stated, "Sherida, this is enlightening information. You are saving Jonathan from wrongly being accused and his wife from embarrassment. I know it took courage, and you felt conflicted, inwardly thinking you were betraying your friend. You are not betraying her, just exposing who she really is. The only person who would have felt betrayed is an innocent man. I appreciate you. You go on home for today with pay and come back tomorrow."

Sherida stated, "Thank you. I was up all night. This was heavily on my mind."

Trent replied, "Okay, you get some rest, and I will see you tomorrow." Sherida went home.

Trent sat in his chair and could have kicked himself. He remembered he had cameras installed in the locker room last week. He had cameras stationed in the front of the store for irate customers or should a robbery occur and cameras in the back for any other activities. He sat at his desk and watched the surveillance. There it was. He saw everything. Jonathan had been in the locker room before Tina. He wasn't all over her. She was all over him. He thought, *I gotcha, Tina. No way you can lie your way out of this.*

When Tina arrived at work, she inquired about Sherida. Trent stated, "She scheduled a personal day today."

Trent was short-staffed and allowed Tina to finish her shift while he made phone calls to replace her. When her shift ended, he called her into his office. "Tina, have a seat. Would you like to recant your story about you and Jonathan?"

Tina replied, "No. Why would I want to do that?"

Trent turned his computer toward her. Tina viewed the footage and was shocked. Her eyes bucked in disbelief. Trent stated, "I had cameras installed last week. You lied to me and accused my friend of sexually harassing you. Tina, you are relieved of your duties. Please clear your locker. Leave the premises to never return."

Tina replied, "Trent, I'm so sorry. Please forgive me. Let me ex—"

Trent interrupted, "I am not the one whom you should explain and ask forgiveness. Please leave."

Tina removed herself from the office and gathered her things. She walked out slowly with her head hung low.

Trent called Jonathan. Jonathan answered, "Hello?"

Trent stated, "Jonathan, it's Trent, man. Can you be here tomorrow at your regular time?"

Jonathan happily replied, "Sure thing, man. What happened? Did she recant her story?"

Trent replied, "No, man. I got one better. I saw everything on my camera. Sherida came in and told me Tina had confided in her about wanting to hook up with you. I had forgotten I had those cameras installed in the locker room. I am sorry, man. Tell Melanie you are in the clear."

Jonathan stated, "Sure thing, man. Thanks, Trent." Jonathan released the line.

Jonathan couldn't wait to tell Melanie the news. He entered the room, stating, "Hey, Mel. I just got off the phone with Trent, and it is over. Trent had security cameras installed last week and viewed them. He saw everything on the monitors. He also told me Tina confided in Sherida, telling her she wanted to seduce me."

Melanie was relieved. "Oh, wow. Thank God, Jonathan. If she had went any further with those allegations, who knows what would have happened."

Jonathan replied, "I know right, baby? It is behind us now. He asked me to continue my shift, so I'll be going back tomorrow."

CHAPTER 13

Insertion of the Cerclage

Melanie was now over three months pregnant. It was time to have the cerclage inserted. Jonathan requested the day off in advance so Trent could arrange coverage for him. The procedure was scheduled for the following week. Jonathan took a trip down memory lane. He thought about the procedure taking place when she was pregnant with JJ. He was counting down the months remaining to meet their baby. He was proud of himself for being there for JJ since birth. He was striving to be an active and present father for his children with Melanie. He never wanted his son, of all his children, to feel abandoned by his father.

Jonathan wasn't feeling any better nor feeling any worse. The medications only masked the pain. He consumed it as scheduled. His pain level increased, but he refrained from dose increase. Jonathan routinely lied about his pain to Melanie. He didn't want her to know how bad he was hurting. He was still convinced that Melanie didn't need to know everything going on. Endeavoring to reach three months of her pregnancy was enough for her to be concerned. Dr. Gharma called periodically, making sure everything was okay.

The following day, Jonathan made breakfast and helped Melanie get ready. Dr. Gharma called, asking that he arrive with Melanie thirty minutes early. He went outside to check the fluids in the car for their trip. After he confirmed the fluids were up to par in the car, he went back inside to get Melanie.

He asked, "Melanie, are you ready, baby?"

Melanie answered, "Yes, Jonathan. I am on my way to the door. I just need to grab my purse, and I'll be behind you." Melanie grabbed her purse. Jonathan was standing at the door, waiting for her. He always walked her to the car, making sure she didn't hurt herself. He was being overly protective with her.

"Melanie, let me get the door and help you get in the car, baby." Melanie moved to the side so Jonathan could open the door for her so she could ease in and sit on the comfortable seat. Jonathan walked over to let himself in the car, and off they drove.

For a moment, there was silence. Jonathan concentrated on driving, and Melanie was looking out at the beautiful scenery. Since she was on bed rest, she wasn't able to go outside to enjoy all the beauty she was consuming. Her whole body was aching. It felt like gravity was working against her. Symptoms surfaced early in this pregnancy. Unlike other expecting mothers, Melanie wasn't permitted to share her pregnancy with the world. She had to stay cooped up in the house, except for doctor's appointments or to stretch her legs. Of course, with an escort for her safety.

Jonathan refused to take any chances and made sure JJ was there to keep a watchful eye on his mother. Every time he left, he gave JJ the speech, "Son, under no circumstances is your mother to go outside this door. She can go sit out on the balcony, but don't let her go out this door. You don't have to do everything for her. It is good for her and the baby that she gets up to keep her body active. She is running the risk of bedsores or hip pain from lying down too much. Don't let her do too much. She tires quickly. So if you see her out of breath, it means she needs to sit or lay to rest. Make her sit down, and you get whatever it is that she needs."

JJ would always tell his dad, "Dad, you tell me this every time you leave. I got this. You go ahead and do what you need to do. Mom is safe with me."

JJ was doing a great job with his mother, and soon Jonathan didn't have to give JJ the speech. He could see how his son was taking charge over his pregnant mother.

Jonathan noticed Melanie was quiet during their commute. He asked, "Melanie, baby, you okay? What are you thinking about staring out the window?"

Melanie replied, "I'm just absorbing all this beauty that I'm missing being cooped up in the house for the last three and a half months. I miss being out here, breathing the air, hearing the birds chirp, seeing the kids get off to school and all. I just miss everything about life."

Jonathan grabbed Melanie by the hand. He squeezed it a little, saying, "It'll all be over soon, baby. You have mastered the first trimester. Now you have two more. When the baby comes, you will feel just like you did when JJ arrived. You missed being pregnant, felt where did the time go, and you wanted to slow it down to enjoy him being a baby for as long as you wanted. Remember that, baby?"

Melanie laughed and replied, "Yes, I do. You always know what to say to me to make me feel better. I am glad you are my husband. You're always making a fuss over and taking care of me when I'm in this condition."

Jonathan said, "You are my wife who's carrying my baby. I am supposed to be this way with you. You're in this condition because of me."

Melanie smiled at Jonathan and continued looking out the window.

They finally arrived at the doctor's office for Melanie's appointment. He helped Melanie out the car and walked her into the building. Melanie checked in to start the procedure.

Dr. Gharma walked in, greeting the couple. "My favorite couple. How are you two doing today?"

Melanie and Jonathan both replied, "We're doing good, Doctor."

Dr. Gharma asked, "Melanie, are you ready for this procedure?"

Melanie replied, "Yes, I sure am. Ready to get stitched up to ensure this baby is full-term."

Dr. Gharma combatted with "All right then, let us get started. Jonathan, let us get you out into the waiting room. We should be no more than forty-five minutes to an hour. If you like, you can always get breakfast downstairs in the hospital cafeteria. The breakfast is good, especially the omelets. I love them."

Jonathan said, "Okay, I'll wait in the waiting room until Melanie's procedure is done."

Jonathan kissed his wife, and the nurse escorted Jonathan to the waiting area.

Melanie was wheeled and taken to surgery. Dr. Gharma prepped for surgery. After prepping, she entered the room, asking, "Melanie, would you place your legs on the stirrups and open for the speculum insertion?" Melanie followed the doctor's instructions. Dr. Gharma added, "Melanie, the anesthesia team is here. Count backward from ten."

Melanie began counting, "Ten, nine, eight." And she was gone to sleep land. The doctor performed the procedure. She opened Melanie up and grabbed the cervix for the stitching process. She had performed the procedure a myriad of times. She was proud of herself each time she performed it. She was making a difference. She was helping women to safely carry their babies full-term, preventing preterm labor. The procedure was an hour. Melanie would need to sleep a while until some of the anesthesia expired.

JJ decided that he would cook dinner for his parents. He removed a pack of ground beef from the freezer. It would take a few hours to thaw. It was 10:00 a.m. He wanted to make this a special dinner for his mother. He watched her make meatloaf and was given lessons on molding and mixing it. His sides would include mashed potatoes, broccoli, macaroni and cheese, and oven bread. And he was making a pitcher of iced tea. Jonathan Jr. was proud of himself. Not too many teenagers, let alone boys, could cook the way he could. He found cooking to be soothing and therapeutic. He enjoyed and took pleasure in cooking. He would turn on the music and cook his heart away. His body moved to the rhythm of the beats. This was his time alone to be free to do what he loved best. He couldn't wait until his parents arrived home so that he could cater to them. He was oblivious to the fact that his mother would suffer from the effects of the anesthesia after waking from the procedure.

JJ loved his parents. They were the opposite of his friend's parents. His friends would tell him how their fathers disrespected and cheated on their mothers, making them cry. JJ could discern the hurt in his friends' eyes. They expressed how much they hated their fathers and wished they would leave. Jonathan was thankful for his parents. He thought about the happiness and love they shared. He often smiled when he would see his dad pat his mom on her butt and tell her how beautiful she looked.

"Man, my dad has mad love for my mom. Hope I can find me someone who makes me as happy as she makes him."

Jonathan sat in the waiting room, patiently waiting to hear his wife's status. He was expected to arrive at his doctor's office in the next hour. The nurse appeared. "Mr. Taylor, Melanie's procedure was a success, and she is resting in recovery."

Jonathan asked "Any idea how long that will be? I have an appointment with my doctor."

The nurse replied, "It will be a while. You will have time to go to your appointment before she awakens from the anesthesia. I will let the doctor know that you will have to leave. Don't worry, Mr. Taylor. We are monitoring her very closely."

Jonathan thanked the nurse and left the hospital. His appointment was only ten minutes away.

Jonathan had forgotten that Melanie would need to rest right after the surgery. It had been over fifteen years since she had the procedure done when she was pregnant with Jonathan Jr. Good thing she would be out for a couple of hours. He would have enough time to see his doctor and get to her before she woke up. Jonathan tried to picture the outcome of his visit with the doctor. Jonathan had been doing only a few of the doctor's instructions. He was exercising and taking supplements but hadn't completely stopped lifting as advised by the doctor. Jonathan Jr., when at home, would help him, and while working, if the guys weren't too busy, they helped with lifting.

Stop the Heavy Lifting

Jonathan arrived at his appointment. He checked in and sat in the lobby for some time before they called to room him. While he sat waiting, a familiar face entered the waiting room.

"Trent? What are you doing here?"

Trent replied, "What's up, Jonathan?"

Jonathan responded, "I'm just here for my appointment. What brings you here?"

Trent answered, "Well, I'm endeavoring to expand my business. I want to get into catering breakfast for close-by businesses." Trent had boxes of donuts, pigs in a blanket, sausage rolls, and all types of goodies for the recipients to sample.

Jonathan stated, "That's a good idea. Generating extra revenue."

Trent smiled, stating, "Yes, those teenagers at home are digging into my pockets. I must make extra cash to keep from going broke."

Soon, the nurse was calling Jonathan to be roomed. Trent and Jonathan said their goodbyes and parted from one another.

Once in the room, the nurse asked, "Mr. Taylor, has anything changed since your last visit with Dr. Henry? Any increased pain, unable to perform daily activities? We were able to procure your medical records from Dr. Henry."

Jonathan replied, "Just a little increased pain. My job requires heavy lifting, but I have my employees to help lift heavy items when we're not busy. I endeavor to prevent hurting myself and increasing my pain level."

Nurse asked, "Is your pain medication working for you?"

Jonathan replied, "Yes, it helps."

Nurse stated, "Okay, well, I'll send the doctor in to see you." The nurse left the room.

Jonathan waited until he heard taps on the door. "Hello, Mr. Taylor. How's it going?"

Jonathan replied, "I'm doing well and making it, Doctor."

Dr. Salazar stated, "I've read your information from Dr. Henry, and according to my nurse, you haven't stopped the heavy lifting. I know you have help, but I need you to stop. Your pain will only worsen if you continue the heavy lifting. I can write a letter to your employer about your restricted lifting. You need to take better care of yourself. I'm going to examine your legs, knees, arms, and hands. I will be just a moment. I'll need to procure instruments for the exam." Dr. Salazar exited the room.

Jonathan's eyes danced around the room. He read literature on the wall and thought about what type of exam the doctor would perform. Dr. Salazar returned to the room with his instruments. He touched, pressed, and squeezed different parts of Jonathan's body for the exam. He asked, "Does this feel uncomfortable?"

Jonathan replied, "Just a tad bit. Not much. I do suffer from stiffness from time to time. It mostly occurs during the morning."

Dr. Salazar stated, "Try applying a cold compression bag of ice or heating paid for about fifteen minutes several times per day if it continues past morning. That should help ease the stiffness. Stop the heavy lifting. Keep up with the stretching and exercising. You will need labs drawn before leaving. I want to see you again in three months."

Jonathan agreed, "Okay, will do."

Jonathan had his labs drawn, and when done, he walked out the office. "This visit was under twenty minutes. Glad we have insurance. For what they charge, I would be mad if I had to pay full price for a visit that only lasts about a quarter of an hour. Let me get back to my baby and take her home."

Jonathan was headed back to the hospital when he received a call. It was the hospital informing him Melanie was ready to go home. He was right around the corner. By the time he arrived at the front desk, the staff wheeled Melanie to the front.

Dr. Gharma stated, "Mr. Taylor, here are the discharge instructions for your wife. She will still be drowsy from the anesthesia and will experience on-and-off sleepiness. Normal spotting may occur from the procedure. She shouldn't do any lifting. We filled a prescription for her at her pharmacy for Tylenol 3. You have my number. Call me if there are any complications. Melanie, you take it easy, okay? Take care of her, Mr. Taylor."

Jonathan stated, "Yes, Dr. Gharma. I will diligently care for her."

Melanie was in and out of it. She could barely speak. Jonathan helped the nurse get Melanie in the car. He buckled her in and adjusted her seat to where she was comfortable.

Jonathan pulled up to the pharmacy's drive-through and looked at Melanie. He asked, "Baby, you okay? Do you need anything? How are you feeling?" Melanie could only mumble when she spoke. Jonathan added, "We're almost home, baby. I'm putting you to bed."

LOSING HER CROWN

Jonathan called JJ. "Son, we'll be there in a few minutes. Turn the covers down on your mother's side of the bed. She is out of it. I will need you to come out and help me get her in the house too."

JJ stated, "Sure thing, Dad. I will turn down the covers now and stay on the phone with you until you are here. How was her procedure? Everything okay?"

Jonathan replied, "Yes, son. Everything is okay. Your mother is just a little out of it from the anesthesia. So she may be talking to you with slurred speech. We are turning into the apartments, son. Come on out and help me with your mother."

They both released their lines, and JJ walked out to the parking lot. Jonathan stated, "JJ, help your mother out the car, son. Be careful with her. Her balance is off. I'll come on the other side to help hold her up, and we can walk her into the apartment together."

Jonathan Jr. looked at his mom. He asked, "Dad, are you sure Mom is okay? She is drooling heavily from the mouth. Mom, are you okay? Can you hear me?"

Melanie moved her lips just a bit, trying to form a sentence. All that would come out was gibberish. Jonathan answered, "She's okay, son. She still feels the effects from the anesthesia. She will be feeling this way until tomorrow sometime. She went through this when she was pregnant with you too. I am not new to this, son. You got her on that side?"

Jonathan Jr. answered, "Yes, Dad. I got her. Come on, Mom. We will get you inside the apartment."

JJ had never witnessed his mother in this state and felt compassion for her. They got Melanie settled on the bed. JJ removed her shoes, kissed his mother on her forehead, told her he loved her, and left the room so Jonathan could remove her clothing. Jonathan removed her clothes and covered her with the covers. He kissed his wife and told her how much he loved her. Melanie smiled and tried to muster up strength to reciprocate her husband.

The Talk with Dad

Jonathan entered the living area to sit and rest himself. JJ was there waiting for him. JJ asked, "Dad, can we talk?"

Jonathan replied, "Sure, son. What's on your mind?"

JJ asked, "Dad, how did you know Mom was the one for you? Did you immediately know she was the one, or did it take some time for you to warm up to her?"

Jonathan looked at his son and immediately thought, *This is the talk*. He smiled at his son and began his soliloquy. "Well, son, your momma was a beautiful sight for sore eyes. Every man in the neighborhood wanted to date her. But none of them approached her. They felt intimidated by her. You see, they were all used to dealing with hood girls. They easy to approach and talk to. When you see a woman like her, you immediately doubt yourself and feel as though she would never be with someone like you. Forbidden fruit, if you will. They didn't know how to converse with her. They all thought she would turn her nose up at them. She didn't hang around outside like the other chicks. She mostly stayed in the house. But just like all females, son, they want someone who will take charge. Someone who's not beating around the bush with them. And since I was that man and was confident about myself, I approached her, and it's all history from there."

JJ asked, "So how did you know she was the one for you?"

Jonathan replied, "Well, son, your mother was different. She wasn't the type to be all up under me, demanding to spend time with me. She let me be free, and I dug that about her. When you find someone like your mother, son, don't let her get away. She is a keeper. Now why do you ask, son? Have you found a little honey you're expressing interest?"

JJ replied, "Nah, Dad. I am sixteen. No time to be thinking about girls. I was curious about you and Mom's story. My friends tell me about their parents. Their parents are different from you two. They tell me stories about how their dads disrespect their mothers, calling them out of their names and cheating on them. Does that mean they are with the wrong woman, Dad, if they are cheating?"

Jonathan answered, "No, son. That means she is with the wrong man. There is nothing wrong with the mothers. The fathers are the problem."

JJ asked, "Dad, I don't understand. Why marry someone you love, only to belittle and cheat on them? My friends hate their dads and wish they would leave. They hate them arguing and hearing and seeing their mothers crying."

Jonathan replied, "Well, son, some men just aren't happy unless they are with multiple partners, and a lot of them just have no conscience about what they do and who they hurt in the process. Son, you just can't have love. There must be respect too. A man can't properly love a woman if there is no respect for her and the marriage. He will resort to badmouthing and cheating on her. If you find someone that is even close to your mother, you treat her with the utmost respect and love her. You only get one great one."

JJ stated, "Okay, Dad. When I meet her, I will treat her like a lady and do everything to not make her feel the way my friends' fathers make their mothers feel."

Jonathan patted his son on his shoulder. "You hungry, son? Want me to fix you something?"

JJ replied, "No need. I am cooking dinner. I already have the meat thawing. I know you are tired after those appointments. I am making a meatloaf, macaroni and cheese, broccoli, pan of oven bread, and a pitcher of iced tea. I didn't know Mom wouldn't be able to join us. I really wanted her to eat a plate of food. I'll start in a little bit and fix your plate."

Jonathan looked at his son and said, "All right, son. I see you're taking charge. Yes, I want a plate with everything on it and some of that iced tea."

After three hours had passed, the meat had thawed. It was 4:00 p.m. JJ went into the kitchen to prepare dinner. It would only take about one and a half hours to prepare. JJ had placed the meatloaf in the oven and was preparing the homemade macaroni and cheese. The potatoes were boiling. He made the batter for the corn bread. The broccoli would be the last thing to cook since it didn't take long at all. JJ had his phone playing music while he cooked. He yelled out, "Dad, we will be eating in about fifteen minutes!"

JJ made the tea hours ago, ensuring it would be nice and cold. Jonathan responded, "Okay, son. I'll be at the table in a few minutes. Jonathan made a trip to the bathroom. The task of zipping and unzipping was tedious for Jonathan. His grip was affected from the arthritis. Lately, he had been experiencing numbness in both hands. He struggled but finally had them zipped and washed his hands.

Five minutes before dinner, Jonathan sat himself at the table. JJ brought his father his food, along with his glass of iced tea. Jonathan thanked him. JJ went into the kitchen to load his plate with food. He returned with food and drink in hand. He noticed his father hadn't touched his food.

"Dad, how come you're not eating?"

Jonathan replied, "I wanted to wait for you, son. Everything looks so good. I didn't want to start eating until you sat at the table. And we need to bless this food. Lord, we bless this food that we are about to receive. Help it to be nourishment for our bodies. Amen."

They both began eating. Jonathan stated, "Son, this is delicious. Your skills are improving. Your iced tea is sweetened with just the right amount of sugar. The woman who snatches you up will be one lucky gal."

JJ smiled stating, "Thanks, Dad. I have you and Mom to thank. Both of you have taught me a myriad of things when it comes to cooking. I wanted to surprise you both. Too bad Mom's unable to enjoy this meal with us. Will she be out for the rest of the day?"

Jonathan replied, "Yes, son. More than likely, she will sleep until the morning. But you can put her food up for her. She loves leftovers. Your mother will enjoy this, son. You really put your foot in this dinner." They both finished the rest of their meals and let out a burp when they finished.

JJ cleaned the dishes and the kitchen. He knew she couldn't stand a dirty kitchen. He was happy to help around the house in any way possible. Jonathan retired to the living room, enjoying a beer and a marijuana cigarette. JJ knew his father and mother smoked them. Melanie would stop smoking whenever she found out she was pregnant. JJ inquired with his father if he needed anything else; otherwise, he was going to check on his mother and go to his room. Jonathan was content and didn't need anything from his son. JJ went to his mother. Melanie was still asleep. He walked over to her side and sat there looking at her. He thought of how beautiful his mother was. He placed his hand on her face and rubbed it.

Melanie felt his rub and cracked a smile. "JJ? Hey, son. I love you."

He kissed his mother on the forehead and told her he loved her. Melanie drifted off again. JJ exited the room and closed the door.

Seeing Her First Baby

Melanie was dreaming. She dreamed of her mother. She came to Melanie and walked in front of her. She was beautiful. She was cancer-free and looked like herself again. Melanie's mother quietly walked into this dream, smiling and holding a baby over her shoulder. She walked by Melanie and stopped. When Melanie saw the baby, the baby lifted its head and looked Melanie dead in her eyes. Melanie knew this was one of her babies she had lost. Her mother never said anything to her. She gave Melanie a look, and it was saying, "Look at my beautiful grandbaby."

Melanie smiled at the baby, and as soon as they came into her dream, they were gone. Melanie had dreamed of her mother another time, right before her and Jonathan reconciled. Melanie's deceased sister, Tosha, along with her living cousin named Sena. Jonathan's daughter's name was also Sena. They were all sitting at a bench, which seemed to be at a park. Melanie's mother looked at her stating, "I know the secret." She asked, "Melanie, why didn't you tell me about Sena?"

Melanie looked at her mother with a strange look because she knew exactly which Sena she was referring to. Melanie shrugged her shoulders and responded, "I don't know." She thought in her dream, *How does she know about Sena?*

Melanie's sister, Tosha, thought she was snitching about something her and their cousin Sena had done together in the dream. So Tosha stated, "Melanie is snitching on us."

Lashon looked at Melanie, stating to her, "Melanie knows what I'm talking about."

It seemed so real, and Melanie sat on the bench, surprised that her mother asked about Sena in the spiritual realm. The dream ended there. Melanie was still holding a grudge against Jonathan for his deception and betrayal. She tried so many times to get over his betrayal and accept the child. The spirit was willing, but the flesh was fighting. All those years of being selfish on her part just to punish him.

Melanie woke up the next morning thinking about her dream. She thought, *How did my mother know about Sena, and why did she ask me why I hadn't told her? I remember the voice telling me Jonathan impregnated another woman, but it was not confirmed until after my mom died.*

Melanie didn't understand that once the deceased crossed over, they knew everything. Every existing secret in the worldly realm, they knew about it. Soon, she couldn't help but smell the scent of turkey bacon, eggs, grits, and French toast. JJ knew that his mother would be hungry once she awakened, after the anesthesia had completely worn off from the previous day.

Jonathan woke up early and was getting out of the shower. He discerned Melanie trying to get up from bed. Jonathan stated, "Let me help you, baby. How are you feeling this morning?"

Melanie replied, "I feel great, Jonathan. I feel so refreshed and rested. JJ, how is he? I want to see my son. Where is he?"

Jonathan replied, "He's in the kitchen making breakfast. Are you hungry? I can have JJ bring you your food served on a tray. You don't have to get out of bed. The doctor says that you are to take it easy. No bending, lifting, and stressing yourself."

Melanie replied, "Okay, yes, that will be fine, but I don't want to just sit and lay in this bed. I want to get up and walk around a bit."

Jonathan stated, "Okay, but not too much. I'll have JJ bring your food to you."

Jonathan left the room to have JJ bring his mother's breakfast to her on a tray. Melanie took a deep breath and rubbed her tummy. "How are you, little one? Mommy loves you with all her heart. Hope the doctor didn't give you a scare while she was securing you. Do you smell that? You hungry, little one? Your big brother will be here shortly to feed you."

JJ was finishing the eggs when Jonathan walked into the kitchen. "Son, your mother will be eating her breakfast in bed. Place her food on the tray."

JJ cracked a smile, saying, "Put her food on the tray without the plate?"

Jonathan replied, "Okay, son. I see you got jokes. No, put the food on the plate and place it on the tray."

JJ stated, "Hahaha, Dad, I was pulling your leg. I know what you meant. Just being funny. I'll get her a glass of water and a little iced tea."

Jonathan placed his mother's food on the tray with the drinks and a vase with a pretty flower in it for his mother. He picked up the tray and walked to his parents' room.

Melanie was flipping through channels when she heard JJ's knock at the door. She knew it was JJ. He had a certain knock that Melanie was no stranger hearing. "Come on in, son."

JJ entered with a smile on his face. His mother adored him. To Melanie, he wore a wardrobe of angelic smiles. Just like when they brought him home from the hospital. His smiles could light up a room. JJ entered, stating, "Good morning, my beautiful queen. How are you?"

Melanie replied, "Good morning, my handsome prince. I am well. How are you feeling?"

JJ replied, "I'm doing well, Mom. I was worried about you." JJ sat the tray across Melanie so that she could eat. He jumped on the other side to sit by his mother so they could talk. "You were out of it when you came home yesterday. I cooked dinner for you and Dad after you came back home. I wasn't anticipating you sleeping for the rest of the day after you had your procedure. Dad explained to me that you were still under the anesthesia, and you would more than likely be out for the remainder of the day until this morning."

Melanie replied, "Son, I am sorry. One of us should have prepared you for my homecoming. I went through this same situation with you."

JJ replied, "Really, Mom? You did? What exactly did you have done?"

Melanie wondered if she should tell him or not. She decided there was no harm in doing so. "Well, son, Mommy needs help carrying my babies full-term. So the doctor manipulates my body so that I can dodge going into preterm labor. It's a simple procedure that requires anesthesia."

JJ stated," Oh Mom. I didn't know that. Is this the case for all women?"

Melanie stated, "No, son. Not all. I am part of the few who require this procedure. Before you ask, my doctor prescribes bed rest as soon as we confirm that I am pregnant. I have a challenging time being in this condition. I stay in pain with no relief. My body is allergic to being in this condition. My body looks at the baby as a foreign object invading me. There is nothing the doctors can give me to alleviate the pain. Any drugs will put the baby's life in danger or cause birth defects. I could have taken something, but because of those factors, I chose to deal with the pain."

JJ commented, "Oh, wow, Mom. You are a strong, tough woman. I couldn't imagine being in pain all the time with no relief. Mom, do you need anything? I don't want you doing anything. You call me for everything, no matter what it is. Okay?"

Melanie responded, "That's nice of you, son, but if I don't get up and move around, I will develop bed sores, my hips will be sore, and I will be burdened with more pain. I appreciate the offer, but I will call you when necessary. Is that a deal, son?"

JJ answered, "It's a deal, Mom. Now finish eating your food. I know my little sister is hungry in there."

Melanie asked, "Now how would you know if it's a girl? We haven't had a sonogram yet, and it's too early to determine the gender."

JJ replied, "Mom, I know the baby is a girl. I been praying for a baby sister to protect her. I mean, even if it is a baby brother, I would still protect him too. But I just want a baby sister. Maybe if I were younger, I would prefer a baby brother. Since I am older, I have the baby sister vibes pulling at me. Does that make sense, Mom?"

Melanie answered, "Yes, baby, it makes sense. I understand exactly what you are saying." Melanie reached for JJ's hand and squeezed it. "Son, you know you are and will always be my special baby, right?"

JJ replied, "Yeah, Mom, I know. Just please don't ever say that in front of my friends or a potential girlfriend. Deal, Mom?"

Melanie responded, "Okay, it's a deal, son."

Jonathan kissed his mom on her cheek. Melanie finished her breakfast. After eating, she told JJ how good the food was and how much the baby enjoyed it. JJ sat with his mother for a while and watched television with her until he received a call from a friend. He excused himself away from Melanie and went into his room.

Jonathan was relaxing in the living area, giving his wife and son quality time. He was drinking a beer and smoking a marijuana cigarette. He loved how JJ was about his mother. JJ had told his father that he was hoping Melanie was having a baby sister for him. Jonathan didn't ask why he wanted a baby sister. He figured if Jonathan had a brother at fifteen, they wouldn't have that much in common.

Jonathan was thinking about his baby girl, Sena. It was still hurtful to think about her. He beat himself up on the inside, wondering if he made the right choice in choosing Melanie over being a part of his child's life. Sometimes he would get angry internally with Melanie. But he couldn't blame her because he should have been honest with her when he first found out about Sena. He knew he had hurt Melanie and betrayed her when she was faithful to him. So many times, he wanted to plead with Melanie to extinguish the fire inside her that ignited the vendetta to punish him. He would give anything for her to accept Sena into their lives. He felt asking Melanie to let go would make her angrier and extend punishing him, adding more time to when she was ready to accept her. So he kept his wishes to himself to keep the peace in the home. It didn't matter in the beginning because he was trying to win Melanie back. He would have done anything, even if it meant abandoning a child he didn't plan. Jonathan didn't realize that this would cause a major problem in his marriage years later.

JJ knew his sister and had met her through Jonathan's mother. They continued contact with each other. Melanie, in the beginning, was against JJ being around her, but one day, while at Jonathan's mother's home, she saw a picture of all three grandkids. The two sisters were hugging JJ. It brought peace to Melanie, and she didn't mind JJ having a relationship with her. It was her first step to accepting her one day. She mentioned to Jonathan that she had seen the pic but didn't make a big deal out of it. She knew eventually it was bound to happen. Jonathan kept his promise to Melanie and made no contact with his daughter. He often prayed that Melanie would one day open her heart to his daughter. He didn't want his daughter to hate him for abandoning her. But deep inside, he knew it was too late. He could feel her festering hate for him. Every time he thought about it, he felt angry and more compelled to tell Melanie his daughter would be part of his life, and if she wanted to leave, then so be it. But he couldn't bring himself to do so. He felt that would have been another part of his life in which he failed. So he sulked in his own sorry plight alone. Jonathan sipped on his beer and pulled on his marijuana cigarette to try and drown out the pain of it all.

CHAPTER 14

Secret Finally Confessed

Three months had passed by since Justin last saw Melanie. He decided to pay his big sister a visit. He had been in prison for one and a half years for an assault weapon. An AK-47 to be exact. When you absolutely, positively must kill everyone in the room, accept no substitutes. Just a quote from a favorite actor. This was his first offense, carrying a five-year sentence, but his lawyer was able to procure a reduced sentence. There was no probation as well. He counted himself blessed and owed all thanks to the Big Guy in the sky. He was checking on his big sister and the baby after her procedure. He remembered how Melanie suffered with her second pregnancy and JJ. He thought Melanie to be one hell of a woman to go through that pain again.

Melanie was sitting in the living area in her recliner when she heard the knock. Melanie positioned herself so that she could get up to answer the door. JJ rushed in to answer the door. "I got it, Mom. You relax." JJ opened the door. "Hey, Uncle! What's cracking?"

Justin replied, "Nothing much, nephew. Boy, you are getting big and tall. You hitting it big with the ladies? I know you have a li'l lady somewhere."

JJ answered, "Yeah, I know I am. Uncle, right now, I am not seeing anyone. But I'm working on it."

Justin stated, "All right. You studying those books in school?"

JJ replied, "Yeah, Uncle. I am staying focused. Things are a little difficult for me, but I receive tutoring at school. That is one of the reasons I don't have a girlfriend. School keeps me too busy to be focused on the girls."

Justin stated, "All right, nephew. Let me get in here to see my big sis. You be straight and call me if you need anything."

JJ stated, "Okay, Uncle J. Will do."

Justin walked into the living area where Melanie was sitting. He leaned over and gave her a hug and kiss. "Hey, sis. How have you been doing? I came by to see you. Making sure my big sis is okay."

Melanie replied, "I'm doing fine, baby brother. Just counting the months before I deliver. I had that cervical cerclage procedure performed. I had it when I was pregnant with JJ. Jonathan and JJ have been making a big fuss over me, making sure that I am not doing too much of nothing. They will only let me do things that are not strenuous and little walking. I get up to walk around the apartment to stretch my legs per the doctor's request."

Melanie was interrupted when she felt a kick from the baby. "Calm down, little one. You will eat when Daddy gets home from work."

Justin asked, "You going through the same symptoms you had with JJ? You limited to your daily activities with this pregnancy too? I remember how you used to hurt, and you were always in bed when you were pregnant with him. You were miserable in this condition."

Melanie replied, "Yeah. So you remember, huh? That was a long time ago. Over fifteen years ago. But when I finally delivered JJ, it was worth every ache and pain. Looking at how perfect he was and the smile he put on my face after holding him. Which is why I always said I would do it all over again for another bundle of joy. I have always wanted at least three kids because I want a mess of grandkids. But this is the last one for me."

Jusin stated, "Man, you are an impressive woman to want to go through not only the labor pains but the entire nine months of pain and bedridden. You ladies are one of a kind. Us men are not built to tolerate that type of pain."

Melanie laughed. "Yeah, you men are wimps when it comes to pain. Hahaha." Melanie's phone was ringing. She excused herself from speaking to Justin to answer. It was a quick call from her doctor's office. Melanie ended her call. She continued, "What you been up to, baby brother? You staying away from that life that sent you to prison?"

Justin replied, "You know me, sis. I keep a low profile now."

Melanie stated, "You are evading my question. Baby brother, it broke my heart that you were away from me. I felt failure with you and Momma. I know you are responsible for yourself as an adult. But I gave her my word I would look after you and keep you out of trouble."

Justin stated, "Sis, Mom shouldn't have placed that burden on you. You have no control over what grown people do with their lives. You taught me well. It was me. I went out there and did what I knew was wrong instead of doing right. It's not your fault that I chose to follow my own path. I had others influencing me, and I saw things I wanted in life, and quick money was how I would procure them. So stop blaming yourself for what I caused in my life. Look at it this way. Did you listen to Momma about Jonathan? She always told you there was someone better out there for you. But you followed your heart and own path in life. I did the same."

Melanie replied, "Okay, baby brother. I hear you kicking knowledge to your big sis. But it sure is good to have you home. You came by after your release three months ago, but as soon as you came, you were gone. So, I didn't get a chance to talk with you. Baby brother, I have been feeling so bad about something. I've kept it a secret for so long, and I need to just talk to someone about it." Melanie began to cry. "If I don't get this out, it's going to keep bothering me. I'm filled with so much guilt."

Justin asked, "What is it? You know you can talk to me. What is bothering you, Mel? Stop crying and tell me what's wrong."

Melanie replied, "Remember when Jonathan and I broke up before Mom passed away?"

Justin replied, "Yes, I remember."

Melanie stated, "Well, when we reconciled, I found out at one of those parties at his granny's that he fathered a child and kept it from me. He impregnated her two months before impregnating me. Our children were to be two months apart. I don't know if my anger intensified toward the fact that we were two months apart, the fact that he deceived me, or how I found out about her. His mother blurted it out at that party while intoxicated. If she hadn't accidentally said something, he would've kept deceiving me for God knows how long. It may be all the above that plays a part in my punishing him. I know it was seventeen years ago, but I should be over this. Should've been over it. But something keeps me hanging on to the hurt, pain, and humiliation I felt. As sweet as Jonathan is to me, I know deep down inside, he feels hate toward me for him walking away from his daughter. He told me he didn't want to have anything to do with her until I was ready. My being ready to accept her has never taken place."

Justin listened to his sister pour her heart to him. He absorbed the information and processed it before speaking. Justin stated, "Wow. That was a lot. Have you just been holding this in all this time? Look, let me tell you what I learned when I was in prison. Whenever you think you are all right and you can move on from life's perils, there the devil is to remind you why you were trapped mentally. He wants you to continue punishing Jonathan. He is tricky, sis. He will make you believe that you are still angry and bitter about things. He needs to keep you in that realm so that he can control you. If it bothers you that much, you need to pray to God to release so you can get on with life, sis."

Melanie was wiping her tears away while listening to Justin. Melanie admitted, "Yeah, you right, and I know you are. Sometimes it is unbearable to look at myself in the mirror."

Justin stated, "Exactly, sis. Surrender your worries to God, and He will make everything better for you. I promise you, He will."

Melanie stated, "Thank you, baby brother. I needed this talk."

Justin stated, "You're welcome. What is that smell? I haven't seen Jonathan, and I know you are not cooking anything. Is that smell coming from your neighbor's cooking through your vents?"

Melanie answered, "No, baby brother. That is your nephew cooking in the kitchen. You didn't know your nephew could cook, did you? He's good at it too."

Justin stated, "Aw, snap. My nephew can cook? It smells good too. I hope he is cooking enough because looks like I came at the right time. I'm staying for dinner and to talk more with my sis."

The three of them talked while JJ made trips back and forth to the kitchen to monitor his food. He was frying chicken wings and baking them in the oven, pouring barbeque sauce and drizzled honey over them. His sides were corn on the cob, mashed potatoes, fresh green beans, and sweet oven bread.

Jonathan arrived home and smelled the aroma outside the door before opening it. Jonathan thought, *My son must be cooking. I can smell the aroma.* Jonathan opened the door and walked into the apartment. The first person he saw was Justin. Jonathan asked, "Justin, what's up, man? What brings you to this part of town?"

Justin rose and gave Jonathan a hug and handshake. "I came to visit and eat up some of JJ's food. He has it smelling good up in here. Who's been teaching him how to cook?"

Jonathan replied, "Yeah, his mother and I both had a hand in that. I told him he should go to school for culinary arts and become a chef or have it as a backup plan."

Justin stated, "My nephew already building his résumé for the ladies. Women love a man who can cook."

JJ was in the kitchen putting the final touches to his dinner. He informed them all that dinner was ready. "Hey, Dad. I didn't hear you come in the door. Mom, I will bring you your food on your tray. Dad and Uncle Justin, you all go on and sit at the table. I will fix your plates and bring them to you. We still have leftover iced tea in the fridge. I'll bring you all a glass of that too."

They both made their way to the dinner table. JJ served his mother first and then the men. Justin was the guest. They asked if he wouldn't mind blessing the food. Justin was honored and said grace. They all dug in and enjoyed the taste of the first morsel of food. JJ made sure he gave them all an extra half serving of everything. They all had their fill from their plates. No seconds needed.

Melanie felt stuffed, she couldn't move. "Jonathan, will you help me up so I can get in the shower? I'm ready to lay down in my bed."

Jonathan replied, "Sure thing, baby."

Justin interrupted, "Here, brother, let me get Melanie up for you. You been away at work, and I know you tired. I will get her to the room, and you can do the rest from there. It is time for me to head back home. Come on, sis. I got you. Just hold on to me."

Jonathan stated, "Thank you. I appreciate that."

Once they were in the room, Justin started the shower for Melanie. "Melanie, you remember what I told you. Pray to God for your release. You call me if you need anything or if you need to talk to someone. I am here for you. I love you and will be back soon to check on you, okay?"

Melanie replied, "Okay, baby brother. I love you too, and come back soon to see me. I miss and love you. Talk to you later." They both hugged and expressed love toward each other. Justin and Jonathan left the room. He shook hands with Jonathan and JJ and promised he would be back soon.

Jonathan went to the room to help Melanie get in the shower. "Hey, baby. Let me help you with those clothes and get you in the shower. I didn't get a chance to hug and kiss you when I came in from work. I saw Justin and completely forgot. How are you feeling?"

Melanie responded, "I'm doing well, and it's okay, Jonathan. I understand your distraction. I forgive you. How was your day today? Any young gals try to steal you away from me today?" They both laughed.

Jonathan replied, "Good one, Mel, but no. No one has stepped out of line. We have a new girl there that Trent hired. He really didn't want to hire another female, but he didn't want Sherida feeling awkward working around a bunch of males, so he hired another girl. She has top-notch work ethics. She mostly keeps to herself and doesn't say too much either. Just clocks in, does her work, and clock outs when her shift has ended."

Melanie stated, "Okay, well, that's good. Can you please wash my back for me? Here is the soap and towel. Please scrub the right shoulder blade. I have been itching in that area and can't reach it. Feels like I am stretching my stomach, making it hurt more when I try. My toes need washing too, baby. I can't reach them at all. Can't pull my legs toward me, nor can I stoop in the shower. I may slip standing or hurt myself trying to wash them. Next time I will sit in the tub. But then it will be hard for me to get up and out the tub. Woe is me."

Jonathan thought, *Woe is you? Woe is me. I'm the one who would have to get you out the tub.*

Melanie continued, "Jonathan, what do you think about me sitting in the tub? I can at least wash my feet, but you'll have to do my back for me."

Jonathan wished she would slow down. She was talking about too many different things to do. He responded, "Melanie, yes, you should sit in the tub next time. I will help you get in and out the tub. Anything else you need me to wash?"

Melanie replied, "No, baby. I can finish the rest. I will call you when done. My clothes are already on the bed, so you can sit and relax."

Jonathan turned on the television and sat in his chair until Melanie called for him to help her. Melanie showered her body, and when she was done, she called out to him to help her. Once out, she pat her body dry to keep from robbing her body of the natural moisture. She dressed into her pajamas and hopped in bed. Jonathan pulled the covers over her and turned the station so that she could watch her cartoons. She would watch them for about an hour and drift off to sleep. Jonathan kissed her good night and went into the living room.

Jonathan grabbed a beer and rolled a marijuana cigarette. He turned on the TV to watch the game. The Mavericks and Warriors were playing. The game had just started. Jonathan pulled on his cigarette and lay back into his chair. He and Melanie had matching recliners, and they were blue. Jonathan felt at ease and relaxed. He heard a voice yelling out to him. "Argh! I was just getting relaxed."

Melanie yelled again, "Jonathan!"

He quickly rose and went to the bedroom. "What is it, Mel?"

Melanie answered, "Could you bring me some grapes, please?"

Jonathan replied, "Sure, Melanie. You need anything else while I'm up?"

Melanie responded, "No, just the grapes, please. And wash them off for me."

Jonathan went into the kitchen to get Melanie her grapes. He grabbed a bowl out from the cabinet and opened the refrigerator for the grapes. He placed them in the bowl, washed them off, and walked back to the room to give them to Melanie. "Here you go, Mel."

Melanie thanked Jonathan for the grapes.

Jonathan went back into the living area to continue watching the game and relax. He had reclined back into the chair and took a sip of beer and a long drag on his cigarette. The Mavericks were in the lead, 13 to 9. No longer had he had himself relaxed than he heard Melanie's voice again.

She yelled, "Jonathan!"

Jonathan thought, *Oh my god, what the hell could she want now? I'm trying to relax here.*

Jonathan rose from his chair and walked to the bedroom. "Yes, Mel. What is it now?"

Melanie replied, "I'm sorry. Can you please bring me something to drink and a bag of chips? I am done with the bowl of grapes. Here you go."

Jonathan retrieved the bowl from Melanie and told her he would be back. He walked into the kitchen and brought back with him the chips and Melanie's 7-Up.

Melanie asked, "How did you know I wanted my 7-Up?"

Jonathan replied, "Because you always have a tough time trying to burp after eating. So I figured your 7-Up would come in handy for you."

Before Jonathan had returned with her chips and 7-Up, Melanie pondered the thought of having a bell to keep from yelling out to her two favorite boys. She asked Jonathan, "Hey, listen. Why don't you get me one of those bells so I won't have to yell out to you guys?"

Jonathan replied, "Melanie, I am not getting you a bell for you to ring at your leisure. You will be ringing that bell just to see if someone will come running to your call. So no bells, okay?"

Melanie responded, "Okay, Jonathan. It just hurts for me to yell, is all."

Jonathan stated, "You can call me on the phone. Do you need anything else, Melanie?"

Melanie replied, "No, I don't need anything else."

Jonathan asked, "Are you sure, Melanie?"

Melanie replied, "Yes, Jonathan. I'm sure."

Jonathan went back into the living area. Melanie was disappointed in Jonathan, and worst of all, she regretted having Jonathan cater to her. "What's wrong with me having a bell? He's getting tired of me calling him. I'll tell you what, Mr. Jonathan, I will not call you for anything else. I need the exercise anyway. Forget him. I'll either call JJ or get what I need myself." Melanie was being extremely selfish and stubborn.

A Father Longing for His Daughter

Jonathan reached into his wallet and pulled out the picture of his daughter, Sena. Melanie didn't know anything about the picture. Sena's mother had given it to him when he secretly visited his daughter. Jonathan felt bad and didn't see her again because he felt he was betraying Melanie. He stared at the photo of his daughter and felt so much pain.

"I'm sorry, baby girl. This is the only way for me to connect with you mentally. Wish I could be there for you. I hurt Melanie, and I hurt you."

Never in a million years did he think when he made that decision many years ago to not be in his daughter's life, he would feel so much regret and hurt. He could only imagine the pain Sena was feeling because he was an absent parent. "I wish I could make things right with Melanie. I really want her to be a part of Sena's life. Melanie is so loving and would be a wonderful stepmother for Sena. God, why can't she accept my baby girl? I know I wronged her, but when will she forgive me for this? I'm tired, Lord, of feeling this way."

He thought he was the only one going through the emotional roller coaster. Melanie was having her share of feelings too. Sometimes, when Melanie would lay in bed, she could hear a voice tell her, "This child needs her father." Melanie didn't understand why she kept hearing this voice and would dismiss it. But God was connecting her to this child so that she could feel her pain. Melanie would think about Sena and would start crying. She couldn't fathom why it was so hard for her. She wanted to accept Sena, but she would always resort to thinking about the deception, pain, and humiliation Jonathan caused her. He didn't respect her enough to come to her and talk to her about what he had done. She would have accepted her within a heartbeat. But Jonathan went two years keeping this a secret. She always told herself the punishment was for Jonathan, not the child. This thinking helped her to always dismiss Sena's feelings invading her. The devil always had a way of reminding us of the hurt so that we could hold on to it, preventing us from moving forward in life.

Sins of the Parents

Sena was sixteen when she started feeling anger toward her dad. She was two years older than JJ. Her curiosity started at the age of eight, with her feeling hurt and wondering why her dad was an absent parent in her life. She frequented friends who had both their mother and father home with them and discerned the father-daughter relationship. She envied their relationships.

"Why does my father not want to be in my life? Does he despise me? What kind of man turns his back on his own flesh and blood?" She plagued her mother with questions. She really didn't know that much about him.

Lisa found herself apologizing constantly to Sena for the unfair perils she endured.

"Mom, what's wrong with me? Why does my daddy not want me in his life?"

Lisa replied, "Baby, it's hard to explain, and it's complicated."

Sena stated, "I have a right to know why. Would you not agree? How am I supposed to accept something that I don't fathom? If you were in my shoes, would you want to know why you have no connection with your dad? I feel empty, Mom, plagued with all sorts of feelings about him. I love him, and then I hate him for abandoning me. I need to know, no matter how much you may think it will hurt me."

Lisa looked at her daughter's desperate face and answered, "You are right, baby. You do deserve to know what happened. First, understand there was no us. He approached me at a club. I liked what I saw, so we started talking and hooked up eventually. I found out I was pregnant. He lived with a relative at the time. When I would call, he was never around to talk so that I could share the news. After so many calls, I finally told her I was pregnant. I asked her to deliver the message. She told me she would. Before she released the line, she told me that he had a girlfriend and that I was wasting my time with him. I had no concern that he had a girlfriend. I wanted to be with him. I had a challenging time trying to get him on the other end of the phone. When I finally spoke to him, he blatantly told me you were not his, and I needed to prove it. I proved you were his. He found out in court I was underage. I believe he was angry that I didn't tell him how old I was, and he took this out on us both. But I told my mother I deceived him. I lied to him about my age. So she didn't pursue any charges against him. I messed up, baby, and I'm so sorry for ruining your life."

By this time, Sena was pacing back and forth, absorbing the bad her mother had done. Sena angrily asked, "Mom, you were just sixteen and at a club! Why would you trick him like that? No wonder he chose to cast me away!"

Lisa stated, "Honey, watch your tone."

Sena calmed herself and began to speak calmly. "I'm sorry, Mom. You both are to blame here, not just you. I don't understand why you lied to him and why you would keep this from me. You saw how bad I was hurting and feeling."

Lisa stated, "I thought I was protecting you, baby. I thought it was irrelevant telling you this. I wanted you to forget about him the same way I did. It pains me to see you suffering."

Sena stated, "Forget about him? Why would I want to forget about my dad? You may want to forget about him, but I want to know him. Adults always think they know what is best. Mom, I am sorry, but you are wrong on so many levels with this one. You withholding this from me hurts even more. I'm angry at both of you."

Lisa could hear the hurt in her daughter's voice and gave her the platform needed to present her case. She listened to every word. "Here I was thinking that it was me he hates when it's you that he hates for not telling him how old you were! You almost ruined his life, Mom!"

Lisa stated, "Yes, I know, and I apologize for this. I just didn't want you—"

Sena had forgotten to calm her voice when talking to her mother. Sena stopped her. "You just didn't want me to what! Hold a grudge against you! Hate you for lying to my dad, almost sending him to prison! What, Mom?"

Lisa replied, "I just didn't want to draw a wedge between you and I."

Sena stated, "You were being selfish, Mom! Parents always use excuses for not telling their children the truth! Don't you adults learn from one another about this very same mistake?" Sena's voice calmed down a little. "I'm sure this isn't the first time this has happened to anyone. You know there are other parents who have done this to their children and how it turned out for them." Her voice elevated again. "Yet you follow to each other's footsteps, knowing one day the truth eventually will be exposed!"

Lisa felt the hairs on the back of her neck stand erect. Lisa felt like she was the daughter and Sena was the mother checking her. She stood all she could. Sena was now taking advantage of the situation. Lisa interrupted, "Now wait just a minute, young lady! I am still your mother! You speak to me with respect!"

Sena humbled herself. She knew her mother was right, and her goal wasn't for things to become escalated. It just happened. She wanted her mother for once to understand how keeping secrets could damage a kid. Especially when it had to do with the absent parent.

Sena stated, "I'm sorry, Mom. Please forgive me. I'm not mad at you. Just disappointed."

Lisa understood stating, "Look, Sena, I know I managed things in a way where they would work in my favor. I never thought how it would affect you, but please believe that I never meant to hurt you."

Sena stated, "Okay, Mom. I prefer to not talk about this anymore."

Sena walked out of the room, but she turned to face her mother to answer one burning question. "I just have one question. Has he ever laid eyes on me?"

Lisa replied, "Yes. He came to the hospital to see you after you were born. And I took you to see him and his family while you were a baby. He saw you another time. He came by when you were a toddler. That was the last time I saw him and his last time seeing you."

Sena replied, "So what happened? Why did he stop coming to see me?"

Lisa replied, "I really can't tell you why. Maybe it was because he married his girlfriend. I assume his wife wasn't ready to accept you into their lives. I guess since she wasn't ready, he wanted to make her happy and felt he needed to keep the peace."

Sena asked, "Okay, so his wife is the reason he abandoned me? Do you know her? Have you ever met her?"

Lisa replied, "No, baby. I don't know her, but I have seen her with no exchange of words."

Sena stated, "Well, at least I know my baby brother. Good thing our grandmother made sure of that. Mom, I just want to be loved by him, is all."

Lisa sat beside her daughter and caressed her locks, which were in braids. "I know, baby girl, and I'm sorry you have to experience this."

They both sat quietly, absorbing and thinking about their discussion.

The Bell Blues

"Melanie, what are you doing? Why are you up and not resting in bed?"

Melanie replied, "What do you mean why am I up? I told you it hurts for me to yell at you. You will not get me my bell like I asked you to. So I'm up getting what I want."

Jonathan asked, "Why can't you text or call me, Mel? You don't need a bell to get my attention."

Melanie replied, "I don't want to call you! I want my bell!"

Melanie's hormones were kicking in overdrive. Her emotions were all over the place. She was snapping at Jonathan and JJ. Mostly at Jonathan. She did this while she was pregnant with JJ. Melanie only wanted that bell because she saw it on her favorite cat and mouse cartoon show. Melanie had a habit of wanting things because she didn't have it and really had no use for it. Now the things she needed in life didn't appeal to her. She loved collecting things that proved little use and loathed things that were necessary to have. She felt things deemed necessary had a tendency of attaching themselves to you, making you feel life was unbearable without them.

Jonathan stated, "Mel, this is selfish of you. What is wrong with you calling or texting me?"

Melanie replied, "You can always ignore my call or text by silencing your phone. Lying to me and telling me you didn't know it was on silent. You can't silence that bell. You will have to answer me because you are going to get tired of hearing me ring it." Mel knew eventually Jonathan would cave and grant her petition. It was only a matter of time. Her telling him it hurts for her to yell out to them would place a guilt trip on Jonathan. But she was being truthful. It really did hurt her to yell out to them.

Jonathan looked up at the ceiling, expressing defeat and asking, "Why me, God?" He did just what Mel's devised plan intended. He gave in, stating, "Mel, I'll get you a bell before I come home tomorrow. You have been getting out of that bed too much today. Make this your last trip. You've stretched out your legs and walked enough in that hall today. Now will you please get back in bed? And whatever it is you need, call me or JJ."

Melanie replied, "Ok. Just make sure you bring my bell."

Jonathan thought, *Selfish bitch! I can't wait until you drop this baby!*

Melanie walked back to the bedroom to relax and watch more cartoons, sitcoms, and movies. She thought, *Yeah, the empress has won that battle. Give me my bell like I asked the first time.*

Jonathan went in the next day to work his shift. He went to a store that sold bells on his lunch break. When he returned, he evaluated the bell. Right off, he didn't like the sound. The thought of Melanie shaking this bell made his blood boil. Bells were for servants. JJ and Jonathan weren't servants. But he knew this bell would make Melanie happy. He had to remind himself that whatever Melanie wanted, Melanie got. He couldn't go back on his word, even if sixteen years had passed by since he made that promise to himself. Of course, Melanie wasn't cognizant of the oath he made to himself. She just knew since he messed up in life, he would be at her beck and call to make things right. Neither one of them understood that this would contribute to the already non-grounded foundation that would start to crumble and destroy their marriage.

Trent came in to see how things were going while Jonathan was sitting in the back, ogling at the bell. Trent asked, "What's up, man? What are you up to? What is up with that bell? Why are you staring at it?"

Jonathan answered, "What's up, Trent? This bell is for Melanie. She says when she yells out to JJ and me, it hurts. So I went to the store on my lunch break to purchase one for her."

Trent asked, "Why can't she just call you guys for whatever she wants?"

Jonathan replied, "Man, Trent, I asked her the same thing. But I tend to place my phone on silent and forget about it. So I miss her calls and texts."

Trent replied, "Ah, okay. I gotcha."

Trent walked over to his desk, asking, "Other than that, what have you been up to lately? It has been a while since we have spent time with the fellas. What say ye we go to the bar and have a couple of drinks and chat casually tonight? I won't have you out late. Melanie won't miss you being away." Trent had spoken to Melanie earlier about surprising Jonathan with a baby shower. She thought it to be a good idea and gave him Justin's number so he could invite him.

Jonathan replied, "Yes, I need a night out, even if it's for a couple of hours. Mel won't mind. She is always telling me to go out and visit with the homies. I worry about her and the baby. But JJ can manage everything while I am away. I try not to put too much on him because Mel is a pain in the ass when she is pregnant."

Trent stated, "From what you're telling me, you really need this time away. What time should I pick you up tonight?"

Jonathan answered, "Come by and pick me up about seven thirty. I will have showered and changed into some decent clothes."

Trent stated, "All right then. I am going to head on out of here and go home to relax for a while before I come for you. We are going to KD's tonight. I'll catch you later this evening."

Jonathan added, "Trent, make sure the whole crew is there. And see you later."

Trent replied, "Will do, man. See you later too."

CHAPTER 15

Jonathan finished his shift at work. He clocked out and closed the store for the day. He went straight home to give Melanie her bell. When he arrived home, Melanie was sitting up in bed with a smile on her face. He walked toward Melanie.

"What's with that smile on your face?"

Melanie replied, "I heard my husband coming through the door. Did you get my bell?"

Jonathan thought, *Damn, she went straight to asking about the bell.* Jonathan asked, "No hi, how was your day? Just straight to do you have my bell? I'm doing fine, Melanie. And yes, I have your bell."

Melanie replied, "I'm sorry about that, Jonathan. How are you? And how was your day at work today?"

Jonathan answered, "It was hectic, but I managed to pull through. I am tired as hell. Trent wants to go to KD's for drinks. Would you mind doing without me for a couple of hours?"

Melanie replied, "Sure. Go ahead and have your drinks. JJ will be here and will take care of me while you're away. He has been wonderful to me. Before he goes to school, he makes sure I have everything I need. I mostly sleep all day until it's time for one of you to come home. So it is as if no one has left me at all. I wake up just to feed the baby and use the bathroom, but then it is back to dreamland for me."

Jonathan kissed Melanie and started cleaning the house. The bathrooms needed cleaning, and the floors needed mopping. It wouldn't take Jonathan long to do. Only the kitchen and bathrooms needed mopping. He could run the vacuum over the other carpeted areas. Melanie loved smelling a freshly cleaned home. He was careful not to utilize too much bleach because the smell would make

Melanie a little dizzy and sick. After Jonathan cleaned the house, he went into the kitchen to cook dinner for Melanie and JJ. He prepared homemade lasagna, broccoli, and a salad. He knew Melanie needed her green vegetables and made sure she had them daily.

Melanie could smell the lasagna baking, and the baby began kicking her. Melanie laughed. "Calm down, little one. Daddy will be here in just a little bit to feed us." Melanie received a kick that was so hard, she sprung forward a little. Melanie thought, *Oh my, that was a hard kick. I have a granola bar to eat until the food is ready.* Melanie grabbed the bar and ripped the colored foil from around it and took a bite out of it. This calmed the little kicker inside her. She looked at the clock, saw that it was 5:30 p.m., and realized JJ's entrance through the door was late. He normally got in about 4:20 p.m. on the dot. Melanie looked at her phone for a message from him revealing his dilatory actions. There was no message. She began to grow weary, wondering about the whereabouts of her son.

Even though JJ had a disadvantage with his disabilities, Jonathan and Melanie always tried to give him leeway so he wouldn't feel detached from the world. He had friends who looked out for him. They made sure no one tried to take advantage of him. Jonathan always made sure to chat with new friends, exposing their reasons for befriending JJ. Jonathan was suspicious of everyone when it involved JJ. Melanie was more lenient with the friends he brought home. She was just happy to see him being accepted and utilizing social skills.

Another thirty minutes passed. Melanie called Jonathan. "Jonathan, it's six. JJ's not home yet, and no messages revealing why he's not home. Have you heard from him?"

Jonathan replied, "Oh, yes. His friend from school gave him a ride, and they are on their way here. They had to make a stop at the store for something. He'll be here in a few minutes, Melanie."

Melanie replied, "Okay, you guys kept that from me. I had been growing concerned. Okay, are you almost done? Your baby smells the aroma coming from the kitchen and gave me a good kick. It was so hard, I almost pole-vaulted across the room."

Jonathan laughed, stating, "Tell him or her I'm almost done and will be there in just a bit."

Melanie stated, "Okay. We'll be waiting for you."

JJ walked in through the door. "Hey, Dad. It is smelling good in here. Is Mom in her room? I got something for her I picked up from the store. That's why I'm late."

Jonathan replied, "Hey, son. Thanks. Yes, go on back there. She has been worried about you not being home on time. I forgot to tell her you would be running late. She called me, and I told her. Let her know I am close to done, and I will bring her food to her shortly. Did you pick up the sugar like I asked you to?"

JJ replied, "Yes, Dad. Here you go."

JJ started walking down the hall and looked at his watch. It was 6:05 p.m. now. He had picked up roses, a box of chocolates, and a card for his mom. He knocked on her door and waited to hear her voice, instructing him to enter.

"Come in, son. I'm dressed."

Jonathan stepped in, trying to hide her gifts. "Hey, Mom. How are you and my baby sister?"

Melanie replied, "We're fine, son. How are you, and where have you been?"

JJ replied, "I asked a friend of mine to take me to the store to pick up some things." He produced her gifts from behind his back and presented them to Melanie. "Mom, these are for you."

Melanie asked, "For me, son? Oh, thank you, son. I love roses and chocolate." Melanie opened her card and read its contents: Jonathan had even written a little note to her: "Mom, I love you, and hope you are having a baby sister for me. Love JJ."

Melanie looked up at her son with tears in her eyes. "Thank you, son. This really made my day. I love you so much."

JJ stated, "It's nothing compared to what you have done for this family, Mom. The greatest mom deserves this and more. And I appreciate you, Mom." He leaned over and gave Melanie a kiss on her cheek. JJ added, "Oh, yes, Dad says that he'll be bringing your plate in a few minutes. He's finishing the broccoli, from what I saw."

Melanie asked, "Okay, son. Would you like to sit with me for a while and watch some *Orbit Ghost Coast to Coast*?"

JJ replied, "Sure, Mom. Let me wash my hands and get out of the clothes before I hop in your bed."

Melanie was strict about sitting or lying in her bed in clothes that had been everywhere else but inside the home.

Jonathan rushed into his room, changed clothes, and washed his hands. He loved spending time with his mother and lying in his parents' comfortable bed. Since Melanie was pregnant, they had to spring for a bed that would contour to Melanie's growing body. The purchase was worth every dollar spent. Melanie was comfortable and had no problems falling asleep in this bed.

JJ went into the kitchen to ask his father if he would fix his plate and bring him a tray so he could keep his mother company. Jonathan gave his son a thumbs up and pulled another tray out for him. JJ made his way back into the room with his mother to watch cartoons with her.

Jonathan was grateful that JJ was spending time with his mother while she remained confined to their bedroom. He despised sitting in the bedroom all day. He did spend time with her, but no more than an hour just to appease her so she wouldn't feel lonely and abandoned by him. Melanie would come to sit in the living area with him in her recliner, but the recliner wasn't as comfortable as the bed. So she only stayed for about an hour and would go back to the room.

Jonathan and Melanie missed each other deeply, especially since there was little intimacy between the two. The lack of intimacy bothered Jonathan, but he knew this was in Melanie's best interest. He often thought about the sexy whispers from them both when intimacy was at an all-time high. Recalling her sexy whispers often had his member growing. He would quickly dismiss the thoughts to keep from missing her more.

Melanie had developed a strong connection to Jonathan that was unbreakable. One Jonathan couldn't fathom. Throughout the years, Melanie was able to hear things pertaining to Jonathan. She had mastered knowing what he desired. The first time it happened, Melanie walked up to Jonathan, handing him a frozen fruit bar. He ogled Melanie and asked, "Baby, how did you know?"

Melanie responded, "I'm your wife and connected to you. I hear what you want, and I bring it to you."

Jonathan had never experienced this type of love from a woman. He never had a deep connection with anyone the way he did with Melanie. He asked, "But how? I don't understand this."

She answered, "I heard a voice telling me to open the refrigerator, grab that fruit bar, and bring it to you." She did this often with different things, and he would be amazed.

Jonathan had prepared Melanie and JJ's plates. He brought Melanie her tray of food first then JJ. They both thanked him. Jonathan told them both to wait before they began eating. He rushed to the kitchen to get his food. He thought it to be a clever idea to eat with his family. There was a chair in the room right next to Melanie that he could sit in to eat. When he came back with his food, it shocked them to see him.

Melanie inquired, "You're eating with us, baby?"

Jonathan replied, "Yeah, I thought it would be nice to eat with you guys back here."

Jonathan pulled the chair closer to Melanie so that he could hold her hand while he blessed the food. After he prayed, they all began to eat. No one was talking. You could only hear Melanie and JJ making sounds from the food tasting good. Melanie grabbed Jonathan's hand and placed it on her stomach. The baby was kicking like crazy. Jonathan put his food aside and started talking to his baby.

"Hey, little baby. Are you kicking you mommy because you happy? You love Daddy's cooking?" He rubbed Melanie's belly as he was talking to the baby. The baby was kicking more from hearing his voice.

JJ had placed his hand on her stomach to feel the kicks. "Oh, wow, Mom! She's kicking up a storm."

Melanie laughed. "Yeah, I feel this all the time. You used to kick like this, too, while I would eat. Both of you have kicked my tail with no mercy. I never mind it one bit. Maybe the both of you can put your kicks to use as kickers in football and soccer." They all laughed.

Melanie took a moment to absorb her atmosphere. She felt good. She had her two favorite guys with her and her bundle of joy safely tucked away in her womb, who was enjoying hearing dad and big brother talking. The kicks calmed a little once Melanie began eating again. They all returned to their meals and watched television. Melanie had started a movie instead of watching the cartoons since Jonathan came to join them. He stayed with them until it was time to shower for his night with the fellas. He collected their plates, kissed Melanie, and told them he had to get ready. JJ stayed until the movie ended and went to his room to play video games. Melanie was satisfied and thanked them both for spending time with her.

Surprise Baby Shower

Jonathan went into the bathroom in the hall so that he could shower. He thought of how much he desperately needed to get away for a while. "Thank God Melanie understands that I could use this time to relax and unwind. I can dismiss her constant pleas and that bell ringing for me. I can't wait until Trent gets here. Uh-oh, I am a little too happy. Should I feel this happy that I'm finally getting a chance to be away from her?"

Jonathan started to feel guilty, but there was no reason for him to. Everyone needed a break every now and then. Melanie understood he needed time with friends. He quickly stopped feeling guilty, stating, "I have denied myself having a night out with any of the fellas since she has been pregnant. I'm a good husband to her and have catered to her every need, so it is okay for me to have a little fun. KD's is the right spot for what I need."

Jonathan exited the shower and walked into the bedroom to dress. He pulled out a pair of his starched dry-cleaned jeans, his Cowboys jersey, and his Dope Man tennis shoes. He sprayed on cologne and removed the rubber band that was holding his braided hair. It was 7:30 p.m. on the dot. Trent was calling Jonathan to come on out the apartment. He was pulling into the parking lot.

"Melanie, I'm leaving. Trent is out here waiting for me. Did you need anything before I leave? I won't be gone long. Just a couple of hours. You make sure you call me should you need me."

Melanie replied, "Jonathan, nothing is going to happen. I require nothing. And if I do, JJ is here for me. You go on and have fun with Trent. You more than deserve it."

Jonathan kissed Melanie and told her thanks and that he loved her. He went to JJ's room to let him know he was leaving. "JJ, I'm heading out the door, and I will be back before ten thirty tonight. Take care of your mother, son."

JJ replied, "Okay, Dad. You have fun. I can take care of Mom. We are good. I will call you if anything goes wrong. See you later."

Jonathan grabbed his wallet and headed out the door. Jonathan jumped into Trent's car. They gave each other fists dap.

Trent asked, "You ready to have some fun, Jonathan? All the guys are meeting us at KD's. I called them all, and they were anxious to hang out tonight."

Jonathan asked, "You kidding, right? The whole crew, Trent? Aw, man, I can't wait to see them all. I haven't seen them in eight months. How were you able to pull this off, man?"

Trent replied, "Well, this has been in the making. I planned this with them about a month ago. The key was getting you to come join us. We knew how busy you were with work and with Melanie, so we held off asking you to come out and kick it with us every other weekend."

Jonathan stated, "I miss you fellas. It'll be good to see them all."

Trent stated, "Well, we here. They already inside waiting for us. I got your cover charge for you."

KD's was only five minutes away from Jonathan's. Trent pulled into the parking lot and parked near the entrance.

Jonathan asked, "You sure about the cover charge? Melanie did not take all my money this pay period." They both laughed.

Trent replied, "I'm sure, man. I got this one for you."

They exited the car and walked up to the door. Jonathan noticed they walked in without paying the cover charge. When Jonathan walked in, he noticed the club looked a little different. There was décor, like a party was happening. Trent had gathered the guys together to give Jonathan a baby shower. Trent was cognizant that Melanie was on bed rest, not working and only getting a percentage of her check. He knew Jonathan was too proud to ask for any help, so he wanted to make sure Jonathan and Melanie didn't have to spend anything for the arrival of their baby.

The guys saw Jonathan and Trent enter the building and walked up to greet them. They all exchanged handshakes and hugs. Jonathan asked, "What's going on, fellas? Why is it decorated in here? What's being celebrated?"

Trent replied, "This is a baby shower just for you. I rented the place so we could have enough space. The guys brought family members to help celebrate you and Melanie's arrival. I hope this is okay. I know how proud you can be."

Deep inside, Jonathan felt love from them all. He was overjoyed, and being embarrassed was the furthest thing on his mind. This was something he and Melanie needed. Not worrying about how they would be paying for the things the baby needed.

Jonathan stated, "I'm speechless. I am going to bask and enjoy this night. Thanks, fellas." They all gave Jonathan a pat on the shoulder.

Justin walked up to Jonathan with a hug, asking, "What's up, brother?"

Jonathan replied, "Justin, they got you here too? Thanks for coming, brother."

Justin replied, "You know I wouldn't miss this. Any chance I get to hang with the fellas who are doing some good, I'm there. Is JJ with Melanie?"

Jonathan answered, "Yes, he is home taking care of his mother. He has helped tremendously with Mel."

Justin stated, "Yeah, I know. He takes care of her hand and foot."

After talking with Justin, Jonathan surveyed the room, noticing the many souls there. Majority of them Jonathan knew, and the others were strangers. But they all felt like family. They all knew Jonathan was affable, so they all introduced themselves and gave handshakes and even hugs. Jonathan needed this. He was glad that Trent extracted him from home, along with Melanie's blessing to have a night out with friends. There were a couple of bartenders and servers to cater to them. Trent's cousin owned the bar. Trent helped him out of trouble years back, and he never forgot what Trent did for him. He was more than happy to reciprocate the favor back to Trent. The beer and alcohol were on the house. There was enough food and drinks for the thirty souls in attendance. They all ate, had libations, talked, played pool and darts.

Jonathan had his mind focused on what was going on at that moment. So much male bonding. Jonathan's gifts were set to the side. There was no time to sit and admire the many gifts. Instead, they all just enjoyed each other's company. Boxes and boxes of diapers, wipes, bassinette, crib, baby bottles, rattles, baby bath and lotion, onesies, booties, baby monitor, pacifiers, mittens to keep the baby from facial scratching, washcloths, baby pillow, car seat, stroller, everything a baby would need. Some gifts were wrapped, and most were brought without wrapping, so no need to sit and waste time opening them. These were men who felt no presentation was needed. Jonathan was grateful and expressed it to all who were there.

To the crowd, he stated, "I sure am glad I came out tonight. Man, so much love here. I am so grateful for you all. There are souls here I've never had the pleasure of meeting before tonight and just want you all to know tonight was needed. I forgot how good it felt to hang out with you guys. I appreciate you all. God is good, and He showed out tonight."

Jonathan enjoyed the remainder of the night and stayed out longer than expected. He couldn't leave the guys to go back home with what they just showered upon him. He knew his son had Melanie, and if anything happened JJ would call him. Jonathan was able to make new friends and strengthen the bonds that existed between these existing and newfound friends. Numbers were exchanged between Jonathan and those brothers he had just met.

It was getting late. The clock read 11:30 p.m. to be exact. Jonathan had stayed out long enough. He made a phone call to Melanie to explain his dilatory actions for the night. Melanie didn't mind. She encouraged him to stay out as long as he needed. He never told Melanie about the shower and all the stuff she was getting for the baby. He wanted to keep this as a surprise for her. All he could think about was the look on her face when he walked through the door with all the gifts received. She would be so thrilled.

Trent had a couple of his family members load all the stuff in their trucks and SUVs after the gathering ended. Jonathan called JJ. "Son, can you come outside for a few minutes? I need you to come help with this stuff out here for your momma."

JJ replied, "Okay, Dad. I'm coming." JJ put on his shoes and went out the door to help his dad. Jonathan was already getting stuff out to haul inside the apartment. JJ asked, "Dad, where did you get all this stuff? I thought you were just going to hang out with the fellas."

Jonathan replied, "Son, I thought so too, but your uncle Trent had a surprise shower for me."

JJ turned to Trent, stating, "Wow, Uncle Trent, you really love my mom and dad. Mom will be so surprised to see all this stuff. Good thing we have an extra bedroom here."

Trent replied, "What's up, JJ? Your dad and mom are special people in my life. Everything here, they both deserve. Grab some of this stuff and help us." The two drivers who transported the items gave a hand too.

Melanie was in the living area when they entered the apartment. Melanie looked confused. She knew about the shower, but she was not expecting everything needed for a newborn. She gave Trent a big hug and kiss.

Trent asked, "How are you doing, Melanie? I hope you didn't mind me keeping him out longer than expected."

Melanie replied, "I'm well, Trent. You are good, and he needed this night out with you guys. I already knew you would be longer than expected."

Jonathan interrupted, "Melanie, look at all the stuff for the baby. Trent had me thinking we were just having drinks at KD's, but it was a shower for me. No need to worry and spend our money on anything. We have everything we need for the baby. They thought of everything."

Melanie focused her attention back to Trent, stating, "Trent, when you told me about the shower, I never thought so much would be given. You organized a daddy shower that had a great turnout for us. That was so sweet of you to do. And who are these souls helping you all?"

Trent replied, "These are my cousins who were a part of tonight's festivities. Again, I am sorry I had him out so late. We were having an enjoyable time and not paying attention to the clock."

Melanie inquired, "How are you all doing? I am Jonathan's wife. Trent, no apology necessary. He's always cooped up in this apartment taking care of me."

Trent's cousins had given Melanie a hug after she introduced herself. This was how the members of Trent's family were. They were very loving.

Melanie stated, "Oh, wow, so much love I'm feeling, and look at all this stuff. Did you all leave anything for us to purchase on our own? This is amazing. I am so grateful to you all for making this happen. Trent, please tell all who were involved how much I appreciate the gifts. This baby is set."

Trent replied, "It's all good, Melanie. But I will make sure to tell them for you."

They made at least five trips, each bringing the spoil in from the shower. They placed everything in the third bedroom, where the baby would be sleeping. After they hauled in the gifts, Melanie thanked Trent and his two cousins and gave them hugs. They said their goodbyes and were on their way home. Jonathan walked the fellas to their vehicles. Before Trent entered his car, Jonathan thanked the host again and went back into the apartment.

Melanie, full of joy, stated, "Man, this is a lot of stuff you procured and brought home, baby. Trent planned this baby shower without you having any idea, huh?"

Jonathan answered, "I had no idea, baby, but I see you were in on it too. I almost broke into tears. I never thought there was so much love for me. JJ and I will have to put the bassinette, crib, and stroller together one day when we are both home and have the time. Right now, I want to shower this sweat off me and go to bed."

Melanie stated, "Okay, Jonathan. Go on and shower. I am going to look through this stuff and see if there is anything we will need to purchase. But it looks as though they purchased everything for the baby."

Jonathan left Melanie and JJ to catalog everything.

Jonathan was tired. He undressed and jumped in the shower. He was reminiscing about tonight's festivities and jumped because the water blasted out and it was cold. He stepped back a little until it was evident that the water was warm. Jonathan thought, *It sure was good to see the fellas and have some drinks with them. Melanie looks to be well pleased with all the baby stuff. I love seeing her smile. She deserves it all. She has been standing by me all these years. She is such a beautiful soul. The smallest things and gestures in life make her smile and laugh. I would never trade her for anything on this earth.*

Since Jonathan had showered before leaving, his shower time was short. The sweat was from the stuffed atmosphere at KD's. None of the guys danced. Just fingers snapping to the music and a little swaying from side to side. He dried off and grabbed his shorts to check on Melanie and JJ.

Jonathan entered the baby's room, stating, "Melanie, come to bed. You can finish this tomorrow. JJ, go on to bed, son. You can help your momma tomorrow. We are all turning in to get some sleep."

JJ kissed and hugged his mom and dad good night. Jonathan took Melanie by the hand to lead her out of the room. If he hadn't done this, she would have still been in the room and looking at everything, filled with excitement. He put Melanie to bed and covered her with just the sheet. Melanie was now seven months pregnant, and her body temperature was at an all-time high. She was always hot and manipulating the thermostat. She would wake up in the middle of the night with her side of the bed, wet from her sweating.

Jonathan sat by Melanie, asking, "How's my baby in there?" Melanie knew what Jonathan wanted. She lay on her back so that Jonathan could talk to his baby. "Hey there, baby. How are you doing? Your daddy's best friend surprised me with a daddy shower tonight. You are set and have everything you need." The baby kicked after hearing Jonathan's voice. Jonathan stated, "Hey, hey, hey. That was a hard kick you gave your mommy. Daddy loves you, and I can't wait to see you. Good night, little angel."

Jonathan kissed Melanie's stomach. The baby wouldn't stop kicking Melanie. It was enjoying hearing Daddy's voice. Jonathan felt the kick on his lips when he kissed Melanie's stomach. Jonathan positioned himself in bed, rubbing Melanie's stomach until they both drifted into dreamworld.

Guilt Settling In

Melanie thought about the dream she had about her mother asking why she hadn't told her about Jonathan's daughter, Sena. While she was alive, she knew something had happened between Jonathan and Melanie. She just didn't know what it was that caused the break in their relationship. Melanie didn't want her mother to know what that voice had told her about Jonathan impregnating another woman. It would only prove that she was right about Jonathan, and her daughter deserved someone better. Sena's feelings were plaguing Melanie's heart and soul more as the years went by. The more she tried to push her out of her mind, the more she felt those emotions. She constantly thought about Sena, asking herself, "Why is it so difficult for me to accept this child?" She cried more and to herself.

Melanie couldn't understand God was convicting her. If Jonathan ever walked in while she was crying, she finagled her way out of divulging the truth for her sobbing. She lied, telling him it was a memory from her childhood that had her in tears. She would go as far as sharing a childhood memory. He listened to her. He knew she needed to get it out of her system. This was therapy for her. Jonathan would console her, telling her it was all in the past. She had her own family now, and they were all that mattered. When he felt she was better, he would leave the room, giving himself mental approval for a job well done. If only he knew what was really causing her heartache.

Pondering about Her Future

Melanie was getting closer to the date for them to remove the cerclage and reveal the baby's sex. She had been making her biweekly appointments as scheduled and was excited about receiving the baby's sex. She was hoping for a girl. She would have her pair, a boy and a girl. She was two months away from delivering. She thought about having to fall back into that same old routine again after she had the baby.

Melanie had been away from work her entire pregnancy. She was dreading going back to that place. She had grown tired of getting up early in the morning, sometimes having to catch the bus to and from work, listening to patients disrespect her and other coworkers with management allowing it. She was tired of hearing management tell her, "Just put yourself in their shoes and try to understand they are sickly." And her favorite was "You shouldn't take things personally."

Melanie didn't care. There was no excuse to allow disrespect to an employee, whether if they were sick, having a difficult day, or just being an asshole. These types of people needed disciplinary actions. You display misconduct, disrespect our employees, you get a warning, and if it happens a second time, you face termination from the facility. This was what a myriad of these people needed. Termed from the clinic. Let your employees know that you are on their side versus making excuses for rude people. They received new patients daily, so if they lost one, here came ten more. Melanie promised if she were able to start her own business, she wouldn't allow her employees to be subject to this type of treatment. But her main reason was that she was tired of making others' pockets fat while she was living paycheck to paycheck, barely making it. What could she do to make her money? Melanie loved writing. She drafted poems, short stories, etc. At one point in life, she started writing about her life months prior to her and Jonathan reconciling. But life happened, and she abandoned what was once one of her passions. She had safely stored away what she composed years ago, and she still had her memory to add to it once she returned to writing. Melanie promised herself as soon as she delivered her baby, she would revisit her innate talent she had abandoned. She remembered how it brought peace to her and took her away from everything that was bad in her life. Reaching deep inside, extracting those events, and transferring them onto paper brought satisfaction to Melanie. It was therapy for her. She could get a feeling and start jotting down her emotions. Sometimes, while she was writing, her words alone would make her cry. She always felt if her own words made her cry, how would they affect those who read her material? She knew it might hit home for a myriad of individuals who had walked in her shoes. This gave her motivation to start her journey again.

CHAPTER 16

Sugarcoating the Truth

Jonathan's condition was worsening. He was keeping his appointments with his rheumatologist. He kept Melanie in the dark about how often he was frequenting his doctor. He was having monthly appointments with his doctor and was informed his condition had progressed and would only get worse. He made it seem as if his appointments stretched out to every three to four months, creating the illusion that everything was okay so Melanie wouldn't raise concern or worry about him. The doctor recommended that Jonathan should stop drinking. The marijuana, he could continue. This didn't pose any threat to his health. Jonathan was weaning himself off the beer. He was drinking two 40 oz per day. After receiving the news about the need to quit, he started having one 12 oz per day. He kept this up for about two weeks. Thereafter, he was down to at least five beers per week. He kept this up for about three weeks. He could feel a difference in his body. He was energetic and wasn't feeling as sluggish and heavy any longer. Eventually, Jonathan was down to drinking less beers per week.

Melanie noticed Jonathan drinking less and less but didn't say anything in the beginning. She wanted to be sure that this wasn't just a phase he was going through, only to return to the habit. And Jonathan didn't want to get her hopes up high by telling her he was weaning himself. He didn't want to disappoint her. He had already done enough of that to her, so he kept it to himself. She was proud of him for taking control of his alcohol intake. When it became evident he was drinking less, she needed to let him know that she had been cheering for him silently.

Melanie deserted her bed, slipped into her robe, and walked into the living area to talk to him. Jonathan was watching the news and looked up at her. Their eyes both met each other's, and they smiled. He grabbed Melanie's hand, asking, "What's up, baby? You tired of being back there in the room? You came to spend a little time with me?"

Melanie replied, "Yes, it's boring back there, and I miss you. I wanted to talk to you, if you don't mind."

Melanie sat in her matching recliner. She stated, "Jonathan, I have been noticing that you have been drinking less and less. If I am correct, I haven't witnessed you drink a beer in a week now. I know it was hard for you to do because you have been drinking beer prior to our relationship. I wanted to express how proud I am to see you taking your health seriously. I know that's a hard habit to kick. May I ask what made you abandon this habit?"

Jonathan replied, "Thank you, Melanie. I was trying to keep it from you. I didn't want to get your hopes up just in case I grew weak and picked up the habit again. It wasn't as hard as I thought it would be. It was something I had to do for you and the children. I have been doing the same thing day in and day out for years. It was time for a change. If I start with this, I can break other habits that I have. I love you guys and our life. I want something better for us."

Melanie stated, "Well, I'm glad you eliminated this habit first, and whatever habit is next, I'll be there cheering for you every step of the way."

Jonathan said, "Now see, that's why I love your ass. I dig your patience, allowing me to work on me without any nagging. I was thinking you weren't noticing my endeavors to stop." Jonathan squeezed Melanie's hand. He added, "I'm glad you're stuck with me, and I'm stuck with you."

Melanie loved these talks with Jonathan. She said to Jonathan, "I've learned a lot about life. I used to see how women would try to make their men do what they wanted and how the men resisted. I promised I wouldn't be that girl. I saw how it rubbed men the wrong way."

Jonathan replied, "Well, it's good to have an understanding woman on your side." They both sat in each other's company, watching the news.

Melanie sat in her recliner longer than usual. She looked at Jonathan, wanting to ask Jonathan if there was any progress with his condition. Something was telling her that he didn't just quit drinking beer and whatever other alcohol he fancied because of her and the children. She asked, "Jonathan, has there been any improvement with your condition? Since you've stopped drinking beer, that should be a plus for you, right?"

Jonathan replied, "So far, everything is going well. I let my doctor know that I was trying to wean myself off the beer. He agreed that I should. I go back to see him soon. I haven't seen him in about three months now. He will be surprised to learn that I have decreased my alcohol intake. He wants to run some lab tests on me and have some imaging done before I see him."

Melanie replied, "Okay, good. I'm glad to hear it."

Jonathan was lying to Melanie. He was just in the office two weeks ago. The doctor had been telling him he needed to stop drinking. He was drinking other alcoholic beverages, but beer was his preferred beverage. And let us not forget about the glasses of sweet tea he loved to drink. Jonathan rarely drank water. All this played a part in what was happening to his body. Jonathan had indeed waited too late to try and keep his condition from worsening. He was hoping Melanie didn't have any more questions. So he was happy when he saw she was feeling uncomfortable and was needing her bed.

She stated, "Okay, I'm going to bed. I'm starting to feel uncomfortable." She gave Jonathan a kiss and excused herself to get back to the comfort of her bed. Once she got all comfortable and about to watch cartoons, she heard that voice. *Jonathan is lying to you.* Every time she heard that voice, it prompted her to investigate. "Tomorrow, I'm going to call his doctor and request that he calls me."

The next morning, after Jonathan left for work, Melanie called his doctor so she could discuss Jonathan's condition with him. She had to leave a message for the doctor to call her. The young lady on the other end of the phone was screening the call and asked Melanie who she was.

Melanie replied, "I'm his wife, Melanie Ashley."

The young lady said to Melanie, "I'm not showing you listed as his PHI, ma'am. There is limited information we can disclose to you."

Melanie asked, "Not his PHI? There must be a mistake. The doctor has spoken to me in the past about Jonathan. Will you just have the doctor call me?"

The young lady replied, "Yes, ma'am. I'll let the doctor know to call you."

The lines released. "I know he didn't remove me from being his PHI. I wonder if he is lying about the children and I being the main reason he has stopped drinking. He wouldn't do that to me. I know him better than that. I'll just wait for the doctor to call me."

Melanie made a quick bite to eat and placed herself in the bed to watch television. Melanie was familiar with the clinic scene and knew it would take a while for Dr. Henry to call her back. If the doctor was in clinic, he was visiting with patients and would only be able to return calls in between seeing his patients. No telling the amount of people calling him and requesting a call back. Since she worked for a clinic, she knew sometimes the doctors wouldn't return calls for days at a time. She was hoping this wouldn't be the case. She was hopeful that he would call her back no later than this afternoon. After she finished eating, she started to feel sleepy. This was routine for her. She tried to fight the sleepiness so that she would be able to hear the phone ring just in case the doctor called. Melanie could sleep through noise that wasn't overwhelmingly loud. A ringing phone was easy to sleep through for Melanie. She sat up in the bed, flipping through the channels and committing herself to not slip into sleep. As hard as she tried, she could fight no more. She gave in and laid her body down and drifted off quickly.

Ringggggg went the phone. As soon as she drifted, the phone rang, and Melanie quickly grabbed her phone and answered, "Hello."

There was a familiar voice on the other end of the phone. "Melanie, this is Dr. Henry. How are you this afternoon?"

Melanie answered, "Hi, Dr. Henry. I'm fine."

Dr. Henry stated, "Good. How can I help you? Is Jonathan doing okay?"

Melanie replied, "Well, Dr. Henry, that's why I'm calling. I am concerned about Jonathan. I have noticed that he has stopped drinking alcohol and wanted to know if it had anything to do with his arthritis? And I want to know if his condition has improved. Or has it worsened?"

Dr. Henry answered, "I'm sorry, Melanie, but I can't discuss his health problems with you. You're not listed as his PHI."

Melanie had a confused look on her face. She asked, "I'm not listed as his PHI? I signed the papers during a visit designating me as his PHI."

Dr. Henry rebutted, "Yes, you did, but Jonathan has reversed his decision and opted to remove you as his PHI. Melanie, hear me out. My guess is that Jonathan felt that your issues with your pregnancy are enough for you to focus on. You will need to discuss his health problems with him. I can tell you that if he has stopped drinking any alcohol, it is a good thing. Beer and alcohol can cause more damage and worsen his condition."

Melanie stated, "Okay, Dr. Henry. Thank you for returning my call. I'll speak with Jonathan." Melanie thought, *I can't believe him. Taking me off as his PHI. What was he thinking? Okay. He wants to play this game with me. I won't say a word to him. I will just remain like I am clueless to him removing me. The nerve of him. If he doesn't want me to know anything, then that is how it will be. I will no longer show any concern about him. I'll let him deal with it on his own.* Melanie meant what she said.

What a Lovely Girl

It was 4:20 p.m. and time for JJ to enter the apartment. He was outside with his soon-to-be girlfriend, Camie, preparing her to meet Melanie. Her name was Camille, but he called her Camie for short. Jonathan warned her, "My mom is pregnant and on bed rest. You'll have to meet her in her bedroom. Is that okay?"

Camie replied, "Okay. Are you sure it is okay for me to come to her bedroom? I can wait in the living area while you talk to her."

Melanie could hear voices in the apartment. She asked, "JJ, is that you, son? Is there someone with you?"

JJ replied, "Hold on, Mom. I'm coming to you." JJ placed his backpack in his room and walked down the hall to Melanie's room. He was nervous about her meeting his potential girlfriend, especially since he never brought one home to introduce to his parents. Jonathan gave a light tap on the door.

Melanie stated, "Come in, son."

Jonathan went to her side of the bed to give her a hug and kiss. He asked, "How are you doing? Are you feeling all right?"

Melanie replied, "I'm good. Now who's in my house?"

JJ answered, "Dang, Mom. No hello, son, how are you, and how was school? Just straight to who's in my house?"

Melanie replied, "Boy, don't play with me. Who's here?"

JJ answered, "It's a girl I want you to meet, Mom. She is a friend, but I like and have feelings for her. We both like each other. Would you mind meeting her? May I bring her here, or would you want to meet her in the living area?"

Melanie asked, "You have a girlfriend, son? How long have you had a girlfriend?"

JJ replied, "Yes, I guess you can kind of say I do, Mom. I haven't asked her on any dates just yet. Sort of a new thing."

Melanie stated, "Okay, well, let me get up and meet her in the living area. Tell her I will be right there. Okay?"

JJ replied, "Okay, Mom. See you in a few."

Melanie thought, *My son has a girlfriend. Well, he is maturing, and it was just a matter of time before he would bring one home for me to meet. I'll have to talk to him after she leaves.*

Melanie grabbed her robe and slippers and waddled down the hall. When she turned the corner, she saw the two of them sitting on the couch, engaged in conversation. She was of average size with shoulder-length hair and a light-skinned complexion. Melanie couldn't see her face because their backs were facing her. Once she was able to look at her face-to-face, Melanie was pleased at her son's choice.

"Oh, my son. She is beautiful. How are you doing, sweetie? I'm Melanie, JJ's mother."

Camille rose from the couch. "Hi, ma'am. I am Camille. It is so nice to meet you. You have a lovely apartment here. I see you are expecting. When are you due, if I may ask?"

Melanie was impressed with her. She was using *ma'am* and *if I may*. Melanie answered, "I'm due toward the end of next month. I have about one and a half months to go."

Camille stated, "Okay, an April baby. My sister is an April baby. She's the baby in the bunch."

Melanie asked, "How many of you are in your family? If you don't mind my prying."

Camille answered, "I don't mind at all. There are four of us. I have two older brothers. One is still in high school, graduating this year, and the other is in college. My parents are divorced and have been for about two years now."

Melanie asked, "Oh, I'm so sorry about that. Is all well with your parents?"

Camille replied, "Yes, ma'am. They are both fine with it. It was mutual between the two of them. They get along like best friends now. They coparent, and it works out for us all."

Melanie didn't have to ask her to tell her about herself. She was doing an excellent job just opening up to her. Melanie asked, "Are you attending the same school as JJ?"

Camille replied, "Yes, I am. We take classes together, and I have been tutoring him. Your son is an amazing person. He is so sweet and kind. I have never met anyone like JJ. Those other boys are disrespectful at school, calling us girls all types of names when we show we're not interested in them. JJ is different. He holds and opens the doors for us and always says ladies first. All the girls dig that about him."

Melanie agreed, "Yes, we have always taught him to be a gentleman to the ladies. Happy to hear that you have witnessed this. Sounds like we taught him well. Camille, would you like to stay for dinner? JJ's father will be home soon and will be cooking dinner for us."

Before Camille could answer, JJ interrupted, "Mom, Dad called and said he would be late. I will be cooking dinner for us. He said he tried to call you, but you didn't answer him."

Camille answered Melanie, "Yes, ma'am. I would love to stay and have dinner with you all. Let me call my mother and let her know."

While Camille called her mother, Melanie looked at her phone, and sure enough, she missed his call. He called her while she was on the phone with Dr. Henry. Melanie asked JJ, "Okay, son. So what are you cooking for us?"

JJ replied, "Mom, let me surprise you guys, okay?" It'll be something good for my baby sister."

Melanie stated, "Sure, son. Go on and surprise us both."

Camille had finished her phone call to her mother. "My mom says it's okay for me to have dinner with you all. When I told her I was having dinner with JJ, she said yes with no hesitation. She is fond of JJ."

Melanie stated, "Wonderful. JJ, go ahead and start cooking, son, while Camille and I talk. So your mother has met my son? I hope he was well behaved meeting her."

Camille replied, "Yes, ma'am. They met last week. His gentleman gestures impressed my mother."

Melanie stated, "Well, good to hear. Now that you both have met each other's parents, it would be nice if we all sit and have dinner one day. I would love to meet your parents."

JJ left the living area, making his way to the kitchen. He opened the refrigerator to retrieve the pork chops Jonathan had thawed overnight. He opened the pack, rinsed, and seasoned them. JJ boiled water for his iced tea. After putting the pot on the stove, he looked in the fridge for vegetables to cook. He saw that there was asparagus, corn on the cob, and fresh green beans. He looked in the pantry and saw canned vegetables and boxes of macaroni and cheese. He loved mac and cheese. He decided that along with the pork chops, he would steam the asparagus, boil thee corn, and make the mac and cheese for dinner. He sat the items on the kitchen counter. He started boiling the corn and would wait until the pork chops were halfway done before cooking his vegetables.

Melanie and Camille were getting along fine while JJ was busy in the kitchen. There was no silence the whole time JJ was in the kitchen. They were like schoolgirls, talking about this and that. Melanie was intrigued by Camille. They had an instant connection. Melanie was enjoying the vibes she was feeling from Camille. She thought, *What a lovely girl.*

After the water boiled, JJ dropped the tea bags in and allowed them to steep for a while. He made his way back into the living area. Melanie was showing Camille family photos. Jonathan asked, "How you all doing? Mom, no! Not the pictures!"

Melanie stated, "Oh, son, hush. These pictures are harmless. I am just showing her a photo or two. Why are you here and not in the kitchen cooking?"

JJ replied, "Well, I'm letting the seasoning marinade into the pork chops before cooking them. They should be ready to cook in a little bit. I'll sit here and make sure you are not sharing anything incriminating about me to Camille."

They all laughed. Camille was such a joy to Melanie. She had not laughed or had fun like this in months. Melanie thought, *This girl is too good to be true. She is an open book. Wonder if there is something that would change my whole perception about her.* Melanie dismissed the idea and basked in the moment. After they shared laughs, JJ noticed that twenty minutes had passed. He excused himself and made his way back into the kitchen.

The pork chops were ready for frying. He pulled out a skillet, poured olive oil into it, and turned the burner on to heat the oil. He added a nuance of seasoning to the pork chops on both sides. He had a paper bag with flour in it, ready to shake and coat the pork chops. He whipped out his phone to play music while he cooked. The oil was at the desired frying temperature, so he placed them in the frying pan. He grabbed something to snack on while he prepared the tea. He made sure to add the right amount of sugar and placed the pitcher of tea in the freezer. After the chops fried on one side, he put the asparagus in a pot to steam and boiled water for the mac and cheese. He waited until he turned the chops over for the opposite side to brown before starting the mac and cheese. JJ thought, *I hope my cooking will leave an impressionable mark on Camille. I really like her.*

Camille was the only girl at school who looked at JJ in a unique way. She knew he was challenged, but she also knew he worked hard and put forth an effort in his education. Unlike the other girls, she wanted more than just friendship with him. Camille was one of the good girls they would take home to mom and dad. She was not into "fitting in," surrounding herself with fake friends and cliques. Her parents taught her being part of a big circle produced fake friends. They also encouraged having compassion and being kind to others. High school was just a popularity facility, and she didn't buy into it. Camille had less than a handful of friends, and she was fine with it. She had been approached by the different girls wanting to induct her into their group. She politely dismissed their invitations to join.

Running into an Old Pal

Jonathan was ending his shift at work. He had to lock the store after the employees were all gone. Trent needed him to lock up because the shift assistant put in his two weeks' notice. So instead of getting off at 3:00 p.m., he was getting off at 5:00 p.m. Jonathan was tired and had a blunt waiting for him in the car. He entered the car, picked up the blunt, and lit it. He took a long drag from it, held it for a while, and exhaled the smoke. He cranked the car and was on his way home. Jonathan was about five minutes away when he looked in the rearview mirror and saw the red and blue lights behind him. Jonathan put the blunt out and had air freshener for occasions like this. He sprayed the air freshener in the vents and turned on the air. He had a bottle of cologne in the pocket of the driver's side door and sprayed himself with it.

The officer ran the plates and saw the name Jonathan Taylor. He wondered, *Is this the same Jonathan I know? I haven't seen him in years.* He exited his patrol unit and walked up to the car about ten minutes later.

Jonathan sat patiently until he saw the officer approaching his car. It felt like forever to Jonathan. Jonathan observed the officer as he was walking to the car. He thought, *This cat looks familiar. Is that Chauncey?*

The officer approached the car. "How you doing, sir? You know why I stopped you?"

Jonathan looked up because he recognized the voice. It was indeed his old high school friend. Jonathan asked, "Chauncey Phillips, is that you? What's up, man?" Jonathan opened the door to exit his car.

Chauncey yelled, "Don't step out of the car!" It was with aggression. But he laughed, stating, "Just kidding. I thought that was you."

Jonathan stepped out of the car while they both laughed and gave each other a hug. Jonathan scanned his old buddy, stating, "I haven't seen you in years. Where you been?"

Chauncey replied, "After we graduated, I went up north trying to get some business ventures started, but it didn't work out for me. I came back here and married Chelsea Johnson. We have four kids, two boys and two girls. But we are recently divorced now."

Jonathan asked, "For real, man? You two got married? I remember Chelsea. How is she?"

Chauncey replied, "She doing good. How about you? You single or what?"

Jonathan answered, "No, I'm married, man. I have a teen-aged son and one on the way late next month."

Chauncy stated, "That's good, man. Good to hear. We should catch up sometimes. Let me give you my phone number."

Jonathan stated, "Yeah, man, sure. I would love to chop it up with you. What's your number? I'll program it into my phone." They exchanged numbers. The two gave fist dap and got back into their cars.

Jonathan stated, "Okay. Talk to you soon."

Jonathan rolled up the window and drove home. He thought, *Old Chauncey. Been a long time. Glad we crossed paths.* Jonathan was home and pulled into the property. He exited the car and walked up to the door. When Jonathan opened the door, the aroma of JJ's cooking hit him strongly. He walked into the kitchen and saw JJ hard at work preparing dinner.

Jonathan stated, "My son got it smelling good in here. What's up, son? How are you?"

JJ smiled and replied, "Hey, Dad. I am good. How was work?"

Jonathan answered, "It was good, son. One of the workers' last day was today, so I had to close. I'll be closing for the next two weeks until we hire a replacement to train."

JJ stated, "Dad, I brought a friend home. It's a girl. I like her a lot, but we're not officially dating. She's in the living area talking with Mom."

Jonathan asked, "Okay, son. So you brought someone home finally, huh? I've always wondered when I would meet a gal you fancied. Is she a looker, son?"

JJ answered, "I'll just say this, Dad. She's the best when it comes to character and heart."

Jonathan stated, "Okay, I will go in to meet her. I knew there was a reason you were questioning me that day about your mother and me. I'll be right back."

Jonathan walked into the living area. Melanie was in good spirits and enjoying her conversation with Camille. Jonathan thought, *Melanie hasn't laughed like this nor been this happy in a long time.* He loathed interrupting their conversation but did so. "Hello, ladies. And who is this beautiful young lady sitting in our home?"

Camille again rose from the couch. "Hi, sir. I'm Camille, a friend of JJ from school."

Jonathan reciprocated, "Camille, it is nice to meet a friend of JJ's." Jonathan walked over to Melanie and kissed her. "Hey, baby. How are you and my little one?"

Melanie replied with little interest, "We're fine." Jonathan tried to kiss Melanie. She gave him a quick peck and immediately continued her discussion with Camille. Jonathan could sense something was wrong. He thought, *Wonder what I did this time? Well, once company is gone, I'll find out why she's acting funny. She usually is happy to see me ready for me to land one on her.*

Jonathan excused himself from their presence. He wanted to have a shower before JJ finished dinner. Before doing so, he went back into the kitchen. "Son, Camille is a special young lady. She has your mother lit up in the living room. I haven't seen your mother this happy in a long time."

JJ stated, "Thanks, Dad. No one comes around to visit Mom. She seems lonely, Dad, so I figured she needed some girl-on-girl conversing for a change."

Jonathan added, "You did good, son. Let me ask you something. Was your mother irritated at all when you came home from school?"

JJ answered, "No, Dad. Well, on second thought, she was irritated that someone was in the apartment, but she dismissed it after she found out I had a friend for her to meet. Why do you ask?"

Jonathan replied, "It's nothing, son. Just concerned about her. What's the ETA on dinner?"

JJ responded, "We should be eating in about twenty minutes."

Jonathan said, "Okay. I'm jumping in the shower and will be done by then."

JJ stopped his dad. "Dad, I did tell you that Camille is just a friend, right? Nothing serious."

Jonathan replied, "Whatever you say, son." Jonathan exited the kitchen. JJ didn't want his dad to assume anything until he and Camille had an understanding about what they meant to each other.

Jonathan went to the bedroom and undressed. He retrieved his clothes from the drawers and laid them across the bed. He turned on the shower and waited two minutes to give the hot water a chance to activate. He gathered his towels, soap, and shampoo. He jumped in the shower and allowed the water to run all over his body. He couldn't get Melanie off his mind. The way Melanie was acting toward him didn't sit right with him. He searched his mind trying to find answers, but there were none. "I hope her reason for speaking to me that way is due to her growing tired of the pregnancy and wanting this last stage to be over sooner than later. Whatever it is, I'll try to make it better as I always do."

Jonathan was in the shower for about twenty minutes. He knew JJ had to set the table and fix the plates, so he had an extra five minutes or so to get himself together. He dressed, combed his hair, and even freshened his breath. He could now join his son, his wife, and JJ's friend. Jonathan chose to be with his son. He'd let Melanie enjoy her time talking to Camille.

Jonathan walked back into the kitchen. "Son, you need your old man to help you?"

JJ replied, "Oh, so you do realize you're an old man now, huh, Dad?" They both laughed. JJ requested, "Dad, would you get the glasses for me? I already have our food sitting at the table for us to eat."

Jonathan replied, "Sure, son. I can do that for you. Would you need me to add ice to these glasses?"

JJ answered, "Yes, Dad, if you don't mind."

Jonathan grabbed the glasses and added ice to them. Three ice cubes to each glass. He placed the glasses on the table. He added an extra glass for Melanie. She always wanted water with her meals and any other available beverage. It was time for JJ to move the party of two to the dining area.

JJ went into the living area. "Okay, guys. We are ready to eat now." Jonathan went to Melanie to help her up off the couch. Melanie clenched on to his arm with an unusual force. He knew she was beyond irritated. She was furious with him.

"Melanie, is everything all right with you, baby? Is there something wrong?"

Melanie replied, "No, there's nothing wrong!" She released his arm and walked to the dining room. JJ and Camille didn't witness her actions. Jonathan decided to play it cool the remainder of the evening. He knew in the past, when she was this way, to leave her alone and let her initiate talking to him. He didn't want to ruin dinner in front of company.

Jonathan pulled Melanie's chair back so she could sit to eat, and so had JJ done with Camille's chair. JJ asked that everyone hold hands so that he could bless the food. After grace, they all began eating.

Camille with surprise stated, "Oh my goodness JJ! This is incredibly good. You left this part out while we were getting to know each other." She couldn't help herself as she spoke with a mouthful of food. JJ, Jonathan, and Melanie all laughed a little.

JJ stated, "Thank you, Camille."

Melanie interrupted, "Camille, I'm glad my son's cooking is to your liking. His father and I both had our hands in showing him how to cook."

Camille stated, "So this is a home full of people who can cook? I can cook, but not like this. When mom works late I cook and dad comes by to help me. He feels he must do extra for us kids because of the divorce."

Jonathan looked at Camille. "They're divorced? I'm sorry to hear that."

Camille answered, "Oh no, Mr. Taylor, no need to be sorry. It was mutual between the two of them, and us kids were all fine with it. We knew it was coming before they announced it to us. So we prepared ourselves. It was best for everyone. And they get along so well now."

JJ shifted the attention from Camille. "Looks like you all are almost done with your food. Does anyone want seconds? There's plenty to go around the table."

They all answered no, except for Melanie. She stated, "Son, your mom is eating for two, and this baby is still hungry. My appetite has just increased since it's close to delivery."

Jonathan insisted, "Let me get your mother's food, son. You sit down and enjoy your company. You have done enough for the evening. Mel, would you like seconds of everything JJ cooked?"

Melanie replied, "Yes, we sure do."

Jonathan went into the kitchen and carefully portioned the food on her plate. Whenever she wanted seconds, it was a small amount. Jonathan thought, *She's still mad at me. I'm lost and don't know what I did to make her feel this way.* Jonathan returned with her plate and placed it before her. "There you go, baby." He sat back down at the table to continue eating the little food he had remaining.

JJ and Camille had the same amount of food on their plates and were nearly done. After the last morsel, JJ picked up their plates and returned them to the kitchen. Melanie was still eating. JJ returned and was about to sit back down next to Camille.

Jonathan stated, "JJ, why don't you take Camille in the living area while I sit with your mom until she's done? I'll take her plate."

JJ replied, "Okay, Dad. Come on, Camille. Let us go watch television until the old folks are done and join us."

Melanie and Jonathan both replied jokingly, "Watch it, son." They all laughed.

JJ and Camille retreated to the living area. Jonathan reached for Melanie's hand, but she didn't give her hand to him. So he gently took her hand and asked, "Mel, what's wrong, baby. Did I do or say anything? Tell me, what did I do?"

Melanie replied, "Nothing, Jonathan. You didn't do anything. I'm just off today and not myself, is all."

Jonathan stated, "Okay, you're a little off and not yourself to only me. I am the only one in the house receiving this energy from you. I know you better than you think. Tell me what's wrong with you."

Melanie replied, "Jonathan, I said it's nothing, okay? So please drop it."

Jonathan knew when Melanie said to drop it, she meant exactly that. Drop it. Jonathan responded, "Okay, baby. I will drop it. If you want to talk, I am here. Can I ask how my baby is doing? Any Braxton-Hicks yet?"

Melanie replied, "The baby is doing fine. Just extra hungry. No Braxton-Hicks yet. Just kicking." Melanie was taking her last bite and said, "Okay, I am full and ready to go back to the living area."

Jonathan helped Melanie up out of her chair and walked her to the living area.

Camille noticed it was getting late and needed to be on her way home. When Mel and Jonathan entered the living area, JJ announced, "Mom, Dad, I need to get Camille home. I'll walk her."

Melanie asked, "Is everything okay, Camille?"

Camille answered, "Yes, ma'am. Mom needs me to watch my baby sister. She is going out to have a night out with her girlfriends. They do this every Friday. They start out with dinner at Gina's, and afterward, they move the party to Elaine's bar. She has been doing this since the divorce, and it makes her happy. But every once in a while, she grows sad about a friend she lost when she was a teenager. She never goes into details about it. Just always saying she wished she could have helped save her friend. But anyways, Mr. and Ms. Taylor, it was nice meeting the both of you. I enjoyed myself. May I have dinner with you guys again?"

Melanie replied, "You are welcome here any time. Jonathan, please take them to Camille's home. I don't want them out this late walking."

Jonathan stated, "Sure thing, Melanie. Are you all ready?"

Camille and JJ both replied, "Yes." They all went out the door, leaving Melanie alone.

Melanie thought, *What a lovely, beautiful girl. I am impressed. There's something familiar about her, and I just can't put my finger on it.*

Melanie didn't put too much thought into it and dismissed it. She was tired and was ready to take her shower and jump into bed. Jonathan always helped her to get in the shower, but she thought she would be able to manage it on her own. She waddled to the bedroom and started the shower.

"Mr. Taylor, turn left here. My house is the second one to the right."

Jonathan pulled up to the house. The two kids exited the car. JJ wanted to walk her to the door. Jonathan thought, *My son, a gentleman. That is the way you do it, son. My boy.* Jonathan could hear Camille's mother thanking JJ for seeing her to the door. JJ said good night and ran back to the car.

"Okay, Dad. Let us get back home to Mom."

Jonathan stated, "Okay, son. We need to dip back home."

JJ laughed loudly, saying, "You know that makes you sound extremely old, right? No one says that."

Jonathan looked at JJ, asking, "So what are they saying now, son? Hip me to the hip talk."

JJ laughed harder, stating, "Dad, give up and just drive home."

Jonathan drove off, and they were on their way back to Melanie.

Mom Finally Dating

Chelsea asked, "Camille, did you enjoy yourself? How was his mother? Was she nosy asking a bunch of questions? Is she a good cook?"

Camille replied, "I had fun, Mom. I really enjoyed myself. JJ cooked the food, not his mother. He is a great cook, Mom. His mother was just the opposite. Not too many questions. She showed me family photos of them. She is expecting another baby toward the end of April. She is a genuinely nice lady. I know she adores me."

Chelsea stated, "Well, who wouldn't adore my baby? You have adorable written all over your face. She couldn't help but adore you. Baby, help me with my zipper, please." Camille helped her mother zip her dress. "Hand me those shoes out the closet. The black ones with the heels, please."

Camille went into the closet, pulled out her mother's shoes, and handed them to her. Camille wondered, *This isn't her usual attire for dinner and drinks with the girls.*

Chelsea stated, "Thank you, baby. I won't be out too late."

Camille asked, "Mom, where are you going, and with whom?"

Chelsea was trying to avoid this question by rushing out the door. She took a deep breath and replied, "Baby, I met someone, and he's taking me to dinner, and we're going to listen to some music."

Camille asked, "Really? That is great, Mom. I have been wondering when you were going to start dating. It has been a while since you and Dad divorced. You deserve to be happy."

Chelsea looked at her and asked, "You mean that, baby? Because I was so scared to tell you kids about him. I thought you would all be against it. My happiness, that is."

Camille replied, "Mom, Dad has someone. It is time you moved on with a mate of your own. You deserve it. You need more in your life than just taking care of us kids and working. Go out and have an enjoyable time. In fact, I order you to do so."

Chelsea embraced Camille, stating, "Thank you, baby. You just don't know how much I needed to hear those words. I love you so much. I'll be back home before midnight."

Chelsea kissed her daughter and went to answer the knock on the door. She stopped and asked, "Would you like to meet him?"

Camille replied, "No, Mom. You get to know him first before introducing him to us. Go ahead. I'll meet him next time."

Chelsea thanked her daughter and answered the door. "Are you ready, my queen?"

Mesmerized by this tall, chestnut-eyed Black male, she replied, "I sure am."

He held his arm out, and Chelsea latched on to it. They walked to his car. He opened the door and closed it for her. She reached over to unlock the door for him. He noticed this and smiled to himself. Camille locked the door behind them and went to check on her baby sister. Little Jasmine was fast asleep. JJ and his father made it home, entering the apartment. Jonathan called out to Mel, "Melanie, baby. JJ and I are back. Where are you?"

Melanie yelled out, "I'm in the bedroom, about to get in the shower!"

Jonathan rushed to the bedroom. "Melanie, you know I always help you in the shower. Your balance is off, and you may harm yourself and the baby. Come on, let me help you."

Melanie was being spiteful toward him still, wanting him to know that she didn't need him and that she could do this all by herself. But deep down inside, she knew Jonathan was right. One small slipup and this could cost her and their baby's life. She always wore her heart on her shoulder when it came to Jonathan because she felt he knew better. He knew who she was in life, so he of all people should know to never do anything to hurt or make her feel betrayed. Silence was her worst revenge against him.

Jonathan hated when Melanie would shut him out and not say anything to him. All the begging and pleading only made it worse. When she was ready to talk, she would open on her own.

She lied, stating, "Well, I just wanted to see if I could do this on my own. But I am ready to get in now. Can you wash my back for me? I can't reach at all back there."

Jonathan replied, "Sure. Anything for you, Mel. Is that all you need washing? You need your legs and feet washed too?"

Melanie replied, "Yes, please." Melanie was getting bigger, and it was harder for her to reach or pull her feet toward her to wash. She was so thankful that Jonathan was around to help her with everything while she was in this condition. So she decided to let go of her anger toward him about removing her as his PHI.

Learning the Baby's Sex

Melanie was now eight and a half months pregnant. They were on their way to her biweekly appointment to see her doctor. This visit was to determine when the doctor would be removing the stitch from Melanie cervix since she was getting closer to her due date and to learn the baby's sex. Melanie wondered if she wanted the baby's gender disclosed to her. She was indecisive while sitting in the room, waiting for the doctor to see her.

"Jonathan, I am unsure if I want to know the sex of our baby. Do you want to know?"

Jonathan answered, "Yes, I would like to know. If you are not ready, it is cool. She can tell me, and I will keep it to myself. JJ wants to know. You know he has been speaking a baby sister into existence. He wants to know if he is right. I will make sure to tell him to keep it to himself."

Melanie agreed, "Okay. That is how I want it. I want to be surprised."

Dr. Gharma walked into the room and greeted them both. She stated, "Melanie, you look like you're ready to pop. Jonathan, I know you are anxiously ready for this baby to be born. Has Melanie been having you do more now that she's approaching nine months?"

Jonathan replied, "Yes, she has, Dr. Gharma. She has been taking advantage of this bell I bought for her. I only bought it because she says it hurts for her to yell out for someone to come help her."

Dr. Gharma laughed, stating, "You know, as crazy as it sounds, she's right. I have had a few pregnant women tell me yelling would cause pain in the abdominal area, and it manipulates their breath. I hope you weren't thinking she had an ulterior motive for wanting it. My bedridden patients, husbands were thinking they wanted the bell just to get on their nerves and to see how fast they would respond to the rings."

Jonathan was embarrassed because he was thinking just what the other husbands were thinking. He falsely replied, "No, Doctor. I did not think that at all. I just thought she wanted it because she has this thing about wanting unnecessary stuff, cluttering up the apartment. Our son helps. He hears the bell, and he will sometimes respond before me. So we both share with taking care of Melanie." Melanie thought to herself, "You telling an L.I.E. You liar. You were thinking just what she said."

Dr. Gharma stated, "Well, that's good to hear. Melanie, are you ready to have your sonogram and eager to know the sex of the baby?"

Melanie replied, "Yes. Ready for the sonogram, but I prefer to not know the sex of the baby. Jonathan would like to know. You can tell him."

Dr. Gharma stated, "Okay, so let us get started. Go ahead and place your legs in the stirrups so we can look at the stitches and cervix." The doctor swabbed Melanie and placed the samples on a sliding glass. She examined the stitch and cervix. Melanie hated the swabbing. She could feel it, and it felt awkward every time she had to have it done. "Okay, Melanie. Everything looks good. We will remove the stitches in two weeks, which would be next month. Now we can conduct the sonogram."

Dr. Gharma rubbed the cold gel onto Melanie's stomach. Then she placed the transducer lubricated with gel across Melanie's abdomen. She turned the monitor toward the expecting parents so they could see the baby. The baby could see a light and turned, looking directly at the light's direction while sucking its thumb.

Melanie laughed, saying, "Oh my god! The baby is looking at us, peeking in there. Look, Jonathan. The baby is sucking on its thumb."

Jonathan replied, "Hey, little one. Daddy is eager to see and meet you."

Dr. Gharma stated, "Okay, guys. Here are some pictures for you. And do you have any questions for me?"

The couple replied, "No, ma'am."

Dr. Gharma stated, "Okay, I will have my staff set up the appointment to remove the stitches. I want you here on April 15 at nine. Jonathan, here is the sonogram of the baby that tells the gender."

Melanie and Jonathan both stated, "Yes, ma'am. We will be here."

Dr. Gharma stated, "Great, I'll see you two on April 15. You all take care."

They both stated, "Okay."

Jonathan led his wife to the waiting room. They could hear the patients saying how big Melanie was and that she was ready to pop. Melanie knew the chitchat was of no harm. This was what's expected at an OB-GYN clinic. It seems pregnant women were at their happiest, most vulnerable, and caring in this condition. Pregnancy and childbirth, the two subjects women loved to compare notes with each other. For them, this was their favorite pastime while at the doctor's office. They all thought they had stories that would outweigh the other. But Melanie's condition would be the winner. If they only knew her story while she was in this condition.

Jonathan reached for Melanie's hand to get in the elevator. Jonathan asked, "Melanie, are you hungry? Would you like to have some Chinese food?"

Melanie eyes bucked. She replied, "Chinese food! How did you know I was thinking Chinese? Yes, I would love to have Chinese. I haven't had any in a while. Can we please go sit and eat at the buffet instead of paying to go? I want to eat a different variety of foods."

Jonathan replied, "Okay, yes. We can sit and eat this time."

Jonathan drove Melanie to her favorite Chinese restaurant, the Happy Palace Buffet. It was right around the corner from their apartment. When they arrived, Melanie opened the car door herself to begin her journey into the restaurant. Jonathan normally opened her door and helped her, but Melanie was too excited to wait.

"Melanie, wait a minute. Calm down, baby. Let me help you out the car. You must be anxious and hungry. That food ain't going nowhere." Jonathan laughed, and so did Melanie.

She stated, "I'm sorry, baby. I know I am a little excited to be here. I have missed this place. I do require your assistance out of the car, please."

Jonathan rushed to her side and let out a loud cry. "Ohhhhh god!"

Melanie asked with concern, "Baby, what's wrong? Are you okay? Did you hurt yourself?"

Jonathan answered, "It's nothing, baby. I just came down a little hard on my leg trying to get to you. I'm okay."

Melanie stated, "Are you sure you're okay? We can weigh our food and go home. It's no bother, baby."

Jonathan reassured her, "No, Melanie. I want you to sit and enjoy yourself. You need this. You've been a prisoner in that apartment for over eight months. I am fine. Come on, we will go inside and eat."

Melanie stated, "Okay, Jonathan. Thank you."

They walked inside and paid for two adults. The staff was surprised to see Melanie was pregnant. They all circled around her, wanting to know why she hadn't been there. She explained to them that she was having a difficult pregnancy and was placed on bed rest. Melanie was a faithful customer. She ate there three to four times per week before she became pregnant. After she was showered with concern from the staff, they were able to get their plates and fill them with their choice of foods. The baby started kicking Melanie, letting her know the food she smelled was to her liking. Melanie ate at least three times before admitting she was full and couldn't eat another bite. Once it was evident she was done, Jonathan helped Melanie up from her chair.

Jonathan stated, "Mel, I told you not to eat too much. You ate too much food in here. We could have weighed the remainder of your food and brought it home."

Melanie stated, "Jonathan, now you know in less than two hours, I'll be hungry again. So I ate enough so that I wouldn't feel the urge to eat until dinner. What are you cooking?"

Jonathan replied, "I'm going to have to rethink my menu. You had too much to eat. More than likely, it will be something not fried. Maybe spaghetti or lasagna with a salad."

Melanie stated, "Oh, yes. Either one of those sounds good, and the side too. You need to stop at the store for the ingredients?"

Jonathan replied, "No, Melanie, everything I need is at home."

Melanie, with disappointment, stated, "Darn it!"

Jonathan asked, "Why you say darn it, Mel? Did you need something from the store?"

Melanie replied, "No. I have just been in the house for so long. It felt good to sit around others, sharing my pregnancy. I never get a chance to share my pregnancy with the world."

Jonathan commented, "Baby, you've had enough awws for today. I noticed how much you enjoyed being the center of attention at the restaurant. Tell you what, next time I go to the store for just a quick in and out, I will take you with me. That way, you won't be on your feet too long and start to tire out and hurt. Okay?"

Melanie answered, "Okay, sure, Jonathan. Thank you."

It was 1:00 p.m. when they returned home. Melanie went into her room to change her clothes, and Jonathan went into the kitchen to start dinner. Jonathan remembered he had thawed frozen catfish, and it needed cooking.

Jonathan asked, "Melanie, would you instead like to have some fried catfish, corn on the cob, baby carrots, and broccoli?"

Melanie replied, "Oh, yes. That sounds good. I would love catfish. It's been a while since we've had catfish."

Jonathan stated, "Good thing I bought them when JJ and I went shopping. You go on and change out of those clothes. I know that's where you were on your way to before I stopped you in your tracks."

Melanie waddled down the hall to change her clothes. She changed into a comfortable duster and was about to go back to the living area to settle into her recliner. She realized she needed to use the bathroom and get her slippers.

Jonathan was in the kitchen placing his ingredients on the counter to cook dinner. JJ walked through the door after Melanie walked to her room. Jonathan asked, "Son, what are you doing home? It's only one thirty."

JJ replied, "Dad, they released us early. The teachers are having a staff meeting or something. Where's Mom?"

Jonathan replied, "She is in the living area. She had her appointment today, and she wanted to eat at her Chinese restaurant. She full as a tick on a dog. Oh, yes, let me show you something." Jonathan handed JJ the envelope that had the sonogram of the baby showing the gender. It was a girl.

JJ smiled and said, "Yes! I was right. I am having a baby sister. I am so excited and eager for her arrival. Dad, I am going to spoil her. Hold her all the time. You and Mom are going to be fussing at me about holding her so much."

Jonathan stated, "Be quiet. Not too loud, son. Your mother didn't want to know the gender. But I know she will be relieved that you will help her take care of the baby. She will need time to recuperate from delivering the baby. It will take her a while to get back into the swing of things. She will be exhausted and out of commission for at least two months. So she will welcome you feeding, burping, and changing diapers for her. Remember, don't tell her the baby's gender. She wants to be surprised."

JJ replied, "Okay, I promise not to tell her. The feeding and burping I can manage, but you and Mom will have to change the diapers."

Jonathan agreed, "Okay, son. I can deal with that. Go say hi to your mom."

JJ went into the living area excited, and he remembered not to mention the sex of the baby. "Hey, Mom. How are you doing?" JJ kissed Melanie on her forehead.

Melanie lowered the volume on the television. She answered, "Hi, son. Why are you home so early? I know it isn't time for six weeks test. So the teachers must be having staff development day today the reason you're home early."

JJ replied, "Yes, Mom. You are right. Dad showed me the sonogram. He told me not to tell you the baby's gender, and I made a promise that I would not."

Melanie stated, "Yes, son. I want to be surprised. So be careful when you are discussing the baby, because it could easily slip from your lips."

JJ stated, "Okay, Mom. I will be careful. Oh, yes, Camille's mother would like to invite you and Dad to have dinner with them. She says her father will be there too."

Melanie stated, "Sure, son. We can arrange that. When would she like for us to come?"

JJ replied, "Well, Mom, I told her about your condition. So she understands if you need to wait until after the baby is born."

Melanie stated, "No, son. I am okay with meeting her parents in my condition. I will talk to your dad about it. I am sure he won't mind. Especially since I've expressed to him today that I would like to get away from this apartment and live a little. Will you let her know?"

JJ replied, "Okay, Mom. That may be hard to do. You know how Dad is about protecting you and the baby. He prefers you not do too much for fear of putting the baby and yourself in danger."

Melanie replied, "Son, I will be okay. We are just visiting a couple of hours for dinner. One night away from here won't hurt me or the baby. We will be fine. I really want to meet her mother. It would do me good to have adult contact other than your dad. What's her name, son?"

JJ replied, "I'm not certain, Mom. I call her by her last name, which is Ms. Phillips. She is kind too, Mom. Almost reminds me of you."

Melanie stated, "Well, I can't wait to meet her. As soon as your dad comes from the kitchen, I am going to let him know I want this dinner invite to happen. He knows that I want to be around people, and he won't deny me. Did he tell you we ate at the buffet after my appointment?"

JJ responded, "Yes, Mom, he did. He also said you were full as a tick on a dog. You ate so much." They both laughed.

"Yes, son, I am full. But I will be hungry again. This baby is greedy. Always hungry."

Jonathan walked into the living area, asking, "What you guys chitchatting about in here?"

JJ replied, "I was telling Mom that Camille's mother would love for us to come to dinner. I explained Mom's condition to her, and she understands if Mom can't make it."

Melanie chimed in, "Jonathan, I want to go to this dinner as soon as possible. I don't want to put this off until the baby is born. Are you okay with that?"

Jonathan answered, "Sure, Mel. We can have dinner with them. JJ, let her know we would love to come whenever she is ready for us."

Melanie was surprised at Jonathan's response. She thought he would try to convince her she should wait.

JJ stated, "Okay, Dad. I will deliver the message. Oh yeah, what are we having for dinner?"

Jonathan replied, "Fried catfish, corn on the cob, baby carrots, and broccoli."

JJ stated, "All right, go, Dad. Can't wait to eat. I love me some fish."

Jonathan had a few moments to spare before heading back to the kitchen to check the food. "Mel, are you comfortable, baby? Do you need me to get you anything? I picked up ice cream sandwiches and sundae cones from the store yesterday. Would you like some?"

Melanie answered, "Yes, please. I will take an ice cream sandwich now and eat the sundae cone after dinner. Thank you, baby."

JJ heard his mother and stated, "I got her, Dad. I was on my way to the kitchen anyway. I'll check the food while I'm in here too."

JJ went into the kitchen to check on the food and get his mother's ice cream sandwich. Jonathan was second-guessing his response given to Melanie and asked, "Mel, are you sure it is safe for you to be visiting people's homes in your condition? The restaurant was one thing, but visiting others may not be the best idea for you at this time. I am just looking out for you and the baby, is all. But it's totally up to you."

Melanie had heard this before so many times. So many times that it was countless. She immediately felt that he was trying to control her. She thought, *Why is he always trying to sway me from my decisions? And he succeeds too. This time, I'm sticking to my decision, and that's that.* Melanie replied, "Jonathan, please refrain from trying to change my mind. I really need this adult contact. Especially with another female. You know I only have two friends who are work colleagues. I really need you to respect my decision. Would you please do that for me?"

Jonathan replied, "Sure, Mel. I was just making sure that this is what you wanted."

Melanie replied, "Yes, it is what I want, and thank you. The baby and I will be fine."

JJ heard them while he was about to enter the living area and stopped to hear the entire conversation. He thought, *I told Mom Dad would be against her meeting Camille's mother and having dinner. I understand his concern, but I'm sure Mom knows her limits.* He walked in and stated, "Okay, the food is coming along, and, Mom, here is your ice cream sandwich. You want me to open it for you?"

Melanie replied, "Yes, please do, after you have washed your hands."

JJ went into his bathroom to cleanse his hands. Once they were clean, he returned and opened Melanie's ice cream.

Melanie stated, "Thank you, son. I appreciate you. Now trash that for me."

JJ laughed saying, "Mom, it's in my hands. Only thing to do is toss it away."

Melanie stated, "I know. I just wanted to make you laugh."

JJ sat with his mother until dinner. She flipped through the channels, searching for a program. She thought about Camille, asking JJ, "How are you and Camille doing?"

JJ replied, "We're good, Mom. We ride the same bus, so I get off with her and walk her home."

Melanie stated, "Okay, son. That is gentlemanly of you to do. She will remember that side of you no matter what happens between the two of you. A girl never forgets."

This was exactly why Jonathan was against Melanie having dinner with her mother. He felt JJ was spending too much time with this girl. He felt she would only end up breaking his son's heart because he was on a different level than the other boys. Pretty girls like her always ended up falling for the bad guys, leaving the good ones confused and hurt. He made up his mind that with intense exertion, he would protect his son from hurt. He would talk to him without Melanie being present.

Jonathan rose, stating, "Okay, let me go check on this food. The fish should be ready for flipping." Jonathan went into the kitchen and flipped the fish and turned the heat from under the baby carrots and broccoli. The corn would finish when the fish would be ready. He could hear laughter coming from the living area. He wondered, *What could they be discussing that was so funny without including me? I hope it's not about that girl Camille.*

He attended to the food. Everything was coming along just fine. When Jonathan returned, the laughter was still present. He was relieved when he saw that they were watching one of Melanie's shows, the reason for all the laughter. He informed them, "Guys, dinner will be ready in a few. The other side of the catfish needs to brown. By that time, the corn on the cob will be ready. Those are the only two items we are waiting to finish cooking."

Melanie and JJ both were pleased to hear dinner was almost ready.

After eating that Chinese food, Melanie was already feeling hungry again. She couldn't wait to eat. And to make matters worse, she knew the baby could smell the food because the baby had been kicking her nonstop for the last ten minutes. She pleaded, "Calm down, little one. Daddy will be feeding us in just a few minutes."

JJ went into his room to play a game or two prior to eating dinner. Since dinner would be ready shortly, he decided to play a game of hunt or martial arts. They would take little time to play.

CHAPTER 17

A Surprised Visit

There was a knock at the door. Jonathan went to answer the door. He opened the door, stating, "What's up, brother-in-law? And you too, Rita? This is a pleasant surprise. Mel will be happy to see her siblings coming for a visit. Are you all hungry? I am cooking up a feast in here. Made enough too."

Justin and Rita both agreed to stay for dinner asking, "What's for dinner?"

Jonathan replied, "Oh, just some catfish, broccoli, baby carrots, and corn on the cob."

Justin stated, "Bro-in-law, you always cooking up something good. I can smell it too. It sure smells good."

Rita stated, "Yes, it does. I haven't eaten since breakfast. Where is my sister?"

Jonathan answered, "Come on, she's right in the living area."

Rita had never been to Melanie's apartment, at least not this one. When she entered the living room, she ran to Melanie's side. Rita yelled, "Hey, sis! How are you doing? My, look at you. You are ready to pop, aren't you?"

Melanie was surprised. Her eyes bucked. "Oh my god! Hey, you!"

Jonathan helped Melanie up so she could hug her siblings. She held on to them tightly. Melanie stated, "Oh, I've missed you both so much. I'm so happy y'all stopped by for a visit. Jonathan cooking. Y'all hungry?"

Justin replied, "Sis, you already know. Yes, we are hungry. You know we ain't turning down no food."

JJ heard all the commotion while he was in his room. He paused his game to come say hello and give his aunt and uncle a hug. When Rita saw him, she couldn't believe her eyes. "Oh, wow! Look at you, JJ. You are so big and handsome. Come give your auntie a big hug."

Justin stated, "What I tell you. I told you he was a big boy, and you wouldn't recognize him when you see him."

Melanie was so happy, full of joy and smiles. Both siblings were here to see her. She missed her siblings, and whenever they came to see her or she visited them, she always felt sad when she or they would leave. She knew it would be a while until their next reunion. She couldn't remember the last time the three of them were in the same room together. It had been that long. They talked and caught up with the current events in each of their lives.

Jonathan had stepped back into the kitchen. All was well, and the food was done. He walked into the living area and informed his family the food was ready. He asked that everyone wash up before dinner. He would get the plates together. He required the assistance of JJ, asking if he would set the table and add the extra leaf.

JJ replied, "Sure, Dad." They both went into the kitchen while the siblings and Melanie washed their hands.

Jonathan placed the food on serving trays, and JJ set the table for them to eat. JJ brought in the pitcher of peach tea his father had made. He filled each glass with ice cubes. Jonathan yelled to them, "All right, y'all, come on and let's eat."

They all came to the dining area to enjoy the night's dinner. Melanie was the last to sit down at the table. When she finally sat with JJ's help, she looked around and felt completely satisfied. She looked at her brother then her sister with a smile that stretched from here to Tijuana. This was what she had been telling Jonathan she missed. The company of adults. Jonathan saw the look on his wife's face, and it pleased him that she was happy. It finally sunk in that she needed this more than he thought. He had never seen her happier than this, excluding the birth of JJ and their marriage. They ate, drank, and conversed with one another, enjoying each other's company.

LOSING HER CROWN

Jonathan felt proud and a little lonely watching them as they shared what all they were up to lately. He was an only child but had a sister that didn't belong to his mother. She was his father's child. He would do anything just to have that feeling Melanie was experiencing with her siblings. But he savored the moment and watched how Melanie kept smiling. Occasionally, they would make eye contact. Jonathan would wink at her, causing her to smile more and bigger. He thought, *How can I deny her anything? She deserves the world, and I want to give it to her.*

Melanie wanted this with her siblings more often, and she expressed it to them. "Guys, please, let us do this more in the future. I miss y'all."

Rita and Justin agreed. After they finished eating, they sat back in the living area for a while and talked. Justin looked at his watch and noticed it was 8:30 p.m. He interrupted Mel and Rita. "Guys, I hate to cut this short, but we must head back to the other side. Rita, are you ready?"

Rita replied, "Whenever you are."

They had a forty-minute drive ahead of them. Melanie understood and rose to kiss and embrace her siblings. "You two, I love y'all so much. Will y'all please come back again soon?"

Justin and Rita both replied, "Okay. We love you too."

Justin added, "I'll try my best to get back out here soon with Rita."

Jonathan and JJ walked them to the door and said goodbye along with an embrace. When they returned to the living area, Melanie was crying. She missed her siblings. Her pregnancy made her more vulnerable and extremely sensitive.

JJ asked, "Mom, what's wrong? You were just laughing and talking. Why are you crying, Mom?"

Jonathan went to his wife and held her hand. He already knew why Melanie was crying. He stated, "Son, she's okay. Just overwhelmed with emotions seeing Justin and Rita. It's okay, baby. You'll see them again."

JJ asked, "Mom, what can I do to make you feel better?" JJ loathed seeing his mother cry.

Melanie whimpered, replying, "I'll be okay, son. I just miss my family. Will you help me up and walk me to the room? I'm ready for bed."

JJ answered, "Okay, Mom, let's go."

Jonathan walked to the room after them. He knew Melanie would be ready to get in the tub, and she would need his help doing so. JJ kissed and embraced his mother and held on to her longer than normal. "I love you, Mom. Please don't be sad."

Melanie said, "I love you too, son. This bath should make me feel better. Son, I'm going to bed after my bath. I'll talk to you tomorrow. Okay?"

JJ replied, "Okay, Mom. Talk to you tomorrow."

Jonathan ran her bathwater and helped her in the tub. She sat in the tub, and the temperature was right. She needed her muscles to relax from all the activity today. Jonathan, without asking Melanie, began to bathe his wife.

Melanie thought about how she acted toward Jonathan about the PHI issue and thought about how he took care of her in this condition. She began to cry again. "Jonathan, thank you for taking care of me. This really means a lot to me."

Jonathan stated, "You don't have to thank me, baby. I am here for you, okay? Come on, I will help you out and into the bed. You've had a productive day today." He had already placed Melanie's pajamas on the bed and helped her dress. He pulled the covers back and helped his wife get in bed. He gave her the remote so that she could watch her programs. He sat with Melanie and knew it wouldn't be long before she drifted to sleep. She was exhausted. Within minutes, Melanie was fast asleep. Jonathan kissed his wife and turned off the television and lights. "Good night, Mel. I love you."

Jonathan had made an appointment to see his doctor. As usual, Melanie didn't know anything about it. When the doctor entered the room, he greeted Jonathan and wasted no time.

"Mr. Taylor, we need to discuss your lab results. Your markers are off, which indicate your condition is worsening. Have you been taking it easy from any heavy lifting? It is time for you to have therapy to address the pain. Is there a specific facility you want me to refer you to? We have a facility here I could refer you to."

Jonathan replied, "No, Dr. Henry. I don't have a facility in mind. I can come here."

Dr. Henry stated, "Okay, I'll put the referral in for you. And make sure you get in some therapy before coming back to see me. Let me examine you."

The doctor had Jonathan lift his limbs, and he evaluated his strength. Dr. Henry stated, "We will have you follow-up in two months to see if the therapy is working. Also, your wife called here about two weeks ago, asking about your condition. I told her I couldn't release any information to her unless you give consent."

Jonathan stated, "Okay, thank you. I'll see you in two months."

It became obvious to Jonathan. He understood why Melanie was giving him the cold shoulder that day when he came home from work. She did exactly what he asked her not to do. After seeing the doctor, Jonathan went back to work to make up the two hours he had missed. The visit plagued Jonathan's mind. He tried not to think about it. How would he be able to make these visits with the copays he would have to pay? The job was only temporary until Melanie's leave from being pregnant ended. He was bringing in enough to meet what Melanie was missing being on long-term disability from work. Childcare for just one child was expensive. He and Melanie weighed the pros and cons of sending their children to day care after delivering each baby. They both agreed it was in the best interest that he would stay home with the babies while she worked. Jonathan had the same job each pregnancy until Trent hired him. Melanie was always the breadwinner of the family. He was making about $2 per hour above minimum wage when Melanie first had JJ. Before he landed his job with Trent, that same job was paying him about $4 per hour above minimum wage after JJ was enrolled in pre-school. Jonathan had to make a way. He would have to get a night job so that he could help Melanie after she went back to work to take the pressure off her. He felt he should be more than just a stay-at-home dad while his wife worked hard just to make ends meet. All sorts of scenarios ran across Jonathan's mind while driving back to work.

Things were good at work. Employees were hard at work. Their production and revenue were at an all-time high. Trent had been away for a while and had trusted the store to Jonathan but understood his commitment to Melanie. When he would have to leave the store, Jonathan would put John in charge. He was the only other adult working in the store. John was dependable, and he loved working with Jonathan and the crew. He kept to himself, did his work, and bothered no one. Sometimes this creeped Jonathan out about him. He rarely ever said anything to the others, but he opened up to customers with no problems. But Jonathan bet he knew why John was this way. And the proof was the incident that happened with Jonathan and Tina. Since John was the only adult other than Jonathan working around teenagers, he thought it best to keep contact to a minimal. He didn't want anyone accusing him of anything that would jeopardize his status at work. Upon Jonathan's return, John was able to clock out and head for home.

"See you tomorrow, Jonathan."

Jonathan said, "Okay, John. Thanks for keeping an eye out on the store for me. See you tomorrow."

Jonathan began to think about his therapy again, but not as much as he thought about the need to get JJ alone to speak to him about Camille. He didn't want his son involved with this young lady to where he loses himself. He wanted JJ to have a better life than him and Melanie. He had plans for his son to go to a college that catered to adults with learning disabilities or a trade school. He reached for his cell phone and went through his contacts to dial his son's number. The phone began to ring on the other end.

"Hey, Pops, what's up?"

Jonathan answered, "Hey, son. I need you to meet me outside in the parking lot to discuss something. I thought I would catch you before you had made any plans. I'll be home in about an hour, so don't go anywhere."

JJ said, "Sure thing, Dad. I'll be here waiting for your call."

Jonathan started getting ready to shut down the store. He would close an hour early. Jonathan announced, "Hey, guys, y'all start wiping the store down so we can get out of here on time. I need the store cleaned and everyone ready to clock out at four p.m."

The time to clock out drew near. The employees cleaned the store, and they all clocked out for the day. Jonathan locked the store, made sure the cameras were still active, and drove home.

Which Advice Is Best?

JJ was on the phone with Camille when his father called him. JJ stated, "That was my dad calling me. He says he wants to talk to me about something when he gets home. Not certain what it could be, but it sounded serious."

Camille responded, "I know what it is. He wants to talk to you about me, I bet."

JJ asked, "Why would you think it's about you?"

Camille replied, "Because, JJ, all fathers want to warn their sons about pretty girls like me. They all have that talk with them about their sons being careful and not getting too involved with the girl because she could break his heart. I have witnessed this talk with my brother, JJ. That talk led my brother to break up with his girlfriend."

JJ stated, "Oh, wow. I won't allow him to make me feel like I need to break up with you just because he has some fears."

Camille replied, "Brace yourself. He will try to reason with you that you need to slow things down with me. But there is nothing to slow down. We're just friends."

JJ and Camille talked for about an hour before Jonathan called him to come meet him.

Jonathan pulled up to the apartment and called his son. JJ looked at his phone and ended his call with Camille. "Camille, this is my dad. I must go. I'll talk to you later."

Camille said, "Okay. Talk to you later."

Jonathan had already called and told Melanie he and JJ would be running somewhere quickly and would be back within fifteen minutes or less. JJ walked out to the car and entered, ready for the talk with his dad.

"What's up, Dad? What you need to discuss with me?"

Jonathan replied, "Son, I wanted to talk to you about Camille. I don't want you to take this the wrong way, but I am just looking out for you, is all. I know you like her. I can see it in your eyes whenever you talk about her. Be careful, son. She is a pretty girl, and pretty girls tend to get attention from the wrong types of guys and sometimes men well older than them. They love that bad boy and older men attention. You are neither of those, son. The good guys always come in last. The best excuse they think of when they break up with you is it's not you, it's me. I just need space to think about things. We can get back on track after I figure things out for us. That is a bunch of bull, son. That is their way of saying they want to break up with you. Do you get where I am going, son? Don't get too involved with this girl. Don't spend so much time with her. Give her space to miss you. You don't want to wear your welcome out with her, or she will get tired of looking at you."

JJ replied, "I hear you, Dad. I hear my friends at school talking about this exact same problem. Their girlfriends, for no reason, start to act like they are not into them anymore. They give them attitudes when they approach them. Look at them funny. All sorts of crazy things."

Jonathan stated, "Son, you also may meet another girl who may turn you away from Camille, which could leave her hurt and brokenhearted as well. It works both ways. Camille, too, will have others expressing interest in her. Now that the girls at your school see that you have pulled a girl like Camille, they will start hitting on you, trying to get your attention. Some will be bold enough to do it in front of Camille. Be careful, son, is all I am saying. You don't want to feel hurt, and you don't want to be the cause of someone hurting. It is one thing to experience heartache, but being the cause of someone else's heart breaking isn't a good thing. Some people don't react well to being hurt."

JJ said, "Okay, Dad. I understand. But remember, even though we like each other, Camille and I are just friends. As soon as Mom has my baby sister, I won't have time for anyone. Camille knows and understands that you and Mom will need me when the baby arrives."

Jonathan replied, "There you go, son. You are right. Your mother and I will need you to help us take care of the baby. We both will be exhausted when the baby arrives."

JJ asked, "You exhausted, Dad? Don't you mean Mom will be?"

Jonathan answered, "Son, your momma is tiring me with the get up, do this, and do that for her. I'm worn out, son."

JJ stated, "Okay, Dad. Are we done?"

Jonathan answered, "Since you have this under control, we can go inside now. I'm sure your mother is hungry."

JJ said, "Yep, you were worried about nothing. I have this under control, old man." They both laughed and exited the car and walked up the sidewalk to enter the apartment.

Jonathan passed the kitchen and dining area to get to Melanie. Jonathan looked at his wife and her belly. It seemed to have grown more since his last focus on her. He saw the misery in her eyes and face. He knew she was tired and ready to deliver their baby. The way she breathed proved it was taking everything within her to catch her breath. He thought, *I can't put her through this anymore. She suffers more than anyone I know in this condition.*

Jonathan also missed loving his wife, holding her, being intimate with her, making her feel good, and she making him feel good.

Jonathan walked to his wife, bent over, and kissed her. Jonathan asked, "Mel, how are you feeling, baby? How are two of my favorite people in the world?"

Melanie answered, "I'm tired, Jonathan. I am so ready to deliver this baby. The baby has been kicking up a storm and has been laying on my bladder like crazy. I've been going to the bathroom nonstop."

Jonathan stated, "Well, baby, you only have a few more weeks before they induce your labor. Have you thought about any boy or girl names yet for the baby?"

Melanie replied, "Yes, I have thought of some names. If it is a girl, I want to name her Ashley Cataleya, but call her Honey. And if it is a boy, I want to name him Christopher William. Are those names okay, Jonathan? I want you to have a say in this too."

Jonathan replied, "Mel, those names are fine. Especially the girl's name. I love it. Ashley Cataleya. It has a nice ring to it. She will be the envy of all little girls."

Melanie laughed, stating, "Okay, that's enough. If you keep talking, you just might give the baby's gender away. I can't lie, I have been itching to know the gender. But I keep telling myself I have waited this long. I can wait a little longer. The suspense is really getting to me, Jonathan."

Jonathan stated, "Well, if you ever decide that you really want to know the baby's gender, I'm still not telling you." They both laughed.

Melanie reminded him, "You know all I have to do is make a phone call to find out, right?"

Jonathan replied, "Oh, yes. I forgot about that. Okay, so I guess if you really want to know, I will tell you. What would you like for dinner, Mel?"

Melanie answered, "Jonathan, I want something light. Noodles, turkey ground meat, and broccoli. I've been craving it, and the baby wants it."

Jonathan asked, "Mel, are you sure that's what you want? I can whip up something that will have you two full."

Melanie replied, "Jonathan, it's what the baby is craving. Yes, I am sure that is what I want to eat. I have been thinking about that dish all day. Will you make it for me, please? I would appreciate it."

Jonathan answered, "Very well, Mel. If that is what you want, I'll make it."

JJ had just finished speaking with Camille about the dinner. "Hey, guys. Camille's mother wants to know if you all want to have dinner this Saturday night with them. Mom, she says if there is something you would like for her to make for you, she wouldn't mind doing so."

Melanie asked, "Really? She would do that for me? Yes, please let her know I love fried breast or catfish with collards, turnip, mustard, and cabbage mixed, mashed potatoes, oven or hot water corn bread, and some sweet baby carrots."

JJ replied, "Okay, Mom. I'll call Camille and let her know now."

JJ went to his room to call Camille. "Hello, Camille?"

Camille answered, "Yeah, this me, Jonathan. What's going on with you?"

JJ replied, "I told you don't offer my mom to choose the dinner menu. She wants fried breast or catfish, mixed greens and cabbage, baby carrots, mashed potatoes, and either oven bread or hot water corn bread."

Camille stated, "Okay. I will let my mom know. Good thing she can cook everything you named. And, Jonathan, it is okay. When my mother offers someone the opportunity to choose the dinner menu, it makes her happy. People get to taste her cooking. She loves making people happy, and she's proud of her cooking skills."

JJ smiled, saying, "Wow, that's your first time ever calling me Jonathan. I will let my mom know that everything is set for dinner. What time will you all expect us there?"

Camille replied, "No later than seven thirty. This is the set time we eat dinner when she cooks. So will you all please be on time?"

JJ stated, "Sure thing. That should be no problem. I'll talk to you later."

Camille stated, "Talk to you later."

JJ went into the living area to let his parents know what time Ms. Phillips expected them for dinner. "Guys, we are expected to be at Camille's at seven thirty on the dot. Please, let us be on time. Mom, if you need me to, I can help you pick out something to wear. That way, you won't be wrecking your brain and stressing yourself."

Melanie stated, "Okay, son. Thank you."

Jonathan interrupted, "Son, you know that's my job. What you trying to say, your daddy doesn't know how to dress your momma?"

JJ knew he could spice her up a little. JJ answered, "No, Dad. But may I this time?"

Jonathan replied, "Yeah. Okay, son."

There was truth to what JJ thought. Anything Melanie bought and wore, Jonathan approved. He always went shopping with her. Melanie thought he was just going with her because she didn't know the first thing about matching clothes, but he did. Jonathan was also making sure she wasn't purchasing anything that would show her curves. Her clothes were all loose fitting, nothing contouring to her shape. She wore minimal makeup, lipstick only, and she really didn't need that. And if he had it his way, Melanie would always have her hair in a ponytail. He had so much control over Melanie, and she didn't realize it. JJ was taking count of all this. He wondered if his dad felt that if Melanie dressed her way and wore makeup, would he feel threatened that it would draw the attention of the other men? JJ felt his father should be proud to have a wife as beautiful as his mother. He always received compliments from his friends that his mother was beautiful and didn't look her age. When Melanie walked into a room, all eyes were on her. Her beauty demanded the attention of any and every crowd.

Jonathan yelled, "JJ! Do you hear me, son? I asked if you were hungry. What would you like? Your mother decided she wants her turkey ground meat, broccoli, and noodles for dinner. I can make something for you and me."

JJ replied, "What Mom is eating will be fine for me. I haven't had that meal in a while, and it's good."

Jonathan stated, "Okay. Well, I guess we all will be eating it then." Jonathan went to the kitchen to prepare the meal. It would not take long at all. This was one of the easiest meals Melanie could ever have him cook. The entire prep and cook time would be no longer than thirty minutes.

While Jonathan cooked, JJ wanted his mom's advice about Camille. He asked, "Mom, can I talk to you while Dad is cooking?"

Melanie replied, "Sure, son. What's on your mind?"

JJ replied, "Mom, I really like Camille a lot, and we've talked about being a couple. But I am afraid of us both getting too involved where one of us hurts the other. She is pretty, Mom. I see how those guys look at her. I know these guys fancy her. I just don't know if she reciprocates. There will be girls I may fancy, or they fancy me. Mom, I am so confused and don't know what to do. I know I should take things slow with her and not get too involved. I don't want to feel hurt by her. I feel something special for her. I'm confused, Mom."

JJ needfully exhaled. Melanie looked at her son and his body language. He really had true feelings for this girl. Melanie stated, "Say no more, son. I know how you feel. You must take chances in life.

There are no guarantees when it comes to the matters of your heart. I don't care how much you try to pull away or forget about someone. The heart will always want what the heart wants. You can't be afraid of loving or caring for someone for fear that you may hurt them or they may hurt you. If you think you are spending too much time with her, let that voice inside you guide you. It is okay for you to pull back. Remember, absence makes the heart grow fonder. You will come across people who may tell you stay away from love. It hurts. Those people forgot about the good times they shared, and now that it is over, they are only thinking about the bad part. It gets better. You grow and learn from your errors. The most important part is to learn from your errors. Don't keep taking route 360 ending up in the same situation. Stop at midpoint and take a journey using route 180. If you don't understand what I mean, you will once life happens."

JJ stated, "Wow. Mom, that was the best advice anyone has ever given me about life. I'm so happy you are my mother."

JJ rose from the sofa to give his mother a big hug and kiss. "Thanks, Mom. I love you. I don't know what I would do without you."

Melanie replied, "No problem, son. I love you too." Melanie told her son what he needed to here. She understood love and matters of the heart.

Jonathan finished cooking their meal and sat everyone's plate on the table. He could hear Melanie giving JJ advice about Camille. He thought, *Damn, she just undid everything I told him. Now I must devise another plan to sever this link. I'll have to think about that later, not right now.* Jonathan announced dinner was ready and for them to come have a seat to eat. JJ helped his mother up and walked with her to the table. They sat and ate dinner together and discussed the arrival of the baby.

Two Souls Reconnected

It was Saturday. Melanie was scurrying around in her closet, trying to figure out what she would wear. She then remembered that JJ would be helping her pick out something special for the dinner with

Camille's parents. It was only five o'clock in the evening. She had Jonathan help her in the shower. She was starting to feel Braxton-Hicks. This was a sign that she would be delivering their baby soon. After she showered, Jonathan was there to help her. He always made sure he stayed in the room until she was out of the shower to ease his mind of something happening and her being alone. JJ had already surveyed the closet containing his mother's clothes. He picked out this nice button-down blue blouse with black maternity pants. He picked out her blue tennis shoes that were comfortable for Melanie. She only wore them when she had to leave the apartment. Melanie loved what JJ picked out for her. Jonathan helped her dress. He stood back and looked at his wife.

Jonathan admired Melanie, stating, "Aw, shucky now. My baby looking good!"

Melanie said, "Stop it, you. Go ahead and dress yourself. It is six thirty. I want to leave the apartment at seven."

Melanie sat herself at her vanity and started applying a little makeup to enhance her beauty. She thought, *I hope no one makes a fuss, thinking they must cater to me. I am sure Camille's mother will know how far to go. We women know these types of things.*

Melanie stared into the mirror. She could see the different lives she lived on earth. The life of a child, being young and carefree. The life of a teenager when popularity, boys, peer pressure, and rebellion existed. The life of an adult when life started to happen, responsibilities, accountabilities, and searching for the right one. The life of being a wife and mother was to be fulfilling and rewarding. Why didn't Melanie feel fulfilled and rewarded? There was something missing. She thought, *I have everything. What more could there be?*

JJ knocked on the door, asking, "Mom, are you dressed? Can I come in your room?"

Melanie replied, "Sure, son. I'm dressed."

JJ walked into his parents' room. He asked, "Mom, how do I look?" JJ had on a pair of starched jeans and a nice gray shirt with gray and blue Dope Man shoes.

Melanie replied, "Oh, my son. You look handsome. You will be the envy of all the guys tonight."

They both laughed. Father and son must have discussed their attire together because Jonathan came out of the closet matching what JJ was wearing. They all looked nice and were on their way out the door. JJ helped his mother get in the car. Melanie couldn't wait until the arrival of the baby so she could get in and out of the car on her own. She was ready to get back to her old self again.

The Taylor clan was ready to drive to Camille's home. Jonathan drove with extra care. Sometimes Melanie could feel every bump in the road, and it would cause more pain to her. Melanie wanted Jonathan to stop at the corner store to get a chocolate bar and a bag of barbecue twists chips. This would take about five minutes or so. This corner store was always busy. JJ went inside with his father. He wanted to get an item for himself. It didn't take long before they both were back in the car.

Jonathan stated, "Okay, guys. We are on our way to JJ's girlfriend's home. Everybody got what they wanted?"

Melanie and JJ replied, "Yep, sure do."

JJ added, "Dad, Camille, for now, is not my girlfriend. I have feelings for her, but not the title."

Jonathan said, "Okay, son."

It was 7:20 p.m. when they arrived at Camille's home. Jonathan helped his wife out of the car while JJ went to the door to alert Camille they had arrived. Camille greeted Jonathan and Melanie.

"Hi, Mr. and Mrs. Taylor. How are you all doing? Come on in. Mom is waiting to meet you."

The guys allowed Melanie to walk in first. Camille escorted them to the family room. Her father was walking in the room, alerting his wife their guests had arrived. It was Jonathan's old friend Chauncey.

Jonathan was surprised and asked, "Chauncey, what's up, man? You're Camille's father?"

Chauncey replied, "Jonathan, you're JJ's father! Aw, man, he told me his father's name was Jonathan, but I didn't know it was you. Good to see you, man." They both gave the brotherly hug.

Camille was surprised, asking, "Wait a minute, you both know each other? You've never spoken about any friends named Jonathan, Dad."

Chauncey replied, "Well, we lost contact right after graduation. We crossed paths two weeks ago. Jonathan here didn't make a complete stop at the stop sign. I ran his plates and saw the car was registered in his name and—" Chauncey looked toward Melanie and stopped midsentence, saying, "My apologies. This must be Melanie. She is beautiful, Jonathan. And you are right. She is expecting. How are you, Melanie?" Chauncey reached out for Melanie's hand and kissed it like a gentleman.

Melanie answered, "I'm doing well, Chauncey. Thank you for asking. Where's your wife?"

Chauncey replied, "She will be out in just a second. She will be surprised that you are JJ's father. I told her about running into you." Chauncey finished the story of his encounter with Jonathan as they waited for Chelsea.

Chelsea was putting on the finishing touch of her lipstick. She heard the voices before she was done applying her makeup. She walked down the stairs into the family room, putting one earring on with her head turned. When she looked in Melanie's direction, they both bucked their eyes.

Chelsea asked, "Mel?"

Melanie returned with "Chelsea?" Melanie had sat in a chair. Melanie rose to embrace her long-lost friend. Chelsea quickly rushed toward Melanie.

Jonathan thought, *Dang, she jetted over there in a hurry.*

Tears filled their eyes. Overwhelmed with joy, Chelsea said, "Oh my god, my friend, my best friend! Where have you been? I have missed you so much."

Melanie replied, crying with a trembling voice, "My goodness, Chelsea, I thought I would never see you again." Melanie knew it was Chelsea because no one else called her Mel but her immediate family and Jonathan.

They held on to each other tightly. They didn't want to release their hold on each other. They both simultaneously had a flashback of how they held on to each other when Melanie's father moved them away. Her father had to break them apart. They were hugging and holding on to each other so tightly. Melanie had her head on

Chelsea's shoulder, crying like a baby. Tears and snot plagued these ladies' clothing.

Jonathan had never heard his wife wail this way. It was as if she was crying over a close deceased relative. Chelsea allowed Melanie to get it all out before she spoke. Once done, she took Melanie by both hands and kissed them both. She placed her thumbs on Melanie's face to wipe away her tears.

She stated, "Look at you. You still have your youthful look. You are going to be a mommy. Remember how we talked about being married and being the best mothers?"

Melanie, eyes still stained with tears, answered, "Yes, I do remember."

They had an audience with tearstained eyes. They could feel the love between the two ladies. Chelsea guided Melanie to the couch and sat next to her. There was silence in the room. They were all waiting to hear the story of how these ladies knew each other.

Chelsea stated, "Chauncey, this is the young lady I always spoke about to you. She is my best friend since we were teenagers. She was my sister. I never allowed anyone else to get close to me. No one was ever able to take her place." Chelsea looked toward Jonathan and knew who he was. She asked, Jonathan? You're JJ's father? It is so good to see you. It's been years."

Jonathan walked over to Chelsea and gave her a hug. He understood why she could not and would not leave Melanie. "Yes, it has been. You two must have been close. I've never heard my wife cry out this way."

Chelsea, while stroking Mel's hair away from her face, replied, "Mel and I had a friendship that no one could ever understand. Guys and gals tried to come between us, but it wasn't happening. I understood what she was going through at home being a teenager. I understood the turmoil she faced every day. I always felt her pain. No one but hers. Always felt connected to her until her dad moved her away from me."

Melanie began crying more and interrupted, "I'm sorry, everyone. I just can't stop crying. And it doesn't help that I'm pregnant."

Melanie was ten times more emotional than the average woman. They all consoled her, letting her know it was okay.

Chelsea remembered she needed to make a trip to the kitchen. "Mel, you just sit here, okay? I will be right back. Your food is ready. Everything you asked for is on the table. I just need to make a quick dash to the kitchen."

Melanie asked, "May I come with you, please?"

Chelsea replied, "Of course, you can. Come on, girl."

JJ helped his mother. They followed Chelsea into the kitchen.

Melanie stated, "Chelsea, you have a beautiful home, and it's so spacious."

Chelsea said, "Thanks, Mel."

As they stepped into the kitchen, Mel's eyes admired the beautiful layout of the kitchen. She stated, "Chelsea, oh my god! You have your dream kitchen, just like we talked about as teenagers." Mel admired every length, width, height, and inch of this kitchen.

Chelsea stated, "Mel, take a look in there."

Melanie walked into the next room. There lay the feast. Melanie confessed, "Chelsea, this food looks good, girl. Nice spread presentation. I skipped lunch to make sure I didn't offend you by not eating enough of your food. From what I see, it looks to be mighty tasty."

Chelsea walked in and sat Melanie down at the dinner table and called everyone in to join them.

Camille's two brothers came out of nowhere with little Jasmine announcing they had plans. Before they left, they introduced themselves to Melanie and Jonathan. Jasmine sat by her mother. Chelsea had cooked both fish and chicken breast, so Melanie could have them both. They all sat, and Chauncey blessed the food. It was like they were a family visiting for the holidays, talking and catching up just like a family with missed relatives would do.

JJ and Camille sat next to each other, holding hands, looking at one another smiling. They felt even closer to each other. Mel noticed that Chelsea had Rice Krispies Treats on the table. Mel stared at them.

Chelsea asked, "Mel, honey, what is it? Are you okay?"

Melanie replied, "Yes, Chelsea. I am okay. I remember how these were our favorite snack. You used to make them, and we would eat them all up one by one."

Chelsea stated, "And it's the same. Eat all you want."

Melanie was so happy that she had crossed paths with her best friend again. She was the only friend Melanie had in high school. When her father moved the family away, Melanie's world crumbled without Chelsea. Chelsea knew the horror going on in her house, and she wanted to save Melanie. Her soul longed for Chelsea, and Chelsea's soul longed for her. The bond between those two girls was incredibly strong. They cried years for each other. Even when life happened, they still longed to have each other in their lives. They never forgot about each other. Chelsea had married Chauncey, so when Mel tried to find her, she was under Phillips. Melanie had given up one day and fell onto her bed crying after she had exhausted all resources to find her best friend. It was one of the worst feelings she had ever had in life. But that all had changed now. She was with her best friend once again. This was one hole existing in Melanie's heart that had finally filled.

Jonathan saw happiness in Melanie. He knew this was a productive dinner invite for Melanie. She was all smiles. Nothing could top this feeling she was having. Seeing her smiling, laughing, and forgetting about the pain from the pregnancy made Jonathan all smiles. He was against this dinner. But seeing his wife her happiest was pleasing to him. They now both had something in common. Four old friends were rekindling friendships.

Jonathan and Chauncey talked about the days of their youth and the trouble they had at school. It was a lovely night. The time had passed them all. It was ten, well past Melanie's time to nestle in bed and fall into dream world within minutes. Melanie was getting tired, and Jonathan could see it in her face.

"Mel, baby, you okay? Are you tired? You ready to go home for bed?"

Melanie replied, "Yes, baby. It's that time. I feel drained and ready to get to bed."

Chelsea interrupted, "Mel, would you like to take some of those Rice Krispies Treats with you? Go ahead and take all you want."

Melanie replied, "Chelsea, you are the best, and yes, I will take me some to go. Thank you."

Jonathan helped Mel from the dinner table. He stated, "Come on, Momma. Let us get you home and into bed."

Melanie stated, "Thank you, Jonathan."

Chauncey and Chelsea walked them to the door. Chelsea stated, "Melanie, I'm so glad we found each other. Here is my number. You call me anytime, and I love you so much."

Melanie stated, "Okay. I will be calling you soon, and I love you too, Chelsea."

The two of them embraced each other so tight that the hug was impenetrable. The link between these two had never withered. Their thoughts of each other helped keep the closeness between them. It was like they had never separated. The friends said their goodbyes for tonight. JJ kissed Camille good night, but like a gentleman would, right on the cheek.

Chauncey closed the door stating, "Chelsea, you two talked as if you all had never lost contact. I can see something special existed between you two. Why did you all lose contact?"

Chelsea replied, "She was abused as a child, and I was her only friend who understood and tried to help her. Her dad was unlike any father I had met. He was strict on her and her older sister Rita. He didn't want them having friends over at their home. He had no trust in her nor Rita. He mentally abused them. He always called them nasty names, lowered their countenance, and made them afraid of him. Every time someone found out how he was treating them, he would move them away. She lived in the neighborhood for about three years. Those were the best three years of her life. She had found me as a friend, her confidant."

Chauncey asked, "Where was her mother? Was she not around while he was abusing them?"

Chelsea replied, "Yes, her mother was around, but he controlled and abused her too. He was no better with her. Those two girls were not the only souls to receive nasty, mean, and hurtful words. He did it to her as well. He wasn't a good husband nor a good father to his family. He treated strangers like they were his family, but his own family, he treated them worse than you treat a stray animal. I didn't like him. She was overweight as a teenager. He used to make fun of her and ridicule her about her weight. He made her cry every day."

Chauncey interrupted, "She cried every day? He must have really had hate in his heart."

Chelsea continued, "She hated when school released because she knew the horror that awaited her. Summers were worse. With school shutting down for summer break, she had no escape. He kept them in the room, and there was where they spent their days and nights. They stayed in that room 24/7."

Chauncey again interrupted, "Damn, they weren't allowed to go outside or anything? No friends, nothing?"

Chelsea answered, "He allowed her one friend. Me. And that was only because I had no brothers. He wouldn't allow any girls who had brothers to come over for fear that they were coming over to hook those girls up with their brothers. He was crazy and evil, Chauncey. I felt so bad for Mel and her sister. I had never witnessed that type of abuse from anyone. A person like that has a demon riding them. I am surprised that Melanie and Rita survived that abuse and didn't commit suicide. It was just that bad. I absorbed her pain, Chauncey, and I wished that I could have done something to bring her out of that realm. Her life was the perfect epitome of a sorry plight."

Chauncey stated, "Man, he was an asshole. To treat your daughters with such disrespect is awful. A father is supposed to nurture his daughters. He is supposed to show them how a man is supposed to treat them in life. Instead, he did the total opposite. Man, baby, I am so sorry you had to witness and go through that horror with her. No man should ever degrade his daughters the way he did."

Chelsea sobbed a little, stating, "Thank you, Chauncey. Seeing her tonight stirred up all those old feelings. Before you go, will you help me with the kitchen?"

Chauncey replied, "Of course I will."

Chauncey had to admit to himself that he still loved his wife and didn't know how she would respond if he declared his love. He kept his feelings to himself for fear she would reject him. They finished cleaning the kitchen.

Chelsea stated, "Thank you for helping me. I appreciate you. I am going to turn in for the night. I am tired. Did you want to sleep in the guest room, or were you driving on home?"

Chauncey replied, "No, I'm going to head home. I will talk to you later. Come lock the door behind me, and good night."

Chauncey kissed his ex-wife on the cheek and left for the night. Chelsea locked the door behind him.

The family arrived home. Jonathan asked, "Mel, did you want to take another shower before bed?"

Melanie replied, "No, Jonathan. I am going to just use those adult wipes and my foam spray to wash myself. I'm not dirty and haven't been doing anything but talking and visiting."

Jonathan stated, "Okay, baby. We can talk about tonight when you're rested. So I'll see you in the morning."

Melanie asked, "Can you help me, Jonathan? I am feeling a little light-headed. There was too much excitement tonight."

Jonathan replied, "Of course, I will help you. Just stand here. I'll wipe you down, and you can get in the bed." Jonathan wiped his wife, helped her with her pajamas, and put her to bed. As soon as Melanie's head hit the pillow, she was fast asleep. Jonathan asked, "Mel, do you want your remote? Mel?" He looked around and saw that Mel was asleep. He was feeling a little tired himself and decided he would go to bed with Melanie and hold his wife and make her feel secure. Those tears of joy between her and Chelsea were more than that. There was something else behind those tears. He would wait until Melanie woke up to ask her.

CHAPTER 18

Reliving the Past

Jonathan Jr. had awakened and made breakfast. He knocked on his parents' door, asking, "Mom, Dad? Are you awake? It is eleven. Are you going to sleep the day away? I cooked breakfast. You want me to bring it in here?"

Melanie and Jonathan were lying in bed, talking. Melanie replied, "Hey, good morning, son. Yes, you can bring us our food in here."

JJ went to get his parents food. Jonathan had asked Melanie about her relationship with Chelsea. Jonathan recalled her talking about her once or twice. He didn't understand how painful it was for Melanie. She felt if she kept Chelsea locked away and not talk about her, those feelings wouldn't surface again.

Jonathan asked, "Mel, I'm sorry to ask you this, but how close were you and Chelsea?" As he was asking, JJ walked in with their food. A tray in each hand was balanced carefully. He could tell by the look on his mother's face that they were talking, and there was no need for him to try and stick around to hear. He excused himself and went into his room.

Melanie began her soliloquy. "She was the only friend I had who understood what I was going through as a teenager. She knew the horror that Rita and I were facing at home. She wanted to save me. But she was a child herself. What could she do?"

Jonathan asked, "Save you from what, baby?"

Melanie replied, "From our abusive dad. He said and did things to us that were just inhumane. It started at the age of seven. I saw him hurting my mother. He was about to break her arm. I went into the kitchen, got a broom, and told him he better get up off my momma. That was the day I lost my dad. From that point on, the abuse started. He would ridicule me, call me names a father shouldn't call his daughter. He did this to both Rita and me. When we became teenagers, he kept us in our bedroom 24/7 except for school, walking to the store, and other errands he had us doing. We couldn't have friends. He feared that they would be coming over to hook us up with their brothers. I loathed when school released for the day, and especially when the weekend arrived. Summers were the worst. At least when school was in, we could get away from him and have peace from his abuse. We knew the horror that awaited us. He would be nice to us for a couple of days, but then something would tick him off, and he would revert to the abuse. He was the epitome of Dr. Jekyll and Mr. Hyde.

"The abuse would last for weeks before he would be nice to us again. That man was evil. He wanted to be nice to us. His soul was willing, but his flesh just wouldn't allow him to. Too much evil had consumed him. He had a daughter before he met my mother. She died at the hands of her boyfriend from an accidental gunshot wound to the face. He told me that God took the wrong daughter. He should have taken me. That hurt me so bad. He has said hurtful things to me all my life. I tried so hard to please him by getting good grades in school, being a good daughter, you name it. One day, I became numb to it all, and it didn't matter anymore. I released my thirst of wanting the daddy-daughter relationship. Just wasn't worth it anymore. Chelsea saw a good portion of this. He only allowed her to visit me because she was an only child, no brothers. He knew she was the only friend I had and purposefully moved us away when people started asking questions about us."

Jonathan, after receiving this information, stated, "Wow, baby. The times that I have encountered him, he seemed humble. Not that type of guy."

Melanie stated, "He wears a mask to prevent revealing his true self. Our mother told him we would hate him, and it became true. Rita and I started to hate him at an early age. It amplified once we became older. He always tried to control us as adults. Every time I try to give him a chance to be in my life, if I didn't walk to the beat of his drum, he curses me out, and we're back to square one again. Years go by before we communicate. I tell myself all the time this is it, I will not have anything to do with him, but I start missing and yearning for him to be in my life. I always put myself through it all over again. I don't fathom why I do this to myself. I just can't completely cut him out my life."

Jonathan held his wife's hand, stating, "I'm sorry, baby, that you had to go through that. That was a lot to deal with at such a youthful age."

Melanie added, "Yes, it was. Only the man up above kept me. I always thought about committing suicide. Sometimes, I would have nightmares about stabbing him to death when I was a teen." It was time for Melanie to end this conversation before the water works started.

Jonathan held his wife, adding, "You got me, baby. I will always be here for you. I will never leave you. Now eat your breakfast and feed my baby."

Melanie laughed, stating, "Roger that." Melanie ate her food and pushed the tray away from her.

Melanie sat in bed until she felt the urge to urinate. When she rose from the bed, she could feel more Braxton-Hicks. She knew this baby was ready to make an appearance. She only had a couple of weeks remaining for induced labor. She was ready to get this over with and take control of her body. She had Jonathan help her get into the shower. As usual, he stayed in the room waiting until it was time for her shower to end. He didn't want anything happening to his two girls. When she would get out of the shower and dry off, she would stand in front of Jonathan so that he could talk and sing to the baby. The baby always kicked Melanie aggressively when she heard her daddy's voice.

"Mel, we need to get your bag ready for your stay at the hospital. They are expecting you in three days to remove the cerclage. Let me know what you want packed, and I will get your bag ready for you. In fact, I already know what you need. You will not need any fancy clothes or shoes. I'll pack comfortable clothes and shoes for you."

Melanie replied, "Okay, baby, thank you." Melanie was constantly giving Jonathan control over her, and because he was her husband, she couldn't see the danger. She just thought of it as her husband looking out for her, nothing more.

Baby Shower Gifts and Dream

After Melanie dressed, she walked into the baby's room. She looked at all the stuff Jonathan had accumulated from his shower. There was really no need for her to have one, but her cousin wanted to throw her one. Besides that, she hadn't seen Melanie in over a year. It was time for a get together. So she called Melanie one week before they had dinner with Camille's parents.

"Melanie, this is Sadie. I am coming to pick you up tomorrow. We are celebrating the baby's arrival with a shower. Make sure you are ready. I'll be there around three o'clock to get you."

Melanie stated, "Okay, Sadie. I don't have anything to do, so I'll be ready for you." That following day, Sadie came for Mel and drove her to the baby shower.

When they arrived at the shower, one of her coworkers sat waiting for Melanie to enter. Melanie's cousin had invited the whole clinic, but her co-worker didn't read the entire invite and thought it was only for her. She had made a pretty pink blanket for Melanie that was just adorable. A host of relatives were there with their gifts. Melanie accumulated things for the baby that Jonathan didn't procure from his shower. She received clothes worn by either gender, booties, walking shoes, hair bows, brushes, combs, and a musical baby crib mobile. They played games and had decent food to eat. They even took pictures for memories. Melanie had so much fun. Her cousin was gifted in hosting parties that everyone enjoyed. Love was surrounding her from family members. She needed this. Just knowing that someone in her family cared enough to celebrate her pregnancy was the best feeling. She savored the moments of being with her family. It was the perfect evening. She spent the entire evening smiling and laughing. She stopped for a moment and looked around at everyone. The looks on their faces, the loud voices, the children playing with each other. This was how family should be. And this should happen more often. A wedding, death and birth shouldn't be the only time families came together.

They moved the party to the patio and sat there talking for a while. The night was ending. Time for everyone to say their goodbyes. This was the hard part. After being around and feeling so much love, it was time to depart. Sadie and her husband loaded Melanie's gifts into the SUV, and they drove her back home. Melanie thanked them for thinking about her and the lovely time she had. They both knew Melanie was on family leave from work, and Jonathan was the only one working, so they felt it was the least they could do to help a family member in need. Melanie was all set. She didn't need anything for the baby. Bobby helped Melanie in the SUV and closed the door. They pulled out of the driveway and took Melanie home. The drive was only twenty minutes. Bobby drove like a bat out of hell. Before they arrived and opened the gate, Melanie called JJ to come out to help Bobby unload. JJ walked outside and helped his mother step out of the vehicle.

Sadie gave Melanie a big hug and stated, "I love you, Melanie. You call me if you need anything."

Melanie stated, "I love you too, Sadie, and I will. Guys, thank you again."

Jonathan had slipped away to Trent's for drinks and relaxation. He made it back home after JJ called him to let him know his mother had made it from the baby shower.

Melanie was exhausted. All her gifts were in the baby's room. There was so much stuff to go through, she started to feel overwhelmed just looking around the room. She rubbed her belly from feeling the baby's kicks.

"Calm down, little one. I know you had an exciting day. So many different voices you heard, different foods you ate, strangers talking to you and feeling your kicks. You were the center of attention this eve."

Sadie and her husband had purchased an expensive rocking chair for Melanie. She sat in it and began rocking back and forth gently. From the exhaustion, Melanie began to drift off. She heard a voice calling out to her, "Melanie." The voice was getting closer to her. The voice said, "Cupcake."

Excitement went through her body. The only person to ever call her Cupcake was her mother. Her mother came closer to her. Melanie was standing up, and her mother hugged her tightly and held on to her. "I miss you so much, my cupcake. Look at you, about to be a mother again. I can't stay long. I wanted to see and tell you how much I love and miss you." Her mother began to fade away.

Melanie called out to her, "Mom, wait. Please don't go. Come back. I need you. I love and miss you too."

Her mother was gone. Melanie opened her tearstained eyes and began to wail loudly. Jonathan had just walked in the house. JJ heard his mother. They both rushed to her aid.

JJ yelled, "Mom!"

Jonathan yelled, "Baby!"

Melanie had her face buried in her hands. They both came to her and consoled her, not knowing why she was crying. Melanie's voice trembled as she began to tell them why she was crying. She cried, stating, "My mother. I saw and talked to her. Please take me to my room."

They both helped her up and felt her sadness. They had never seen her in this state. She buried her face in Jonathan's side as they walked her to the bedroom. Jonathan helped her sit in her chair.

JJ stated, "Mom, it's okay. She wanted to let you know she is still with you."

This made Melanie cry even more. The emotions and cries had surpassed the reunion with Chelsea. She stated, "I know, son. It just hurts to hear and see her and then she just fades away. It's just not fair. No fair!"

JJ didn't know what else to say to his mother. JJ stated, "Mom, I love you."

Jonathan stated, "Son, I need a few minutes with your mother. Okay?"

LOSING HER CROWN

JJ stated, "Mom, when you are better, I can come in here with you and watch cartoons or whatever you like."

Melanie accepted, "Okay, son. I would love for you to."

Jonathan held his wife and asked, "Are you okay, Mel? Do you need anything? Tell me, what can I do?"

Melanie replied, "Please don't leave me in this room while I'm awake. She hugged me and told me how much she missed and loved me. She called me Cupcake. I miss her so much, Jonathan. It felt so real, her visiting me."

Jonathan stated, "I know it did, baby. She is always with you. I was not planning to leave you by yourself, Mel. You know that I am here for you and the baby, right?"

Melanie replied, "Thank you, Jonathan. Will you pop some popcorn so we can all watch a movie or something together?"

Jonathan replied, "Sure, Mel. I will have JJ come in here. You want the kettle corn, right? Anything to drink?"

Melanie replied, "Right, and some iced tea, please."

Jonathan stated, "Okay, kettle corn popcorn, iced tea, and JJ. I'll get those for you."

Melanie cracked a smile. Jonathan always had that effect on her.

Jonathan wasn't the type to dwell on things. Especially while Mel was pregnant. He didn't want anything happening to the baby with her being upset. He was good at taking things off her mind. He headed to JJ's room to tell him they were all going to eat popcorn and sit with Mom until she fell asleep. JJ was talking to Camille and explained to her that he had to hang up and keep his mother company. By the time he finished talking to Camille, Jonathan had all three bags of popcorn, along with Melanie's iced tea. JJ freed his father's hand of the iced tea so he could deliver it to his mother. They both walked down the hall to join Melanie. They could hear her laughing while they were walking toward the room. They all sat together, ate popcorn, watched cartoons, and laughed.

Melanie looked at her two favorite boys, and a smile appeared on her face. She thought, *They are good to me. Sitting here with me just to make sure I remain happy and content.*

Cerclage Removal and Delivery

It was less than two weeks for them to induce Melanie. Dr. Gharma was examining her and removing the cerclage. The removal took less than five minutes with no anesthesia. Mel was a very delicate patient to her. Dr. Gharma could see how she waddled into the exam room. Melanie was tired and ready to deliver her baby. She wanted to see Melanie early on April 29 to induce labor. Melanie was relieved to hear this. She was feeling low on energy. She was out of breath more than ever. Her feet were severely swollen. She was short-tempered with Jonathan and JJ. Anything and everything rubbed her the wrong way. She was constantly hot and was barely able to walk. She counted the days down every day.

Finally, it was Melanie's day to be induced. Jonathan did everything, from making phone calls to having her bag packed and ready. Jonathan phoned their families, letting them know Melanie was going to the hospital and they were welcome to come to the hospital for a visit. The night before, Melanie consumed a big dinner. Jonathan made her catfish fillets, corn on the cob, broccoli, and baby carrots. She knew she wouldn't be able to eat anything after they induced her. JJ didn't want to miss the arrival of his baby sister and went with them. Once they arrived at the hospital and induced her, she called Chelsea to let her know. Chelsea had cancelled all plans a week before Melanie's admittance to the hospital. Since the dinner, Chelsea and Melanie talked every day. It was as if they had never lost contact and picked up where they had left off all those years ago.

Chelsea scurried around the house, searching for her keys. "Camille, have you seen my keys?"

Camille laughed, answering, "Mom, you always do this. You lose your keys all the time. We have suggested you place them around the doorknob or on the table when you enter."

Chelsea, puzzled, said, "I checked everywhere. They are nowhere to be found."

Camille asked, "Mom, did you check the jacket you wore last night?"

Chelsea remembered they were in the jacket. It was chilly at the restaurant her date had taken her. She was no stranger to the facility and knew they kept it cold there. Chelsea knew they did this on purpose. That's how they got you to leave after eating. No lingering around so other patrons wouldn't have to wait long to be seated. She asked Camille if she wanted to attend the trip to the hospital. Camille hurried to put on her shoes for the trip.

When Chelsea arrived, Melanie was so happy to see her. She asked, "Mel, how are you? So they induced you, huh?"

Melanie replied, "Yes, they shoved a pill behind my cervix to break my water. I remember how bad it hurts for them to shove that pill inside you. I was so hoping there was an alternate method since I last had JJ."

Chelsea stated, "Well, I'm here for you. If you need me in that delivery room to hold the other hand, you let me know."

Melanie stated, "Friend, you took the words right out my mouth. Yes, I would love for you to hold my hand."

Melanie started feeling contractions. It had been three hours since they had placed the pill behind her cervix. Melanie tried to hold off on receiving the epidural to have a natural birth, but once those labor pains hit hard, she quickly changed her mind. About two hours after the epidural, she felt her water break. Nurses came in every so often to check her cervix. She was moving right along. Soon Melanie was having contractions that were thirty seconds to one minute apart, according to the monitor.

Dr. Gharma walked into the room. "Melanie, are you ready to deliver this baby?" Dr. Gharma didn't want anyone else to deliver this baby. She made sure to clear her schedule.

Melanie replied, "Yes, ma'am, I am." They instructed Melanie to scoot closer toward Dr. Gharma. The baby was ready to come out, but something happened. With all the commotion going on, the baby decided she was not ready to meet what was at the end of the tunnel. The baby's heart rate was dropping. Dr. Gharma immediately took Melanie to another room to perform an emergency C-section. Jonathan began to worry because they wouldn't allow him in the room. Chelsea kept him calm and assured him everything would be okay.

He kept asking the nurses, "Ma'am, are my wife and baby okay? Please tell me something."

They replied, "I'm sorry. We don't have any information right now. We will update you once we know something."

Jonathan felt the nightmare happening again. "Not another baby born with complications. First my boy, now my baby girl. Lord, please let them be okay."

Once they had her in the room, they made the incision and quickly extracted the baby from Melanie's womb. Melanie was scared. They started trying to revive the baby. It was a repeat of JJ's birth. She thought about her baby having defects. She tried to discern what they were doing, but the nurse noticed Melanie looking and lifted the sheet just enough so Melanie couldn't see. A couple of moments later, they were handing Melanie her baby girl. She was okay, giving her parents a scare.

The staff retrieved Jonathan, allowing him to come in the room with her to meet his baby girl. She was perfect and beautiful, with a head full of hair and all fingers and toes. Melanie thought she was perfect and ogled her the entire time she had her.

Melanie was so exhausted. They asked if she would be breast-feeding. She informed the staff she would be using formula. Melanie knew she would start drinking her wine. And she had heard how saggy the breast would appear if she allowed the baby to feed from them. Melanie was wheeled into her private room, where everyone was waiting to see the baby. Jonathan's mother, JJ, Chelsea, Camille, and a host of other relatives were all there waiting to meet the new addition to the family. Every one of them made a fuss and ogled the tiny and perfect baby.

Chelsea grabbed Melanie by the hand. "Friend, she is perfect and so beautiful. You rest yourself. I am going to take Camille and JJ home now. I will be back to see both of you tomorrow. You have a lot of family here visiting."

Melanie stated, "Okay, Chelsea. Please come back tomorrow."

Chelsea promised, "I will, sweetie. You try to get some rest, and I'll see you tomorrow." Chelsea kissed Melanie on the forehead and took Camille and JJ home.

JJ allowed family to have this time with his sister. He knew he would have her to himself after today. He kissed his baby sister and mom, telling them both he would see them later.

An hour had passed. It was time for everyone to leave the room. Melanie didn't want any more visitors in the room, so she allowed staff to take baby Taylor to the nursery, so she could sleep. There were family members arriving to see the baby. Jonathan was there to meet each of the visitors, explaining how Melanie was exhausted and needed rest. After each family member paid a visit to the nursery to look at baby Taylor through the glass, they all told Jonathan how beautiful she was and wished the family well. Once visiting was over, the nurse asked if she wanted the baby in the room with her and Jonathan. They both agreed to have the baby in the room with them. Melanie always had a fear about a non-staff member stealing her baby from the nursery. So what better place for their new addition to sleep. Mother and baby slept through the whole night, with nurses coming in periodically to check on them. Jonathan also slept through the night. He was exhausted, but not as much as Melanie.

Melanie's body was too weak to return home due to the c-section and her restricted mobility. Her body had to get back into the swing of things. And the cesarean section didn't make things easier for her. She was sore and would require two months to recuperate from the procedure. The doctor didn't want to release her until it was certain that she could move around to care for her newborn. Her stay was five days after having her C-section. The hospital was depressing for her, and she missed being home with Jonathan and JJ.

Jonathan and JJ kept the house germ-free, waiting for the day the doctor's would release Melanie and the baby. Jonathan and JJ missed her those five days. Jonathan kept working until Melanie's release. That way, he would not miss too much work. Trent understood Jonathan would be taking family leave to care for Melanie and the baby. Jonathan would continue to receive 60 percent of his pay.

Bringing Baby Home

It was Melanie's release date and time to take Ashley "Honey" Cataleya home. JJ and Camille were there for the ride. Camille, while looking at the baby, thought how tiny and beautiful this being was. She allowed the baby to hold on to her finger and awed at her making those baby noises. She held the baby until the nurse came in to get mom and baby. The nurse wheeled mommy and baby to the car. Camille carefully placed the baby in her car seat. Jonathan and the nurse helped Melanie get into the car. They were careful to not cause any rips or tears to the stitches from her cesarean section. All were nestled in the car. JJ and Camille sat in the back with the baby. JJ ogled her and couldn't take his eyes off his baby sister. He brushed his finger across her face. She latched on to his finger and wouldn't let go. JJ cracked a smile. He thought, *How precious and peaceful she looks with no care in the world. I am going to spoil you rotten, little girl. You won't ever have to worry about anyone messing with you. I got your back.*

JJ couldn't wait until they arrived home. He wanted to remove her from the car seat and cradle her in his arms. He only held her a little while when she was born. She had so many visitors, and everyone wanted their chance to hold her. Tonight, it was just her and her big brother. No visitors tonight. Melanie made everyone aware that she wouldn't be up for any visits. She wants to spend a quiet first night at home with her newborn baby, husband, and son. Camille and Chelsea were the only visitors allowed. Chelsea had things that needed addressed before she could visit. Once they arrived home, Jonathan and JJ helped the new mother exit the car. They were careful and took their time with her. Melanie was desperate to enter her apartment and get into her bed after taking a nice quick shower to remove the hospital smell from her.

When Melanie walked in, she smelled nothing but bleach and lemon all-purpose cleaner in the air. This was validation the boys had been busy sanitizing the home for the baby's arrival. Melanie was pleased with the smell and scenery. They removed clutter to make space for the baby's things to be within Melanie's reach. Jonathan knew she would be showering as soon as they arrived home and started Mel's shower. Camille and JJ took the baby into the living area to watch her until Jonathan and Mel returned.

"Hey there, little Cataleya. It is me, your big brother. You are so perfect."

Camille could see JJ was enjoying his time with his baby sister. It made her imagine how he would be with his own kids one day. She asked, "JJ, you want something out the kitchen? I'm going to grab a water."

JJ replied, "Yeah, get me one too. And thanks for asking."

Camille went into the kitchen. When she returned, the baby began crying. JJ had reached into the bag and pulled a bottle out for her. He removed her from the car seat to hold her while he fed her. He had her in his arms and bottle in her mouth, but she was still crying. Camille stated, "Here, place her close to you with her head cradled in your arm. Make sure to hold the bottle up to keep her from sucking air."

The baby ceased crying and sucked on the bottle. She wanted to feel JJ's warm body for security. Camille kept an eye on JJ, making sure she corrected any errors on his part. He was doing wonderfully with her. He needed little help from Camille.

After the baby finished feeding, Camille showed Jonathan how to burp her. Camille stated, "JJ, you can burp her two ways. Hold her over your shoulder and pat her back or sit her up and gently pat or rub her back in circular motions."

JJ put her over his shoulder and burped her that way with a burping cloth to catch any regurgitated milk. When he heard her burp, he responded, "Oh, wow. That was a big one." He laid her in the bassinette and watched her sleep. He stated to Camille, "Camille, thank you for helping me with her."

Camille responded, "No worries. I have had tons of practice with babies. I have always had to babysit my sister and little cousins. It will get easier for you. You will become a pro in no time. You can always call me if you're home alone with her and need some advice, or I can come over and help you."

JJ stated, "Thanks, babe. I mean friend. You are the best. They won't have anything to worry about when she is with me. I will protect her at all costs."

Camille stated, "And I'm sure she appreciates her big brother."

JJ said, "When I first looked at her at the hospital, my heart raced. I became excited because the waiting was over. She is finally here. I get to initiate spoiling, protecting, and being the best big brother here on earth and in her life. What do you think?"

Camille replied, "You will make a great protector and big brother. She is lucky to have you in her life. You know, once you start spoiling her, she will look for you to be this way with her always. You can't pull back. She won't understand it."

JJ replied, "I'll be able to manage it. Shouldn't take that much spoiling for someone so tiny."

Camille educated JJ, stating, "Let me just let you in on a secret. Don't hold her all the time. When she is calm, quiet, and asleep, let her lay there to herself. They find all kinds of things to play with, like angels and their feet. They love putting their feet in their mouths. But that won't come until much later. Just try not to hold her too much, or she will want you holding her all the time. It will make things hard for your mom. Especially with her having to recuperate from the cesarean section."

JJ replied, "I'll keep that in mind."

Jonathan helped Melanie in the shower. "Mel, I'll get your pajamas to slide into once you are done showering. Is there a particular color you want?"

Melanie replied, "Yes, something neutral. Nothing that stands out. Just neutral."

Jonathan ran across a pair of red pajamas, and he knew that was out the question. He saw red on Melanie, and a certain member of his body would erect and throb. He grabbed her tan-colored pajamas. He laid them across the bed, along with a pair of underwear. Melanie wouldn't wear pajamas without any undergarments.

Melanie asked, "Jonathan, can you bring me some water, please? I'm thirsty."

Jonathan replied, "Sure."

Jonathan walked to the kitchen and overheard Camille instructing JJ with the baby. He grabbed two waters from the refrigerator and walked back to the room.

"Here you go."

Melanie stated, "Thanks, Jonathan. I am almost ready to get out of here. Have you checked on the baby?" Melanie opened the water and drank until it was gone.

Jonathan replied, "Baby, I went to the hall and overheard Camille telling JJ how to hold and feed her. He was listening and did everything she told him to do. He even burped the baby."

Melanie stated, "Oh, okay. So my baby is safe until I get her? Camille must have tons of experience with babies. Well, duh, she does have a baby sister. I'm so ready to hold my little princess."

Jonathan replied, "Yes, the baby is safe. I have been peeking around the corner, watching and listening to everything while you were showering. Would you like me to bring her in here?"

Melanie replied, "No, let her stay in there with them for a while. We have all night to get her to ourselves. She is fine for now. Can you help me out, please?"

Jonathan answered, "Sure, baby. Don't move."

Melanie had to be extra careful getting out of the shower. She didn't want to cause any tears or rips from the procedure. It took almost a minute to help her get out the shower, but she finally made it.

Jonathan helped her with her underwear and pajamas. Melanie was exhausted. Jonathan asked, "Are you ready to go into the living area to witness what I have been seeing?"

Melanie replied, "No, Jonathan. As much as I would love to walk in on JJ taking care of his baby sister, I need to take it easy. Can you bring her here to me?"

Jonathan replied, "Sure, Mel. Anything for you." Jonathan walked into the living area to bring baby Cataleya to her mother. "JJ, your mom wants me to bring the baby to her. She's done getting herself together and is now asking for your sister."

JJ replied, "Okay, Dad. Let me walk her back there with you. I can't seem to take my eyes off her, nor do I want to lay her in her bassinette. She looks so peaceful resting in my arms."

They both walked to the room together. A smile appeared on Melanie's face. She would finally have time alone with her baby. She requested, "Please hand her to me, son. Thanks for watching her for us while I was tidying myself. Did she need changing while you had her with you?"

JJ answered, "You're welcome, Mom. No, she didn't need changing. Mom, I am not ready for that yet, so I had Camille check her for that. She mostly just slept and kept holding my finger."

Melanie stated, "Yeah, they tend to latch and hold on tight for dear life. Thank Camille for me too, son. She has been great with your little sister."

JJ stated, "Sure thing, Mom. I will leave you two alone with her. Call me if you need me for anything."

Melanie was still tired, and so was Jonathan. Melanie placed the baby in her bassinet next to her. They both fell asleep for a much-needed rest.

Continue Therapy and Nutrition Consult

Jonathan had been going to therapy two times weekly. The therapy was giving him a little relief. The condition had damaged his joints, causing pain. This explained why Jonathan, at times, could not perform simple tasks while at work or home. He could barely produce a fist without it resulting in pain. He continued telling Melanie his health was okay. He didn't want her to worry about him. She had the new baby to occupy her mind and getting herself back into the swing of things.

Jonathan had been doing research about his condition, and had he caught it earlier, things would be different for him. He went in to see Dr. Salazar for assessment. The doctor looked at his labs and the report from the therapist. Jonathan wasn't getting any better and not getting any worse. If he followed the regimen, he would stop it from progressing.

Dr. Salazar stated, "Mr. Taylor, you should take the initiative and start doing therapy at home. Whatever you have learned during therapy sessions, continue it at home. Your insurance will only cover so many visits within a calendar year. I also know how expensive therapy can be when asked to attend two to three times per week. I have patients who tell me the cost fits nowhere in their budget."

Jonathan replied, "Okay. I do find myself doing those exercises at home. Anything I can do to keep from being on medication?"

Dr. Salazar answered, "Well, you can talk to a nutritionist and explore nutritional options that may eliminate medication. You can see a nutritionist without a referral because of your PPO plan. Find one and talk to them."

Jonathan stated, "Okay, will do, and I'll see you for our next visit in three months." Jonathan left the doctor's office feeling a little better. This appeased Jonathan's mind after hearing the doctor say his condition hadn't worsened.

A Much-Needed Visit

Melanie's phone rang. She picked up and heard a familiar voice, asking, "Hey, Mel. How are you doing?"

Melanie replied, "Hey, you. I'm fine, Chelsea. Just adjusting to being a new mom for the second time. When will you be by to see me and the baby? I haven't seen you since the hospital. I miss my best friend."

Chelsea answered, "I know, Mel. I have been so busy. I haven't forgotten about you. In fact, it is my reason for calling. I have free time after work. Do you feel like company?"

Melanie answered, "Sure. I would love company. I love Jonathan and JJ, but I need some gal friend time."

Chelsea stated, "Okay, so I will be done in thirty minutes. I will clean myself up before coming around you and the baby. I'll see you about four, okay?"

Melanie replied, "Okay, Chelsea. Sure thing. See you then." Melanie had Jonathan help her dress before he went to see Dr. Henry. He also placed a pan of lasagna in the oven that would take about two and a half hours to cook thoroughly. It had been in the freezer. Melanie wanted to sit in the living area and visit Chelsea. She was spending so much time in her bedroom and needed a change of scenery.

Chelsea, eager to see Melanie and Cataleya, drove ten miles over the speed limit. She arrived home, jumped out of the car, and ran to the door. Once inside, she removed her attire and jumped in the shower. She cleansed her body. As she washed herself, she began to remember the times she had in the shower with her ex-husband.

"Stop it! Stop thinking about Chauncey." After showering, she made haste getting dressed. She grabbed her keys and a plastic bowl, heading out the door.

Chelsea finally arrived and had a batch of Rice Krispies Treats for Melanie. The two ladies greeted each other with a hug and kiss. Chelsea stated, "Look at you. You are still glowing after having the baby. What's been going on with you?"

Melanie answered, "I have been doing nothing but sitting in my bedroom watching television." Mel noticed the bowl Chelsea brought, stating, "Oh, my favorite. Rice Krispies Treats. You read my mind. I thank you kindly. I have seven more weeks before they release me back to work. I must admit, I really don't want to go back at all, but I know I have no choice. Wish I could work from home. Jonathan and I have already discussed that since I am the bread winner, I will continue working, and he will stay home with Cataleya. I just can't trust my baby with these day cares. I feel better knowing she is with one of us."

Chelsea sat there listening to Melanie and wondered if she should say something about her plan. She knew the dangers this might cause. Chelsea asked, "Really, Mel? I mean, if that is how you both see things, then make it work. Just make sure this is what you want, Mel. Have you really thought about it? Weighed the pros and cons? It sounds like a smart idea, but is it the best? You don't want a man to become reliant on you, even if he is your husband. Once a woman takes on that role of being the head of the house, it is hard for you to step down and for him to step back into that role. Are you willing to risk being put in alpha position?"

Melanie looked at her friend and had no answer. She hadn't questioned it, nor had the decision thoroughly been discussed. Mel wanted it to be this way. It didn't make sense to work just to pay for childcare. Not only that, the day cares had been targets of the media because of abuse, neglect, you name it. Melanie didn't trust them.

Melanie answered, "Chelsea, please let me make this decision without any interference."

Chelsea stated, "Melanie, it's not just about Jonathan. It's about losing yourself. You are a loving and nurturing person. I just detest the idea of you becoming someone other than who I know you to be in life because you have assumed a role that's not yours to have."

Melanie rebutted, "Chelsea, I am okay with this. Jonathan is okay with it. We will deal with whatever comes toward us."

Chelsea stated, "Men are okay with it in the beginning, but after a while, they begin to question who they are in the relationship. They feel as though they have become the female in the relationship, and the only way to reclaim their dominance is to exit. They don't know how to get themselves back from it, so they take the effortless way out and don't care who they hurt during the process. Please reconsider. This is how men and women lose their crowns as the King and Queen of the home. Figure out another way to do this so that it won't harm your family. Maybe Jonathan could find a night job."

Melanie always made her decisions based on how it would affect her. It didn't matter to her who else it would affect. Melanie and Jonathan had switched roles in the marriage. She had become the man of the house and Jonathan, the woman of the house.

Melanie stated, "Oh, wow, I never thought about it that way. We did the math. With both of us holding onto our jobs, day care would take his entire check, leaving me to pay for everything anyway when he could just be at home."

Chelsea said, "Yes, it's expensive, and it does seem like the smart thing to do. You feel as though he is working to pay day care when he can be at home with her. It looks like an approachable option, but just think. If he keeps working and seeing you all are getting nowhere, he may opt for a higher paying job. Sometimes you must allow men to get into a situation to see how they will manage it. Give them control of the situation. Motivation comes from a worrying man to make things better. He won't be able to sleep at night until he finds a way. Let him iron out the complications and come up with a solution. Never give a man an easy way out of things. He just needs to know you have his back."

Melanie stated, "Now see, that's why I'm so happy to have you as a friend. I never see things that way."

Chelsea stated, "No problem. I have been through it. That is a part of why Chauncey and I divorced. I learned once a man loses his place in the home, he's not the same person in that relationship. He feels it is necessary to start all over just to find himself."

The two friends briefly stopped talking to play with Cataleya. She was stretching from a nap. They watched in awe as she opened her eyes from stretching. She started sucking her thumb. Melanie knew her baby was hungry. Chelsea went to the kitchen to grab a bottle to warm up. She thought about her and Chauncey while waiting for the bottle to warm. She couldn't understand her thoughts of him. She was thinking about Chauncey more. She thought, *I thought I was over him. Why am I thinking about him so often lately? Could it be I still love him? Nah, that can't be. I shouldn't love him after what he did.*

Chelsea returned to the living area with the bottle. "Mel, I still love him. I don't know, I mean I think I do. Listen to me. I'm not making any sense. I want to hope he loves me, but a part of me wants to deny that we both still love each other. We just don't know how to get it back on track."

Melanie stated, "Chelsea, love will always find a way to bring people back together. Just give it time. Sounds as though loneliness has settled in and you miss him. Everyone who is single goes through it. You just need to keep yourself busy at all times. Occupy your mind as much as possible. You two have a special connection, and it is beautiful. I know he loves you. He looks at you as if he's apologizing. He's just waiting for a sign or gesture from you."

Chelsea asked, "You can see that just by looking at him?"

Melanie replied, "Yes, and I can feel his feelings for you pour into me when I am in the room with you both. Whatever he feels at that moment concerning you, I can feel. That is the life of an empath.

I always get these uninvited feelings from other people. Sometimes they just invade me, and there is no reason for me to feel what I am feeling. I never know where it is coming from until I confirm the origin. We are all connected, you know. Sometimes it rocks, and sometimes it is depressing. You feel the good, the bad, and the ugly. Not just one but all of them. Sometimes I forget that I'm an empath and question the feelings."

Chelsea stated, "Wow, that is amazing. How did you know you were an empath?"

Melanie answered, "One day, I was in the elevator on my way up to my clinic. I stood behind this lady who worked in the same building. While in the elevator, I couldn't help but focus my attention to the back of her head. I started feeling compassion for her and didn't understand why. Two weeks later, another coworker and I were talking about an employee that had been in the hospital. She died from a brain tumor. Her description matched the lady in the elevator with me. I told my coworker about the elevator incident. Later that day, I cried. Because when I think about that day, God was telling me to pray for her, and I didn't. I didn't know at the time. It was a new feeling for me. I had never, to my recollection, experienced that feeling. When I told a friend the story, she told me I was an empath. She's one herself."

Chelsea stated, "I always knew there was something special about you. You always appeared fragile and so bashful when we were younger, but that was because of your trials at home. People like you go through things in life to prepare you for a special gift. You have yours, and it is cool. You look at it as a blessing and curse, which is understandable. Melanie, I must be honest with you. The other reason for our divorce, there was an indiscretion with another woman that caused the final rip in our marriage. His betrayal made me feel unattractive to him. He made me feel I wasn't good enough for him. All sorts of thoughts invaded me. They were extremely profound. I couldn't take anymore of those thoughts, so I purposely became distant and standoffish. Then I finally filed for divorce at his request. I thought the only way to obliterate them was the divorce. I was wrong. They still invade me to this very day."

The baby let out a cry. "Oh, my little Cataleya, what is it, momma's baby? You want your pacifier?" Melanie placed the pacifier in the baby's mouth. It appeased her. "There you go, my sweet love. Mommy loves you so much." Melanie kissed her baby on the forehead. Cataleya gave her a smile. Melanie asked, "Chelsea, would you please lay her in the bassinette for me?"

Chelsea answered, "Sure thing, Mel." Chelsea placed her in her bassinette and returned to her seat.

Melanie asked, "You still love Chauncey, right?"

Chelsea answered, "Very much so."

Melanie stated, "Then work it out, Chelsea. You only get one great one in life. I'm certain Chauncey feels that about you."

Chelsea asked, "Okay, if he feels that way, why won't he just come out and say it?"

Melanie replied, "Same reason you haven't. You both feel it is over and are afraid of rejection. Sometimes just a small gesture from us gals gives them that sign that there is still hope."

Chelsea asked, "So I could initiate a meaningful hug or something like that when he comes by to see the kids? Holding on a little longer but not too much?"

Melanie responded, "There you go. Give him a welcoming and meaningful gesture. You got this, Chelsea."

Chelsea stated, "Thanks, Mel. I'm elated that I talked to you about this. It's hard for me to discuss this with others." Mel and Chelsea talked for an hour before Jonathan and JJ arrived home.

After Jonathan left Dr. Henry's office, he called his mother for her nutritionist's number. "Hey, Mom. How are you feeling?"

Ms. Taylor replied, "I'm doing fine, son. I just came home from work, and I'm making my dinner. How are my grandbabies?"

Jonathan replied, "The kids are fine, Mom. I'm calling to get the number of your nutritionist."

Ms. Taylor asked, "Why do you need her number? Does Melanie need it for a nutritional consult?"

Jonathan replied, "Yes, Mom. It is for Melanie. She has been complaining about how she misses her shape before her pregnancy. May I have her number please?" Ms. Taylor gave him the number.

Jonathan didn't want his mother to know about his condition. She would have plagued him with questions and her advice. The less she knew, the better. Jonathan called the nutritionist and made an appointment. After scheduling his appointment, Jonathan made a phone call to Melanie. "Hey, Melanie. How are you and my little princess?"

Melanie answered, "We are fine. I am tired as usual, and she is sleeping right now. She been sleeping for the last two hours. When you get home, I am waking her up so she will sleep all night. Chelsea is here with me. We can discuss your visit later tonight." Melanie didn't want to say anything about him being at the doctors in front of Chelsea out of respect for Jonathan.

Jonathan stated, "Okay, but it was a productive visit. He says nothing has changed. I am on my way home. Do you gals need anything while I'm out before I come home?"

Melanie replied, "Just a second. Chelsea, you need anything before Jonathan makes it home?"

Chelsea answered, "Have him to bring me a bottle of Pinot Grigio."

Melanie asked, "Did you hear what she asked for, Jonathan?"

Jonathan replied, "Yes, I heard her. I will get the bottle of wine for her. Is JJ home?"

JJ and Camille just stepped through the door. Melanie answered, "He and Camille just walked in here. Son, you all want anything while your dad is out before he comes home?"

They both replied, "No, thanks."

Melanie added, "Jonathan, you already know what I want, and please hurry home. I miss you."

Jonathan stated, "Sure thing, baby. I will be home in about twenty minutes or so. I love you, Mel."

Melanie replied, "I love you too, Jonathan."

Hearing that JJ and Camille had just stepped inside irritated Jonathan. He was certain his talks with JJ about Camille would cause conflict between the two. He just wanted JJ to be careful and not limit himself to one person. But JJ never disclosed to his parents they were dating. Jonathan was under the impression that they were because they spent too much time together, and all he talked about was Camille.

Melanie looked at JJ and Camille. Melanie would love to have Camille as her daughter-in-law. She was respectful, smart, didn't give her mother problems, and she was very pretty. Her genes, along with JJ's, would give Mel and Jonathan beautiful grandchildren.

Chelsea asked, smiling, "And where have you two been? It is five o'clock. I have been here since four. I thought you two would have been here."

Camille replied, "We were at the house, waiting for you to show up from work. You didn't tell me you were coming here, Mom, or we would have come here right after school."

Chelsea stated, "You're right. I never told you I would be visiting Melanie today."

JJ interrupted, "Where's my baby sister? I missed her so much and thought about nothing but her all day."

Melanie replied, "She's in her bassinette. Your dad will be here in about twenty minutes. You all can hold her after I wake her from this short nap."

JJ asked, "Mom, are you hungry? You want me to cook something?"

Melanie answered, "No need, son. Your dad put a pan of lasagna in the oven before he left. It should be ready when he gets home. If you like, you can put the salad together. That way, when he gets home, we can all eat dinner."

JJ stated, "Okay, sure thing, Mom."

Melanie asked, "Will the two of you please join us for dinner? We have more than enough."

Chelsea and Camille both agreed to stay and have dinner. JJ checked on the lasagna. It had a nice, almost done baking look. He opened the refrigerator to grab the lettuce, tomatoes, cucumbers, avocados, shredded cheese, spinach, grilled chicken strips, and salad dressing. JJ thought about the conversation he had with his dad about Camille. He thought, *What does Dad know? He seemed bitter when he talked to me about my relationship with Camille. Wonder what's his beef with me being with her.*

Jonathan had arrived home, bearing gifts for Melanie's guest. He walked by the kitchen and saw JJ making the salad for their dinner. "Hey, son. What's going on with you?"

JJ replied, "Hey, Dad. Nothing much. Just getting this salad together. We will be eating in a couple of minutes. Mom invited Chelsea and Camille to eat with us."

Jonathan replied, "Okay. I'm quite sure at least one of them will want a glass of wine." Jonathan entered the living area where the ladies sat. Jonathan stated, "Well, hello, ladies. You two good in here? Chelsea, would you like me to crack open and pour your wine into a wineglass?"

Chelsea replied, "Hey, Jonathan. Yes, please, if you don't mind. Melanie invited us to stay for dinner."

Jonathan walked over to Melanie and kissed his wife. He walked back into the kitchen to fetch the wine opener to pour Chelsea a glass of wine. While getting the wine opener, Jonathan thought back to the day he and JJ had their talk about his relationship with Camille. He noticed that they seemed to have become closer. He surely thought his son would take his advice and get rid of her. He knew the first conversation about Camille should be the last. He knew if he kept talking to JJ about Camille, he would only draw JJ closer to her. So instead of reminding JJ of their conversation, he casually asked how things were going at school, homework, sports, and eventually worked his way to ask JJ the one question that plagued his mind.

Jonathan asked, "Meet any pretty girls lately?"

JJ didn't want to have this conversation with his dad. He knew he would try to sway him into not pursuing a relationship with Camille. Nothing sexually was going on with them, but JJ didn't want to be the type to talk to other females while he was endeavoring to be with Camille.

JJ replied, "Dad, with school, sports, Mom, and the baby, I just don't have the time. Besides, Camille for now would be the one I would like to date, just not yet."

Jonathan stated, "I understand, son. Just remember to keep your options open. You are still young, is all I am saying. Let me get this wine out to Chelsea. Are you good? You need any help in here?"

JJ replied, "Yes, no, and I'm setting the table."

Jonathan returned with the glass of wine for Chelsea. "Here you go, Chelsea. If you ladies will excuse me, I will be showering for dinner. I will see you ladies in a few." Jonathan thought about his angel in the bassinette. He walked over to kiss her. She gave her daddy a smile.

Melanie stated, "By the time you return, she will be awake."

CHAPTER 19

Plans to Detour JJ from Camille

Jonathan jumped in the shower. He thought about his conversation with JJ and how he still clung to Camille. Jonathan's plan to influence his son to date girls other than Camille had to be carefully planned. "I know what I'll do. Trent has a son and a daughter. This will stir things up between JJ and Camille. If he won't listen to what I say, then I will just have to take a different approach. I'll have Trent bring them over for dinner one night." Jonathan finished showering and was drying off his body. He thought about his plan, and a smirk brushed across his face. He would entertain the idea to Trent when he got in for his shift tomorrow. He joined the others.

JJ had the table already set for dinner. He brought in the lasagna and salad. JJ thought about his mother, wondering if she wanted to eat at the table or in the living area. "Mom, did you want to eat in the dining room with us or here in the living area?"

Mel answered, "I can join you guys. Just bring the baby in here with us."

JJ did as his mother asked. They all sat at the table and enjoyed the meal and each other's company. After dinner, Camille and Chelsea ended their evening, leaving for home.

"Mel and Jonathan, thank you both for having us. It's time that we go. It's getting late."

Jonathan said under his breath, "It's about time."

JJ heard him and looked at him with disdain. Melanie and JJ kissed and hugged their guests. JJ walked them to their car.

Cataleya was awake but didn't bother her parents while they ate. The noise entertained her. Jonathan retrieved his princess from her resting place and held her. Mom and dad, sitting close to each other, gazing at the beautiful life they produced. Jonathan Jr. returned and wanted to confront Jonathan, but this was his dad. He had authority over him. Jonathan didn't want to argue with his dad, causing Melanie and the baby to be upset. So he brushed it off and joined his parents. Soon, they all felt tired and prepared for bed, turning in for the night.

Trent was at the store before Jonathan arrived. Jonathan noticed the unlocked door and knew Trent was there. "Good. He is here. I can ask him to come to dinner one night with his kids." Jonathan could hear that voice telling him to leave things alone, but he was headstrong about JJ allotting so much time with Camille, and he needed to break the hold he thought Camille had on his son.

Trent heard Jonathan coming into the back and saw him through the cameras. He greeted Jonathan, "Hey, my man, Jonathan. How's it going?"

Jonathan walked up to Trent as he was pulling himself up from his chair. They gave each other the brotherly hug and handshake.

Jonathan replied, "Aw, man, I can't call it, but you got it. How you been?"

Trent answered, "Same here, man. I have been so busy with the store and trying to expand in other cities. But all is well. It's time for a night out with the fellas."

Jonathan stated, "I have the perfect solution. Why don't you and the kids come over for dinner with us? It's been a while since the last dinner invite. JJ and Mel haven't seen the kids in a while. I'm sure they will be thrilled to see them."

The children had known each other for about ten years. Trent's daughter, Naomi, was sixteen, and Trent Jr. was seventeen. Trent replied, "Okay, sure. We can do that. I will even bring their mother so that Mel can have someone to talk to. Do you need me to bring anything? I have some nice liquor we could drink while the gals are talking."

Jonathan answered, "Hey, if you want to, I'm cool with it. I'll let Mel know when I get home later."

Trent had to leave, stating, "Well, man, I'm out, okay? You let me know when you all want us to come over, and I'll make sure to clear my calendar, unless it's something that I just can't cancel."

Jonathan stated, "Sure thing, Trent. But tell you what. It would make sense that you let me know when you are free, and we will work from there. Mel and I are open for dinner anytime. Deal?"

Trent answered, "Sounds like a plan, man. I will call you and let you know. I have some out-of-town business to conduct."

Jonathan stated, "Okay. See you later, and look forward to your call."

Jonathan's plan now was in motion. Jonathan thought, *Operation JJ looking elsewhere in full effect. I know he is going to want to spend time with Naomi. Especially since it's been years since they've seen each other.*

John arrived to work on time as usual. He had been in the back when he heard Trent and Jonathan talking. Jonathan asked, "How are you doing this morning, John?"

John replied, "All is good, Jonathan. Ready to start this day and get it over. I have everything prepped and ready to make these pastries and breakfast sandwiches for the people. You need anything before I start?"

Jonathan replied, "No. I am good. Go ahead and do what you do, John. I'll be in the office if you need me." Jonathan and John were able to work the register and fill orders with no problems.

Business was starting to pick up, and Jonathan had pitched the idea to Trent that an extra hand was necessary. Trent did agree. He had been looking at the profits his business was generating. So the extra hand was justifiable. There were five applicants that caught their attention. Trent and Jonathan both did the interviewing for the shop as a team. Since they needed an adult, it was necessary for them both to be present. One would be checking body language, eye contact, and awareness, while the other conducted the interview. They did switch up roles as well for each interview. There was one candidate who proved to be the perfect person for the position. Sharon was a great employee. She remained gainfully employed and didn't jump from job to job. Both former and current employer deemed her as an exemplary employee. They both agreed Sharon would be their best candidate and hired her. She would be helping John and Jonathan to open and prep the store.

Sharon was surprised to see Jonathan sitting across from her during the interview. She never said anything to Jonathan. It wasn't the right time to reveal to Jonathan her identity. Jonathan didn't recognize her, but Sharon certainly knew Jonathan.

Dinner and Game Night

Jonathan arrived home. He kissed Melanie, stating, "Mel, I invited Trent and his kids over for dinner. He is also bringing the kid's mother. I hope you don't mind. He wanted a guy's night out, but I thought it would be okay to invite them over for dinner. I don't want to leave you alone with the baby." He was determined to cool things down between JJ and Camille.

Melanie said, "Okay, Jonathan. I look forward to seeing them and meeting their mother. They can come this Saturday night. JJ is planning to make something special, so I will have him to make enough for extra guests. Have you met their mother?"

Jonathan thought, *Extra guests? Chelsea and Camille must be coming. I am tired of seeing those two. They are always here eating up my food. But this will be perfect. Camille will see how beautiful Naomi is and instantly feel some type of way about her being around JJ.* A devious smile brushed over his face. Jonathan answered, "Yes, I met her once. It was a while back. She came to the store to drop off papers for Trent. Let me text him right quick to let him know clear his calendar for Saturday. Do you know what JJ is cooking?"

Melanie answered, "No, I sure don't." Trent responded rather quick and accepted the invite. Jonathan's plan was in motion.

Jonathan headed to JJ's room to tell him the news. "JJ, son, how's it going with you? Anything new going on you wish to talk about with the old man?"

JJ replied, "Hey, Dad. Things going good with me. Nothing new. What's going on with you?"

Jonathan answered, "I'm good, son. I wanted to tell you Trent is bringing Trent Jr. and Naomi over for dinner this Saturday. Will you be available?"

JJ replied, "Sure, Dad. In fact, I am planning to cook something special that night. I can't tell you what it is. I want to surprise you all."

Jonathan stated, "Cool, son."

Jonathan turned to walk away, but he had one last thing to say to JJ. "Son, your old man is proud of you. You have soared with your cooking skills. This may be something you could venture off to in life. You would be a great chef."

JJ stated, "You know, Dad, I have pondered that idea. I have done research about their salaries. Their salaries are okay, but the money in that field would be personal chefs or a catering business. They really make a handsome salary. I would just need to build my clientele. This field could be lucrative for me. If I strategize correctly, my plan is to meet a bunch of privileged individuals my age and do a little cooking for them while I am in school. They will spread the word, and in no time, the requests will pour in abundantly."

Jonathan looked at his son, amazed. "That is a great business plan. Where will you meet these individuals?"

JJ replied, "That's easy, Dad. My friends and I are always spending time together downtown. We meet interesting people our own age, especially those with money who want to hang out with us while we're there. They are always picking up the bill for us. They just whip out their credit cards, saying it is on them. They tell us they tired of hanging with the stuck-up people in their own environment. They are always calling for us to come hang out with them. The cultural difference intrigues them. They are different, Dad, from the usual privileged folk that I have encountered. They genuinely have an interest in being friends with us. They don't judge us, nor do they flaunt their money and possessions. I will just use those connections to my advantage. Peep this, Dad. I never told you, but when police officers harass us, those guys tell them to leave us alone. We have done nothing wrong for their harassment. Dad, they stand up for us, embarrassing and dismissing the police."

Jonathan said, "Now, son, those are the type of privileged people you want to have in your circle. There are some good ones out there. Officers are afraid of people with status. For us, we must know our rights and be smart when they approach you. Always remember that, son."

JJ answered, "Sure, Dad. I'm already a step ahead of you."

Jonathan went into the room with Melanie and Cataleya. He looked at Mel while she played with his daughter in her arms. "Here, Mel, let me hold her for a spell."

Melanie handed her over to her dad. "Hey, my sweet baby girl. It's your daddy. I love you so much." He kissed her on her forehead.

Cataleya gave him a big smile and began to coo at him. This put a big smile on Jonathan's face. She was one and a half months now.

Jonathan stated, "Mel, Trent accepted the invitation to dinner. I told him to be here seven thirty on the dot. I can't wait to see the kids. Seems like forever since our last visit. I know it's been at least three years since we last saw them. We used to see them all the time before Trent and their mother split."

Melanie replied, "Yes, it has been a while since we last saw them. I am anxious to see them too. Glad you invited them." Melanie had to relieve herself and went to the bathroom. She thought about Jonathan, hoping he was following doctor's orders. She asked, "Jonathan, how are things going at work?"

Jonathan replied, "Well, we just hired someone to help open and prep the store. Her name is Sharon. She started two days ago. So far so good."

Melanie added, "Well, I'm glad you two entertained the idea of an extra hand. The business is increasing, and you do need the help."

Jonathan stated, "Yes, much needed. Hey, Mel, by chance, did JJ tell or hint about what type of food he plans to cook for dinner this Saturday? He seems excited about it. Thought maybe he gave you an idea."

Melanie replied, "No. I asked, and he will not tell me. Says just mentioning the ingredients will ruin the surprise. He says he also doesn't want us coming into the kitchen while he is preparing the food. So anything we want from the fridge, we will have to ask him for it. I don't know why he is so secretive about this dish. Whatever it is, it must be big for him to not want to share with us."

Jonathan added, "Yeah. Must be, Mel." Jonathan and Mel continued playing with their princess.

Melanie had two weeks before she was to return to work. She was not looking forward to going back. But she tried not thinking about it. The suspense of JJ's dinner did just that. She had offered to take JJ shopping for all ingredients needed for his dinner. JJ dismissed her idea of traveling with him. He asked Camille if she wouldn't mind shopping with him. Camille would keep his secret. He knew his mother would follow him to each aisle in the store, so traveling by himself ensured she wouldn't be privy to his menu. Just a glance of what he was purchasing would immediately tell Mel what he was planning to cook. He was going to surprise his parents and guests with New Orleans dishes. JJ was making jambalaya, chicken, sausage and shrimp gumbo, corn okra creole, and sweet oven bread his mom taught him to make. JJ had confidence in himself and knew he would get good reviews from everyone. With items purchased, he exited the store.

JJ arrived home with bags in each hand. Melanie asked, "Did you get everything you need, JJ?"

JJ answered, "Yes, Mom. I did. I think you all will be pretty impressed with this one. And, Mom, remember, you and Dad stay away from the kitchen. Whatever you need from the kitchen, I will get it for you. Okay, Mom?"

Melanie replied, "Okay, son. I will stay out of the kitchen. Your dad won't be so easy to steer away from the kitchen. You know how he is. He will ease in there, being inquisitive about things other than your meal. You know how he loves holding conversations with you in the kitchen."

JJ laughed, "Hahaha. Don't worry, Mom. I will handle Dad. One thing I have noticed about Dad, he respects boundaries between us." Except for boundaries dealing with JJ and Camille.

Unforgettable Dinner

It was Saturday. JJ was up early getting the apartment cleaned prior to preparing his dinner for the evening. JJ was smart. He prepped everything the night before just in case there were roadblocks along the way. In addition, he purchased a little extra of everything to be on the safe side. JJ wanted everything to be perfect. Since he prepped and stored everything in the refrigerator, he started cooking at three that evening. This would give him enough time to cook and shower before the guests arrived. His parents kept their oath to not access and enter the kitchen. Whatever they needed from the kitchen, he procured it. Melanie and Jonathan endeavored to not bother him too much to keep his focus on the surprise dinner. JJ had the apartment drenched with an amazing aroma. He had his three dishes cooking on the stove. When it was time for the corn bread, he had to inquire with Melanie about the amount of sugar because there were other people eating who might not fancy sugar in their bread.

"Mom, do you want me to add any sugar to the bread?"

Melanie answered, "How much are you making? Is it a small or big pan? Half a cup if it's small and three-fourth of a cup if large should suffice."

JJ stated, "Okay, thanks, Mom." JJ was preparing a large pan of oven bread, so he used three-fourths cup of sugar. He wanted to wait a while prior to placing the batter in the oven. He gave the gumbo the most time to cook. He waited about forty-five minutes prior to the gumbo's completion to cook the jambalaya and corn okra creole. After he placed them in the cookware, he would go ahead and place the corn bread in the oven. He endeavored to have all dishes completed simultaneously. JJ was proud of himself, allowing his chest to protrude.

After JJ placed the remaining dishes in their cookware, he decided to get himself cleaned up with a nice shower. He approached his parents, stating, "Mom and Dad, I have everything cooking, and it should be done in about forty-five minutes. I am going to take a shower. Before I shower, do either of you need anything from the kitchen?"

Melanie and Jonathan replied, "No."

Jonathan stated, "Okay, good. So there's no reason for either of you to go to the kitchen."

Jonathan stated, "Right, there is no reason, son. Your mother and I were discussing there's no wine. I am going to the store to buy two bottles. I will be back son. And it smells good in here."

JJ said, "Okay, Dad, and thanks."

Melanie was alone in the living area, soaking up the impeccable aroma her son created. She kept herself busy playing with Cataleya. Melanie thought, *That food smells good and familiar. If it is creole food, my son is doing an impressive job.*

JJ hopped in the shower, cleansing his entire body. He thought about Naomi and Trent Jr. It had been years since their last encounter, so he was anxious to see them. He was in the shower for about twenty minutes. He already had his attire laid out across his bed for the dinner. It was seven. Everyone would be arriving around seven thirty. The food would be ready in about twenty minutes. JJ had his boxers and a wife beater on and walked into the kitchen to check on the food. He was incredibly pleased. He thought, *Only a few more minutes to go and I'll let you cool a little. Can't wait until they sink their teeth into this meal. This is my best meal ever.*

JJ opened the oven door and removed the bread from the oven. It was ready. It had a golden brown color to it. He placed it on top of the stove. JJ asked his mother, "Mom, are you okay in there? Do you need anything before I get dressed?"

Melanie answered, "No, son. I'm good. You go on and get yourself together before someone knocks on the door. I am still a little sore, and your dad may not be back in time to answer it."

JJ stated, "Okay, Mom. I'll be out in about ten minutes or so."

JJ made haste dressing. He moisturized his face and sprayed on some cologne, walking into the mist. He slipped on some socks and put on his tennis shoes. He had a full-size mirror in his bedroom to check his attire. He was pleased with his reflection. He heard a knock at the door. He left his room to answer. It was Trent and his family, minus the mother. She had an emergency at work and had to cancel her plans. Trent and Trent Jr. greeted JJ with a handshake. When

Naomi appeared before JJ, he couldn't believe his eyes. She developed in every place imaginable. Last time he saw her, she wore glasses, was skinny, had no shape, and was flat chested.

Jonathan ogled her, stating, "Wow, Naomi, you look really great since the last time I saw you."

Naomi replied, "Thank you, JJ. It's good to see you." Naomi walked in, and JJ looked at her from the back.

JJ thought, *She looks good. Stop it! Camille is the one for me. No one else.* After they were situated and greeted Mel, there was another knock. JJ knew it was Camille and her mother. He opened the door and welcomed them into the apartment.

Trent walked over to Melanie greeting her with a hug and kiss. "Mel, I'm sorry, but my ex-wife couldn't make it." Melanie responded, "No worries Trent. I'm just happy to see you and the kids made it." Trent averted his attention to little Honey. "Hey there little one." Little Honey cooed at Trent with excitement.

When Naomi saw Camille, she couldn't help but stare at her. She rose from the couch and extended her hand. "Hi, I'm Naomi."

Camille accepted her hand, stating, "Hi, Naomi. I am Camille. I'm a friend of JJ's."

Naomi added, "Well, Camille, you are very pretty, and it's nice to meet you."

The girls began conversing with each other. Trent and Chelsea exchanged hellos. Trent also kissed her hand. Chelsea stated, "My, what a gentleman. Where is your wife?"

Trent stated, "I am recently divorced. How about you?"

Chelsea replied, "So am I."

Trent and Chelsea conversed innocently. Neither opened that door, insinuating the other was interested. Just friendly conversation between the two.

Jonathan had arrived with the bottles of wine. Trent had made it clear through text message that he would bring something for him and Jonathan. It was an expensive brandy. Jonathan said hello to everyone and brandished the bottles of wine he had for the women.

Jonathan noticed Trent's ex-wife wasn't present. He asked, "She couldn't make it, huh?"

Trent replied, "The life of a lawyer, man."

Once Jonathan arrived, JJ informed everyone to take their places at the table. JJ had presented the food in serving dishes. He wanted to make a grand slam impression to all. They looked at what had been prepared and immediately inundated him with compliments of how good the food looked and smelled. Everyone began serving themselves.

JJ went to the kitchen to get wineglasses and glasses specially designed for drinking the Courvoisier Brandy. The group was impressed and enjoyed every morsel taken. There were so many "Oh my god" and "This is so delicious" remarks at the table. The guest stroked JJ's ego that night. He sat next to Camille as always and mentally gave himself a pat on the back when he sampled his entrée.

Naomi thought, *They are such a cute couple. Wonder if there is something I can do to change his mind about her. I have never looked at him this way. But it has been years since we have seen each other. Why does he look so good to me? And he has impeccable culinary skills too.*

JJ looked extremely attractive to Naomi. Naomi had to cease the transparent gaze she had on JJ before someone noticed. It was too late. Jonathan saw how she ogled JJ, and a smile brushed across his face. He understood exactly what was on her mind.

Jonathan thought, *She's contemplating and soon will initiate the first move. My son looks incredibly attractive with Camille on his arms. I thought this might detour her. But I see having Camille here is helping. I will make sure Trent leaves well after Chelsea and Camille. That way, they can get to know each other.*

After dinner, Chelsea had four glasses of wine. She looked at the time, stating, "Melanie, Camille and I need to head on home. We have some plans for tomorrow and need to get up early."

Melanie stated, "Okay, Chelsea. Thank you guys for coming to dinner. I'll talk to you later." They both kissed and hugged Melanie.

JJ walked Camille and her mother to the car, giving her a kiss on the cheek. Jonathan saw Melanie getting up from her chair. He rose, stopped her, and stated, "Melanie, are you ready for bed? I can bring Cataleya in the room. I know you are tired and want to be in bed. JJ can entertain Trent Jr. and Naomi in his bedroom while Trent and I talk."

Melanie stated, "Okay. Sure thing, Jonathan. Please place Cataleya in her bassinette close to me." Melanie said good night to the remaining guests and went to bed. Jonathan followed her with Cataleya in his arms. He kissed his two girls good night and went into the living area to continue conversing with Trent. JJ, Trent Jr., and Naomi all went to his bedroom to play video games.

Naomi wasn't interested in any games. She was interested in JJ and how she could get him interested in her. She asked, "So, JJ, how long have you and Camille been an item?"

JJ replied, "Right now, Camille and I are close friends."

Naomi asked, "So you two aren't dating? Have you kissed?"

JJ replied, "Not dating, but we have shared a kiss here and there."

Naomi asked, "How much do you like her?"

Trent Jr. interrupted, "Damn, Naomi! Why are you asking him about his business? Leave him alone. We trying to play a game. You are distracting him, causing us to lose."

Naomi looked at her brother with disdain, rolled her eyes, and silenced herself. JJ was relieved that Trent Jr. came to his rescue. JJ knew why she was asking those questions. Inquisitive minds weren't a challenge, even with his learning disability. It was obvious to him where she was going with those inquiries.

Jonathan and Trent enjoyed their drinks, conversing about the new employee. Jonathan remained disciplined, limiting himself to two drinks. He kept wondering if Naomi was making her move on JJ. He knew JJ would be coming to him about her, asking his dad about those transparent stares from Naomi.

An unwelcomed yawn broke from Trent. It was time to go home. He and Jonathan had talked and drank their fill for the evening. He called out to his offsprings that it was time for them to head home. The teens said bye to one another. Before leaving, Naomi gave JJ a hug and whispered in his ear to call her, slipping her number into his hand. Jonathan and JJ walked their guests out the door.

Jonathan checked in on Melanie and Cataleya, finding them both fast asleep. He noticed Melanie had a smile on her face. He thought, *She must be having a nice dream.* He walked back to the living room to smoke a joint before going to bed.

Melanie was lying in her bed with Cataleya next to her. She watched her baby girl sleep. She was the center of attention for the entire evening and had fallen asleep when Chelsea and Camille went home. Melanie sat up in bed and started watching reality shows on television. She loved watching the celebrity hip-hop shows. They were entertaining to her and full of drama.

Melanie thought, *I saw how Naomi was watching my son and Camille. The two of them are close. I know Camille is extremely fond of JJ, and he feels the same way about her. They are always hanging around each other. We had that talk about his feelings for her. I wonder what is keeping the two of them from connecting. JJ will soon be seventeen in a couple of weeks. I will have to talk to him about it. Approach it delicately with no pressure.*

Melanie soon fell asleep. With JJ and Camille on her mind, she dreamed of the two. She dreamed of them being married, and grandchildren were also in the dream. Jonathan was not part of the dream, like he had no place there. Cataleya was there, playing with the children. There was a smile on Melanie's face as she dreamed of them all.

Conversation with Mom and Dad

Jonathan Jr. knocked on his parents' bedroom door. "Are you guys awake?"

Melanie heard the knock and replied, "Come on in, son."

JJ entered the room and noticed his dad wasn't present. "Mom, where is Dad? I didn't hear him leave, and he's not in the living room or the kitchen."

Melanie pulled herself up and stated, "He was in the mood to wash the car. Why? Is something wrong, son?"

JJ replied, "Good, he's gone. I wanted to talk to you alone."

Melanie asked, "Okay, about what, son?"

JJ answered, "Last night, I kept getting this strange feeling that Naomi was watching me while we were having dinner. I didn't make eye contact with her because Camille may have caught me looking at her, and I didn't want her feeling uncomfortable. And when she, Trent Jr., and I went into my bedroom to play video games, she was questioning me about my relationship with Camille. But Trent Jr. shut her down and demanded she stay out of my business. Before they left, she hugged me, whispered in my ear to call her, and gave me her number. Mom, I must admit, she is pretty. I find her attractive. Does that mean anything?"

Melanie was thinking while JJ was feeding her this information, *I knew that girl was up to something.* Melanie answered, "Son, maybe you should call her and answer those questions for her. Let me ask you, and you don't have to answer me now. Let it marinate a while. How do you feel about Camille? If you like her, is Naomi worth the effort of you destroying what could be with you and Camille? Do you like Naomi? Is she cognizant of your feelings for Camille? You should call her and talk to her. She may sense that there's nothing going on between you two and she wants to take this chance to declare how she feels."

JJ stated, "Okay, Mom. I will do just that. Mom, are you hungry? I can cook you some breakfast."

Melanie answered, "No, thanks, son. Your dad fed me prior to leaving to wash the car."

JJ rose from the bed, stating, "Well, if you need me, just ring your bell."

JJ left the room, thinking, *I have Mom's thoughts. Now I want to get Dad's thoughts about this.* JJ opened the refrigerator and grabbed items needed to cook him breakfast. He was especially craving grits. Melanie had made them for him since he was a child. He was ecstatic that she kept a box or two in the house.

After he cooked his breakfast and ate, Jonathan walked in with bags and placed them on the table. "Hey there, son. How's it going?"

JJ answered, "Hey, old man. What's up with you?"

Jonathan replied, "Oh, just washed the car and did a little shopping is all."

Jonathan sat in his recliner and turned on the television. JJ sat in his mother's recliner, ready to converse about last night. "Dad, I need to talk to you about something."

Jonathan stated, "Okay, son. Tell me what's on your mind."

JJ said, "Well, Dad, seems as though Naomi likes me. Don't get me wrong, she is pretty and all, but I really like Camille. Before Naomi left last night, she gave me her number and asked that I call her. I am conflicted, Dad. Camille and I are not in a relationship, but I feel like I would be cheating or something on her if I call Naomi."

Jonathan thought it was good that he invited them to dinner. Jonathan asked his son, "Well, JJ, has Camille shown any intentions of being your girlfriend or interested in a relationship with you, son?"

JJ responded, "No, but—"

Jonathan interrupted, "No but, son. If she has not shown the least bit of interest in being in a relationship with you, she only wants to be friends. Nothing more. As long as you two have been around each other, something should have transpired, leading up to more than just friends. Remember, I told you not to get yourself hooked on this one girl. There are other girls out there who would be interested in you, and vice versa. Why don't you give Naomi a call and see where it goes? You have known each other for years. Just check into it and see if it's something you would want to pursue."

JJ stated, "Maybe you're right, Dad. I'll call her later sometime."

Neither Melanie nor Jonathan were cognizant that JJ had conversed with them both.

JJ was conflicted on the inside. He hadn't called Naomi. He had spoken to friends about Naomi. A couple of friends wanted to know why he was waiting to call her. One knew how he felt about Camille and told him to follow his heart. And there was one who secretly liked Camille and would betray JJ's trust. Steve had always had a crush on Camille and thought JJ was moving too slow to make her his. This was the perfect opportunity for him to steal Camille from him. After JJ confided in Steve, as he was walking away, the paper with Naomi's number on it had fallen from his pocket. Steve picked it up, and the words on it read, "Call me, JJ." It had the number and

Naomi's name on it. He put it in his pocket and knew this was the chance he needed to turn Camille against JJ.

Melanie was planning JJ's birthday party. She invited his friends, along with Chelsea and Camille. This was a special birthday. He was turning seventeen and would be a senior for the upcoming school year. Melanie and Jonathan went all out for their son. Melanie was making his favorite foods. He loved Mexican food. So she had chicken/beef fajitas, taco bowls for salads, beans, rice, the whole works. She had his favorite strawberry cake with pastry images of all his favorite horror film stars. Jonathan had even purchased a nice birthday attire for him to wear. Jonathan Jr. was pleased with the birthday surprise. He thanked his parents. Jonathan had invited Trent Jr. and Naomi to the event.

The guests arrived, presenting JJ his birthday gifts individually. Camille was saving hers for last. She hadn't spoken to Jonathan in a while. He was acting distant toward her. So she planned to pull him aside after opening her gift she had for him.

"Hey, Jonathan. How is it going? I haven't heard from you in a while. Is everything okay with us?"

JJ replied, "I'm sorry. I have a myriad of things on my mind, is all. Nothing to do with you." He had Camille by the hands while telling her this and gave her a hug for reassurance.

Steve was watching them. Melanie called JJ. He released Camille's hands to answer his mother.

Steve had taken out the piece of paper, pretending Camille or JJ dropped it on the ground. He approached Camille from the back, asking, "Hey, Camille. Did you or JJ drop this?"

Camille received the folded paper and opened it. She read the words, saying, "JJ, call me, Naomi." There were hearts on the paper as well as her number. Camille responded, "Thank you, Steve." She spotted Naomi and kept her eye on her. She made sure to not be obvious and kept a smile on her face the entire time.

Naomi, at times, would go to JJ, playing with him and trying not to look obvious to Camille. With a smile on her face, she asked JJ, "Why haven't you called me? I have been waiting for your call. I like you, JJ, and want to get to know you. There is nothing going on between you and Camille. You can have all you want right here. Why not come over to my side of the fence? I will make you feel extremely good too. Just think about it." Naomi walked away.

Jonathan was even more confused. Here he was, wanting Camille, but Camille hadn't given any gestures of wanting to be together. And on the other hand, Naomi was throwing herself at him. It was sounding tempting as hell to JJ. He had never been with anyone at all. His friends always talked about their experiences, but he refrained from this activity. He liked Camille and wanted his experience to be with her, even if he had to wait.

Camille, for the remainder of the evening, didn't approach or or say anything to JJ. In fact, she would play his game. She thought, *If he wants to be silent toward me, then I'll respond the same way. I've already approached him.* Camille asked her mother if they could leave. She fed her an excuse that she wasn't feeling well. Chelsea excused them both and left the party.

Jonathan had been sitting back, watching everything unfold. He saw how Camille looked at Naomi after reading the note. What Steve did was an addition to Jonathan's scheme. He didn't know how Steve procured the note, but it worked well with his plan to sever Camille and JJ. There was a big smile on his face. Now he could enjoy his son's birthday party without having to look at Camille.

It was time for the party to end. Melanie was tired. The three of them began cleaning up the mess from the party. JJ's mind was on what Naomi was doing to him. He hadn't realized that Camille had left the party. Melanie and Jonathan both could see there was something bothering their son. Melanie had an idea why he seemed burdened. Having Camille and Naomi attend his party might not have been the best idea. She hoped he would come to her and talk about what was on his mind. JJ always came to her when something was bothering him.

Succumbing to Temptation

A week had passed by without JJ and Camille talking to each other. JJ decided to call Naomi. He just had to see why this girl was pursuing him the way she was. He dialed the number, and the phone rang. On the other end, he heard, "Hello?"

JJ followed up with, "Hello, Naomi."

Naomi stated, "Hello, JJ. Took you long enough to call."

JJ asked, "How did you know it was me?"

Naomi responded, "I know your voice, JJ. What are you up to today? You have any plans with Camille?"

JJ responded, "No, I don't. I haven't spoken to Camille in a week."

Naomi had a devious smile on her face. She smiled and asked, "So you haven't talk to her in a week, huh? Well, would you like to hang out with me?"

JJ asked Naomi, "Hang out and do what?"

Naomi replied, "Come on, JJ. You already know why I want to hang out with you. You know I am feeling you. I can tell you feeling me too. If you weren't, you wouldn't have called me. Am I right?" JJ had never had anyone come on to him as strong as Naomi. There was silence. She asked, "Are you there, JJ?"

JJ answered, "Yeah, I'm still here." JJ asked, "Why me? Out of all the fellas you could have, why are you targeting me? Is it because you see me with Camille?"

Naomi was being manipulative and replied, "No, silly. I really like you and want to be with you. Is that hard for you to understand? I am trying to get to know you on a personal level. We have known each other for a long time, and I just want something on a more intimate level with you. Is that okay?"

JJ thought about Camille, and since she hadn't approached him with her feelings, he would entertain Naomi. JJ replied, "Sure, why not? We can see where this goes."

Naomi stated, "Okay, great. Would you like to hookup today? I can come by and pick you up before my dad gets home. We can chill for a couple of hours, and I'll take you back home before he is due to return."

JJ replied, "Okay. Sure. Why not? See you in a few."

Trent Jr. was on the other line and heard everything. "You a ho. Straight up ho, Naomi. You know how much he likes Camille. Are you okay with messing up what they have? You do this all the time. You always want something that belongs to someone else."

Naomi replied, "You shut your ass, TJ! If I want to have sex with someone, I am going to have sex with them. You can't talk with all the hoochies you be with up in here."

Trent Jr. said, "I'm a man. That is what men do. We are supposed to get in where we fit in every chance we get. You should be ashamed taking advantage of JJ like that. You know he has a learning disability and can be easily manipulated."

Naomi rebutted, "Well, he has the sense to say no. I am not forcing him to come here. I simply presented an idea, and he accepted. Now shut up. I'm going to go pick up my plaything for the day."

Trent Jr. shook his head in disappointment with his sister. But he knew he couldn't snitch on her because she had twice as much on him to tell their dad.

While she was driving, Naomi thought about how she would sex JJ down and taste him in her mouth. She couldn't wait to get him home. JJ had told Melanie that he would be going out with a friend for a couple of hours. He talked to his dad and told him the opposite. "Dad, I'm going to hang out with Naomi, but don't tell my mom. I don't want her to know."

Jonathan stated, "Okay, son, have fun. Please take condoms with you. Play it safe, okay, son?"

Jonathan replied, "I know, Dad. I keep them on me."

JJ saw Naomi's text that she was outside waiting. He exited the apartment and hopped into the car. They exchanged greetings. JJ looked at her and what she was wearing. She had on a low-cut shirt with Daisy Duke shorts fitting every curve. They pulled off for their journey to Naomi's house. JJ was nervous, and she could tell. To ease his nerves, she picked up his hand and held it. She could feel the tension fade away, and he started to relax.

She stated to JJ, "There's no reason to be nervous. I won't bite you. Just want to have a little fun with you, is all. You look nice today, and smelling good too. Did you do all this just for me?"

JJ replied, "I was already dressed when I called you. Wasn't expecting for you to want to hook-up today."

JJ certainly didn't want her thinking he did anything special just for her. He wasn't feeling Naomi the way he was into Camille. He thought, *This is just a hookup, nothing more. The guys always talk about random loose girls and their interest in sex with no strings attached. I can do this. But why am thinking about Camille and feeling the urge to have her take me back home? I can't stop now. She will think of me as a wimp and tell everyone she knows.*

JJ hadn't been with anyone. This was his opportunity to break away from being a virgin. It would be cool to join in with the guys engaging in conversations of sexual encounters. This didn't help him from feeling conflicted. He couldn't fathom why he even agreed to this. He grew nervous again after they pulled up to Naomi's home. No one was home. Trent was away on business. He wanted to expand in another city about thirty miles away. He would be there for the entire weekend, analyzing location, the number of similar businesses, and human traffic in the area. Trent Jr. had left to spend the evening with a friend. Naomi led JJ into her room and told him to relax. She would be right back. He studied Naomi's room. It was tidy and had a nice smell. Naomi came in with drinks in her hands.

"Drink this, JJ. It'll help you relax."

JJ took the drink without investigating or questioning the contents in the half-filled glass. He knew it was alcohol, judging by the smile and look on Naomis' face. JJ had faith that Naomi wouldn't do anything to harm him. He looked up at Naomi. She had already gulped down her drink.

JJ thought, *Damn, she gulped that down like a pro. She's already finished.* JJ looked at his glass, thinking, *It's now or never.* He tried to gulp it down, but this was his first time having any alcoholic beverage. He coughed from the burning sensation.

Naomi asked him, "Are you okay? Is this your first drink, JJ?"

JJ, still coughing, answered, "Yes, it is."

Naomi asked, "Why didn't you tell me? I would have told you to take sips and not try to gulp it down. Just sip on it." A thought came across Naomi, and she asked JJ, "JJ, is this your first time having sex too? Is that why you were nervous during our drive here? Oh my God, you are a virgin! Why didn't you tell me?"

JJ didn't know how to answer her. She asked and said so much. He just ignored her and placed the glass on the table.

Naomi continued, "Don't worry, JJ. I'm going to take good care of you."

There was a ring at the door. JJ was a little jumpy and nervous. Did someone know he was here? Naomi saw the look on JJ's face and stated, "Relax, JJ. I told you I would take care of you."

Naomi went to answer the door. JJ could hear another female inside the house. He didn't think much about it. Just thought a neighbor had stopped by for something. JJ started to feel the effects of the alcohol. It didn't help that he had taken his medications for anxiety and ADD. The girls entered the room. With his vision compromised, JJ couldn't focus to see the friend Naomi invited. Naomi came over and pressed downward on JJ, forcing him to lay on her bed. JJ tried to resist, but he couldn't. The alcohol and medication kept him from doing so. Naomi realized that JJ wasn't responding to any of their advances. JJ couldn't see, and he slowly felt himself drifting.

Naomi discerned he was zoned out and started yelling, "JJ! JJ! Oh my god, are you okay? JJ! Say something, please!"

Naomi's friend had gotten scared and ran out the house. Naomi tried slapping and shaking JJ to bring him back. Nothing worked. She called 911 and told them there was a male who had passed out and wasn't responding to any attempts to awaken.

The voice on the other end stated, "Calm down, ma'am. Did he take anything or have anything to drink?"

Naomi responded, "No, he didn't take anything, but he did have a small drink."

The voice asked, "How old is he? And what did he have to drink?"

Naomi replied, "He is seventeen and only had a half glass of fireball."

The voice asked, "Is he breathing, ma'am?"

Naomi replied, "Hold on."

Naomi looked at his chest to see if inhaling and exhaling was taking place. "Yes, ma'am, he's breathing. Ma'am, please send someone quick. He's not waking up at all."

The operator had Naomi give her the address and assured her the arrival of an ambulance. Naomi kept trying to awaken JJ, but he still didn't respond.

The ambulance arrived. Naomi led them to her bedroom, where JJ lay unconscious. They checked his vitals. His blood pressure was a little high. They opened his eyelid to check his pupils.

"Ma'am, did he take anything that you may be aware?"

Naomi replied, "Not that I know of, sir. Is he okay?"

The EMT replied, "We need to take him to the hospital. Are you his sister or relative?"

Naomi replied, "No, I'm not. I'm a friend of his."

The EMT replied, "You may want to call his parents and have them come out to the Dallas Medical Center located on Colorado Road. It's the closest hospital."

Naomi called her father and told her what had happened. Trent immediately called Jonathan. Melanie's brother, Justin, had come over to visit them. Jonathan delivered the news to Melanie about JJ being rushed to the hospital.

Melanie cried, asking, "What happened to my son, Jonathan? Who was he with, and where was he?"

Jonathan stated, "He was with Naomi at Trent's house." Jonathan couldn't tell her no more than what Trent told him. Justin overheard the conversation. He knew this wasn't the time for them to have the baby with them.

Justin volunteered, "Go ahead, guys. Go handle whatever is going on with my nephew. I will sit here with the baby until you all come back. Make sure to call me and keep me posted about my nephew." Jonathan and Melanie promised to call him.

Jonathan and Melanie rushed to the hospital. Melanie kept saying, "I knew this girl was trouble! I just knew she was! What was he doing with her anyway?"

Jonathan knew all along and was feeling regret for influencing his son to pursue this girl. Once they arrived, Melanie saw Naomi. Melanie aggressively walked up to her, asking, "What happened to him, Naomi! What did you do to my son!"

Naomi answered, "I'm sorry, I'm so sorry. I didn't know."

Melanie asked aggressively, "You didn't know what!"

Jonathan grabbed Melanie, pulling her into his chest and comforting her. She burst out in tears for her son. Jonathan held on to her, stating, "Calm down, Mel. We'll go to the nurse's desk for information."

They walked to the nurses' station, asking for information about their son. Jonathan asked, "Can you give us information about our son, Jonathan Taylor Jr., brought in about twenty minutes ago?"

The nurse searched the database. "Yes, here he is. His condition is stable. I will have the doctor come out and speak to you all. Have a seat, please."

Jonathan led Melanie to the lobby's seating area. The doctor came out to speak with them. He approached them. "Mr. and Mrs. Taylor?"

They both responded, "Yes, we are the Taylors."

The doctor responded, "Hi, I'm Dr. Tessnow. Jonathan's condition is stable. According to the 911 call, JJ had been drinking, but it was a small amount."

Jonathan immediately told the doctor JJ was on routine medication for anxiety and ADD. Dr. Tessnow responded, "That explains why he reacted to the alcohol. I was waiting for tests results to come back confirming if there were other substances in his bloodstream. Well, now we know. But I still want to look at the results to make sure there was nothing else other than his two medications in his system. You all can go in and see him. He will be fine, guys."

Naomi heard what the doctor said. She walked up to Melanie with a trembling voice. "Mr. and Mrs. Taylor, I'm so sorry. I didn't know that JJ was on any type of medication."

Melanie had calmed down after hearing the doctor tell them her son was fine. Melanie said, "Naomi, thank you, but I really wish to not talk to you right now."

Naomi said, "Yes, ma'am, Mrs. Taylor." Naomi was relieved to hear that JJ would be okay. She called her dad to let him know. Trent was on his way back home when she first called him. He informed Naomi he would be dealing with her once he arrived home.

Brokenhearted Camille

Camille wanted to talk to JJ. She just couldn't get over how he had been treating her. So she made her way out the door to talk to him. She had asked permission to drive her mother's car. Once she arrived, she saw JJ slide into the car with Naomi. She saw it was Naomi. They were pulling out to leave in the opposite direction from the way Camille came. Camille turned around. She was heartbroken with tearstained eyes. She thought, *I've lost him to her. He could've just told me instead of ignoring me and treating me as if I didn't exist.* She drove back home and cleaned her face before entering the door. *If I cry, it'll be in my room where eyes won't be able to see me.*

Chelsea was watching TV when she heard Camille. She asked, "Why are you back so soon? Did you forget something?"

Camille replied, "No, Mom. I didn't forget anything. I had just missed JJ."

Chelsea asked, "Did you want to have a daughter-mommy day with me? We can go to the spa, and afterward, we can go sit at a nice restaurant for a bite to eat. Would you like to do that?"

Camille replied, "No, Mom. Not today. I want to catch up on abandoned activities. Maybe tomorrow."

Chelsea stated, "Okay, sweetie." She knew her daughter wasn't okay, and JJ was the reason. She noticed the distance between them. She would wait until Camille came to her without any influence or pressure.

Camille went into her room thinking how much she liked Jonathan. She reminisced on the dinners he would invite her to, playing with his baby sister, and talking with his mother. She felt adored. But when she thought about his dad, she felt he didn't care for her.

Camille thought, *So that's what it is. He is the culprit. I bet he influenced JJ that he was spending too much time with me and should explore potential options.* Camille lay on her bed and had fallen asleep. Shortly after, she heard her phone ringing. She quickly rose to reach her phone to answer. She said, "Hello?"

It was Mrs. Taylor on the other end with a frantic voice. "Camille, JJ is in the hospital! We're on our way there now!"

Camille asked, "Mrs. Taylor, he's in the hospital? What happened? Why is he there?"

Melanie replied, "I just know he had some liquor, and he's not responding. Can you and Chelsea come to the hospital here on Colorado Street?"

Camille answered, "Yes, ma'am. Mom and I are on our way."

Camille ran in her mother's room, yelling, "Mom, Mom, it's JJ! He is in the hospital! Something happened to him! Let's go now!"

Chelsea stated, "Wait a minute. Calm down, Camille. Baby, where is he? What happened to him, Camille?"

Camille replied, "He's at the hospital on Colorado, and Mrs. Taylor said something about liquor and him not responding. I bet that Naomi had something to do with this."

Chelsea asked, "What? Who?"

Camille replied, "Mom, I'll explain on the way. Please, come on, Mom. Let's go. We need to leave now!" Camille wasn't trying to yell at her mom. She was just worried about JJ, and her mother knew this. Camille told her about Naomi and that she had been the reason she had returned home so quickly. When they arrived at the hospital, Camille saw Mrs. Taylor speaking to Naomi.

Camille could see Melanie, and they walked her way as she was telling Naomi that she wished to not speak to her right now. Chelsea rushed to Melanie, stating, "Mel, we're here. How is he?"

Melanie turned to the familiar voice and replied, "Chelsea, thank God you're here."

Chelsea pulled Melanie in for a hug. "How is JJ, Mel? Is he okay?"

Melanie replied, "The doctor says he will be okay. He had some liquor after taking his medication, and it caused a reaction."

Naomi stood there with her head down, waiting for all eyes to turn to her, fueled with anger. Mel didn't want to do that to her. Instead, she took Camille by the hand to show Naomi this was who would be going in with her to see JJ and walked away.

Naomi didn't blame Melanie for how she felt. She could've caused serious medical issues to JJ. She didn't know what to do. Should she leave or stay? She felt leaving would prove she had no remorse for her actions. If she stayed, she would be subject to consuming fiery eyes, finger-pointing, etc. She pulled herself together and decided she would stay. She wanted them to know she was owning up to her wrong, and she wanted to right this wrong with them.

Jonathan started to revisit his thought about interfering with JJ's love life. He thought, *What have I done to my son? This is all my fault. Had I not interfered, this wouldn't have happened.* Jonathan diverted his attention to Naomi. He began to despise her action, even though he knew he played his part in getting them together. Jonathan wanted to approach her and question what happened. But he preferred to do so in the presence of Trent. When he discerned Chelsea and Camille expeditiously walking into the hospital, he saw the look on Camille's face. She was worried about JJ. They bypassed Jonathan, approaching Melanie. He smiled and thought, *She is expressing undeniable concern for our son. My interfering days between the two are over.*

There were lessons to be learned for three people. Jonathan learned Camille was good for JJ, and interfering could've cost him JJ's life. Naomi learned her lascivious behavior could've cost JJ his life, and the respect and trust of her father. JJ would learn to open his heart to the person he fancied.

Jonathan reached for Melanie's hand, and they all, with the exception of Naomi, walked toward JJ's room. As they were walking, Melanie thought about Naomi. She decided to permit her to attend their visit so that she could see what she had done to her son. She stopped Jonathan. She stated, "Wait, Jonathan. I want Naomi to come with us."

Jonathan asked, "Are you certain about this, Mel?"

Melanie replied, "Yes, Jonathan, I'm sure."

Camille didn't understand why Melanie would want Naomi anywhere near JJ, but Chelsea fathomed Melanie's exact intentions of inviting her. Melanie asked Naomi, "Would you like to join us to see JJ?"

Naomi answered, "Yes, if you wouldn't mind me doing so." Naomi, with haste, removed herself from her seat to follow them. She wanted to show how grateful she was, so she thanked Melanie.

Feeling Ashamed

Trent arrived just as the ladies were about to visit JJ. He called out to Jonathan, "Jonathan! Hey, man. I got back as soon as I could after Naomi called me. How is JJ?"

Jonathan turned to Melanie, stating, "Mel, you all go on and visit JJ. I will stay here and speak to Trent and Naomi. We'll go in to see him after you all have visited with him."

Melanie stated, "Okay, Jonathan."

Jonathan took a deep breath to prepare himself to question Naomi about the events that took place at Trent's home. Jonathan stated to Trent, "JJ will be fine, according to the doctor. I wanted to make sure you were present prior to questioning Naomi about what happened at your home."

Trent looked at Naomi, asking, "Yeah, Naomi, what happened? Why was JJ at my house? You know my rules about having company while I'm away. Now what happened?"

Naomi replied, "Dad and Mr. Taylor, I'm sorry. I picked JJ up to just hang out, and that is it. When we arrived home, we went into the living area to watch television. I wanted to show him how cool I was, so I fixed us each a glass of fireball. I only filled them halfway, so it wasn't much at all."

Trent, enraged with his daughter, yelled, "Naomi, how could you be so irresponsible! Do you see what you have done to JJ and his family? You shouldn't be drinking, and you had no business offering an underaged person alcohol under any circumstances!"

Naomi replied, crying, "I'm sorry, Dad. I understand. It will not happen again. I promise, I didn't mean for this to happen."

Trent averted his attention to Jonathan, stating, "Man, Jonathan, I'm so sorry about this. I feel bad this happened to JJ. Is there anything I can do?"

Jonathan replied, "Trent, I just ask that whatever insurance won't cover, you pay the balance. They still kids, Trent, and learning as they live life. Judging from Naomi's concern, I feel she has learned a valuable lesson about her actions. Just her witnessing the outcome is punishment enough for me."

Trent calmly stated, "Okay. You're right. This is a lesson for her. I wasn't going to be lenient at all with her. I will still punish her for disobeying my rules. Thanks for understanding." They all continued talking until Chelsea and Camille were visible, walking from JJ's room.

Melanie, Chelsea, and Camille had walked into JJ's room. He was awake, looking at the covers. He felt disappointed with himself. He knew from reading the side effects on each medication bottle that alcohol shouldn't be mixed with any of them. He was also thinking about how he had been treating Camille. He loved her, and his heart jumped when he looked up and saw that she had come to the hospital to see him.

Melanie rushed to JJ's side, grabbed his hand, and ran her hand on top of his head. Melanie asked, "Son, are you okay? Can I get you anything?" Melanie was careful about the questions she asked, Camille was present, and she didn't want to embarrass him by asking anything that would result in hurting Camille's feelings.

JJ replied, "Mom, I'm okay, and no, I don't need anything. I just want to go home."

Melanie stated, "Well, the doctor says you are okay and can be released once he receives your test results. No need for an overnight observation."

Jonathan acknowledged Chelsea and Camille in the room. "Hi, Ms. Phillips and Camille. Sorry you all had to hear about and see me in this condition."

Chelsea stood next to him, saying, "Don't you worry about that, sweetie. We're relieved you are okay."

Camille added, "Yeah, JJ. We're just happy what happened wasn't serious."

Camille forgot about her aching heart and wasn't as disappointed in JJ. She thought, *This may have prevented him from going all the way with her. There hadn't been much time passed from when I first saw them leaving and receiving the phone call from his mother.*

She felt relieved on the inside after processing her thoughts. Chelsea informed Melanie they would step out so Jonathan, Trent, and Naomi could visit him. She didn't want Camille in the room with Naomi. She knew the tension between the two girls wouldn't be good for JJ. Chelsea and Camille seated themselves until further information would be divulged about JJ's discharge.

Jonathan, Trent, and Naomi walked into the room. Jonathan approached his son, asking, "Son, how are you?"

Trent gave Melanie a hug. "Mel, are you okay?"

Melanie replied, "I'm fine, Trent. Thank you for asking."

Trent turned to JJ, asking, "How's it going, young man? I rushed here from being out of town as soon as I heard. I didn't know how bad your condition was."

JJ replied, "I'm good, Uncle Trent. I'm sorry for being at your home and ruining your out-of-town travel."

Trent stated, "Don't worry about that. You are more important. Good thing I was able to wrap up business prior to getting the call."

JJ looked at Naomi, and she looked at JJ. She approached his bed, saying, "JJ, I'm so sorry for what I did to you. Please forgive me. I didn't know you were on any medications. More importantly, I should've never fixed those drinks knowing we are both underage."

JJ said, "It's okay. I forgive you." The two realized at that moment that nothing more than friendship should exist between them.

JJ's mind was on Camille the whole time. JJ asked his mother, "Mom, will you get Camille for me? I would like to talk to her alone."

Melanie kissed her son on the forehead. "Of course, I will, son. All right, guys, you heard JJ. Everyone out so he and Camille can talk."

The group removed themselves. They all walked to the waiting room. Melanie approached Camille. "JJ would like to speak to you alone."

Camille and Naomi looked at each other. Camille brandished a victorious smile, basking in the fact that he asked for only her.

Camille walked into JJ's room and stood by the bed, waiting for him to state his reason for wanting to converse with her. JJ stretched his hands out, gesturing for Camille to come to him. Camille gave her hand to JJ. JJ stated, "Camille, I'm sorry for how I've been treating you. Will you forgive me?"

Camille replied, "Of course, I forgive you, JJ. You're a very dear friend to me."

JJ looked at her and asked that she sit on his bed facing him. He took her by both hands. Camille sat facing him, ready to hear his speech.

"Camille, I almost did something stupid today. Since I have been in this room, all I have been thinking about is you. You have always been there for me. I see your beautiful smile when I go to sleep and when I wake up each morning. When I look at you, your eyes light up like they're dancing. I was wondering if we could take this a step further. I would like to be in a relationship, if that's okay with you?"

Camille responded, "Jonathan, I've waited so long to hear you ask me this. I would love to be in a relationship with you."

JJ pulled her in for a kiss. After their kiss, Camille laid her head on his chest. "JJ, please don't ever scare me like that again."

JJ lifted her head from his chest, stating, "I promise, baby. I love you, Camie."

Camille replied, "I love you too, Jonathan Jr."

Dr. Tessnow read the remaining test results and concluded there was no reason to keep JJ. "Mr. and Mrs. Taylor, I have your son's tests results. Everything has checked out, and I've already arranged his discharge."

Jonathan extended his hand stating, "Thank you, Doctor. We appreciate all you've done for our son."

Dr. Tessnow stated, "You are both welcome. You all take care."

The group was relieved to hear the news. Trent told Jonathan he and Naomi would be leaving and to give JJ their regards. Melanie, Jonathan, and Chelsea went to deliver JJ the good news. As they were walking in, they could hear the two professing their love to each other. Their parents knew all along how they felt about each other. The mothers never interfered and just wondered which of them would be the first to admit their feelings. JJ looked up and noticed they were the center of attention.

He stated, "Come on in, eavesdroppers."

The three of them entered the room. Melanie shared with Jonathan Jr. the good news that he could leave. She gathered his things while they waited for the discharge nurse.

Camille pulled her mother to the side. She wanted to ride with the Taylors and JJ. "Mom, is it okay if I ride with JJ?"

Chelsea didn't mind at all. She stated, "Sure, baby girl. I'm going to head home and relieve your brother from watching your sister." She gave JJ a kiss on the cheek and gave Melanie and Jonathan a hug. There was no need to stay since the hospital was releasing JJ.

Camille told her mom that she would be home after she visits with JJ for a while. The nurse entered the room about five minutes after Chelsea left to procure signatures from a parent, completing JJ's discharge to go home.

During the drive home, neither Mel nor Jonathan mentioned what happened. There was no need to. JJ had learned his lesson about mixing his medicines with alcohol. When they arrived home, JJ felt tired and wanted to sleep. Camille sat up next to him in his bed, watching television while he slept.

Left from Little to No Contact

Jonathan couldn't help but notice there was something familiar about their new hire, Sharon. He couldn't pinpoint just what it was, but every time he looked at her, he just felt he knew her. Sharon, after working there for about a month, would soon reveal to Jonathan who she was. She didn't know Jonathan was married with children. They never talked about their personal lives. They just kept it professional on the job. It tickled Sharon that Jonathan hadn't figured out who she was yet. She was getting ready for work. There was a bracelet she had kept given to her by Jonathan when they were in high school. The bracelet had her name engraved. The two had lost touch after she had to move to another state. Her father was in the military and stationed in Utah. Things never really ended between the two of them. They still called each other, until one day, the calls ceased. As if Sharon had fallen off the grid. This hurt Jonathan, and for a while, he moped around, wasn't himself and became distant.

Sharon was Jonathan's first girlfriend, and he didn't take her rejecting him well. He endeavored to figure out why she no longer had an interest in him. He understood a long distance relationship between teenagers wouldn't work, but what about friendship? Couldn't they at least remain friends? He still wanted to hear her voice. After so much time going by from little to no contact, eventually, Jonathan went on with life. He eventually changed his number, figuring Sharon wanted nothing to do with him. Jonathan felt anger toward Sharon and on purpose began to match the energy he was receiving from Sharon.

"Since she doesn't want to call or talk to me, I don't want to contact or talk to her. Two can play this game."

While getting ready for work, Sharon thought wearing the bracelet would succor identifying to Jonathan who she was. She knew she would be taking a chance because she recalled how she left things between them shortly after moving away. She gathered her things and exited to begin her journey to work. While driving, she kept contemplating if she should wear the bracelet. Was it too soon to wear it? Was it just not the right time? Would he instantly remember this gift given to her by him? Sharon's mind was plagued with thoughts, wondering if she should reveal herself. Once she arrived, she sat in the car. She took a deep breath and decided she would wear the bracelet, hoping Jonathan would remember. She also thought how he would react. She knew she was playing Russian roulette with this decision. The store was open when she arrived. She entered the building and greeted Jonathan and John. She walked back to the locker area to put away her purse. Before storing it away, she removed the bracelet and slid it around her right wrist. She thought, *Okay, it's now or never. Here we go.*

She walked toward the front of the store to begin her shift and help them make the pastries. Jonathan walked three trays of donuts from the oven and placed them on the racks. When he returned, Sharon initiated preparing the remaining dough for the pastries. Jonathan looked down at her wrist and noticed the bracelet. Sharon saw the look on Jonathan's face. It was a look of confusion and something looking familiar.

Jonathan thought, *That bracelet, it looks just like the bracelet I gave my girlfriend Sharon back in high school. I had that bracelet made and engraved especially for her. No, that can't be her.*

Jonathan kept his thoughts to himself and didn't say anything to Sharon about the bracelet. He remembered how Sharon treated him after she moved away. Jonathan asked John, "Big man, y'all got it from here?"

John responded, "Sure. Do your thing, boss."

Jonathan excused himself, went into the office, and closed the door. He sat at his desk in shock. His mind was just racing. He knew she had done this on purpose and was wanting him to remember who she was. He thought, *I know her raggedy ass ain't trying to waltz back into my life after what she pulled in high school. She ghosted me after being in Utah for two weeks. She stopped calling and receiving my calls. Why didn't she say anything during or after her interview with Trent and me? I should fire her ass for this. I loved her.* Jonathan vented for about a minute and calmed himself. *I have got to have some composure when I return. I can't let her know her actions affected me.* Jonathan realized he had harbored feelings about Sharon ghosting him those many years ago.

Jonathan returned to the front and continued with daily operations as usual. Sharon immediately realized her plan backfired on her. She wanted to leave and internally punish herself. She thought, *This isn't the end result I expected. I didn't think this through thoroughly. I know I caused him heartache years ago. And to add insult to injury, I never gave him any closure. How could I be so stupid? I thought he would have been happy that it was me after seeing the bracelet.* Sharon dared not say anything to Jonathan during her shift. They avoided each other the entire time.

The workday had come to an end. Jonathan drove home thinking about Sharon's actions. He wasn't in the mood to listen to music as usual. He just wanted to clear his head with no interference. He felt there was no need to tell Mel until he figured out what to do about it. He knew he would be talking to Trent to terminate her.

CHAPTER 20

Forgiveness

Jonathan had arrived home and found Melanie crying. Jonathan rushed to her side, asking, "Mel, what's going on, baby? Why are you crying?"

Melanie, with a trembling voice, replied, "Jonathan, I'm tired."

Jonathan inquired, "Tired of what, baby?"

Melanie replied, "I'm tired of pretending. Pretending that Sena doesn't exist. I am so conflicted on the inside about her. She is your daughter. Your flesh and blood. I'm tired of this burden weighing heavily on my heart. I know you feel resentment toward me because I haven't accepted her. I want to end this feeling. I am not a bad person, Jonathan. I'm not."

Jonathan stated, "I know you're not a bad person, Mel. Stop crying, and we will figure this out together."

Melanie agreed, "Okay. I want her to know her baby sister. She knows JJ. And I want to accept her in my life."

Jonathan asked, "Are you sure about this, Mel? Whatever you decide, I am for it. How would you like to approach this?"

Melanie replied, "Well, you can start by calling her mother to see if she would like to come over for a visit one weekend. I will let you manage all of this. I'm fine with the whole thing."

Mel was right. Jonathan did feel resentment toward her, but he never divulged this to Melanie.

Jonathan had been waiting for the day Melanie would accept his daughter. Finally, all the arguments, accusations, and hurtful words used by Melanie toward Jonathan were coming to a halt. The hurt and pain he had caused her was no longer the catalyst that would keep his daughter singled out as a member of their family. He was proud of Melanie for putting her feelings aside. He didn't bother asking what brought those guilty feelings. He just hoped Sena would want him in her life. Three ladies he had wronged in his life. Betraying Melanie, impregnating Lisa, leaving her alone to take care of their baby, and abandoning Sena. She suffered the most, and Jonathan could blame only himself for the pain he caused.

Jonathan contacted his mother for Sena's number. His mother cultivated a healthy relationship with her son's offspring since birth. Jonathan dialed the number. When his mother answered, he asked, "Mom, how are you?"

She answered, "I'm fine, son. And yourself?"

Jonathan answered, "I'm good. Can I have Sena's number?"

She asked, "Why? What do you need it for?"

Jonathan answered, "I want to talk to her and invite her to spend time with us."

His mother asked, "Is Melanie okay with this?"

Jonathan replied, "Melanie asked that I do this, Momma. This is her idea."

His mother stated, "Oh, wow. After all these years, she has finally accepted her, huh? I had always prayed that one day she would put her feelings aside. Looks like my prayers were answered."

Jonathan asked, "Momma, can I have the number please?" Jonathan didn't want to chitchat with her. He was too excited about calling his daughter. Ms. Taylor gave Jonathan the number and wished her son the best.

Once Jonathan had the number and looked at it to dial, he started to feel nervous. What was he going to say to her after all this time? How would she receive him reaching out to her? Jonathan dismissed what he was feeling and dialed the number. The phone rang, and he heard a sweet angelic voice stating, "Hello."

Jonathan's heart started to beat fast once he heard the voice. Jonathan asked, "Yes, this is Jonathan. Is Sena available?"

The voice replied, "This is Sena. Who is calling, please?"

Jonathan felt nervous again, stating, "Hi, Sena. This is your dad, Jonathan. How are you doing?"

Sena was shocked. This was what she had been waiting for her entire life, hearing her dad on the other end of the phone. She asked, "This is my dad for real?"

Jonathan, relieved from her excitement, stated, "Yes, it's me."

Sena stated, "I'm doing good. How about yourself?"

Jonathan answered, "I'm good, baby girl."

There was a pause. Sena broke the silence, asking, "What made you call?"

Jonathan replied, "Well, I wanted to know if you would like to visit for the weekend with us. If that's okay with you and your mother. I know you don't know me, but—"

Sena interrupted, "Dad, I would love to come spend the weekend."

Hearing her call him dad confirmed to Jonathan she wasn't resistant to meeting and spending time with him. He was incredibly relieved and hoped she wouldn't question him over the phone for his reason for abandoning her. This was a conversation he wanted to avoid over the phone. The two of them sitting down and talking was the ideal setting for Jonathan. They ironed out the details and talked a little more. She promised to tell Lisa about her plans for the weekend.

Once they released the line, Jonathan's phone rang a couple minutes later. He looked at the phone and noticed it was Sena calling back. Jonathan answered, "Hey, baby girl. You forget something?"

Lisa answered, "This is Lisa. Sena told me you called her. Jonathan, I don't mind you calling her. Please don't disappoint her. She has been through countless sleepless nights thinking about a reunion with you. If you are going to be in her life, be consistent and please keep your promises. Okay?"

Jonathan answered, "I understand, Lisa."

Lisa added, "I will make sure she is ready for you to get her this weekend as planned."

Jonathan stated, "Okay. Thank you, Lisa." He wanted to keep his conversations with her as short as possible. He didn't want her initiating a conversation that would turn into a blame game, causing him to feel guilty.

Jonathan went to Melanie with the details. "Melanie, Sena will be coming over this weekend. I hope that's okay with you."

Melanie responded, "Of course, it's okay. I told you I was leaving everything up to you."

Jonathan grew curious and asked, "Mel, can I ask you something?"

Melanie replied, "Sure, what is it?"

Jonathan asked, "Why the change of heart? What made you want to accept Sena in our lives?"

Melanie replied, "Well, there were two events taking place that caused the change of heart. I kept having these awkward feelings when I would be in bed, trying to sleep, thinking about her. While thinking about her, sadness would overcome, leading me to cry. I would hear a voice tell me she needs her father in her life. I knew it was God convicting me about her and how bad she was suffering without you. The other reason…I was taking a shower, and I heard His voice again. He asked me why I continued to punish you for hurting me. Jonathan, I cried uncontrollably when He asked me that question. I told Him I didn't know why. He told me I needed to forgive you if I wanted Him to be a part of this marriage. I knew it was time for me to stop reminding you how bad you hurt me. I was hurting you on purpose so you could feel what I was feeling. I'm sorry, Jonathan. I just want to move on and be happy."

Jonathan uttered, "Okay, I see. I was just wondering. So you can hear Him talking to you?"

Melanie answered, "Yes, I can hear Him speaking to me. You can hear Him too. Just listen, you'll know that it's Him talking to you."

Jonathan uttered, "Maybe I heard Him but just didn't know He talks to us. Thought it was just my thoughts."

Melanie stated, "He talks to you through your conscience. When you are warring mentally with yourself, usually it's Him speaking to you."

Jonathan replied, "Okay. I'll keep that in mind. Baby, I want to thank you for accepting my daughter." Jonathan walked toward Melanie and gave her a kiss and a pat to her backside.

Jonathan went to work that following day. He and Sharon were still avoiding each other. Jonathan was helping John when she arrived at the store. When she walked over to help, Jonathan excused himself to attend work in the office.

Sharon stopped him, asking, "Jonathan, can we talk for a moment?"

Jonathan's eyes rolled to the back of his head, but he agreed to speak to her. Jonathan asked John if he could handle things until Sharon returned.

Jonathan led her to the office. He gestured for her to have a seat. Sharon began her soliloquy. "Jonathan, I really don't know what to say or how to begin. When I interviewed and saw who you were, I wanted to say something, but I just couldn't bring myself to do so. I didn't know how you would respond after all these years. The only way I knew how to reveal my identity was through the bracelet. But that proved to be an epic failure."

Jonathan stated, "You should've just excused yourself and walked away from the interview. You didn't think working together would put us both in awkward positions? You stopped calling and receiving my calls with no explanation. You just should've walked out of my life again that day. That was not cool at all for you to do this."

Sharon agreed, stating, "Okay. You are right. That wasn't cool. But seeing you stirred up those old feelings. I couldn't believe I was seeing you. Never in a million years did I think I would see you again. But the reason I stopped calling and receiving your phone calls was—"

Jonathan interrupted her, "No worries. Just save it. There was no respect then, so no need to tell me now. Listen, John is out there by himself. Someone needs to help him. We are done here."

Sharon continued, "I was in a car accident, Jonathan! That's why you couldn't recognize me!" She calmed down and continued with a trembling voice, "It was almost life-threatening. I spent six months in the hospital recuperating, six months of therapy, and another six months of cosmetic surgery. By the time I healed, I reached out to you, but your number had changed." She began to cry.

Jonathan felt terrible. He walked over and consoled her. "Oh my god, Sharon, I'm so sorry. I never knew you went through this. I thought you found someone else and ended things without telling me. I feel so stupid."

Sharon continued, "I never stopped loving you, even to this day."

Jonathan's mind was set on handing Sharon a tissue from his desk. He never heard she still loved him. He insisted that she take a little time before going back up front to help John.

Sharon stated, "Thank you, Jonathan. I didn't mean to yell at you, but it was the only way for me to get your attention. Will you forgive me?"

Jonathan, with compassion, replied, "It's okay, Sharon. I understand now why my calls were unanswered. I feel bad for hating you all this time. Listen, take all the time you need. I am going to the front to help John. Will you be okay?"

Sharon answered, "Yes, I'm okay. I'll be there in just a minute."

Jonathan made his way out the office to the front, helping John until Sharon was able to gain composure. John asked, "Is Sharon okay?"

Jonathan replied, "Yes, she's okay. She's just having a moment and needed some time."

John stated, "Okay, well, let's make these donuts for the world." They both laughed and continued making the pastries.

Sharon sat in the office for a while. She couldn't believe she told him she never stopped loving him. She thought, *Since he didn't respond, maybe he didn't hear me. That must be the reason he didn't respond.* She gathered herself together and made an appearance back to the front to help with the pastries.

Missing Appointments and Increased Symptoms

Jonathan was on his way home when pain struck him. He hadn't been keeping his appointments regularly as suggested by Dr. Henry. He grinded his teeth, stating, "Lord, have mercy! This pain is no joke! I need to get home soon."

Jonathan had been missing appointments because there was so much going on in his life. Jonathan told himself the well-being of Mel, the baby, and JJ would supersede his health. This was an excuse he fed to himself. Jonathan didn't take his ailment seriously. He kept lying to himself that he had enough time to address his health issues. Each time Melanie asked Jonathan if he had been keeping his appointments, he would lie, telling her yes. But Melanie knew he was lying to her. She always knew when he lied and told the truth. It was all about how she questioned him. She could catch him lying, and he wouldn't even know he told on himself.

Jonathan called JJ, "Son, I need you to come help me out the car. I'm in pain, and please don't say anything to your mother."

JJ replied, "Okay, Dad. I just put the meatloaf in the oven. I'm on my way out now."

Melanie couldn't help but hear JJ talking to his father. JJ was walking to the front door, hoping his mother wouldn't see him and start asking questions. Melanie was smarter than the two of them thought. JJ had never went outside just to meet his Dad coming home from work. She knew something was wrong. JJ walked out the door without his mother hindering him. As soon as he walked up to the car to help his dad, he could see Jonathan slumped over the steering wheel.

He asked, "Dad, how bad are you hurting so I'll know how to get you out the car?"

Jonathan answered his son, "I'm having a flare all in my back, son. I just need you to help me get out of the car. I can manage it from there."

JJ said, "Okay, Dad."

JJ carefully helped Jonathan out of the car, ensuring he caused no additional pain to his father's back. Once Jonathan was out the car, he looked at JJ, stating, "Thank you, son. Your old man appreciates you. Your mother didn't question you, did she?"

JJ replied, "Oddly, no. That's not like her either. Normally, when I leave out the door, she asks where I'm going."

Jonathan stated to JJ, "Well, good she didn't inquire."

JJ asked, "So what are you going to tell her the reason that I came out to meet you?"

Jonathan answered, "Look in the back seat son. Something told me to grab those before leaving work."

JJ saw that there were about two dozens of honey glazed donuts in the car. JJ laughed and stated, "Even if she is thinking something, these donuts are sure to throw her off, Dad."

Jonathan agreed, stating, "Right, son. Grab them and let's go."

Melanie was sitting in the living area and playing with Ashley Cataleya. Jonathan walked in, greeting his two favorite girls. He asked, "How are my two favorite girls?"

Melanie smiled and answered, "We are doing fine. And how was work today?"

Jonathan replied, "Work was okay. I brought donuts home. JJ, bring your mother a donut, son."

JJ brought his mother one of the boxes for her to choose her own donut. Jonathan excused himself to take a shower. Melanie noticed that Jonathan wasn't walking right. Jonathan tried to mask it, but she could still see the unnatural way he walked.

Melanie thought, *If he wants to keep me in the dark, then so be it. I can't help someone who's not willing to help me help them.*

She averted her attention to JJ. She asked her son, "JJ, what are you making with that meatloaf?"

JJ replied, "I have some asparagus, squash, and zucchini." While JJ was listing the sides to his mother, Cataleya cooed at them both. JJ laughed, asking, "You trying to get my attention, baby sis? You want big brother to play with you?" JJ walked over to little Cataleya and retrieved her from her playpen. She was four months now.

Melanie had started working, and she detested going back more than ever. She wanted to be home with her sweet baby, but Jonathan's income alone wouldn't cover all expenses.

Melanie asked JJ, "Son, how are you and Camille doing?"

JJ responded, "We're fine, Mom. I gave her a scare when I was in the hospital. She brought it up almost every day for two weeks."

Melanie informed JJ, "She really likes you. You do know that, right?"

JJ answered, "Yes, Mom. I'm so glad I finally asked her to be my girl."

Melanie confessed to JJ, "Chelsea and I could see how you two felt about each other. We were just waiting for one of you to confess your feelings to the other."

JJ asked his mother, "Mom, if she liked me, why wouldn't she tell me how she felt? She should have said something as soon as she knew, right?"

Melanie responded, "Son, you must fathom this about a woman. We give you signs. Signs that are easily noticeable. Sometimes you all overlook the signs, but everyone else can see them but the intended recipient. They overlook the signs or deny the girl is interested in them. We don't like for you all to feel we are forcing our agenda on you. Men want to be in control. They want to be the chaser. She did it the right way. She had to wait for you to tell her how you felt. A myriad of men lose interest when the woman is chasing him. We leave it up to you all to approach us. I'm sure she fought hard to keep from disclosing her true feelings for you, son."

JJ looked at his mom, stating, "Okay, Mom. That makes sense. I just know I fought hard not to tell her how I felt about her because of rejection. I always thought my disability would prevent girls from wanting to be in a relationship with me. I know I'm not like the other guys, and I'm a little slower than they are. It's no problem for them to walk up to a girl, talk to her, and get her number."

Melanie disagreed with him, saying, "Son, it's not that you're slow. You take your time and consider what type of girl you want to pursue. Most guys just want to have sex with these girls and toss her away. You are smarter than they are, son. Give yourself some credit. You have come a long way in life. You amaze your dad and me all the time."

Melanie and Jonathan made sure they kept JJ up to par with how the world operated. And intentionally didn't use simple words with JJ. They wanted him to have an expanded vocabulary. They would use the words and give him their meaning, just to see if he retained. To their surprise, he would retain the meaning and knew how to use the words.

JJ stated, "Mom, I love talking to you. You have a way of explaining things to me. You deliver with love. Whenever I talk to Dad, I always get these doubts about his speeches. I had to stop approaching him with my problems. I knew deep inside he was coming from a place of hurt and what he had been taught as a young man."

Melanie was blushing and stated, "Well, I'm glad one of us makes sense to you."

Cataleya was chiming in on their conversation with her baby talk, demanding their attention.

Jonathan had walked into the living area and heard her making a fuss. He walked over, asking Cataleya, "What are you making a fuss about, little girl?" Jonathan gestured for JJ to hand her to him. Jonathan continued talking to Li'l Honey, stating, "What's my baby girl fussing about this time?" Li'l Honey began to coo even more. Jonathan loved talking to his baby girl. Jonathan thought, *I will never abandon you the way I abandoned Sena. I have to do better with her.*

JJ came out the kitchen, announcing, "Okay, guys, the food is done. I will get the plates together and put them on the table. I have iced tea in the fridge if you all want any. Dad, I'll help you up after I'm done." JJ thought about what he said. He thought, *Oh, shoot. I hope Mom didn't hear what I just said. I didn't mean to say that and draw attention to Dad.*

Jonathan ignored JJ and continued playing with Cataleya. Melanie heard him loud and clear. Melanie looked at Jonathan with anger. He could feel her eyes piercing through him, but he continued playing with Cataleya, giving her no indication that he knew she was ogling him.

Melanie rolled her eyes. She thought, *Okay, so there was something wrong with his ass. I wonder why he is being so secretive. I am not pregnant anymore. So there wouldn't be any reason for him to think he is imposing stress on me by talking about his condition. Since he wants to keep this a secret, I will not say anything to him. Selfish ass!*

Weekend with Sena

It was the weekend. Jonathan was on his way to bring his daughter home to meet Melanie and her new baby sister. Jonathan thought about his other daughter he abandoned. This child was produced before Melanie was in the picture. Her mother would keep the child away from him using her as a pawn because she wanted to be with him. If he didn't commit to her, she would keep him from seeing her. Jonathan grew tired of her behavior and never pressed the issue by taking her to court for visitation rights. Another reason he didn't pursue visitation was because of money. He felt he needed to have money if she were to come visit. Melanie would constantly tell him, "Your child doesn't care about money, she just wants to spend time with you." But he never listened. Sena was all ready when he arrived. She was grateful that Jonathan kept his promise and didn't renege. They bonded on the way to Jonathan's home. He told her about Mel and her baby sister. She couldn't wait to meet them both. She wondered how she and Melanie would respond to one another.

She thought, *Will she accept me or feel threatened that my dad is making me a part of this family? I am the reason for the heartache he caused to her and Mom.* Sena asked Jonathan, "Dad, is your wife truly okay with me coming over for the weekend? She won't change her mind, will she?"

Jonathan replied, "Baby girl, don't you worry about that. We have already discussed it, and she is perfectly fine with you spending the weekend with us."

Sena was relieved to hear those words. They finally arrived and were walking toward the door. Sena took a deep breath before entering the apartment.

Jonathan opened the door and announced, "Hey, guys, we're here."

JJ was playing with Cataleya when they entered. He walked toward her with the baby in his hands and hugged his sister. "What's up, big sis? How are you doing?"

Sena, hugging him back, replied, "I'm doing fine, little bro. How have you been doing?"

JJ answered his sister, "I'm good."

Sena asked, "Is this my baby sister?" Sena grabbed ahold of her little fingers. Cataleya leaped toward Sena.

"Whoa, little girl," said Jonathan.

Melanie walked over and introduced herself. "Hello, Sena. How are you? I am Melanie, Jonathan's wife. It's good to have you for the weekend."

Sena replied, "I'm doing good, ma'am. Thank you for having me. May I hold my sister, JJ?" JJ handed Cataleya to Sena. Sena asked, "How old is she? She is so cute and adorable."

Melanie answered, "She'll be five months in two weeks. She is a handful too. Come on in the living area and have a seat. JJ, take your sister's bag to your room for her. She will be sleeping there for the weekend."

JJ uttered, "Sure thing, Mom. I'll change the sheets while I'm in there."

Melanie wanted Sena to feel as comfortable as possible. Sena felt nervous, but Melanie conversed with her as if she had already been part of the family. The weekend was off to a good start. The family gathered in the living area, laughing, talking, and playing with Cataleya. Jonathan looked at Melanie, adoring how she was making Sena feel at home. He thought, *I knew she could do this. I am so proud and at the same time happy for her. She finally stepped away from hurt and anger at me. Now she can be happy in life.*

Jonathan had the weekend planned out for Sena. He had talked to JJ about spots parents could take their teenagers for fun and if he knew what his sister's interests were. Jonathan went down a list, stating, "Dad, she enjoys painting, skating, laser tag, paintball, and a few other things."

Jonathan called the local recreation facility, and to his surprise, three of her activities were available. They would spend one and a half hours painting and one and a half hours with laser tag. On Sunday, he wanted to take the family out for dinner prior to taking her home. Melanie declined the painting and laser tag but wanted to be there with them for dinner. She felt Jonathan and JJ should have the recreational time with Sena. Cataleya was too young for those activities, and Melanie didn't have anyone to care for her, so they would've been tagalongs, not being able to enjoy the activities.

A Surprise for Chelsea

Chelsea was on the phone with Chauncey. He was calling to let her know that he was outside waiting for her and Camille. He was sponsoring and driving them to a much-needed spa day. Chauncey would always eliminate any plans he had to cater to his two favorite girls. It was no secret that Chauncey still loved Chelsea. He had been missing the family structure he shared with them. His career, unemployment, and a discretion with one woman had caused the strain in their marriage, leading to their divorce. Chauncey, while seeing this woman, became irresponsible and neglected his job, resulting in his termination. But after some time, Chauncey was able to convince with the help of his friend/partner William, the chief to rehire him. Chelsea was employed as a district manager for a chain of restaurants, supporting the family. She carried the weight for a year, leaving Chauncey to care for the kids. Chauncey started to resent Chelsea. He felt less than a man. He wasn't able to care for his family financially. He felt she resented him for his unemployment status and abandoned his family to live with a friend. Chelsea never belittled him for not having a job. They were in this together. Chauncey didn't see it that way. Soon after leaving, he asked for a divorce. Chelsea was confused, hurt, and didn't understand the logistics of his decision. She respected his decision and never pressed the issue for him to return. She felt he needed that time to think and sort through some things.

Chelsea called out to her daughter, "Camille? Honey, what is taking you so long to get ready? We need to leave. Your dilatory actions will cause us to be late for our spa appointment. Your father is outside waiting for us."

Camille was almost ready, stating, "Okay, Mom. I am tying my shoes and grabbing my cap to leave."

LOSING HER CROWN

Chelsea was walking out the door, telling her daughter, "Okay. I will be in the car. Make sure you lock the house and activate the security system."

Camille uttered, "Okay, Mom, will do."

Camille was thinking about her brothers, Chauncey Jr. and Lonnie, and how she wished the two of them were present to be home with the family. She missed them deeply. They both were off to college and couldn't make it home for the weekend. While thinking about her brothers and tying her shoes, she noticed JJ was calling her. She answered, "Hey, JJ. How's it going?"

JJ replied, "Hey, it's going well. My sister is here for the weekend. I would like for you to meet her before we leave. Dad is taking us to the recreation center for some painting and laser tag."

Camille answered, "I would love to, but right now, Mom and Dad are waiting for me in the car to join them. Dad is paying for a three-hour session for Mom and me at the spa and no telling where else. Is your sister visiting just for today?"

JJ replied, "No, she will be here until Sunday. Dad will be driving her back home around six in the evening."

Camille stated, "Okay. If I can't make it sometime today, I'll be there before she leaves."

JJ stated, "Okay, we'll see you when you can make it."

Camille heard a car's horn honking. She yelled out, "All right! I'm coming!" Camille activated the security system, walked out the door, and locked up the house.

After Camille entered the car, Chauncey asked, "Well, how are you two doing today? Y'all ready for this spa treatment I have planned for you two? Oh, and thanks for allowing me to drive you there. I haven't spent any time with you all lately."

Chelsea and Camille replied they were fine, and both thanked him for the tickets he procured from the police department from which he worked. Chauncey had a surprise up his sleeves in which both Chelsea and Camille were oblivious. They all engaged in the conversation of wishing Chauncey Jr. and Lonnie were present. Chauncey kept the secret, not revealing they would be home for a surprise.

They finally arrived at their destination. Chauncey reached into his glove compartment and removed the tickets, allowing Chelsea and Camille access into the establishment for much-needed pampering. He handed the two to Chelsea, stating, "You all go in and enjoy yourselves. Afterward, we will be having dinner at a restaurant close to downtown. It is new, and coworkers stand by the service and food. I will see you gals about five thirty. I will drive you all home, and from there, we will change and then off to the restaurant. While you are here, I'll be at the gun range target practicing."

Chelsea stated, "Okay. Be careful. And again, thanks for this, Chauncey."

Camille added, "Yes, Dad. Thank you so much."

Chauncey drove off, and the ladies walked into the spa.

Chauncey lied about where he would be until it was time for him to retrieve his ex-wife and daughter. Chauncey and his girlfriend were no longer together. She just couldn't measure up to Chelsea, so he decided before any serious feelings were to be involved, he would call it quits with her. The split was amicable between the two. Chauncey was on his way to get everything ready for the evening. One of his old partners, William Jedar, had quit the force and opened his own restaurant. It was family oriented, and he named it Jedar's Restaurant. He owed Chauncey a favor and reserved the restaurant for Chauncey to execute the night's event he had planned. Chauncey had called his and Chelsea's family members to join in on the surprise he had planned. Even the two sons knew about it and were part of the surprise. They were all to meet at the restaurant at 7:30 p.m.

Once he arrived at the restaurant, he could see his two sons were there decorating and getting everything set up for the night's event. The boys, in the past, told Chauncey that even though Chelsea dated a couple of times, their mother was still in love with him and hadn't moved on with anyone. Chauncey didn't want to waste any time with the news and immediately started planning his move to win her back.

The Other Woman

Camille was confused, stating "Mom, why didn't you just drive us here to the spa in your car? And after we're done, Dad could've just met us at home."

Chelsea responded, "Your dad insisted that since he procured the tickets, he felt it was his duty to drive us here. He said since we were being pampered, we might as well let him chauffer us here."

Camille stated, "Okay. That makes sense."

The ladies presented their tickets and were ushered to a room to remove their clothing and cover themselves with beautiful blue robes in the changing rooms. Since Chauncey was an officer of the law, the robes would be theirs to keep.

Camillie stated, "Mom, these robes are beautiful, and they feel so soft. I am going to enjoy this robe every winter night."

Cheslea replied, "Yes, baby. I agree. They are beautiful, but you may have to bear not having it for a day or two at time. I plan on sending these to be professionally cleaned." Camille agreed.

Chelsea didn't want to damage these in a washing machine. They stepped out of the change room and were greeted by two young ladies. They led them to a room to get their nails manicured.

Camille said, "Mom, this is a beautiful establishment, and it's owned by African Americans. It's about time we as a community opened an establishment just for us. I'm tired of spending my money in communities who prove to not appreciate us." Camille waited for her mother to add to her statement but saw that she was in deep thought and asked, "Mom, did you hear me?"

Chelsea replied, "Huh? No, baby. I am sorry. I was thinking about something."

Camille stated again, "I was saying how beautiful this place is, and I'm glad it's owned by one of us. Tired of going to those other folks who don't appreciate our business. They treat and talk to us with such disdain."

Chelsea stated, "I was thinking that exact thing, sweetie. This will be our spot from here on out if they remain in operation."

After they got their nails done, the same two ladies escorted them to their pedicure seats. They offered Chelsea a glass of wine and whatever nonalcoholic beverage Camille wanted. The ladies accepted and enjoyed their drinks and pedicures.

While they were waiting for their toenails to dry, Chelsea recognized a familiar face walking into the spa. Chelsea thought, *What is this jezebel doing in here? If I wasn't in this establishment with my daughter, I would whip her ass!*

This was the woman Chauncey had his indiscretion with and one of the reasons they divorced. She looked Chelsea's way, gave her a smirk, and rolled her eyes while walking into the changing room. It took every fiber in her bones to keep her composure while in the company of her daughter. Camille discerned their looks at each other. Camille was curious about their eye contact.

"Mom, who is that lady? Do you know her? Why are the two of you giving each other those looks?"

Chelsea broke contact to answer her daughter. She never wanted the kids to know about their dad's infidelity, but just in case, this woman felt feisty at the spa, revealing herself in front of Camille. She thought it would be best she told her.

Chelsea looked at her daughter, stating, "Camille, I didn't want you kids to know about this. I kept a secret from you all so that you wouldn't look at your father in a disgusting way. She is a part of the reason your dad and I divorced."

Camille responded, "Dad? No, Mom, he wouldn't cheat on you. Dad loves you. Who told you that? Did she tell you?"

Chelsea confessed, "No, baby. I caught them in the act. Your dad used to blame his job for his late nights out, and sometimes he wouldn't come home until the next day. I knew he was cheating. I could feel it. He was careless one night and had the nerve to talk to her on our home phone. I picked up to call my sister when I heard them making their plans to meet. She gave him her registered name, the place, time, and room number. She was waiting for him. I knew the place where they were meeting. I gave him a head start before I left to catch him. Once I saw him leave the front desk and enter the room, I went to the front desk and told them I was her and that I had mistakenly left the key inside along with my purse and needed their assistance to open the door. When they opened the door, there he was on top of her. I screamed all types of obscenities at him. He jumped up, trying to elucidate that it wasn't what I was thinking. I yelled, 'So this is where you have been all those times you told me you were working mandatory overtime!'"

Camille interrupted, "Oh, Mom. I'm so sorry. You actually caught them in the act? Did she say anything?"

Chelsea continued, "She just sat up in the bed, looking at your dad and telling him to tell me how long they've been seeing each other. It proved she knew he was married and didn't care. It didn't matter to me how long he had been cheating behind my back. I just knew I could no longer trust him. I couldn't let him touch me. The vision of them permanently branded in my mind was too much."

Camille stated, "Now I see why he's always at your beck and call and volunteering to do things for you. He is trying to make up for what he did to you. I am so proud of you, Mom. You knew your self-worth. He was the one who couldn't see your worth to him."

Chelsea added, "I did give that front desk person a scare when I rushed the door after he had it unlocked." They both laughed and changed the subject.

Chelsea and Camille heard a voice saying, "Ladies, we're ready to move you on over to have your facials."

Chelsea and Camille were escorted to the facial chairs. The ladies massaged their faces prior to applying the mask. Chelsea, while getting massaged, felt calmed and relaxed. Camille saw the look on her mother's face and latched her fingers onto her mother's hand. The ladies applied a clay mask, leaving it on for twenty minutes. Once they rinsed off, they moved over to the massage tables. Their tickets allowed them a one-hour massage. Mom and daughter remained quiet while getting pampered for the full hour. Camille couldn't help but think about her father's indiscretion, and Chelsea was enjoying the hands of the massage therapist.

Chauncey noticed it was time to retrieve his ex-wife and daughter. He told the boys to go home to get ready. There wasn't that much left to do. They could continue after they came back. He wanted them ready and out of the house before he brought Chelsea and Camille home.

Chauncey Jr. stated, "Okay, Dad. We'll go home and get ready. We only need to hang the banner when we arrive." Chauncey Jr. added, "Don't forget to text me and let me know when you all are arriving, so we won't be visible to Mom when she walks into the restaurant."

Chauncey replied, "I won't, son."

The boys left. Chauncey hung around to make sure everything was set in perfection. After thirty minutes, he received Chelsea's text to pick her and Camille up. Chauncey texted her back, letting her know he was on his way. As they walked to the front, Chelsea and the other woman had eye contact again prior to leaving. Chelsea decided to be mature and gave her a killer smile, not breaking eye contact. Her enemy couldn't stand looking at Chelsea's beautiful face and smile, so she broke eye contact with her. Chelsea thought, *Yeah, bitch, that's what I thought!* And she walked to the waiting lobby with her daughter.

The two of them sat, waiting for Chauncey to appear. Camille stated, "I saw that, Mom. You gave her a confident smile and didn't break eye contact. Way to go, Mom!"

Chelsea laughed, stating, "I had to show her that her appearance didn't mean a thing to me."

Chauncey finally pulled up to take them home. The two ladies entered the car. Chauncey asked, "So how was it? Did you all enjoy being pampered?"

They replied, "Yes, we did."

Chelsea added, "I had fun with my baby today, and we discussed some things."

Chauncey asked Chelsea, "Okay. What did you guys discuss?"

Chelsea answered, "Just girl talk, is all."

Chauncey texted Junior, making sure they would be out the house before bringing Chelsea and Camille home. The boys were already out of the house and on their way back to the restaurant. Chauncey kept thinking about the surprise he had in store for Chelsea. He carefully planned the décor to every detail. He knew

Chelsea loved purple and gold colors. Every anniversary, he endeavored to purchase her gifts with those colors. He anticipated her facial expressions from the two surprises in store for her—their two sons being home from college and family members she hadn't seen in years witnessing his proposal to her. Chauncey's thoughts, for some reason, expeditiously went to Melanie. He thought, *Oh no, I forgot about Melanie and Jonathan. How could I have forgotten to invite them? I will call them as soon as they both are out of sight. How could I have been so careless not to invite the most important person besides me and the kids in Chelsea's life? I hope they have no plans for the evening.*

They were finally home. Chauncey stated, "Guys, we have one and a half hours to dress."

Chelsea and Camille responded, "Okay." They both made their way upstairs to dress for dinner. It wouldn't take long. They all had a bathroom to bathe and dress. Chauncey remained standing near the car to call Jonathan.

Jonathan picked up, asking, "Hey, Chauncey, man what's happening?"

Chauncey replied, "Hey, Jonathan. I am so sorry this is last minute. With all the excitement, I neglected to call you all and invite you to a surprise gathering for today. I'm asking Chelsea for her hand in marriage again."

Jonathan asked, "Is that right? Ready to take that plunge into marriage again, huh? I am happy for you, man. I am out with JJ and my eighteen-year-old daughter, but we will be finishing here in a bit. I'll call Melanie and let her know to go ahead and start getting ready."

Chauncey, confused, asked, "Your eighteen-year-old daughter? You have an eighteen-year-old daughter? I didn't know you had a daughter older than JJ. You never mentioned her."

Jonathan answered, "It's a long story, man. I'll tell you about it."

Chauncey said, "Okay. We are all meeting up at Jedar's at 7:30."

Jonathan stated, "I know exactly where it is. We may be a little late, but we'll be there."

Chauncey was relieved, stating, "Thanks, man. And again, I apologize for such short notice." Chauncey released the line and entered the home to tidy up for the engagement party.

Melanie was at home with Cataleya. The baby had been asleep since the trio left for their evening entertainment. She was about to awaken Cataleya when Jonathan called her. She answered, "Hey, Jonathan. How's the evening with JJ and Sena going?"

Jonathan replied, "Mel, you need to get ready. Chauncey just called and invited us to attend a surprise party for Chelsea. He's going to ask her to marry him again."

Melanie was shocked asking, "Are you serious? Oh my goodness. I just knew that one of them would come around one day. I can see and feel the love between the two of them. I was about to wake the baby for her feeding. I've already taken my shower, so I'll get us both ready."

Jonathan stated to Melanie, "Okay, we'll be there in a bit. We're almost done with laser tag."

Melanie ended with "Okay. I'll see you in a little while."

Melanie was ecstatic to hear the news. She knew it was only a matter of time before one would break their silence and confess their love to the other. She walked into her closet, gathered her attire, and laid them on the bed. She sat at her vanity and applied just enough makeup to enhance her beauty. After applying the makeup, she dressed herself. She turned her attention to Li'l Honey and what outfit she would be wearing. While she was searching for an outfit, the trio walked in the house.

Melanie asked, "How was the painting and laser tag?"

Jonathan replied, "Baby, you should've been there. We enjoyed ourselves."

Melanie looked at their faces, stating, "Good. Now you all can get ready."

The men agreed they wouldn't be in the shower long because they had taken one prior to leaving this afternoon. Sena would wait until JJ finished before taking her shower.

Sena watched as Mel tried to pick an outfit for Ashley Cataleya. She initiated talking to Mel. "Thank you for having me over this weekend."

Melanie walked over to her and embraced her, stating, "You are welcome, sweetie. Would you like to get Cataleya ready for me?

I need to make sure your dad and JJ are dressed appropriately for the occasion."

Sena was shocked that she embraced her. Sena replied, "Sure, I would love to."

Melanie handed Cataleya to Sena, along with her beautiful pink outfit and booties to match. Melanie went into their closets to retrieve nice attires for Jonathan and JJ. Once both men simultaneously exited the showers, they discerned the clothes Melanie had picked for them. They showed their appreciation to Melanie for getting their clothes together. Sena carefully dressed her baby sister. She played with her until JJ announced the shower was all hers. She delivered the baby into the hands of her big brother.

Melanie asked, "Sena, do you have something to wear?"

Sena replied, "Yes, ma'am, I do. Mom made sure that I packed something nice for such an occasion as this."

Melanie stated, "You have forty minutes to shower and get ready. We need to leave soon."

Sena said, "Yes, ma'am. Good thing my hair is in braids and no ironing is needed."

Sena went to shower. She knew it would only take her fifteen minutes or less to dress, so her shower time was about twenty-five minutes. While showering, she began to cry. She never thought she would be a part of her dad's family. She was so happy that Melanie was making her feel at home. She finished showering and dressed herself in JJ's room. Melanie had brushed Cataleya's hair, and it was time for the family to be on their way to the party.

Jonathan had a smile on his face as they were leaving the parking lot. He thought, *My family all together, finally.* Jonathan asked, "Does anyone need anything before we pass by this convenience store?"

They all responded, "No."

Jonathan was relieved. He didn't like stopping while driving to his destinations.

Chauncey's Proposal

Chauncey yelled out, "Guys, it's time to leave for dinner! Are y'all ready?"

From upstairs, Chelsea and Camille yelled, "In a minute!"

Chauncey looked at his watch. It was 7:00 p.m. They had thirty minutes to get there. There was no traffic, so they should arrive there in about ten or fifteen minutes. He went upstairs so he wouldn't have to yell. "Guys, you have no more than fifteen minutes. We need to leave around 7:15 p.m. No later."

Chelsea, applying her makeup, stated, "I'm almost done applying my makeup. I'm already dressed."

Camille, fussing with her hair, stated, "I'm almost ready. Just getting my hair together."

Chauncey went downstairs while calling Chauncey Jr. "Hey, Dad. You on your way? Everything is ready, and everyone is here."

Chauncey replied, "We'll be there shortly. Also, I failed to tell you. We have five more guests arriving. You remember meeting my friend Jonathan and his family?"

Chauncey Jr. replied, "Yes, I remember, and we have more than enough for them. In fact, I see them walking in now."

Chauncey stated, "Okay, good. Everything is going according to plan. I'll see you when we arrive, son."

Chauncey Jr. stated, "Okay, Dad. See you when you get here."

As he was hanging up the phone, mother and daughter made their way downstairs. Chauncey asked, "All right, you guys ready?"

They replied, "Yes."

Chauncey activated the alarm system and opened the door for Chelsea and Camille. They walked out, and he locked the door. He rushed to the passenger side to open the door for Chelsea. She thanked him. He opened the door for his daughter. She thanked him as well. Chauncey did this on purpose for his daughter. She needed to know how a man should treat her. They were off to the restaurant.

Chelsea and Camille continued their conversation about their visit to the spa. Chelsea added, "You have started something that you will, from now on, have to continue."

Chauncey uttered, "That's what I aim to do for my favorite girls. You ladies look exceptionally beautiful tonight."

Chelsea and Camille both said, "Thank you."

Chelsea added, "I can see the effort you have put into this evening. That is good. I like it. And you are looking, dapper yourself tonight."

Camille sat back, listening to her parents. Her dad's behavior had been a little eccentric lately. She thought, *Dad has something up his sleeve. I wonder what he is up to tonight.*

Jonathan pulled into the restaurant and had no problems finding a place to park. "Okay, guys. We are here. We need to enter before Chauncey gets here with Chelsea so we won't spoil the surprise."

They all exited the car. JJ removed Cataleya from her car seat. He handed her to Melanie. Jonathan popped the trunk to get her stroller out for Melanie.

Melanie asked Jonathan, "Do you want me to place her in the stroller? I know you've been in pain."

Jonathan pushed the stroller to Melanie. Melanie turned her body, placing her feet on the ground as she sat in the car to situate Cataleya in her stroller. JJ took control, pulling the stroller away from Melanie so he could chauffer his baby sister. Jonathan helped Melanie from the car.

Chauncey Jr. met the Taylors at the door. He stated, "Hi, Mr. and Mrs. Taylor. I just spoke to Dad. He told me you all were arriving. Please take a seat at the table where we will be sitting. If I know my mother, Melanie, she would want you close to her."

They all took their places and waited for the couple and Camille to arrive. Melanie and Sena were admiring the décor. Melanie knew Chelsea would love Chauncey's choice of colors for her.

Chauncey Jr. received a text from Chauncey, announcing they were outside and headed for the door. Chauncey Jr. announced to everyone, "Okay, guys. They have just arrived. When they enter, we all yell surprise."

Everyone's attention was focused on the door and the parties entering. Chauncey opened the door for his ex-wife and daughter. Camille saw the audience and confirmed her dad was up to something. Chelsea was busy making sure her hair and clothing were intact. When she looked up, they all yelled, "Surprise!"

Chelsea's eyes bucked with surprise. Chauncey took her by the hand and led her to the table where her best friend sat. Camille noticed JJ and claimed her seat next to him. JJ stood erect, and they embraced each other. JJ pulled her seat out for her. JJ noticed Mr. Phillips was standing in front of everyone for an announcement and would introduce his sister to his girlfriend later. Melanie rose from her chair and gave her best friend the warmest, tightest hug imaginable. Chauncey rushed back to Chelsea and pulled out her chair so she could sit. Everyone was quiet, and Chelsea wondered why they were all staring her way. He stepped in front of her, positioned himself in the proposing position, pulled a ring from his pocket, and asked, "Chelsea, would you do me the honor of accepting my hand in marriage again?"

Chelsea was in tears, and she cradled her face with her hands. Chelsea replied, "Yes! I will marry you again!"

Chauncey placed the ring on her finger and pulled her close to him and gave her a big kiss and hug. The whole crowd clapped and cried with joy. Chelsea turned to Melanie and asked, "You knew about this?"

Melanie replied, "I just learned about it this evening. I had no idea. Oh, Chelsea, my friend. I am so happy for you and knew you two would find yourselves back to each other." Melanie had tears of joy streaming down her face. Her friend pulled her in for a hug.

Chelsea cried, stating, "I'm so happy I have you, my friends, and family here to celebrate this with me. You are all here with me to witness this occasion. Can you believe it, Mel? I'm getting another chance with him. Things worked out just as they were supposed to. How blessed can one be?"

Melanie replied, "All it took was just one of you acknowledging the love is still there and to act on it. You both knew it was there. You two were just mirroring each other, endeavoring to see which of you would make the first move. You were patient and allowed him to do so."

Family members approached the couple to congratulate them. This was JJ's opportunity to introduce Camille to Sena. He pulled his sister near, stating, "Camille, this is my sister Sena. Sena, this is Camille."

They both exchanged hellos and hugged each other. Both parents of Chauncey and Chelsea were present at the evenings event. When Chelsea's mother laid eyes on Melanie, she couldn't believe her eyes. Melanie looked the same as she last saw her. She walked toward Melanie. Melanie knew exactly who she was. They instantly greeted one another with a hug.

Chelsea's mother stated, "Oh, Melanie, it's so good to see you. Chelsea told me you two had found your way back to each other."

Melanie stated, "Mrs. Johnson, it's good to see you. Yes, we found our way back to each other."

Mrs. Johnson asked, "You remember Mr. Johnson, don't you, Melanie?"

Mr. Johnson reeled Melanie in for a hug. "Of course, she remembers me. It is good to see you, dear. Chelsea told us you are married with two children."

Melanie stated, "Yes, sir. I am. This is my husband, Jonathan, and our son, JJ."

Mr. Johnson extended his hand to Jonathan and JJ, stating, "It's good to meet the both of you. Chelsea has told us so much about you two."

Jonathan and JJ both exchanged handshakes with Mr. Johnson, stating, "Good to meet you, sir."

Jonathan stated, "I hope she said good things about us."

Mr. Johnson stated, "It was all good."

Melanie interrupted, "Mr. Johnson, this is Jonathan's daughter, Sena. And last but not least, here is our Cataleya."

Mr. Johnson said to Sena, "Hello, lovely young lady. It's a pleasure to meet you."

Sena stated, "It's a pleasure to meet you as well."

Mr. Johnson set his eyes on Cataleya. She was smiling at Mr. Johnson. "Well, look here. Aren't you just the cutest, most adorable baby I've seen?" Mr. Johnson's hand made its way to Cataleya.

Cataleya grabbed his finger, pulled herself upward, and cooed at him. They all laughed at Li'l Honey.

Mrs. Johnson stated, "Guys, she is beautiful. You all have a beautiful family here."

Mr. Johnson added, "Yes, Jonathan, always remember to cherish them always. There's nothing like having your family with you standing by your side."

Jonathan uttered, "I hear you, Mr. Johnson. Nothing like having your family beside you."

Chauncey's parents met Jonathan and Melanie. They met everyone there and were adored by the crowd. Everyone kept telling them they were an attractive couple with beautiful children.

It was time for the food to be served. There was a buffet prepared for everyone to eat from their choice of food. There was fried fish, fried chicken, baked fish, grilled chicken, spaghetti, meatloaf, steak, mashed potatoes, corn on the cob, steamed baby carrots, broccoli cheese, mac and cheese, red beans and rice, cabbage, and a mixture of collard, mustard, and turnip greens. For dessert, there was ice cream, strawberry cake, German chocolate cake, banana pudding, and chocolate chip and peanut butter cookies. Everyone ate their fill. There was even enough for them all to take food home. Chauncey hired a band for the evening. Good music played for the couples dancing on the dance floor. This was a fun evening for all who attended.

After everyone ate and prior to their leaving, Chauncey had an announcement, demanding their attention. Chauncey looked over at Chelsea and stated, "I hope you all enjoyed yourselves tonight. I thank you all for coming out this evening to celebrate with us. I must thank my old partner, William, for sponsoring this event for me. Chelsea and William, would you both mind standing here by my side?"

Chelsea and William walked up to Chauncey and stood by him.

Chauncey went on to say, "I've been in law enforcement for twenty years now. I have encountered the good and the bad. Since I was a little boy, I would see the police cars riding through the neighborhood with those cool lights on top. I used to tell myself how cool it would be to drive one of those and get rid of the bad guys. I always wanted to make sure my mother and father were safe. Becoming an officer of the law, I tried my best to do just that. Making sure all my loved ones were safe. You know how you have that fire in you that is so strong it keeps you going each day with hope that you can make the world a better place? For twenty years, I have walked and rode the beat. That flickering flame, bit by bit, extinguished until there was nothing left. I will miss my colleagues. But it's time for me to retire and advance to better things."

Chelsea thought, *What is he doing? Is he quitting the force? The force was all he used to talk about when we were married.*

Chauncey continued, "My partner here has this thriving and successful restaurant and has offered me to be his partner. After weighing the pros and cons, I have accepted."

Chelsea couldn't believe what she was hearing. Chelsea thought, *Oh my god! He is quitting the force! Yes!*

Chauncey turned to Chelsea, stating, "This was the other surprise I had in store. I had wondered if it would make you happy. But in making the decision, I realized how happy I was making myself. Having a piece of something to call my own brings happiness to me. I want to do this while I'm still young with the woman of my dreams and the beautiful children we have together."

Chelsea was teary-eyed and speechless but was able to muster up a small reply. She stated, "I'm with you all the way, Chauncey."

Chauncey took advantage of the moment to embrace and kiss her. He turned to William and stated, "William, you were my partner all those years. I was a rookie when they paired me with you. You taught me much about the beat. The dos and don'ts of the force. How to have respect for even the criminals out there. I couldn't have asked for a better partner. I thank you for having me as a partner."

Chauncey turned it over to William. William stated, "I don't know what to say. This guy here was a pain in my butt when I first met him. He was so eager to take down the bad guys. The work and years of experience I had put into this job succored with shaping and molding him into the police officer he became. He had my back, and I had his. We were one hell of a team together. He came to me a few months ago. He said, 'William, the fire that once burned in me to be a cop is no longer there. I thought I would always have it until I reached full retirement. It is just not the same without you, partner. That was when the fire in me burned its most.' That statement alone made me think about the rides we had taken, the bad guys eliminated off the streets, and many other things we did together. Which is why, out of all the souls I considered co-owning this restaurant, my heart led me back to wanting my old partner for another adventure."

Those two souls hugged, and the whole crowd let out a tumultuous shout. The two calmed the crowd.

Chauncey made his last speech, stating, "It's time to end tonight's affair. Thank you all for coming, and have a good night!"

They all approached one another for some last words and gathered their things. They all said their goodbyes and were out the door for their journey home.

Mr. and Ms. Johnson, before leaving, approached Melanie, giving her a big hug and kiss. Mr. Johnson stated to Jonathan, "You remember what I said, young man. Nothing like having your family by your side."

Jonathan uttered, "Yes, sir. I won't forget that."

Chauncey walked his parents out the door after they hugged Chelsea and the grandkids. Melanie and Jonathan lingered around offering to help tidy up the place. William insisted that everyone go home. There was a cleaning crew already hired to clean up the place. Chauncey asked, "You need me to hang around until they arrive?"

William stated, "No. You go on home and enjoy your time with your soon-to-be wife for the second time."

Chauncey wished his old friend a good night. The Phillips and Taylors walked out of the restaurant together. Before Melanie and Chelsea placed themselves in their vehicles, they shared one last hug for the night.

Melanie stated, "I love you so much, Chelly."

Chelsea laughed and stated, "All this time, I thought you had forgotten you used to call me Chelly."

Melanie stated, "Nah, just saving it for the right time."

Chelsea ogled Melanie, saying, "I love you, Mel. Call me when you get home so I'll know you all made it safe."

Melanie promised, stating, "Okay. I promise to call you."

JJ walked Camille to the car and opened the door for her. "JJ, thanks for being here. I really appreciate you."

JJ held both her hands, stating, "You know I wouldn't miss anything when it involves me seeing you. I'll call you when I get home, okay?"

Camille replied, "Okay. Talk to you later."

The guests were almost gone. The Taylors walked away to get in their car until Melanie remembered Sena. She turned and called to Chelsea and Chauncey. "Oh, guys, with all the fuss this evening, we failed to introduce my stepdaughter. This is Sena. Sena, this is my best friend, Chelsea, and Chauncey is a friend of your dad's. And the lovely young lady standing with JJ is their daughter, Camille."

Camille stated, "Yes, we met."

Chauncey and Chelsea were happy to meet her. Sena was pleased to meet them.

Sena asked JJ, "Baby brother, can we all hang out sometimes?"

JJ answered, "Sure. The three of us can hang out on your next visit."

Jonathan interrupted, "If it's all right with your mother, you can come back anytime you like."

Sena laughed stating, "Dad I'm almost 19, mom really doesn't have a say about this."

Melanie stated, "Yes, anytime you want to come back is fine with us all. Cataleya has taken a liking to you." Cataleya had let out a big yawn. Melanie stated, "Awe, Momma's baby is tired. Okay, guys, let's get her home. Chelsea, I'll call you when we make it home."

The two families went their separate ways. As promised, Melanie called Chelsea to let her know they were home. JJ was already talking to Camille, wishing her good night.

Driving Sena Back Home

Jonathan received a call from Lisa that she would be home all day Sunday and that he could bring Sena home anytime he wanted. Jonathan asked Sena, "What time would you like to go home tomorrow?"

Sena replied, "I want to stay as late as y'all will have me."

Jonathan stated, "Okay, JJ and I will drive you home at about eight. Is that okay?"

Sena answered, "Sure, Dad. I would love to stay that late."

Jonathan told her he would be taking her home after dinner. Sena loved feeling like she was part of the family. She was grateful for Melanie opening her heart to her.

Melanie was getting Cataleya ready for bed. She heard a knock on the door. She answered, "Come on in."

Sena entered, asking, "Is she asleep? I wanted to kiss her good night."

Melanie replied, "No, she isn't. Would you like to hold her a while before I lay her down in the bed?"

Sena became excited, stating, "Sure!" She rushed over to pick her baby sister up from the bed and held her."

Melanie stated, "She likes you. I have never seen her take a liking to anyone the way she has with you. She's never seen you, and it's as if she knew you were her sister the first time she saw you. The next time you come back, her room will have a bed for you. You can bunk with her."

Sena, overjoyed, stated, "Really? Oh my goodness. Thank you so much."

Melanie stated, "You are welcome, sweetie." Melanie asked, "Have you spoken to your mother to let her know when you plan on arriving home tomorrow?"

Sena replied, "Yes, I told her I would be home after we eat dinner tomorrow, if that's okay with you."

Melanie stated, "Of course it's okay with me." It was time to put little Cataleya down for bed. She started yawning.

Sena asked, "Would you like me to put her to bed?"

Melanie replied, "Yes, please. I'm going to freshen up before I go to bed."

Sena laid Cataleya down for the night. Jonathan was walking in to turn in himself. Sena gave her dad a hug and said good night to him and Melanie. Sena went to her brother to tell him good night. Everyone had turned in for the night.

It was Sunday morning. Everyone had slept late from the previous day's activities. JJ made breakfast when he had awakened. They all sat at the table as a family to eat. After eating, Sena felt compelled to wash the dishes and insisted. Everyone went to the living area and spent the remainder of the day watching television until it was time to fix dinner. Melanie wanted to turn things around and cook dinner for the family vs. Jonathan taking them out for dinner. It had been a while since she had been in the kitchen. She was frying catfish, made mashed potatoes, greens, hot water corn bread, sweet oven bread, and macaroni and cheese. The ingredients were already available at home, so there was no need to make a trip to the grocery store.

Melanie wanted to set the mood right while cooking and turned on her music. She danced around in the kitchen, grooving to music. Melanie felt like a little girl at heart. She missed cooking. She forgot how good cooking made her feel. And the music, well, it made her just tingle all over. Melanie forgot she was at home and flowed into the groove of the music. She was dancing and singing in the kitchen. She had even grabbed the remote and used it as a microphone. She was listening to "I Will Be Loving You Always" and "What a Fool Believes." She kept repeating those two songs and mixed it up with others. But those two, she loved. They reminded her of happier times. The family had their eyes on her. They loved the energy she was releasing. They all ogled her and began dancing and singing along. When Melanie realized what was going on, she laughed and made her way into the living area to join them while the food was cooking. Sena and JJ didn't know all the lyrics to the songs, but they were enjoying themselves and could repeat the chorus. Sena was feeling vibrant and didn't want her stay to end. Even little Cataleya was clapping and cooing with everyone. Melanie would dance her way back into the kitchen to check the catfish. The hot water corn bread, greens, and mashed potatoes were ready. They were just waiting for the fish and oven bread.

Time was passing quickly. Finally, dinner was ready, and it was time for them to sit and eat as a family. They all enjoyed every morsel. Sena looked at her watch and knew it was getting close for her to end her weekend.

JJ offered to wash the dishes. He wanted to ride with his dad to take Sena home but felt compelled not to ask. He thought his dad would want alone time to talk to Sena privately about her weekend stay. Jonathan was scurrying around, trying to find the car keys. It was time to get her back home.

She hugged her baby sister, JJ, and Melanie. Jonathan walked with his daughter to the car and opened the door for her. After he entered, he turned the ignition and pulled out of the parking lot. He asked Sena, "So did you enjoy yourself?"

Sena replied, "Yes, I certainly did. Everyone went out of their way to make me feel welcomed."

Jonathan stated, "That was our mission. We wanted to make you feel accepted. You can come anytime you like."

Sena said, "Thanks, Dad. I would like to come back next weekend too. I want to spend more time with Cataleya, JJ, and Melanie."

Jonathan asked, "What about me, your old man?"

Sena replied, "Yeah, you too, Dad." They had a nice engaging conversation. Their ride seemed short. Jonathan pulled up to her home and walked her to the door. He gave her a kiss and hug. He waited until she unlocked and opened the door to enter before leaving.

Jonathan turned his music on as he left the neighborhood. Jonathan thought, *A big accomplishment has been made this weekend. Everything is finally coming into play now. Melanie has accepted Sena. My children are getting to know one another. I feel blessed.* Jonathan cruised down the avenue without a care in the world. "What the! Oh shit!" Jonathan started to feel excruciating pain in his legs and back. Jonathan wasn't paying attention to the red light in front of him and ran it. He could see another car coming from the opposite direction. Jonathan screamed out, "Oh shit!"

All he heard and saw next was CRASH!

To be continued.

ABOUT THE AUTHOR

The author experienced mental abuse at an early age from her father. The abuse stemmed from name calling, being held prison to her room, denying her of food, denying her of a healthy father/daughter relationship, etc. Having no proper guidance from a strong male figure would prove failed relationships and repeated cycles of accepting unattractive behavior from the men she allowed in her life. Her choices in life produced spiritual wounds attached with a myriad of lessons to be learned. Her life's experiences were the catalyst for her writing this book for you, her audience. For years the author dealt with her mental abuse alone leading her to low self-esteem and a repeat cycle of choosing the wrong mate. She encourages mothers to protect their children, and all whom have suffered any abuse to seek help through a licensed encouraging clinical therapist for support. The author is a mother of two who resides in Dallas. She loves singing, dancing, cooking, and spreading positive spiritual energy.

Printed in the USA
CPSIA information can be obtained
at www.ICGtesting.com
CBHW020538151124
17428CB00001B/48